Visual Journalism
A Guide for New Media Professionals

Visual Journalism
A Guide for New Media Professionals

Sudhanshu Digal

RANDOM PUBLICATIONS
NEW DELHI (INDIA)

Visual Journalism A Guide for New Media Professionals

ISBN 978-93-5111-927-2

Published in 2016 in India by

RANDOM PUBLICATIONS

Reprint 2018

4376-A/4B, Gali Murari Lal, Ansari Road
New Delhi-110 002
Phone : +9111-43580356, 011-23289044, 011-43142548
e-mail: sales@randompublications.com,
info@randompublications.com, randomexports@gmail.com

Reprinted 2022

Type Setting by : Friends Media, Delhi-110089
Digitally Printed at : Replika Press Pvt. Ltd.

Preface

Visual journalism is the practice of strategically combining words and images to convey information.

Visual journalism is premised upon the idea that at a time of accelerating change, often words cannot keep pace with concepts. Visual journalism incorporates ancient symbols that resonate with humans across cultures and time and conveys meaning instantaneously at a deep level.

In exploring visual journalism from these two angles, and across a range of contemporary media platforms, the text evaluates the extent to which visual communication comprises a significant part of what content means to audiences. As such, the book is an invaluable resource for students of journalism, media studies and photography, as well as for practising designers and journalists.

Journalism is the work of supplying content, primarily news, for the ever-expanding world of mass media. Journalists are responsible for gathering information, analyzing and editing it for a mass audience, and dispensing it using some form of media platform. Increasingly the methods of distribution have become more complex, but the basic mission of a journalist remains the same: to serve the public by finding, defining, writing and editing information.

This book is the practice of strategically combining words and images to convey information. It covers the professions of photojournalism, reporting, writing, and graphic design, is a challenge to teach and a challenge to perform.

Visual Journalism presents a unique, critical investigation into this area. In this book the chapters integrate the experiences of practitioners working in photography, visual design and set design, including insights into how they work and the changing environments they find themselves in, with an innovative theory of visual communication – multimodality – that enables the text to break down and analyse the key elements and patterns of visual design.

– ***Author***

Contents

1

Visual Communication in Journalism

A comparison of the design and photography of public journalism projects with non-public journalism shows there is a difference, but not a radical one. Between 1990 and 1996, more than 400 media outlets in the U.S. had undertaken public journalism projects. Much has been written about the philosophy behind public journalism, its goals, and techniques.

Individual public journalism projects have been analysed and compared against these goals and philosophies, and also compared to traditional journalism to see what, if any, difference exists. However, no study has yet focused on the visual communication of public journalism in newspapers. Public journalism practitioners and theoreticians argue that the content of stories generated through public journalism methods is significantly different from the content generated by traditional reporting methods. News designers are taught that the form of their designs must reflect the content of the stories rather than artistic preference or trends.

This prompts the question: If the content of stories generated through public journalism methods is different, and design is driven by content, doesn't it follow that design for public journalism will be different than design for non-public journalism? This is a key question that visual communicators and public journalists must address if the final product is to truly integrate verbal and visual meaning.

The purpose of this research, the first of a two-phase study, is to explore how public journalism projects have been visually communicated in newspapers practicing this approach, and how they differ from the visual communication of non-public journalism.

Through content analysis, textual analysis and telephone interviews, this exploratory study examined the design and photography of projects at six newspapers; four practicing public journalism and two practicing non-public journalism to explore how public journalism projects were visually communicated in newspapers that practiced the genre, and whether the visual communication of public journalism differed from the visual communication of non-public journalism.

Public journalism is a product of the 1990s — its first well-documented experiment was in late 1989 in Columbus, Georgia. Even a decade later, there are as many operational definitions of public journalism as there are media outlets that practice it. For a conceptual definition that speaks to the developing theory of public journalism Jay Rosen has said: "Journalism can and should play a part in strengthening citizenship, improving public debate and reviving public life." Public or civic journalism is widely understood as an approach designed to address issues that readers say are important, rather than only those issues identified by experts. It seeks to promote a public conversation about those issues that will result in a collective working through of the problem to resolution. Among its goals are strengthening citizenship, improving the quality of public debate, and reviving public life. It proposes a more active role for the press than has traditionally been adopted.

Public journalism derives many of its philosophical foundations from the social responsibility theory of the press and agenda-setting theory. While some scholars of public journalism trace its roots as far back as Thomas Jefferson, John Locke and John Stuart Mill, it seems unarguable that the development of the ideas that infuse public journalism were an outgrowth of the debates between John Dewey and Walter Lippmann over the proper role for the press in a democracy.

Dewey and other scholars helped lay the foundation for a gradual shift towards the emerging social responsibility theory of the press, which was akin to Dewey's proposal of the role of the press in helping build a more pluralist and tolerant society. The evolution of the social responsibility theory culminated in the Commission on Freedom of the Press' report in 1947.

The Hutchins Commission's work can be seen as a forerunner of public journalism in that it called for the press to offer "a method of presenting and clarifying the goals and values of the society" and for reporting to project "the opinions and attitudes of the groups in society to one another." Although social responsibility theory has been challenged as a product of its time, the developing concept of public journalism has drawn heavily from the Hutchins Commission and expanded on the role of the press by incorporating ideas from Dewey, philosophers Jurgen Habermas and Hannah Arendt, and political scientist Michael Sandel. Arendt, Habermas and Sandel all acknowledge the important role media play in society — without communication there is no public sphere. Contemporaries whose thoughts have added fuel to the public journalism fire include Daniel Yankelovich in Coming to Public Judgement, Russell Neuman, Marian Just and Ann Crigler with Common Knowledge, Clifford Christians, John Ferre and Mark Fackler's Good News, James Carey, Jay Rosen, and Davis Merritt.

Public journalism also incorporates aspects of agenda-setting theory, which says that one of the effects of mass communication is to direct the audience's attention to certain problems or issues. By conducting focus groups and taking polls of what the audience considers important before reporting on issues, public journalists make a self-conscious effort to avoid agenda-setting by the media or others, including government and special interests.

While there is no consensus on what public journalism is, or even on what to call it, the premise that all agree on is that it is the duty of the press is to improve the quality of public life by fostering public participation and debate. Some of the methods and techniques public journalists are best known to have used towards these goals include focus groups and citizen advisory boards to discover issues of importance to people; avoiding conflict framing of stories; using ordinary citizens as sources as well as officials and experts; seeking to clarify the core values behind opinions and underlying causes of problems; focusing on solutions and success stories; and taking an active role in promoting discussion among citizens with public forums and town hall meetings.

While public journalists are still focused on inventing their craft, they are understandably concerned with fine-tuning the proper reporting and writing techniques. As is historically typical in journalism, the visual aspects of journalistic storytelling — photography and design — are postponed for attention after the verbal aspects have been worked out.

While they may momentarily forget this essential element, journalists have come to realise that visual communication can be just as important, if not more so, as verbal communication. Inherent in all definitions of design is the idea that it is not simply decoration or dressing up a page, but that form carries a content of its own. The literature laments the use of designs that overemphasize form to the detriment of communication. Originally, design developed in response to the mechanical needs of page make-up. With the advent of photocomposition, mechanical concerns were eliminated as well as the design conventions they necessitated. Today, the story content and needs of the reader drive design.

It is the consensus in design theory that form is inextricably linked to message meaning. The form, or design, of news changes the perception of its content. If newspaper page design is truly to be used to communicate meaning derived from the story's content, and if public journalism has changed that content, then design must change to reflect that. Design must now communicate the public agenda.

If public journalism is an attempt to better address the goals laid out by the Hutchins Commission, how can design and photography encourage this? Perhaps public journalism photographs should reflect citizens more often than candidates. Photojournalists might also refuse to participate in photo opportunities organized by public relations people in the interest of letting the public set the agenda, rather than PR professionals. Public journalism design could also make use of design elements which help communicate its goals, such as summary boxes describing the values in conflict over a certain issue, or graphics telling readers how to get involved, express their opinions, or get more information on an issue. These and other topics must be addressed by public journalism's visual communicators if the final product is to truly integrate verbal and visual meaning.

There is some indication in the public journalism literature that design is beginning to be considered. Most are references made in passing with little follow-up as to how the goals of public journalism might be achieved with visuals. Others offer some specifics. For example, in a speech to the Regional Reporters Association, Jan Schaffer of the Pew Centre for Civic Journalism suggested building in "graphic devices that invite and encourage readers and viewers to contact the news organization and react to an issue, a controversy, a public problem." Jay Rosen made the connection between public journalism's goals and design when he commented that, "If the pages of the newspaper are thought of as a public space designed by journalists, then what the (Wichita) Eagle did is arrange this space so that the proper concerns of politics (`issues in depth') shone through." He then described how the Eagle accomplished this with visual elements.

For each of the major issues, the Eagle published a list called Places to Start, with the names, addresses and phone numbers of organizations and agencies working on the problem. Repeated invitations were issued to readers to contact the paper with their comments and suggestions. At the Charlotte Observer, the Where They Stand feature was more than a voter's guide. If candidates refused to answer the questions the public posed, then a blank appeared under the candidate's name. This was a powerful use of space, charged with visual meaning.

A survey found that one of the most useful features was the Where They Stand box. The Pew Center's Schaffer also reported that a focus group at one newspaper responded differently to information conveyed graphically than when the same information was reported in a bylined story: "They loved the voter's guide in a grid and asked why we didn't give it to them earlier and repeat it often.... It seemed to them fairer and more factual. There was no byline and no news peg, just distilled information. Even though it was from bylined stories, the way it was presented seemed to make a difference in how much people believed it."

At the Virginian-Pilot in Norfolk, a new feature was inaugurated on the front page to stimulate more productive dialogue about controversies in the news. The paper also created a new design element that graphically conveyed its new treatment of controversy. After summarizing the themes of the issue, readers were directed to question themselves. For example: "If you tend to disagree... in what part of (his) argument can you find merit? Even if you tend to agree... what part of (his) argument do you have problems with? Where is the common ground?" It is much harder to find discussions of photojournalism that promotes the ideals of public journalism. One example that was widely discussed appeared in the Wisconsin State Journal when citizens gathered in the seats of their representatives at the state capitol to question candidates. The result was "a startling visual," according to Rosen, a visual symbol that things had changed. The value of visual communication to public journalism's goals is even beginning to be addressed tangentially in some scholarly research. Paul Riede concluded that, in the Wichita Eagle's The People Project, the most journalistic depth came in the form of the graphics: "the graphic goes beneath the surface, personality-based coverage of politics typical of traditional journalism." This same study called the "innovative use of the `core values' graphics'... the project's most promising attempt at depth in coverage." In order discover how public journalism projects have been visually communicated and whether they differ from that of non-public journalism, one research question and six hypotheses regarding visual communication were developed based on public journalism characteristics derived from the literature.

They are:

H1: Public journalism will visually convey more mobilizing Information to help citizens participate in their communities than non-public journalism.

H2: Public journalism will visually convey more interactivity, *i.e.*: ways to contact the media.

H3: Public journalism photographs will use fewer managed photo opportunities than non-public journalism.

H4: Public journalism will use more photographs of citizens and "real people" versus candidates or experts than non-public journalism.

H5: Public journalism will use more visual devices to convey views of citizens and "real people" than non-public journalism.

H6: Public journalism will use more visual devices to convey common ground and solutions than non-public journalism.

RQ1: Does the visual communication of public journalism differ with circulation size?

The unit of analysis was all the stories on the public journalism topic in one day's issue of the newspaper. Forty-one newspaper issues were sampled. The 41 issues were drawn from six newspapers in two circulation sizes using one week from each paper. For this study, large newspapers were defined as greater than 200,000 daily circulation. Small newspapers were defined as less than 100,000 daily circulation. Medium newspapers, 100,000 to 200,000 daily circulation, were not included in order to maximize comparisons. It was postulated there would be little difference, for reasons such as resources, between medium and large papers, but the difference would be greater between small and large papers.

One week's issues from two large-circulation non-public journalism newspapers were compared against one week's issues from four public journalism newspapers (both large and small circulation sizes); one week's issues from two small-circulation public journalism newspapers were compared against one week's issues from two large-circulation public journalism newspapers; and one week's issues from two large-circulation public journalism newspapers were compared against one week's issues from two large-circulation non-public journalism newspapers.

This allowed comparison of the presentation of public journalism against non-public journalism two ways, and also allowed comparison of the presentation within the genre of public journalism.

Sampling time was limited to one week because one newspaper's series ran for only six days. In addition, the large number of variables examined made a larger sample unwieldy. All elements associated with the stories in each issue, including stories, headlines, photos, illustrations, sidebars, boxes, logos, refers, graphics, charts, maps, tables, schedules, lists, pullquotes, readouts, and jumps, were coded for size and presence of public journalism criteria.

Since the purpose of this exploratory project was to learn as much as possible about a subject which has not previously been studied, examining all relevant appearance variables was deemed to be more important than a large sample. If even small differences were detected, the results of this exploratory study could help point the way towards future research.

The public journalism stories were sampled using the latest public journalism projects at each newspaper; the non-public journalism stories were sampled using the newspapers' latest series that was on a similar topic as the public journalism series in its comparison paper, or, if that was not feasible, a project that ran as a series of similar magnitude was chosen. This study analysed the content of the appearance variables of all stories dealing with the subject except opinion pieces and letters to the editor.

The focus of this study was on differences in photography and design. Editorial pages are highly formatted and generally do not vary in presentation, so they were not deemed suitable for this study. Purposive sampling with newspapers stratified by circulation size and chosen for their experience with the public journalism approach was used because it is better suited the purpose of comparing the visual presentation of public journalism to see how it varies within the genre, and of comparing the visual presentation of public journalism to non-public journalism. The four public journalism newspapers were initially chosen for a different study by the Pew Centre for Civic Journalism. The basis for this decision included the level of experience each paper had with public journalism philosophies and techniques, and Pew's director's and assistant director's assessment that these particular papers were doing some of the more interesting work within the public journalism genre.

Because of their early entry into the movement, the philosophies and practices of public journalism at these papers are assumed to be more highly developed than those of papers just beginning to practice public journalism.

Therefore, the visual communication of public journalism stories should have achieved a deeper level of consideration in these newsrooms. Also, by experimenting with the photographiy and presentation of public journalism for a longer period, their practices should be more finely tuned and may represent the direction that other newspapers will take in public journalism.

The two large circulation newspapers not practicing public journalism were chosen by this researcher for their similarities with the public journalism newspapers in circulation size, morning publication, and market demographics, and also to represent specific regions of the country. Their editors have publicly stated their opposition to the public journalism approach.

The differences in design styles across the different newspapers were taken into account in the textual analysis.

The characteristics of each newspaper sampled are:

Public journalism - large circulation:

- San Francisco Chronicle: 489,238 daily circulation. Public journalism project on commuter transportation. Published October-December 1996.

The public journalism stories were sampled using the latest public journalism projects at each newspaper; the non-public journalism stories were sampled using the newspapers' latest series that was on a similar topic as the public journalism series in its comparison paper, or, if that was not feasible, a project that ran as a series of similar magnitude was chosen. This study analysed the content of the appearance variables of all stories dealing with the subject except opinion pieces and letters to the editor.

The focus of this study was on differences in photography and design. Editorial pages are highly formatted and generally do not vary in presentation, so they were not deemed suitable for this study.

Purposive sampling with newspapers stratified by circulation size and chosen for their experience with the public journalism approach was used because it is better suited the purpose of comparing the visual presentation of public journalism to see how it varies within the genre, and of comparing the visual presentation of public journalism to non-public journalism.

The four public journalism newspapers were initially chosen for a different study by the Pew Centre for Civic Journalism. The basis for this decision included the level of experience each paper had with public journalism philosophies and techniques, and Pew's director's and assistant director's assessment that these particular papers were doing some of the more interesting work within the public journalism genre.

Because of their early entry into the movement, the philosophies and practices of public journalism at these papers are assumed to be more highly developed than those of papers just beginning to practice public journalism. Therefore, the visual communication of public journalism stories should have achieved a deeper level of consideration in these newsrooms. Also, by experimenting with the photographiy and presentation of public journalism for a longer period, their practices should be more finely tuned and may represent the direction that other newspapers will take in public journalism. The two large circulation newspapers not practicing public journalism were chosen by this researcher for their similarities with the public journalism newspapers in circulation size, morning publication, and market demograph.

COMMON GROUND AND SOLUTIONS

Results showed that the public journalism issues sampled in this study used significantly more visual devices to convey common ground or solutions than non-public journalism issues. None of the non-public journalism issues sampled used visual language to convey common ground or solutions, while 21 per cent of the public journalism issues sampled did so.

Reporting common ground and solutions is fairly unique to public journalism, with non-public journalism traditionally focusing on past events. Common ground and solutions speaks to Yankelovich's idea that media should facilitate a working through stage that ultimately leads to solutions, rather than stopping at the consciousness-raising stage. That none of the non-public journalism issues sampled visually conveyed common ground or solutions reinforces the belief that non-public journalism limits itself to issue-raising.

Even though there is a significant difference between public and non-public journalism in this sample, fewer than one-quarter of the public journalism newspaper stories sampled (21 per cent) used visual devices to convey common ground and solutions. It is hoped that higher ratios would be achieved as public journalism develops. However, this is a sign there is beginning to be an awareness of the need to visually communicate this information. This hypothesis also showed a marginally significant difference between small and large papers within public journalism in this sample.

Larger papers in this study used visual devices for common ground and solutions in 36 per cent of their issues, while only 7 per cent of issues sampled in small papers did so. Perhaps this speaks to the difference in resources between small and large papers. It may be that common ground and solutions are harder to conceptualize, thus, small papers with smaller design staffs, more inexperienced designers, and less time to design each page, will not have the resources to devote to such complex issues. The other side of this argument is that a box conveying possible solutions with typography is neither hard to conceptualize nor time-consuming to execute.

Alternately, it could mean that reporters and editors at small papers are not including common ground and solutions in stories, thus the designers are not either. This seems to be the case with one small public journalism paper sampled. In the textual analysis, the Wisconsin State Journal's We the People project on the fall 1996 election showed no common ground or solutions in either the text or visuals.

The possibility that the topic may not lend itself to exploring common ground and solutions is unlikely since the other public journalism paper that covered the election, the Charlotte Observer, did visually present common ground and solutions. On most days, the Observer had a box on the issue of the day (*i.e.*: crime, school vouchers, etc.) that outlined different sides, gave background, and told where there was agreement or not. The solutions box on school tuition vouchers explained three reasons for supporting vouchers and three for opposing them. Common ground was explained this way: "Critics and supporters agree that school vouchers, if offered on a national scale, have the power to dramatically change the face of public education. Where both sides disagree is whether those changes will improve or ruin public schools."

Public journalism election coverage in the Wisconsin State Journal more closely resembled non-public journalism in the Omaha World-Herald. Both focused on differences in the candidates' positions rather than where there was agreement on issues. The main difference was that the public journalism election treatment included forums for citizens to question candidates, whereas the non-public journalism coverage did not.

This difference between the small public journalism issues and the large non-public journalism issues could still be partly due to staff resources. But the possibility that journalists at the small paper did not have as great an understanding of public journalism is another likely explanation. In the informant interviews, two designers at the small public journalism paper indicated they had received no training in the philosophy, goals and techniques of public journalism, while the design director at the large public journalism paper said design staffers had been included in educational sessions with one of the founders of public journalism, Prof. Jay Rosen.

THE DIFFERENCE BETWEEN HISTORY AND JOURNALISM

Even if one accepts the dominant view about the nature of history, what, if anything, does it say that will help us distinguish history from journalism? First, we must be careful not to be misled by one obvious but not unimportant difference. Journalism is a type of communication. History is not that. If one accepts Kahler, it is what has been going on.

If one accepts Collingwood and most other historians, it is knowledge, organized knowledge, of what has been going on. Thus the parallel with journalism is not history itself but rather the *communication* of history. But this is not the crucial point. Both journalism and history deal with knowledge. Journalism is the communication of a type of knowledge that has been acquired.

History is the acquisition of a type of knowledge that will be communicated. Both are concerned with the communication of knowledge. But the important factor is neither when the knowledge is acquired nor *when* it is communicated. Rather, what requires our attention is the *type* of knowledge that is acquired and communicated. Traditionally, two broad categories of knowledge have been recognized. One is knowledge that is acquired for the sake of knowledge. It is knowledge for its own sake. It is knowledge for the sheer pleasure of knowing. This is called theoretical knowledge. The other is acquired to procure by some kind of activity the good of people. It is knowledge that is put to use. This is called practical knowledge. In *How to Read a Book*, Mortimer Adler and Charles Van Doren explain the difference this way:

Some books and some teachers are interested only in the knowledge itself that they have to communicate. This does not mean that they deny its utility, or that they insist that knowledge is good *only* for its own sake. They simply limit themselves to one kind of communication or teaching, and leave the other kind to other men. These others have an interest beyond knowledge for its own sake. They are concerned with the problems of human life that knowledge can help to solve. They communicate knowledge, too, but always with a view to and an emphasis upon its application.

Historians are interested in this first kind of knowledge. If one asks why historians do what they do, Toynbee answers that there can be several reasons; "the strongest and most estimable of these" is simply to satisfy curiosity. "In the field of human affairs," he says, "curiosity prompts us to seek a panoramic view in order to gain a vision of reality that will make it as intelligible as possible for a human mind." When historians communicate their historical knowledge they do so, dominantly and most properly, simply to help people understand what has happened. But journalists, to the extent that they are practicing journalism, have a practical goal in mind. They acquire and communicate knowledge for the sake of providing people with what they need to know to make good decisions about what should be done or what should be avoided concerning the issues currently facing them.

If one wants to distinguish historians from journalists, one can say that the former are concerned not only with the past but with the past primarily as merely something to be known. In one sense, this type of knowledge might be viewed as useful, but it is useful for increasing understanding, not for determining future actions. Journalists, on the other hand, are ultimately concerned with helping people decide what would be good things to do or to avoid doing.

BOTH CAN BE MISDIRECTED AND MISUSED

As events discussed by historians creep closer to the present, a temptation tags along to apply historical knowledge to the solution of contemporary problems. If historians give way to this temptation, however, they edge into the domain of the journalists. But journalists also face their own temptation. They may fall short of the practical goal that is their reason for being.

Perceiving, achieving, and maintaining the distinction between the theoretical and the practical are enormously difficult, for they require the concurrence of message senders and message receivers. History and journalism both can be misdirected and misused.

For example, a historian examining the letters of Thomas Jefferson finds they set forth some radical changes in his attitudes towards newspapers. Before he became president, Jefferson esteemed the press highly, writing that, if he had to make a choice, he would prefer newspapers without government rather than government without newspapers. But after he was president, Jefferson criticized the press mightily, claiming it was so filled with lies that a man who never reads a newspaper is better informed than one who does.

Now the historian's proper task is to discover what, in many contexts, Jefferson's letters mean and to find, if he can, the reasons for the changing attitudes reflected in them. But instead of communicating to us this knowledge, he might discard the historian's garb and, using these letters as evidence, try to convince us that we should not trust the campaign words of presidential candidates when they laud the press, for even the best of them is bound to have a change of mind once elected.

Sometimes we can spot what pseudohistorians are doing, especially if they are blatant in their misuse of documents or relics of the past. We might even charge that, no longer historians, they have become propagandists. By that we probably mean that they are trying to mislead us, trying to incline us towards what we believe to be some inappropriate course of action. We are less likely to spot the sacrifice of history if the writers are proposing something with which we agree. Yet whether we agree or not, propaganda is not good history.

Even when a piece of writing *is* historical writing, some readers might misuse it by attempting to turn it to some practical purpose.

Just as Pablo Pi- casso's great painting *Guernica* might be cut in half and hung sideways merely to cover a long crack in the wall, so one might try to turn Thucydides' *History of the Peloponnesian War* into a guidebook for fighting a twentieth-century battle.

In a more recent example, General Albert Wedemeyer book *Wedemeyer Reports!* was intended to help us understand the major battles of World War II, but it could have been misused as a handbook for conducting the war in Vietnam. Journalism, too, can be misdirected or misused. But for now and throughout the succeeding pages, we must keep in mind one dominant characteristic of journalism: properly done, it deals with useful, practical knowledge. If we lose touch with this core, the effort to discover journalism will fail.

OTHERS ALSO COMMUNICATE PRACTICAL KNOWLEDGE

Journalists, however, are not the only ones who communicate useful knowledge. Parents, profiting from their own experience, advise their children on how to make the first car purchase or diaper the first grandchild. A dietician informs a heart patient of the foods that will lower fat and cholesterol. A psychiatrist tells an overworked employer how to reduce stress. All of these tend to work on a one-to-one, face-to-face basis. Perhaps more instructive for our purposes would be the comparison between journalists and trial lawyers, since lawyers, in addition to their one-on-one dialogues with judges and witnesses, often have a group of people—a jury—with whom to communicate.

In addition to their mutual interest in the recent past, trial lawyers, like journalists, have practical goals in mind. Their ultimate goal in criminal trials is ostensibly to help assure that the guilty are punished and the innocent set free and exonerated. Both journalists and lawyers engage in communications to help others determine what ought to be done or avoided. But how do they differ?

Once again, some of the most obvious differences may not be the most important. Whereas journalists communicate about a wide range of topics, lawyers travel within the relatively narrower compass of the law. More significant, however, is the extent of the communications, and the number and type of persons reached by the communicators.

Lawyers who communicate in the process of a jury trial attempt to reach several people, thus exceeding the one-to-one communications previously mentioned, but they are not engaged in what is usually called "mass communications." Journalists, however, whenever they are functioning as journalists, are always participants in mass communications. But how does communicating with several or even many persons differ from communicating with a mass of people?

JOURNALISM AND THE NEWS

As we continue to examine the nature and functions of journalism in greater detail, we see immediately that another term is so closely associated with journalists that it is sometimes used as a synonym.

During the prolonged Society of Professional Journalists-Sigma Delta Chi debate on the meaning of journalism, for example, Edward Lindsay, editor of the Lindsay-Schaub newspapers in Decatur, Illinois, sometimes substituted "fraternity of newsmen" for "society of professional journalists".

Indeed, in the mind of many persons, news reporters and newswriters seem to occupy the centermost chambers in the house of journalism. Therefore, although journalism consists of much more than the acquisition and presentation of news, it is appropriate that we now turn our attention to that important but highly ambiguous term.

READER-REPORTER INTERACTION

The hypothesis that public journalism designs would visually convey interactivity between readers and the media more than non-public journalism (H2) was also significant. Seventy-five per cent of the public journalism issues in this sample used visual elements to encourage readers to contact the media, while 46 per cent of non-public journalism issues sampled did so. In addition, the number of different ways public journalism provided for readers to contact them (address, phone, e-mail, web site, fax) was highly significant. Small circulation mean = 2.1, large circulation mean =.5. There were no significant differences between small and large circulation issues on this variable, as would be expected if all size papers were practicing public journalism the same way.

PHOTO OPS AND PHOTOS OF 'REAL PEOPLE'

The two public journalism characteristics that were not significant when public and non-public journalism issues were compared but whose means were in the direction hypothesized both dealt with photographs; whether public journalism relied on managed photo opportunities less often than non-public journalism (H3), and whether public journalism photos featured citizens and real people more often than candidates or experts (H4). The non-significant findings may be due to the low number of cases sampled (N = 41), but it is important that for both hypotheses the mean ratios of non-managed photos and photos of real people to total photos showed that the public journalism issues sampled used fewer photographs from managed photo opportunities and also used more photos of citizens and real people than candidates or experts.

Comparisons within public journalism showed no significant differences between small and large papers' photos in this sample regarding photo opportunities or the use of citizens and real people in photos versus candidates or experts. Textual analysis revealed both small public journalism papers, Binghamton and Wisconsin, used all photos of real people from non-managed photo sources. In the large public journalism category, San Francisco used all non-managed photos featuring citizens in its series on transportation.

Since Binghamton's series was on the local economy and primarily covered the citizen's forums, and San Francisco's series was on commuter woes, it is perhaps not surprising that they were able to find photo subjects that did not involve officials and experts. It is more unusual for election coverage to avoid photos of candidates, yet that is just what the Wisconsin paper did. It achieved this goal mainly by running only one photo (citizens at a forum) over all seven issues; six issues had no photos at all. In the large non-public journalism genre, Omaha used all photos of candidates, as would be expected for traditional journalism.

The variation is mainly explained by the non-public journalism Philadelphia paper's use of all non-managed photos of real people, and the public journalism

Charlotte paper's heavy use of managed photo ops of candidates — findings that are counter to what would be expected in ideal public journalism. The story subjects provide partial explanation. In its series on a typical suburban neighbourhood, Philadelphia used five to eight pictures every day in its non-public journalism series, all were of real people and none were from photo opportunities. In its election coverage, the public journalism Charlotte paper used mug shots or photo collages of candidates on nearly every cover, plus cutout photos of candidates in its full-page graphic of candidates' answers to voters' questions. In addition, Charlotte used four conventional campaign trail photos over the course of the series, in traditional political photojournalism style.

The only real-people photos Charlotte used were approximately three to five photos daily of the citizens who asked questions of the candidates or whose opinions were quoted. The Charlotte design director indicated in a telephone interview that the amount of campaign-trail photographs shot were "not nearly as many as five years ago... An effort was made to take photos of real people, but that makes things harder." The convention of candidate photographs for election coverage apparently remains strong, even at papers that have embraced public journalism principles. The design director's acknowledgment that finding photos of real people is harder than attending photo opportunities is a candid admission that goes to the root of the difficulty of altering established conventions.

Comments by designers at the public journalism papers in Binghamton, Madison, and San Francisco, all indicated their photographers tried to avoid photo opportunities in favour of real people; however, photo ops could not be entirely eliminated. The former graphics editor at the Madison paper provided some background on the thinking:

The photo staff hates dull pictures, first of all. There is nothing worse than a talking head (politician) or a grip-and-grin. They do try and look for action or images from the issue they are addressing. It is a combination of public journalism and aesthetics.

He also attributed the lack of photos (one photo over seven issues) to aesthetics:

With 'We the People,' the premiere events are these town meetings. They don't make particularly good photos. They are often held in the capitol, which has miserable lighting, and it's a sea of people sitting around. The marching orders are we will shoot that, but we would probably try to limit that to one. Otherwise, we would have photos and stories about journalists from different media getting together to organize 'We the People'."

The idea of using photos of real people that are not the result of photo ops orchestrated by people seeking to manipulate publicity goes to the heart of public journalism philosophy and reflects a conscious effort to avoid agenda-setting effects. The use of this type of photo would be a sign that public journalism's goals are beginning to be translated into practice. Helping citizens participate in civic life. Of the two remaining hypotheses, neither showed any significant differences between public and non-public journalism. One was the hypothesis that public journalism would visually convey more mobilizing information to help citizens participate in their communities than non-public journalism (H1). There were no significant differences between the sampled public and non-public journalism issues' use of mobilizing information.

However, when comparisons were made within public journalism between large and small papers' issues, there was a highly significant difference in the visual communication of mobilizing information, with small papers scoring better. Only 14 per cent of large papers' stories used visual elements to convey mobilizing information, whereas 71 per cent of small papers' stories used one visual element, and 7 per cent used two.

In the public journalism genre, issues from both large papers sampled used no mobilizing information in visual format. However, both small public journalism papers sampled visually conveyed mobilizing information.

The topics—the Charlotte Observer's election coverage — cannot be the reason, however, since the two other papers which carried election coverage, including one non-public journalism paper (Omaha), listed mobilizing information. The other large public journalism paper, San Francisco, gave almost no mobilizing information on its transportation series. Both small public journalism papers listed mobilizing information frequently; Wisconsin had the most and most regular mobilizing information with its boxes for forum broadcasts, call-in lines and registration information for upcoming town meetings. Wisconsin even developed regular graphic devices its designers called democracy boxes. Perhaps the convention of having these boxes to fill kept mobilizing information in the forefront for Wisconsin designers. Binghamton usually publicized an upcoming priority setting conference or results of the economic teams' reports.

One reason for these results could be that mobilizing information is not new or unique to public journalism the way other variables can be. For this study, mobilizing information consisted of news citizens could use to participate in community life. However, the importance of information which allows people to take action has been discussed in scholarly and trade publications since at least the 1970s.

Well before the advent of public journalism, traditional journalism has offered dates of neighbourhood watch meetings, names and addresses of redevelopment agencies that offer grant money, etc. Because of the length of time over which journalists have been aware of the importance of mobilizing information, and the ubiquitous nature of such information, it may not be surprising that there are no significant differences in the amount of mobilizing information conveyed visually in public and non-public journalism. The greater resources at larger papers cannot help explain why small papers used more visual devices for mobilizing information than large papers. Mobilizing information should be quite familiar and top-of-mind to designers at both small and large papers, public journalism and non-public journalism. Perhaps another explanation for the highly significant difference between small circulation and large circulation public journalism designs that visually convey mobilizing information can be found in James Lemert and colleague's findings.

Because small papers may better reflect their small communities, there is more awareness of readers' desire for visual display of mobilizing information. If large public journalism papers are not providing mobilizing information, this supports Lemert's theory that mobilizing information is regularly missing when issues are located outside of town, where audiences ordinarily can't look up addresses and phone numbers. This may be the case for large newspapers that cover many different communities.

VIEWS OF REAL PEOPLE

The other hypothesis that was not significant was that public journalism would use more visual devices to convey views of real people (H5). This non-significant finding between the public and non-public journalism issues sampled is interesting because views of real people rather than experts or politicians are one of the central tenets of public journalism. Although all designers interviewed said they tried to include views of real people, two said it was a copy desk decision and would be done mainly through pullquotes.

However, textual analysis revealed that not all public journalism papers visually displayed views of real people. Both Wisconsin and San Francisco used no graphics or design elements for views of real people, although these views were carried within the text.

A lack of significant difference between public and non-public journalism's use of views of real people may signify that visual journalists do not fully understand or embrace this idea. If a significant difference were found to exist in the written communication of views of real people, but not in the visual communication, this would have implications for the integration of the designers and copy editors with the reporters and editors.

It may indicate that designers have not been included in sessions devoted to explaining the philosophies of public journalism and do not understand its principles fully, or, they are aware of the importance of views of real people but are leaving it to reporters to include in stories rather than employing content-driven design to convey this visually. There was also no difference in the sampled issues between small and large public journalism's use of visual devices to convey views of real people, but this would be expected if all papers practiced public journalism the same way.

THE IMPORTANCE OF UNDERSTANDING

Two final points of interest were revealed in the interviews when designers were asked whether they designed differently for public journalism than for non-public journalism. Designers at two papers said yes, public journalism design was different from non-public journalism design, and designers at the other two papers replied no, there was no difference. Interestingly, the no difference responses came from designers whose papers did not have training sessions on the concepts and techniques of public journalism, or who did not include visual journalists in those sessions.

Both affirmative responses came from newspapers whose designers did participate in public journalism education sessions. Understanding of public journalism principles was one of the explanations offered for some of the findings in this study, and the perception of designers regarding the difference in designing for public journalism reinforces such an explanation. Visual journalists who did not attend sessions aimed at explaining public journalism's goal and principles may not understand it as well as those who did and, therefore, may not consider ways to visually communicate those goals and principles.

Also, one of the designers interviewed complained that too many journalists at the paper felt like they had been ordered to do public journalism with no opportunity for discussion or input. This chapter did not offer training sessions in public journalism. "If they're really going to get people on board to do this and do this well, there has to be that discussion," said the designer, who asked to remain anonymous. "There are numerous ethical challenges in doing this, and they need to at least be explored, as do the possible pitfalls." Both these insights have implications for managing editors contemplating introducing public journalism into their newsrooms.

This study has used the emerging theory of public journalism, which claims a significantly different content than non-public journalism, and the theory of content-driven design, which says that visual meaning must reflect the written content, to examine the question prompted by these theories: If the content of stories generated through public journalism methods is different, and design is driven by content, shouldn't design for public journalism be different than design for non-public journalism?

The results from this study are mixed. Of six hypotheses that speak to the question of whether public journalism is visually different from non-public journalism, two showed significant differences among the newspaper issues sampled. Public journalism stories in this study used more visual devices to convey common ground and solutions, and ways to contact the media than did non-public journalism stories.. Four hypotheses showed no significant differences between public journalism and non-public journalism, but two had means in the direction hypothesized.

The public journalism issues sampled were more likely than non-public journalism to use fewer managed photo opportunities and more photos of real people than candidates or experts, but the differences were not significant These are signs that some of public journalism's goals may be beginning to be translated into practice by visual journalists, but that there are other goals that are not being addressed visually, at least in these newspapers.

The fact that the public journalism issues sampled were not significantly different from the non-public journalism issues in how they visually conveyed views of real people — one of the central tenets of public journalism — should be of concern. That the public journalism issues sampled visually communicated no more mobilizing information than the non-public journalism issues is less cause for worry because mobilizing information is not unique to public journalism the way the other characteristics can be. This study has also found that, in some cases, public journalism papers that have established new conventions in place of the old have found it easier to adhere consistently to public journalism principles; for instance, the development of standing graphics such as democracy boxes for mobilizing information.

One problem in the consistent communication of public journalism characteristics seems to be with journalists' fundamental understanding of public journalism. Confusion over and even unawareness of public journalism principles seems to be a basic, underlying reason why the practice of public journalism is not significantly different from non-public journalism in terms of visual communication. In addition, it appears that not all designers are practicing content-driven design.

For instance, this research found stories which included views of real people in the text but not in the design. In conclusion, there appear to be some significant differences in this sample in the way public journalism is visually communicated compared with non-public journalism. However, there is not enough significance to say that it represents a radical departure from non-public journalism, at least in the issues studied here. It appears another researcher's conclusion regarding the content of public journalism may be correct for the visual display as well: "there is no overriding, core philosophy of public journalism at some of the papers practicing it; instead it has become a label used to name a variety of special projects."

TEXTUAL ANALYSIS IN JOURNALISM

Textual analysis is sometimes called careful reading, and it is as important to a journalist as good listening. Textual analysis is a method that communication researchers use to describe, interpret, and evaluate the characteristics of a recorded message. This type of qualitative research and analysis focuses on a particular text to determine its characteristics and place it in a category shared by other similar texts for comparison and contrast purposes.

Qualitative textual analysis can lead to quantitative research methods such as content analysis or Q methodology, which can be used to analyse publications or opinions about texts. For example, researchers might categorize the types of message strategies that politicians use in public campaign speeches as fear-appeals and reward-appeals by studying individual texts, and then conduct a quantitative study.

This research project might study how the *New York Times* and the Los *Angeles Times* covered campaign speeches over the period of a year by focusing on the textual attributes of each paper's campaign coverage. Reporters who write the news stories also use some level of textual analysis to compare and contrast oral and written language. Reporters at the *Washington Post* use personal computers to search for key words in bills and legislation that indicate stakeholders—winners and losers—in the documents.

Mass media textual analysis is closely related to literary criticism, which, broadly used today, encompasses any discourse on any literature, including three distinguishable but overlapping areas: history, theory, and evaluation. Many scholars view literature as part of an historical process, a phenomenon that can be described by internal principles such as types, techniques, and functions, or as objects to be studied, analysed, and judged. Several methods and approaches to criticism fiercely compete for attention in the field. Wellek commented on this new age of criticism:

The variety of voices today is so great that the situation has been compared to the Tower of Babel, with its mutually incompatible languages.

Never before has there been such a ferment in criticism, and critics have never before attracted so much attention and fervent loyalty ... Indeed some scholars argue that this is the age of criticism, since literary critics now often function not only as specialists in literature, but also as general critics of society and civilization.

This chapter focuses on only the most common terms of textual analysis that are used by journalists. It addresses how journalists read, analyse, categorize, describe, and evaluate their own writing as well as the writing and oral language of others.

PURPOSES AND TYPES OF TEXTUAL ANALYSIS

There are two basic uses of textual analysis for practicing journalists. The first is to study the language of their sources for specific stories; the second is to study the language of journalism to refine their art of writing. This broad approach to criticism is relatively new; it has been advanced in recent decades by critiques of English composition and rhetorical analyses of speech communication. In their 1991 book, Investigating Communication, Frey and colleagues explained that textual analysis stems from a systematic attempt to understand how meaning moves from author to audience and how the text is related to other variables that precede it. Ultimately, textual analysis is a scientific attempt to evaluate a text based on a set of established standards or criteria. Several organizations and publications have begun criticizing the content of the news media on a regular basis for the general public.

They include *News Watch, MediaChannel, Brill's Content, Fairness and Accuracy in Reporting, CounterSpin, Medianews,* and *Media Watch*.

Textual analysis can be applied to any communications medium because photos, illustrations, graphics, and video images can be reduced to textual summaries before analysis. Some language theorists claim that history in general consists of texts to be analysed.

Scripts of radio and television news and entertainment are more readily available than ever, and they often can be secured over the Internet for textual analysis.

Five types of media criticism use textual analysis: Aristotelian, genre, historical, dramatic, and fantasy theme. The first is a return to Aristotle's judicial, logical, and formal analysis centered on the work itself rather than its historical, moral or religious context.

Genre critics group texts that are similar in function, purpose, and form, and then evaluate each text based on the established attributes of the genre. An example of genre criticism is Cawelti's *Adventure, Mystery, and Romance: Formula Stories as Art and Popular Culture,* published by the University of Chicago Press in 1976. Historical criticism consists of oral histories, case studies, bibliographical studies and social movement studies.

The historical critic attempts to evaluate the influence of events on the creation of the text. Dramatic critics study principles drawn from theater—act, purpose, agent, agency, and scene—to evaluate texts. Finally, fantasy theme critics focus on stories with characters that symbolize cultural moral principles or philosophies. Examples of this type of criticism include Chance's *The Lord of the Rings: The Mythology of Power,* published by Twayne Publishers of New York in 1992.

Each of these critical approaches used to study journalism and media share a common list of textual attributes that can be identified and then described, analysed, and evaluated by a community of readers.

Careful and comparative reading and analysis by knowledgeable critics help to create a richer understanding of the function and value of any single text, and such case studies contribute to the general knowledge in the field.

While some media criticism attempts to measure the influence of the mass media on society, in general, textual analysis attempts to categorize, analyse, and evaluate one particular text. Visual forms such as the inverted pyramid are tools of textual analysis that critics use to classify one piece of writing as a report, another as a story, and still another as an essay. Careless use of these forms contribute to confusion and imprecision in the profession.

Thus, textual analysis is an activity that reporters, editors, publishers, news directors, producers, media critics, and researchers use on a daily basis.

For example, a reporter writes a 25-inch news story on Afghanistan, but how good is it.? How can working journalists evaluate the quality of the texts they receive and create on a daily basis? Textual analysis can help.

Attributes of non-fiction prose, including journalism, can be used to categorize, analyse, and evaluate any news report or feature story.

Many of these textual attributes can be applied to texts of sources, too, but some other specialization, including terminology from a field other than journalism, may be required for such an analysis.

THE MEANINGS OF MASS COMMUNICATIONS

The term "mass communications" means different things to different writers and speakers. Another excellent scholar, Charles R. Wright, a contemporary of Schramm, presented a somewhat clearer explanation—clear enough, at least, to show what modifications must be made if we are to see the relationship between journalism and mass communications.

Wright makes quite clear that he is writing about "modern mass communications", but he does not identify or describe any mass communications before the modern period. At least he does not do so explicitly. One can look at what he has to say about modern mass communications, subtract the modern and qualify a few other items, and then set forth the characteristics of basic mass communications.

But why go to all this trouble? Why not simply accept Wright's formulation as he expressed it? Well, even if one extends the modern period back to the middle of the last century, limiting mass communications to that time forces a dilemma: either journalism did not exist before approximately 1850 or journalism, if it did exist before that time, must not be a type of mass communications.

The first choice would ignore the hundreds of books on the history of journalism that set earlier dates for those working in this field, including one of our prototype journalists, Horace Greeley, who was already an experienced journalist when he founded his *New York Tribune* in 1841. The second removes an effective means by which we can distinguish journalism from other practical communications, such as law.

Another, perhaps stronger, reason for removing the "modern" qualification is that the notion of "modern mass communications" is no longer apt. Wright distinguishes modern mass communications from earlier individual communications in this way:

Mass communications is organized communication. Unlike the lone artist or writer, the "communicator" in mass media works through a complex organization embodying an extensive division of labour and an accompanying degree of expense. To be sure, in the 1950s when Wright was preparing his book, mass communications seemed to be moving in the direction of complexity, expensiveness, and a division of labour that resulted in more workers per communication enterprise but fewer and fewer independently controlled media institutions. What Morris L. Ernst had ironically called the "sweep of progress" had continued, seemingly unabated, a decade later. The tide apparently was moving towards bigger but fewer media institutions. Both print and broadcast outlets were getting larger, but their number, and the competition between the members, was decreasing.

This movement, especially among daily newspapers, had flowed along steadily since the second decade of this century. A new type of mass communications, therefore, seemed to be acquiring characteristics that were the inevitable flooding from the past. Thus it could have seemed quite reasonable to Wright to ignore the fact that the communications operations of a century or two earlier were *not* complex and expensive, for the flow of history seemed to show that those days were gone forever.

But technology outwitted the course of history. The machines that had been growing larger, requiring more people to operate and vastly more money to acquire, suddenly began to move in the opposite direction. Computers that had occupied enormous air-cooled rooms shrank until they fit on the lap of a businessman jetting from Chicago to Los Angeles. Minicams plus public access channels brought the possibility of television journalism within the financial range of even the lower middle class.

Desktop publishing moved the production of periodicals into small offices, even into homes. Computer bulletin boards opened a vast range of new ways of distributing messages.

In other words, technology opened doors back into the mass media environment that had existed at the beginning of the nineteenth century: once again, a single person with only a modest investment could convey messages to large numbers of persons in a very short period of time.

If those processes that possess the characteristics of mass communications, except that they involve simple and inexpensive production, are not included in the category of mass communications, then we would have to create another category to accommodate them. But what are we to call the broadsheets introduced by the missionaries in Nigeria a century before that country's independence? They were examples of mass communications, but they were not produced through complex or expensive facilities.

The handwritten newsletters circulated among the refusniks in the USSR; the wall posters that appeared in China during the Cultural Revolution; the mimeographed sheets of church agencies, universities, and justice and peace groups in South and Central America; the *Drudge Report* that appears on the web pages of the Internet: these and many other relatively contemporary communication activities have all the characteristics of early nineteenth-century mass communications. It seems unnecessary to invent another name for the category that merely lacks the complex organization, the division of labour, and the great expense mentioned by Wright.

Many others of Wright's points about mass communi-cations, however, help clarify this confusing term. He says, for instance, that the audience of mass communications is relatively large and that so many people are exposed to the message in a short period of time and are of such numbers "that the communicator could not interact with its members on a face-to-face basis". He also says that the audience is anonymous so that its members "generally remain personally unknown to the communicator".

Moreover, mass communications are public; because the messages "are addressed to no one in particular, their content is open for public surveillance." Also, "They are rapid because the messages are meant to reach large audiences within a relatively short time, or even simultaneously." And, "They are transient because they are usually intended to be consumed immediately".

Even so brief an account tells us enough to help us distinguish journalistic communications from lawyer-courtroom communications. When lawyers address juries, they are addressing several people, but not so many that the lawyers are unable to be aware of them as individuals.

Jurors cannot normally respond verbally to the words of the lawyers, but they have available many non-verbal means of communicating. If one jury member's facial expression indicates skepticism at what the lawyer is saying, the latter can modify his or her communication to take that into consideration.

If another juror shows surprise, the lawyer may realise that an opportunity for pressing a point now exists. If still another juror is falling asleep, that may tell the lawyer it is time to request a recess.

Thus interpersonal communication can exist even when a number of people are involved. How large can that number be? There is no magic figure. Normally, the limit is the number of people to whom the communicator can react as individuals when they provide verbal or non-verbal responses to what the communicator is saying. Consider, for example, the politician who is addressing a thousand people at a political rally. They may cheer or they may boo at what the politician has to say.

The speaker may modify what he had intended to say as a result, but the reaction is to the audience as a collectivity, not to them as individuals. The speaker is engaging in mass communications. But let's say that one person leaps up and begins to engage the speaker in a debate. If the speaker responds, what had been only mass communications then becomes a mixture of mass and interpersonal communications.

When a young couple sends out a thousand wedding invitations to friends and relatives, the process is interpersonal communications in spite of the large number of persons to whom the message is sent. Each person to whom that message is sent can--and is probably expected to--respond individually. Some will attend. Some will send regrets. A few might ask whether they may bring a friend. But when the commander of a thousand troops orders them to attack at dawn, no individual responses are expected and none is likely to take place.

Then the process is solely mass communications. Thus, although in mass communications one or a relatively few people send a message to relatively many people, the exact size of that receiving group is not important.

More important is what Wright refers to as the anonymity of the audience. The audience may be known as a certain category of persons, as when the army commander knows he is addressing infantrymen rather than pilots or when the publisher of a religious newspaper knows the readers are Lutherans rather than Methodists. But these people are not individually spoken to or even precisely thought of as individuals.

Likewise, when a magazine publisher goes to a list broker to buy a thousand names and addresses of people who the publisher hopes will become subscribers, the subscription offers will go out to individually named persons, but they are persons unknown to the publisher. They are as anonymous as "occupant."

The last example reveals a slight modification of Wright's statement that mass communications messages "are addressed to no one in particular" and that the messages are "open for public surveillance." What Wright says is very often true, especially when broadcast mass communications are involved.

But it is less true when the mass communications medium is a periodical sent to a list of subscribers. Large circulation magazines are usually open for public scrutiny at newsstands and libraries, of course, but there are many hundreds of highly practical and specialized publications--for example, trade journals such as Implement and Tractor, China Glass and Tableware, and Western Outfitter-that are not. They are rarely available for inspection by anyone other than subscribers.

Wright's point concerning the transience of mass communications also needs qualification. Mass produced novels, poems, and other works of fiction may endure for centuries, and so also may theoretical non-fiction works such as books of philosophy or natural science.

Such works as Charles Dickens A Tale of Two Cities and Albert Einstein The Meaning of Relativity possess all the qualities Wright attributes to mass communications except transience.

Interestingly, however, the mass communications that are transient are likely to be the journalistic ones, for once they have served their practical purpose, once the decisions have been made from the knowledge that journalism supplies, then the messages cease to be useful, cease to be journalism, and become, like treaties, diaries, and other artifacts, the raw materials of history.

BASIC MASS COMMUNICATIONS

Thus there is a type of mass communications that not only exists in the modern period but also has existed for many earlier centuries.

In this basic mass communications, one person or a relatively few people (relatively few in comparison to the number of people who receive the message) convey one or more messages to a relatively large number of persons.

Often the receivers perceive the messages simultaneously; if not simultaneously, at least they perceive them more quickly than they would if the message had to be originated for each individual. Even if the messages are individually addressed, the receivers are not thought of as individuals; they are thought of as groups or types or masses of people; for all practical purposes, the receivers are anonymous.

Each of those who receive the message does not prepare and deliver an equivalent response to those who send the message. They may, however, respond as a group (as when Pontius Pilate asked the people what he should do with Jesus and they all replied, "Let Him be crucified!"). Sometimes the group reply will be through action rather than through words (as when soldiers, in response to the commander's order "Charge!" go dashing into the field of battle). Thus, although mass communications seem to be one-way, they are not totally so; the sender may well get a response, but not an equivalent response, from each one who receives the message.

A few situations require special attention. Although not all the receivers will give an equivalent response, some of them might do so. For example, a newspaper reader might respond to an editorial with an equivalent letter to the editor. If this letter is delivered to the editorial writer, that person may or may not provide a personal reply.

If the editorial writer does so, then there has been a transition from a mass communication to an interpersonal communication between the letter writer and the editorial writer. Or the editor may decide to publish the letter in the newspaper; if so, a new phase of mass communications takes place, one in which the letter writer is the sender and the other readers of the paper are the receivers.

Quite clearly, not everyone who is involved in a mass communication process is a mass communicator. That name is reserved for those who have control over the content of messages and intend to deliver their messages to masses of people. The readers of newspapers, although participants in the mass communications process, are not normally mass communicators.

Nor are the printers, delivery people, newsstand salespersons, and others who lack the authority to originate or modify the content of the messages. Writers, speakers, editors, photographers, cartoonists, and the like, however, can be mass communicators, if they intend their messages to go out to the masses.

To clarify this latter point, let us consider for a moment the call-in programmes often heard on radio, often late at night. The subjects discussed are sometimes quite personal: the sex life or economic problems of the callers, for example.

The host of the show is clearly a mass communicator. He or she wants the program's messages to be heard by as many people as possible. The host's popularity and income depend upon a wide, anonymous, unrestricted audience.

The host, in other words, is not communicating only with the person who calls in; the host would like to think that he or she is communicating with "the world." But what about the person who calls in? That person is also involved in a mass communications process and originates a portion of the messages that are sent out. But is that person also, like the host, a mass communicator? Perhaps not. Although the caller participates voluntarily in a mass communications process, he or she does not, in many instances, really desire to do so. To obtain free advice, the caller tolerates one type of communication, mass communication, but would probably prefer another type, interpersonal communication.

If the caller happens to be an exhibitionist or propagandist, however, then the caller does become, like the host, a mass communicator.

But because we cannot always establish the truth of intentions, it will sometimes be difficult or impossible to know whether or not a certain person is a mass communicator. Yet in most instances, the evidence and circumstances are so clear that we have no doubts. To those who participate in the mass communications process regularly and for a living, it is particularly easy to grant the title of mass communicator.

Two additional glosses on Wright's mention of anonymity as a characteristic of mass communications are relevant. First, not only do mass communicators not know the recipients of their communications as individuals, but those recipients usually do not know one another as individuals.

They often think of themselves as existing in isolation. Second, partly because of the anonymity of the audience, mass communicators must guess at the level of background knowledge, literacy, and sophistication of the message recipients. The messages are often directed at a level somewhat below the median, to the distress of those who exist at the extremes.

LAWYERS AND JOURNALISTS RECONSIDERED

With all this in mind, we can perhaps better understand how journalists differ from lawyers, even when both groups employ the communication of literally true, practical knowledge.

The former are mass communicators; the latter are not. Courtroom lawyers may direct their messages to a number of people—the judge, jurors, witnesses, the other lawyers—but they are people with whom it is possible for the lawyers to interact as individuals. Although there are prominent exceptions, most lawyers in the courtroom are not interested in addressing the nebulous, anonymous public at large.

The lawyers defending civil-rights activists in the 1960s and 1970s may have been extending their remarks to an audience far outside the courtroom. They may have wanted their words to be political statements to the entire nation about racial injustice.

If so, to that extent they were assuming the role of mass communicators. But, usually, trial lawyers direct their messages to the limited group of persons at hand in the courtroom.

Their aim, like that of journalists, is a practical one, but their audience is the relatively few people who are able to determine the outcome of legal proceedings. In most instances, lawyers control their messages so that they impact on that select group.

In addition, this is an immediate group, one whom lawyers, simply by a turn of the head, can address face-to-face. Any overt reactions by members of this group can be readily known and dealt with by the lawyers. Thus, not only in their private relations with clients in their offices but also in the public arena of the courtroom, lawyers are normally interpersonal communicators. Journalists, on the other hand, are mass communicators.

THE GENERIC MEANING OF JOURNALISM

We have reached the point where we are ready to set forth the basic definition of journalism. Many refinements will be added in the succeeding pages, but the following seems to sum up the comments we have made so far.

Journalism is a type of mass communications:

- That provides useful and practical (rather than theoretical) knowledge;
- That actually is or at least purports to be literally true, rather than invented or fictional;
- That is provided by persons who have at least some control over the content of the messages that are communicated;
- And that aids the recipients of the knowledge in making decisions on issues presently facing them.

Journalism is the type of activity that has all of the attributes just described. Journalists are the persons who engage in that type of activity.

Journalism does not exist aside from the persons who practice it. It is not like a tree or a frying pan or a light bulb; it cannot grow by itself, nor, once made, can it exist by itself. The *products* of journalism—news stories, editorials, video tapes, photographs—can have an independent existence, but journalism itself cannot.

Journalists, however, do exist independently of their journalism. A sleeping Horace Greeley, Frederick Douglass, Ida Tarbell, or Edward R. Murrow would have been identified as a journalist even though, while sleeping, he or she was not practicing journalism.

All of this seems quite clear. What may not be so clear is the correlative point: just as those readily identified as journalists often continue to be called journalists even when they are not practicing journalism, so also those who are not ordinarily identified as journalists ought to be called journalists as soon as they begin to practice journalism.

Journalism is not a custom-made dress or suit available to only a few select people. It is a cloak which almost anybody can throw on.

Journalism is an activity that can be employed by everyone except those who have not yet acquired or who have lost their communicative faculties. Whenever plumbers or clerks or architects or musicians become participants in the activities identified earlier, *they become journalists*.

This point, sometimes ignored, becomes especially important when questions concerning the legal protection of journalists arise.

Such protection belongs to all of us. It is also important when we consider our national educational system, for it means that all citizens should be prepared to practice the arts of journalism, should they ever desire to do so. Thus one of the dangers of attempting to define journalism, now becomes less worrisome. There is no need to license journalists as a restricted class of people when nearly everyone is or legitimately can be a journalist.

SOME OF THE SPECIES OF JOURNALISM

Some people would grant the title of "journalist" only to those for whom the work is a full-time job. But such a viewpoint not only carries with it some of the dangers already mentioned but would be analogous to denying T. S. Eliot the title of poet because he made his living working at Lloyd's Bank or saying William Carlos Williams should not be called a poet because all his life he was a practicing physician.

Thus it seems much better to recognize that, although for some their regular, full-time job is doing the work of journalism, there are many more who practice journalism only occasionally. *New York Tribune* editor Horace Greeley belongs to the first group; Robert Dale Owen, a Democratic congressman from Indiana, who wrote a letter published in the *Tribune* on October 23, 1862, appealing for a Proclamation of Emancipation, belongs to the second.

The first are often called professional journalists in the sense that the principal source of their livelihood is the practice of journalism. For the second, we have no well-accepted designation. Perhaps it is adequate simply to call them amateur or occasional journalists.

Although professional journalists are sometimes given privileges not available to occasional journalists, access to a press box at a baseball game, for example, or access to the press gallery in the U. S. Senate chambers, the legal rights of both the amateurs and the professionals are the same, and whenever they are doing the work described earlier they deserve to be called journalists.

Another set of species is quite obvious, for it is based on the medium employed by journalists to convey their messages to the public. Thus there are newspaper, magazine, radio, television, film, book, and other types of journalists, even though no journalist is inextricably tied to a single medium. Many, in fact, move from one to another, as did William L. Shirer, who switched from the *Chicago Tribune* to radio, television, and books.

Others use several media at the same time, as did David Gergen, who was an editor of *U.S. News and World Report* at the same time that he was a news analyst on public television. But most professional journalists are usually identified with the medium to which they devote most of their time and from which they derive the greater part of their income.

PUBLIC AFFAIRS AND PERSONAL AFFAIRS JOURNALISM

One of the most important, yet also one of the most ignored, divisions of journalism is that into public affairs journalism and personal affairs journalism.

It is easy to understand why it receives so little attention: although both journalists and the public have a quiet awareness that the distinction exists, they seldom discuss it explicitly. But it is so essential to an understanding of journalism that explicit discussion is essential, briefly here and more extensively later on.

The brief description of the generic meaning of journalism is that it provides useful, practical knowledge. But useful for what purpose? Useful to help those who are consumers of journalism decide what should be done or what should be avoided concerning the issues currently facing them. Journalism exists to help all of us decide what is good to do and what is good not to do.

The concept of good, of course, has a multitude of meanings. Here we think of it in relation to those for whom something can be considered good. We can say that something is good for me or we can say that something is good for us. That is, we can make a choice in order to improve, profit, delight, enhance, benefit our individual selves or to do one or all of these things for the improvement and benefit of the community, group, organization, or society of which we individuals are members.

For example, let's consider a fictitious Hiram. Hiram never married and is now retired from his job as a clothing salesman. He lives in a small apartment, is in good health, likes spectator sports, has a satisfactory income from Social Security and a few investments, pays taxes, and is, in general, a rather average person.

Every day, Hiram has to make thousands of decisions. Some are so personal—shall I sleep another five minutes or should I get out of bed right now?—that no other person can be of much help to him in deciding what is the good thing to do. But hundreds of his decisions can be more or less well made depending on the knowledge that is communicated to him from the outside world.

He likes to watch the local baseball team. Is the team playing today? Is the weather likely to be good for baseball? Are the normal means of transportation in operation? Is the admission price the same as last time he went to a game? What time of the day will the game be played? Will it also be shown on television?

How well has the team been doing? Has any starter been injured and thus is unavailable to play? He can probably find the answers to these and to numerous other questions affecting his personal welfare by consulting his daily newspaper or listening to the news reports on radio or television.

The knowledge he receives will help him decide whether or not it would be good for him to attend the baseball game. Learning that the game will be shown on television, Hiram may decide to watch it at home rather than go out to the ballpark. Many others, receiving the same information, may decide just the opposite. Hiram's decision is a personal decision in the sense that he decides what is good for himself. Other baseball fans can make similar or different personal decisions. It is not necessary that there be just one decision.

Now let's say that while reading the newspaper Hiram learns that next Tuesday the city will hold a referendum to determine whether or not money will be borrowed to build a new high school. In this situation, the decision to be made is not what is good for Hiram but rather what is good for the city, not "for me" but "for us." Whatever the decision is, it will be one decision. It will be assumed that even those who might have preferred a different decision will go along with the one that is made.

If the voters decide to approve of the borrowing, that decision will be against Hiram's personal welfare: his taxes will probably increase, and he has no children who will benefit from the new school.

But if the new school is truly needed, the public welfare might well require that money be borrowed to build it. In fact, Hiram himself, recognizing the dominant character of the public welfare, of the common good, might put aside consideration of his own personal good to vote in favour of the referendum.

What, then, is the difference between personal affairs journalism and public affairs journalism? The first type provides the knowledge people can use to make good decisions about their personal, current welfare. Each person decides what is good for him or her, independent of the decisions being made by others. Much of the journalism dealing with sports, business, and entertainment (just to name a few possibilities) is of that type.

The second type of journalism provides the knowledge people need for decisions concerning the current welfare of some community, group, organization, or society of which they are a part. Here a decision will be made (perhaps by all the members, perhaps by one or a few) concerning what will be good for that community or group. It will be a decision concerning the welfare of the whole collectivity, and the members will be expected to go along with it even if they would have preferred some other decision.

Most of the activities of federal, state, and local governments are the business of public affairs journalism, but the latter can also extend to private groups: fraternities or businesses, for instance.

The welfare of these, too, requires decisions concerning the good of the whole, and public affairs journalism contributes to the goodness of those decisions. If one company is considering a merger with another, this decision concerns the welfare of both companies and is a decision in which the managements, stockholders, and employees have a stake.

All need knowledge so that the decision can be well made, and most of the knowledge that is needed comes through the work of public affairs journalism. One might ask: Why should members of a public pay attention to issues-such as a proposal to raise tax rates—which seem beyond the public's powers of determination? Some answers will be found in our later discussions of public opinion and electoral processes.

For now, it may be sufficient to recollect that mass communications always extend messages to more people than have a direct need for them. Can we also say that the communications tasks associated with public relations and with advertising ought to be viewed as additional types or species of journalism? That question has been the source of many heated disagreements.

One of the most vigorous of these disagreements took place in the 1950s when Sigma Delta Chi, the Society of Professional Journalists (SPJ), debated the problem of membership eligibility. Having already excluded advertising people from the organization, the members now decided that, in the future, public relations practitioners would also be excluded because neither group was composed of true journalists.

Some public relations practitioners do spend their time analyzing situations and providing interpersonal consultation to their clients. Similarly, some advertising people spend time in market and media research and in similar interpersonal communications.

Thus, to the extent they are not engaged in mass communications, they would not fit the definition of journalists.

But the activities of most people in both fields culminate in their preparing messages for the mass media. To the extent that those messages convey useful knowledge that at least purports to be true, the work they do fits the concept of journalism.

Why, then, did SPJ claim they were *not* journalists? For years, the society had differentiated between those acceptable persons who prepared and disseminated information in the "public interest" and those non-acceptable persons who did so in what the members called the "private interest." They concluded that all advertising people were in the latter category; but in 1952, they admitted, at least for a few years, that this was not true of all public relations practitioners.

Those who wrote for civic organizations, social agencies, benevolent foundations, educational institutions, and governmental departments (with the interesting exception of the military) and who had an "acceptable background of experience in news work for newspapers, magazines or in broadcasting" could be considered to be working in the public interest and thus be eligible for membership.

But in the summer of 1958, a select panel had second thoughts about even these exceptions and submitted a report proposing, among other things, that there be no initiation of public relations men in the future. A heated and extensive debate ensued, much of it carried out in the pages of *Quill*, the society's journal, concluding with a vote at the 1958 national convention that endorsed the report.

One of the more interesting contributions to the debate came from a group of distinguished public relations persons themselves. Although they were grandfathered into the society, they said they recognized differences between their work and that of many other members:

We accept your tighter definition of journalism. Although we prepare and disseminate news stories, we admit we do so, at least in part, in the interest of our clients and employers. Newsmen, on the other hand, generally work without obligation to any special interest. Both activities may well be in the public interest, but there is a fundamental difference which is important to Sigma Delta Chi.

Several years later, David Berkman seemed to express a similar thought. In discussing whether public relations courses have a place within journalism programmes, he wrote, "If we accept—and how can we not do so?—that the purpose of the journalist is to discover and report truth, while that of those in public relations is to serve the interests of their clients or employers, then the answer is clearly 'no'".

Even though public relations practitioners serve the interests of clients or employers, it does not necessarily follow that such a type of service precludes the discovering and reporting of truth.

Journalists, no matter whether they are newswriters, public relations practitioners, or advertising personnel, can have a variety of motives when they do their work. They can be working for their own welfare, for the welfare of a cause in which they are interested, for the welfare of their employers, for the welfare of the public, or for many other possible objectives. To say that only one of these goals is good and all the rest are suspect is to assume an arbitrary and unreasonable moral standard. Any or all of them can be good, and no one of them need necessarily exclude the others. Any moralistic approach to the definition of journalism depends in part on the precarious possibility of detecting the intentions of message senders.

Although some journalists are morally good and some morally deficient, it is not the case that all newspeople are in the first category and all public relations and advertising people in the second.

It did not seem, for instance, that former *Wall Street Journal* reporter R. Foster Winans had been acting as a very ethical journalist when he was convicted in 1985 of using his "Heard on the Street" stock market column to further an insider trading scheme that netted him $31,000.

Unfortunately, deceptions on various levels have not been infrequent among newspeople during the history of journalism.

During the first months of 1998, Stephen Glass of the *New Republic*, Patricia Smith of the *Boston Globe*, and April Oliver of CNN lost their jobs for concocting material that turned out not to be factual. But they certainly are not typical of all reporters, columnists, and television producers.

Likewise, some advertising and public relations practitioners lack the integrity we ought to expect of people who work in those fields even though most of them adhere to the goals of their professions. The Public Relations Society of America*Code of Professional Standards* says, "A member shall conduct his or her professional life in accord with the public interest."

Also, advertising personnel aim at stimulating business competition, resulting in improved products and more economical ways to produce and distribute them; thus in the end "the consumer benefits by the availability of new and better products".

To increase the likelihood of such good performance is one reason for incorporating advertising and public relations instruction in journalism programmes.

The journalism/advertising identification is further complicated because some advertising, like newspaper, magazine, and broadcast editorials, argues for or against public issues.

The Mobil Oil Company produces this type of editorial advertising frequently. The American Federation of Teachers buys space in the *New York Times* on the first Sunday of each month so that its president can discuss matters of public policy.

Similarly, political public relations contribute to the public discussion of public affairs. The public relations writer, of course, advances the position of the person or party who is paying the bill, but print and broadcast editorial writers also advance the positions of the editors, publishers, or station managers who employ them. Ideological, ethnic, religious, and other special interest newspapers, magazines, and cable systems are as much devoted to advancing private agendas as are public relations and advertising practitioners. And at least since the period of the penny press in the 1830s, a strong feeling has existed that some members of the information media function more to sell copies and enrich their owners than to serve the public. The contemporary members of this trend might be the tabloids conveniently placed along the supermarket checkout lanes.

ADVERTISING AND PUBLIC RELATIONS ARE SPECIES OF JOURNALISM

Thus it seems that as long as advertising and public relations people use the mass media to convey purportedly true knowledge that can help people make good decisions about what to do and what to avoid in regard to issues currently facing them, advertising and public relations people ought to be considered journalists as much as anyone else who does that type of work.

They are, in particular, much like print and broadcast editorial writers, columnists, and commentators. Like them, advertising and public relations practitioners are persuaders. It is true that they advance products or causes in which they or their employers are interested, but so also did Greeley, Douglass, Tarbell, and Murrow—and nearly all of those whom we are proud to identify as journalists.

It is also true that, unlike some other journalists, advertising journalists buy space or time in media that they do not own. This makes them different from those who own or those who are employed by those who own their media. But every type of journalist is different from other types: photojournalists differ from word journalists, broadcast journalists from print journalists, public affairs journalists from personal affairs journalists.

The fact that a person is this type of journalist rather than another *type* of journalist need not deprive that person of identification as *a journalist*. Many public relations practitioners produce their own media: newsletters, company newspapers, brochures, slide presentations, annual reports, and video- tapes.

Many of the others supply, at no cost, informational, analytical, and persuasive material to the general mass media. Some studies indicate that more than half of the non-wire, non-syndicated editorial content of newspapers comes from releases or memos generated by public relations sources. Some press agents have misused their abilities, it is true, but the same can be said of those in any field of endeavor. Nothing in the nature of the work they do requires either the lying or fictionizing that would exclude them from journalism.

TEXTUAL ANALYSIS OF NEWS WRITING

Evan Mahoney, a reporter for the Fund for Investigative Reporting and a professor at University of North Carolina at Asheville, uses the following terms when teaching, analyzing, and evaluating news writing: abstraction, attribution, connotation, denotation, contrast, lead, nut graph, narration, exposition, form, induction, deduction, tone, voice, mood, style, thesis, quotation, and metaphor.

Consistently careful use of such attributes of language can enrich the experience of reading in addition to simply informing the public. For example, smell and fragrance have the same denotative (literal) meaning, but one has a positive connotative (suggestive) meaning while the other is negative. A quick reading, without textual analysis, can miss connotations. Exposition is logical explanation, and form is the overall structure of an article.

Induction is reasoning that moves from specific details to a generalization, while deduction moves from a generalization to specifics. Tone and mood refer to word choices that indicate seriousness, humour, glee or depression, to name only a few emotions.

Paying careful attention to these attributes of language can lead to an enriched understanding of a text. Mahoney urged writers to check for these attributes when revising their texts to enrich their writing and make it more engaging.

Diana Fishlock, diversity reporter for the Harrison (Penn.) Patriot-News, considered brainstorming, ambiguity, cliches, character, close-ups (concrete, sensory details), and editorializing when evaluating her own writing and the writing of others.

Brainstorming is a method for analyzing topics or ideas for a news story. It ranges from making simple lists of ideas and ranking them in importance to semantic webbing, in which the writer begins with a key word and diagrammatically connects it to another word, whatever comes to mind, and so on, through lines and circles. New connections are made in this playful act of discovery, and the process helps the writer see new possibilities for the article.

Fishlock explains: Brainstorming often is extremely useful. Brainstorming and simply having time to let a concept percolate in my mind help me to explore more facets of the idea. Is there a historical context? What about religion? Given the time (or brainstorming input from other people) the story becomes much more complete ... Often character makes or breaks a story. If the character is compelling and the writer is able to show that, I'll read about someone doing almost anything-even something I may have no interest in.

Media criticism is growing as a classroom and newsroom practice, so news writers must become more sophisticated about their use of language. Textual analysis is a qualitative method that can be used to create, defend, and improve writing skills. "Making meaning clear does not mean making the copy tedious," Peter Jacobi explained during the Association for Education in Journalism and Mass Communication's Gannett Teaching Fellows Workshop at Indiana University. "Exposition [information delivery] must go beyond a dictionary definition and be as bright and intriguing as narration [story telling]."

TEXTUAL ANALYSIS OF CIVIC JOURNALISM

Reporters conducted textual analysis of community conversations that were conducted with a wide range of citizens in Columbia, Missouri. The project began with University of Missouri School of Journalism Professor Edmund Lambeth who studied and taught civic journalism, a movement debated in research and trade journals throughout the 1990s.

Lambeth established the Civic Journalism Interest Group of the Association for Education in Journalism and Mass Communication and guided the university's Columbia *Missourian* newspaper staff through a civic journalism project that became known as "Faith in Our Community". Lambeth said public journalism could be viewed as a form of journalism that seeks to:

- Listen systematically to the stories and ideas of citizens even while protecting its freedom to choose what to cover.
- Examine alternative ways to frame stories on important community issues.
- Choose frames that stand the best chance to stimulate citizen deliberation and build public understanding of issues.
- Take the initiative to report on major public problems in a way that advances public knowledge of possible solutions and the values served by alternative courses of action.
- Pay continuing and systematic attention to how well and how credibly it is communicating with the public.

To test the effects of one of civic journalism's reporting tools, community conversations, a group of radio, TV, and newspaper journalists worked together to conduct a civic journalism project and publish a series of news stories during the week of May 26, 1996. With the support of their editors and station managers, the group planned a week-long collaborative strategy that included all three media because Lambeth's earlier research indicated that citizens learn more from multimedia presentations.

Missourian Managing Editor George Kennedy said the media managers selected the topic during a discussion session. They settled on religion because it had high relevance to the community and inadequate coverage. He said the goal was to raise the level of public awareness concerning the relationship between religion and public life.

Research began in Fall 1995 when five resource panels were conducted. Each resource panel consisted of about five experts who were knowledgeable in some aspect of religion and public life. Media managers moderated the panels, and the audience consisted of reporters and editors. These panels were used for background information only.

Eight community conversations were planned. These, too, were used only for background information. Participants were told in advance that they would not be quoted in the newspaper or recorded for radio or TV, although minutes of the meetings were recorded and reported to project members. Confidentiality enabled participants to speak more openly and freely, said a reporter who conducted the public policy conversation.

Otherwise, the citizen-participants might have been reluctant to be honest and forthright about controversial issues, he said, adding that the conversations were good for generating sources and story ideas. One reservation was expressed by a reporter who said the time and effort required to organize, conduct, and analyse community conversations could be costly in day-to-day reporting.

The advantage of using them on a collaborative project, he said, was that several reporters could attend and benefit from one community conversation. Throughout the civic journalism project previously described, Lambeth met with graduate journalism students to study and analyse the significance of these practices to working journalists. One of his classes discussed a list of characteristics of civic journalism, which could be used to identify the Language of civic journalism.

These characteristic attributes of civic journalism were identified as coverage of citizen viewpoints, invitations to action in news stories, reporter-reader interaction, identification of personal and social values, identification of consequences associated with the events-issues covered, and identification of the stakeholders involved in the coverage.

This list of attributes complemented the attributes of traditional news stories that researchers have previously identified as characteristics of news: impact, proximity, timeliness, prominence, novelty, and conflict.

Two hypotheses emerged from this exercise:

- Textual analysis of a civic journalism news story should produce attributes significantly different from those of a traditional news story;
- At least most of the attributes of civic journalism identified by Lambeth and his students should be found in civic journalism texts. The original list was modified according to suggestions in a memo from newspaper editor Davis Merritt, one of the founders of the public journalism movement:

The objective isn't to quantify things and make a judgement about whether or how much a newspaper is succeeding, though that might be a small side effect. Rather, the objective is to provide a list of traits that we think constitute public journalism and examples to illustrate those traits—and how they differ from traditional practice —as a step towards a working definition that journalists can understand.

A sample of readers was asked to rate these news criteria from low to high on a 7-point scale after reading several blocks of news coverage that resulted from the civic journalism project titled "Faith in Our Community" and samples of more traditional news coverage from the same period and newspaper.

Some blocks contained traditional news coverage, some civic journalism style reporting, and some were mixed. The following are the textual attributes and their definitions that were rated in this pilot study.

- *Citizen viewpoints*: Citizens are identified as contributors in solving a public issue.
- *Impact*: Many citizens are likely to be significantly affected by this news.
- *Invitations to action*: This news coverage presents ways readers can actively respond.
- *Proximity*: This takes place close to readers' homes.
- *Reporter-reader interaction*: This indicates reporters have communicated with citizens.
- *Timeliness*: This news is based on recent events.
- *Values*: The values (moral—ethical principles) under-lying courses of action are explained.
- *Prominence*: This news includes well-known person-alities or celebrities.
- *Consequences*: Consequences (the outcome or end results) of actual or possible decisions are explained.
- *Novelty*: This news is based on the odd or unusual.
- *Stakeholders*: Who (individuals or groups) stands to gain and who stands to lose are clearly identified (in the news story).
- *Conflict*: This news emphasizes opposing sides.

A procedure was designed to test two hypotheses about the characteristics of the news coverage.

The researcher wanted to learn:

- Whether readers would identify civic journalism stories,
- Whether readers would rate civic journalism stories differently from traditional news stories.

The readers for this pilot study consisted of 12, specifically selected journalism students who had completed a basic news writing course and were in a media history course. This sample was used because the members possessed a basic knowledge of the elements of journalism.

Each subject was asked to read five to six blocks of news and rate each block, which represented part of a newspaper page and contained some of the "Faith in our Community" project. The block included headlines, teasers, photos, captions, and other news devices. The blocks were rated according to the 12 textual attributes previously listed.

At least two readers rated each block, and scores for each of the criteria were averaged for each copy block. The scores were grouped into a public journalism (PJ) index (statements 1, 3, 5, 7, 9, and 11 previously mentioned) and a traditional journalism (TJ) index (2, 4, 6, 8, 10, and 12). Each block received

PJ index and TJ index scores. Scoring on a 7-point scale, the readers gave the public journalism blocks an average of 4.62 for public journalism and only 3.62 for traditional journalism; they gave the traditional journalism blocks a 4.16 for traditional journalism and a 3.67 for public journalism.

The public journalism index score was a full point above the traditional journalism index score for the blocks that contained the public journalism news. This shows that the readers correctly identified which news blocks contained more public journalism language attributes. They had identified public journalism by its textual attributes.

Textual analysis can be useful to reporters, editors, news directors, and researchers, who use it to explain how mass media affect our everyday lives. Mahoney and Fishlock used textual analysis to help strengthen individual journalists' writing skills by offering models to identify, describe, and evaluate vari ous types of news writing. Miller and Dewar used textual analysis of complex government documents to uncover important issues clouded by legalese.

Finally, textual analysis offers benefits through identifying, describing, and evaluating various genres of journalism as shown by the civic journalism project in Missouri. That textual analysis revealed that a purposive sample of journalism students could identify public journalism texts by language attributes.

Manzella frames the civic journalism debate of the 1990s as a battle between the news of record, inverted-pyramid journalists versus the narrative, storytelling journalists. Before deciding which is the one best style tor journalism, media critics, editors, and news writers must carefully identify, describe, and evaluate the various genres of news writing. After seeing valid alternatives, the questions to ask, as Merritt suggested, involve the characteristics of various forms of journalism, and the set of circumstances that call for the use of each form.

The questions that can be addressed through textual analysis are qualitative. As researchers analyse a text, they ask the overarching question, "What are the qualities of this particular text, and how does this text compare and contrast to other texts?" Under this umbrella, they may ask other questions such as, "Can readers distinguish a public journalism text from a traditional journalism text?" or "What's the difference between a story and a report?" or "How does interactivity affect the language of journalism?" Textual analysis takes more time than routine reading, and it may require some computer hardware and software, but it is an effective method for understanding and evaluating news writing, complex documents and journalism genres.

2

Framing and Temporality in Visual News Discourse

In what is now a classic treatise, Goffman argues that human beings organize or "frame" everyday life in order to comprehend and respond to social phenomena. When applied to studies of news, "media frames" allow readers to "locate, perceive, identify, and label" the multiple happenings of the social world in a way that will be meaningful to them.

Media sociologists have found the framing metaphor to be of heuristic value for understanding how journalists process and package large quantities of information, quickly and routinely.

For instance, Gitlin argues that media frames are "largely unspoken and unacknowledged [and] organize the world both for journalists who report it and, in some important degree, for us who rely on their reports."

According to Gitlin, media frames "naturalize" the social world apropos certain discursive conventions. In other words, media frames function as the centre or core of a larger unit of public discourse and are intelligible beca use they are "tacitly presupposed within a particular linguistic practice". According to Snow et al., media frames have the capacity to do more than merely organize experience for newsreaders—frames also serve as a "guide to action".

Conceptualized in this way, framing essentially involves selecting "some aspects of a perceived reality [to] make them more salient in a communicating text, in such a way as to promote a particular problem definition... frames, then, define problems... diagnose causes... make moral judgements... and suggest remedies".

Political cartoons operate as frames for the organization of social knowledge insofar as they make use of various rhetorical devices— metaphors, catch phrases, depictions, etc.—that purport to capture the essence of an issue or event graphically As Gamson and Stuart have argued, cartoons "offer a number of different condensing symbols that suggest the core frame" of the issue.

Cartoons help to render infinite amounts of detail into practical frameworks that are relevant and appropriate to social actors understanding the everyday world. In this sense, political cartoons channel the discursive possibilities for making sense of social phenomena; they legitimate (and thus facilitate) the grounds upon which some things can be said and others impeded.

The structural organization of knowledge about the world within visual discourse may lead to what Mumby and Spitzack (1983) call "metaphoric entrapment": "The way in which a concept is understood becomes so tied up with a particular metaphoric structure that alternative ways of viewing that concept are obscured, or else appear to make less sense".

The visual image, its caption and the accompanying label or "punch line" provide clues to the preferred meanings and the types of outcomes or consequences that the artist feels may legitimately result from the activity, issue or event being depicted.

Despite offering a rather useful framework for examining the selectivity, partiality and inclusion or exclusion of particular claims, the "framing" metaphor is theoretically limited in terms of being able to properly capture the temporal or unfolding character of social reality.

Indeed, Goffman readily acknowledged that the rules of a frame are analogous to the syntactical structures of language, a position which led some observers to critique frame analysis as far too static a model for capturing social process as it actually unfolds.

To account for the shifting and temporal character of the social world, our understanding of it and how political cartoons capture this process, Mead's theory of temporality may be useful as a complementary framework to the approach developed thus far.

According to Mead, neither the past nor future exists as an objective social fact in the sense that there is no definitive claim to universal understanding about what has already happened, what is currently going on or what is likely to happen in the future. Rather, for Mead, "every conception of the past is construed from the standpoint of the new problems of today".

Furthermore, to find justification in a permanent or "irrefragable past" is, according to Mead, an endeavour hampered by awareness that "different minds within a generation will discover different pasts".

In Mead's view, the definition of the present is always subject to change in light of the claims-making activities of social actors in the real world. Moreover, as real world events change over time, news frames must become "flexible to accommodate new contents and perspectives, and to rearrange what is already [embedded] within the frame".

When applied to studies of media discourse, this suggests that news coverage organizes our understanding of everyday life in its temporal sense, *i.e.*, it structures our awareness of the past in ways that are shaped by, and become meaningful for, claims about current or future needs. Indeed, as Schudson argues, journalistic accounts of the past not only legitimate the authoritative status of newsmakers as storytellers but they al so provide newsmakers and readers alike with analytic tools for describing and constructing meaning about future problems.

The temporal dimension of visual news discourse is of sociological importance not only because cartoons provide a lens through which an implied version of the past may be examined vis-a-vis present conditions but also because media accounts of social phenomena have repercussions for how societies relate to their own histories.

The claims constructed in political cartoons are illustrative of whether a society will see itself as a collective or a mosaic of different groups, whether it will interrogate its past critically or accept it as given, and whether and how it will see the past as relevant to the needs of the present and future.

Thus, political cartoons not only grasp the way in which visual discourse conveys social experience, but cartoons also help constitute the subjectivities and identities of social subjects, their relations, and the field in which they exist.

Of course, this is not to say that political cartoons causally affect how individuals and groups will define themselves in moments of stability or crisis. Rather, in speaking of visual discourse, it is probably more accurate to refer to "the persuasion to attitude, rather than persuasion to out-and-out action". Political cartoons are an optic to a "timely topic that exploits commonplaces of a transitory nature". Political cartoons are thus both informative and persuasive.

Cartoons render normative judgements about social issues by employing a variety of journalistic conventions, such as figures of speech, metaphors and irony As Savarese notes, persuasive techniques such as the aforementioned are used either "deliberately or unwittingly to convince the public of a certaln point of view (for or against something) without being explicit."

As the empirical portion of this study will endeavour to show, the persuasiveness of any claim about a given "social proble m" will resonate only when the audience being addressed is living in and experiencing a set of socio-historical conditions that enable those claims to make sense," that is, when the temporal positions of social actors correspond to the structural organization of discourse about phenomena in a meaningful way.

This chapter employs a hermeneutic framework for the analysis of political cartoons as visual news discourse. In doing so, it takes seriously Thompson's statement that discourse analysis should involve "a synthetic construction, a creative projection, of a possible meaning".

A word of caution: the political provenance of an approach of this sort requires methodological clarity, for as Purvis and Hunt state, "the discursive practices through which subjects are constituted... may have, but do not necessarily have, ideological effects."

Thus, visual discourse analysis does not reveal how newsreaders will actually interpret the content of a cartoon in the context of everyday life.

Rather, hermeneutic analysis of political cartoons allows the analyst to describe the "materiality" of discourse at the point of reader contact and provides clues to the range of possible readings readers may construct. Though a reader may be able to decipher, in whole or in part, the preferred interpretation of t he cartoon, this is not to say that s/he will accept it ipso facto.

Whereas most studies of social problems construction criticize news media for amplifying the situation and exaggerating the general public's level of anxiety, significantly less attention has been paid to examining the visual signs and symbols that accompany written news reports.

A hermeneutic analysis of political cartoons and its relation to social problems construction acknowledges the role that cultural and symbolic representations, myths, narratives and meanings play in organizing everyday experience and the interpretive process that ensues. Such a framework "accords to the various levels of human consciousness a fundamental role in the ontology of social problems".

In making a case for the sociological import of political cartoons, this study draws upon the methodological schema developed by Morris's sociology of visual rhetoric. Morris argues that cartoons capture the endless binary oppositions that organize social representations about the world and provide, as it were, a "cognitive map" for understanding everyday life.

According to Morris, cartoons establish social goals and devise the division of labour needed to attain these by:

- Establishing the source of the cartoon (*i.e.*, artist, newspaper) as an authority or expert in relation to the event or problem in question and identifying, locating and labelling certain "other" elements as "troublesome";
- Constructing a specific frame and setting an agenda that will "create or excite interest in a problem, generate a sense of intellectual crisis, identify the nature of the crisis, pinpoint its symptoms, and propose a course of action as the effective remedy";
- Constructing a normative agenda against which newsreaders may evaluate the cartoon's characters in moral terms; and
- Promoting the "desire for action" by ensuring that the preferred message resonates with the lived experiences of the audience.

Morris also argues that four rhetorical devices will affect the contents, intended meanings and negotiated meanings of political cartoons. First, condensation involves the compression of disconnected or complexly related events to a common, singular frame. Second, combination involves the construction and organization of various elements or ideas from different domains with numerous and perhaps conflicting meanings. Third, opposition is a process whereby the complexity of a problem or event is reduced to a binary struggle. And fourth, domestication occurs when distant events remote from the everyday experience(s) of the reader are translated into concrete happenings that can be experienced as close and familiar.

To enrich Morris's schema, it is instructive to consider the ways in which visual discourse of the world transfers meaning and causal blame along a referential chain of signifiers within a particular image. Thus, I propose an additional analytic device: the notion of "transference."

Transference normally operates in an implicit way that absolves the cartoon's actors of their absurd actions or commentary by displacing blame to another, normally non-visible, actor. The notion of "transference" fits neatly within the rhetorical framework of opinion discourse in that it not only evaluates social phenomena and social process, but it also explains these events in ways that have first and foremost to do with the allocation of blame and attribution of responsibility.

One final caveat is worth mentioning here, which is that when performing empirical analysis, each of these processes—condensation, combination, opposition, domestication and transference—should not be treated independently but, rather, as strategies of "meaning-making" that operate within a broader "repertoire of cultural evaluation".

CIVIC UTILITY OF THE NEWS

All three publics for the news intuitively grasp the idea of civic utility, and among all three publics there are strong beliefs that much of what one finds in the daily news lacks relevance.

Public opinion polls and focus groups can detail these views with considerable specificity—whether ascertaining overall evaluations of news media performance or evaluations of the coverage about individual issues, public figures and other topics.

This kind of research is needed on a continuing basis to measure exactly how effective the news media are as public communicators, to measure how relevant citizens find the content of the news media, and how much the public has learned from this content.

Moreover, this research should go beyond general descriptions of how the public responds to the daily news and measure the performance of the news media against some very specific criteria. One source for these criteria is the venerable Hutchins Commission report, "A *Free and Responsible Press.*" However, before reviewing the criteria for media performance advanced by that commission, some important aspects of its background need to be noted.

Although this report is most frequently discussed in the idealistic context of social responsibility theory—one of the grand macrotheories, along with the libertarian and authoritarian theories, of how the mass media are organized in various societies—the origins of this report were imminently practical. The commission was suggested to University of Chicago Chancellor Robert Hutchins by *Time* magazine founder and publisher Henry Luce and substantially funded by Time Inc. However, the members of the commission, distinguished academics and public officials of their day, enjoyed complete freedom in their deliberations.

Their comprehensive analysis of the mass media, not just the news media of their day but also movies and books, identified five requirements for a free and responsible press in a democratic society:

- A truthful, comprehensive, and intelligent account of each day's events in a context that brings out their full meaning. There is already enough in this initial criterion of media performance to fill the questionnaire of a public opinion poll or discussion guide for focus groups. And numerous examples already have been offered here of gaps and irrelevancies in daily news coverage. But there is more to consider.
- A forum for the exchange of comment and criticism, a requirement that advocates of public journalism contend goes considerably beyond letters to the editor, op-ed pieces and occasional news reports on public hearings, civic debates and other incidental public affairs events.
- A representative picture of the various social groups that constitute American society, a requirement that has taken on considerable significance since September 11th. The importance of understanding people who trace their ethnic and cultural background to the Middle East, other parts of Asia, and to Latin America was further underscored by the 2000 Census with its detailed findings on the substantial immigrant population of the United States. It is also particularly important to take note of the long history of public reports seeking better understanding of racial relations and tensions in our country.
- Presentation and clarification of our country's goals and values, a requirement inextricably linked with the previous requirement because of the increasing cultural complexity of the country as a whole and its individual cities, towns and neighbourhoods. Noting that the mass media are "an educational instrument, perhaps the most powerful there is, " the Commission also observed, "The mass media, whether or not they wish to do so, blur or clarify these ideals as they report the failings and achievements of every day. "
- Facilitation of citizens' full access to information about the current state of public affairs. Facilitating full access does not ignore differences in an individual citizen's need for orientation or the existence of multiple publics for the day's news.

We do not assume that all citizens at all times will actually use all the material they receive. By necessity or choice large numbers of people voluntarily delegate analysis and decision to leaders who they trust. Such leadership in our society is freely chosen and constantly changing; it is informal, unofficial, and flexible. Any citizen may at any time assume the power of decision.

In this way, the government is carried on by consent. To paraphrase a more recent *New York Times* advertising campaign touting that newspaper's extensive news coverage, "You may not read it all, but isn't it comforting to know that it is there." Especially in a time of declining political participation, maintaining the option for every citizen to participate in a knowledgeable way is critical. There are three publics for the daily news, and news media have a responsibility to be effective communicators to all three. This requires careful professional reflection about the choices made each day for the media agenda. It also requires precise measurement of the public's response to this agenda, explicit feedback that measures the effectiveness of journalists as public communicators with a vital social role.

Much like those swelling waves that can move across the vast reaches of the Pacific Ocean, steadily growing in size and momentum until their gigantic flood engulfs some isolated island, a vast technological wave moved relentlessly across the 20th century and pounded onto our shores in this new millennium.

Early in that century, radio—the first of the electronic mass media—supplemented the hundreds of newspapers and magazines. By midcentury, television added to the reach and power of mass communication, soon augmented by ever expanding cable television channels.

As the century moved towards its close, the personal computer and the Internet opened a vast new universe of information, a combination of an international yellow pages targeted at specific individual needs and an international newsstand offering mass media from every corner of the world with every perspective on the day's news. Technological marvels—the gee-whiz stuff of feature stories— had created a gigantic wave of information.

Although there always has been a tendency to view new communication technologies as unmitigated blessings, as a panacea for our social problems, it also always has been the case that reality soon provides a corrective discount. This already is apparent in regard to the flood of information chan nels now available to us. The lessons to be learned from Postman and Thoreau in this regard were cited at the very beginning of this book. More is not necessarily better.

MEDIA COMPETITION AND DIVERSITY

In elaborating why more is not automatically better, we preface our discussion of the situation here in the new millennium by reviewing a widely shared belief about mass communication, the belief that competition creates diversity.

As the number of daily newspapers in the United States receded from 1,772 morning and evening papers in 1950 to 1,480 dailies at the end of the century, leaving more and more cities with a single newspaper voice and an ever-smaller number of companies owning a larger and larger proportion of the newspapers still publishing, critics viewed these trends with great alarm.

In their view, the marketplace of ideas—the supply of news and opinion—became significantly less diverse when a competitor disappeared from the market and left a city with only a single daily newspaper.

In those earlier times when daily newspapers were the dominant mass media, the presence of competing daily newspapers in a community was taken as prima facie evidence of diversity in the supply of news and opinion. But was that true? Or, alternatively, is the menu of news and opinion available to the audience largely determined by the traditions and practices of journalists regardless of the ownership structure?

The traditions of journalism centre on news values and ethical standards, such as balance and fairness, and the homogenizing influence of these traditions on news content have been traced as far back as the 19th century. The routines of news gathering—for example, the organization of news beats, reliance on press releases, and covering events, many of which are staged specifically to attract press attention—further define the homogenous behaviour of journalists across news organizations. The social perspectives of journalism are a centripetal force for a centrist convergence on social and political issues.

In short, this body of evidence on the sociology of news collectively predicts that news media competing in the same geographic and demographic markets will produce highly similar, not diverse, products. Back in the time when there were competing newspapers in many cities, a detailed content analysis of the situation in 23 cities across the United States found minor differences at best between the "leaders" and "trailers" in 22 categories of content.

Nor was there any difference in the proportion of the newshole that was devoted to news and editorial content. This null relationship between competition and diversity of content is succinctly summed up by the title of another article on this topic, Rivals in Conformity.

Further perspective on this question is gained from a comparison of competing newspapers in Cleveland, Ohio, Winnipeg, Manitoba, and Montreal, Quebec prior to the end of competition in those cities and a further comparison of the surviving newspaper before and after the suspension of its competitor. Detailed comparisons of general content categories for the entire newspaper, of more specific categories for the news of the day appearing in the front section of the newspaper, and of the geography of the news coverage essentially produced portraits of rivals in conformity.

An additional qualitative analysis of the Montreal newspapers' coverage of an extensive regional power blackout indicates that the readers of both Montreal papers received virtually the same facts from the same sources over a three-day period. Nor were there any major changes for better or worse in these three surviving newspapers a year after the disappearance of their competitors.

A comprehensive look at the broad mix of nine news media available to Chapel Hill, N. C., voters during the 1972 presidential election is compelling testimony about the homogeneous nature of the marketplace of ideas. There was no local daily in Chapel Hill, but voters used four dailies from nearby cities, the *New York Times*, two television networks, and two newsmagazines as major sources of information about the issues in the campaign.

Comparisons of the pattern of news coverage among these nine news media can be summarized by correlation coefficients in which 1.0 is a perfect match and 0.0 is no match at all. Among the four local newspapers, the median correlation is +.90. Across this entire mix of news media the median correlation is a hearty +.78.

Despite the technological diversity of these media of communication and the significant diversity in the geography spread and demography of their audiences, when these news organizations look out at the issues of the day, their observations are virtually identical. A multiplicity of media voice is no guarantee of diversity in content.

There is a tremendous amount of redundancy across the news media. More frequently means more of the same. Professional norms of journalism, more than the presence of competition from other news media, determine the range of content available to the audience.

As to the quality of that content, little seems to have changed since Raymond Nixon and Robert Jones drew this prescient conclusion after an extensive mid-20th-century examination of 420 competitive and non-competitive U. S. daily dailies:

Differences in quality seem to hinge upon the "social responsibility and professional competence" of those who own and operate the papers, irrespective of whether they have competition.

At the time of this observation, a media company typically was a corporation that owned a large number of newspapers and perhaps a scattering of broadcast properties. Over the last half of the 20th century the media companies grew ever larger, frequently buying smaller groups of newspapers and adding a variety of other communication operations ranging from cable television franchises to outdoor billboards.

By the new millennium, the reach of the major media companies included various mixes of newspapers, magazines, broadcasting, cable television, book publishing, television and feature film production, and dot-corn ventures on the Internet. In this setting, the magic word was *synergy*, the business world's equivalent of "the whole is greater than the sum of its parts."

It was anticipated that the presence of so many outlets under a single umbrella would generate greater momentum and excitement. But in many cases the result was no more than the redundancy of existing material across more outlets. In the case of the online versions of many daily newspapers, the jargon for the software used to transfer this material to the Web was "shovelware."

Just shovel the stuff from the newspaper onto the Web. For the producers of media content, particularly news, there are now more outlets for the distribution of this news. More channels create greater convenience for the public, but not necessarily any greater diversity in the availability of useful content.

From another perspective, more channels create greater inconvenience both for the public and for journalists and other producers of media content. For journalists, the basic problem is that by traditional definitions of what is news there is only a limited supply of news most days. How to fill all these outlets—and attempt to maintain some appearance of differentiation among them to attract an audience—is a major problem.

Contemporary solutions to this problem have produced two trends: fragmentation and the blurring of the line between news and entertainment. The news cycle—once a relatively clean dichotomy between morning and evening newspapers and a distinct set of television news programmes spaced across the day—has grown ever shorter for all the electronic media.

To reduce the sheer repetition of the same news over and over, new stories often are rushed onto the air or onto the web site in rudimentary outline on the flimsiest of sourcing. Audiences are bombarded with scattered fragments, many of which are later retracted. This approach to news reporting is more likely to produce bewildered citizens who are not sure how to assemble these scattered fragments into any meaningful mosaic.

But even this strategy is dependent on the existence of real news, which is a relatively scarce commodity. So the set of acceptable stories for the news report has expanded, a strategy that helps solve the problem of how to fill voracious newsholes and that offers the potential of creating synergy between the news report and other media products produced by the same corporation.

In practice, the frequent result has been a blurring of the line between news and entertainment. The focus of the synergy often is a new television programme or feature film that receives a level of attention far beyond any thing that press agents or publicists of past decades would have imagined in their wildest fantasies.

There is, of course, another form of entertainment that is wholly journalistic in its origin— scandals and sensational behaviour. Once virtually the exclusive province of the supermarket tabloids, the last decade has seen a running catalog of these stories. O. J. Simpson and Monica Lewinsky were just the most visible tips of an ever growing iceberg.

Journalists have always sought good stories to attract the interest of an audience. But in recent times this narrative imperative—the urge to tell a good story—has taken on startling dimensions. Is it possible that the deluge of these salacious tidbits from running stories that offer little more that the satisfaction of curiosity— some would say prurient interest—are linked to the steady decline in the news audiences for all media and in the continuing decline of public trust in the news media?

THE END OF MEDIA AGENDA SETTING

A vast array of agendas are now readily available to the public, leading some social observers to predict the end of agenda setting as audiences fragment and virtually everyone has a unique media agenda that is a highly individualized composite constructed from a vast wealth of news and information sources.

The result of these idiosyncratic personal agendas will be a public agenda characterized by diversity and the scattering of attention, some observers predict. Perhaps it is even incorrect to speak of a public agenda in these circumstances, they suggest.

This perspective on the future is the antithesis of the long-standing situation in mass communication characterized by large audiences receiving highly redundant agendas from the media. As previously noted, the initial observations in Chapel Hill, NC, of the agenda-setting influence of the news found substantial similarity—a median correlation of +.78—among the nine media agendas that were the dominant sources of news and information for voters.

Obviously, this degree of similarity is not found across the total array of Web sites on the Internet, leading to the prediction that the era of agenda setting is coming to an end. But like so many prognostications about the magic of a new technology as the source of radical change, these predictions about the disappearance of any substantial agenda-setting influence simply may be wrong.

Predictions about the disappearance of agenda setting as a potent social force are grounded in a broad assumption that audiences will fragment and avail themselves of vastly different media agendas. Corollary to this assumption is the expectation that the redundancy across outlets characteristic of mass communication for many decades will be greatly reduced as niche media offer very different agendas.

Moreover, there is the expectation that a substantial number of individuals will use a significant number of these multiple sources of news and information, patterns of behaviour that will result in a large number of highly idiosyncratic personal agendas. At present, there is little evidence to sustain these assumptions.

Most of the news sites on the Internet are subsidiaries of traditional media, the online versions of newspapers, magazines and cable TV news channels. In this setting, it already has been noted that the popular buzzword synergy means amortizing the costs and increasing the profits of news by distributing the same basic content through numerous channels.

It also is the case that, currently, the audiences for all Internet sites are very small. In short, the redundancy in the media agenda to which most of the public is exposed is likely to continue for at least the near future.

An additional major constraint on exposure to the agendas of multiple Web sites is time and effort. Few people have the time or wish to expend the effort to explore this virtual library in any depth except under extraordinary circumstances.

Despite the plethora of sites that could be accessed, there already are suggestions of the existence of a news and information oligopoly in which a small number of sites command the largest proportion of the Internet users. Even when software allows members of the public to specify their categories of interest in advance, most people also want to know about the day's most important events regardless of the category in which they fall.

Under these circumstances, editors will continue to edit—that is select and summarize from the vast daily array of news. The fundamental nature of the front pages of newspapers and the opening segments of TV newscasts as a showcase for the day's most important events is likely to remain largely the same.

There still will be a relatively homogenous media agenda, at least until someone invents a new kind of news that eclipses the traditional news audience. If that happens, it will be the result of journalistic creativity, not technology, and it will shift the agenda-setting influence of the news media to a new source.

New technologies offer vast new opportunities. But technology is only a means of distribution, not a substitution for content that citizens find compelling in their personal and civic lives. Success in the new millennium will be measured by the quality of journalists' daily response to the question, "Why do we do journalism?"

For 60 years, the prevailing model of public affairs journalism in the United States has been one in which reporters and editors "cover" people and events that they deem to be important or newsworthy. They write about those people and events with the aim of informing citizens about public matters.

The flow is from source through journalist to citizen. Reporters and editors assume the posture of neutral observers, detached conveyors of information. Sometimes because of the complexity of events, they become analysts and interpreters, but only out of the necessity of helping people understand, not out of any admitted desire to affect the flow of events. The goal is to present information in a "journalistically objective" way—that is, fairly, honestly and accurately, with proper balance—and let citizens make of it what they will, do with it what they will, or ignore it altogether.

Limiting the role to neutral observer and conduit is both compelling and convenient. It allows journalists to focus on the singular task of transmitting information and absolves them of any other responsibility. The simple, straight-line model is based on several assumptions:

- Those citizens are, or at least should be, intensely interested in being well-informed about public affairs and thus are eager receptors of what journalists consider important.
- That "truth" put to the test in fair contest will always prevail over "untruth."
- That new information has intrinsic, utilitarian value simply because it is new.
- Those governments and other institutions are inevitably the "actors" and citizens the "acted on" and therefore the journalistic conduit need only be one-way in design.
- That "giving people what they need" and "giving people what they want" are distinct functions, and the former is far more important and valuable than the latter, which is somehow seen as fundamentally threatening to journalism's foundations.
- That the public sphere, the private sphere and the journalistic sphere are necessarily separate, like atoms held in eternal stasis by immutable natural forces and connected only by the flow of information.

These assumptions, each of which is arguable in today's world, form the basis for journalistic reliance on the model of detached observer and transmitter of information from source to citizen.

That efficient though simplistic model has ceased to well serve either public life or journalism, and a more sophisticated model is needed. The new model challenges the dynamics of the old one and involves two fundamental shifts: repositioning journalists and repositioning citizens, that is, challenging the stastis model of the three spheres. "Positioning" in this usage is not a mechanical event; it is a conceptual one. It is the picture in the journalist's mind of the relationship among citizens, journalism and public life; conceiving of those spheres not as in stastis but as a dynamic.

Nothing in this model suggests that journalists abandon what is commonly called journalistic objectivity, that is to say, the imperative to be fair, honest, accurate, and clear-eyed about facts. It does suggest that journalists move away from the idea of detachment, that is, the mistaken notion that journalists are and necessarily must be separate from the consequences of their decisions.

While the terms *objectivity* and *detachment* are often used interchangeably and sometimes in the same sentence, as in "detachment and objectivity are fundamental to good journalism," our model makes a distinction between the two. That distinction is best illustrated this way. Jonas Salk discovered a vaccine for polio.

As a professional scientist, he had to be objective about the facts of his research, if for no other reason than those scientific protocols require that other scientists be able to replicate his results.

But he was not detached. He did not enter the lab willy-nilly, wondering what he might find. He had a purpose: finding a cure for a dread disease. And he cared very much whether or not he discovered it.

Another way of thinking about the difference between objectivity and detachment is this. You want your doctor or lawyer to be objective. That is, you want her or him to be clear-eyed and clear-minded about the facts of your case, to be truthful with you about it, to be fair in the way your case is treated. But you do not want him to be detached. You want her to care very much about a successful resolution of your situation.

Likewise with professional journalists, it is both possible and desirable to be objective without being detached. Objectivity reflects intellectual and professional honesty; detachment reflects a lack of concern.

Moving away from DE-tachment does not mean moving to full AT-tachment; for instance, caring about whether a problem is solved does not mean dictating how it is resolved.

Detachment-attachment do not lie on separate sides of a single, fine, bright line; they constitute a continuum. Imagine two vertical lines, one to the left of this page, the other to the right.

The one on the left represents the pole of total detachment that positions journalists at a far remove from the events they cover, free from all consequences of their decisions, able to say, "We just tell the news and have no responsibility for anything other than doing that fully and honestly."

The other line represents total attachment, which positions journalists as fully engaged in the events they cover. Just as full engagement by journalists is obviously unacceptable, so is the other position. Journalists in today's world necessarily must operate somewhere in that middle ground between the poles, for reasons that have to do with the preservation of both the profession and democracy.

The paraphrase from John Dewey at the opening of this chapter reflects a concern about the usefulness of the profession of journalism. Dewey's original comment was about his profession, philosophy.

As a pragmatist, Dewey was interested in having the work of philosophy resonate in society in a useful and important way. It cannot be influential if the central concern of philosophers is insular—the problems of philosophy. What is necessary is to address, among other things, the concerns of democracy and its people, Dewey felt.

Traditional journalism can sometimes slip into insularity, in part because journalists fail to distinguish between objectivity and detachment. Defining and operating within that middle ground between dangerous total detachment and equally dangerous total attachment is what the balance of this book is about.

Only a limited number of journalists are available to monitor daily life. Even if there were an infinite supply of journalists, the capacity of the various news media could not accommodate all their reports. This is true even though with Web sites and all the other new technologies, there is far more capacity than at any time in the past.

Even this enlarged capacity poses a problem for the public, whose available time, range of interests, and span of attention are limited. Of necessity, the reported and received news is a tiny sample of all the daily happenings in the world.

More important, the news is a highly idiosyncratic sample of each day's events and situations. A grab bag of professional routines and traditions largely inherited from the past define how journalists sample the world around them—what they pay close attention to and what they ignore as they prepare their news report for the public.

More than 75 years ago, Walter Lippmann talked about the beat system and its dominant underlying rationale that news is not a mirror of social conditions but the report of an aspect that has obtruded itself. Good sources for information about situations in which daily life departs from its normal, mundane channels include the police station, fire department and court house.

The contemporary expression, "If it bleeds it leads, " is a culmination of this perspective about news that results in some local television news relying on a heavy diet of stories about accidents, crimes and fires. In less spectacular fashion, the beat system expanded to include a wide variety of officials at all levels of government—everything from the local zoning board to the White House—is a productive source of reports and statistics about non- routine events that are grist for the journalistic mill.

Of course, not everything that occurs at these locations or that is reported by these routine sources of news is sampled by journalists, only those occurrences that pass muster in terms of the traditional litany of news values. The resulting sample of the day's happenings that is presented to the public is a highly peculiar one, a set of events mostly involving government officials in some role and heavily weighted towards conflict and bad news.

Nowhere is this latter aspect of the sample—conflict and bad news—more obvious than in the reporting of presidential campaigns over recent decades. Think about the total set of events that make up a presidential campaign each day or each week. Then compare the sample presented in the news. To use the language of mathematics and polling, it is not a representative sample. In public opinion polls, which have become a staple of both the news media and political campaigns, achieving a representative sample of the public is the central goal. The core idea is to convey an accurate picture of the prevailing views among the public.

To achieve this representative sample of the public, pollsters utilize the technique of random sampling, a procedure in which at the outset of the selection of persons to be interviewed for the poll, every person in the relevant population has an equal opportunity to be selected.

Obviously, this kind of random sampling would not work for observing the occurrences of each day. The vast majority of these occurrences are of no interest to the general public. Who cares that Fred had a beer after work and talked sports with his friend, Bob; that 86 people renewed their drivers' licenses that day in Austin, Texas; or that Amtrak Train 27 arrived in Chicago five minutes ahead of schedule?

Actually, there are a few people who care about each of these things, but these people are not a very large proportion of the public. So, to use the technical language of sampling, journalists employ the technique of stratified sampling. That is, they divide the events of the day up into various categories or strata. To use Lippmann's term, a simple, first cut at sampling the day's events is to group them into two strata, the obtrusive and the unobtrusive.

The latter strata, the unobtrusive and routine, are deleted from any further consideration, just as many political pollsters define persons not registered to vote out of their picture of political trends. One of the purposes of stratification is to focus attention on particular kinds of events or persons.

A major part of the problem with existing definitions of news, which fewer and fewer members of the public find relevant, is that the strata of daily occurrences defined as newsworthy are too narrowly focused. Put the other way, too many strata are defined out of the picture. First, consider the sampling of obtrusive events from a limited set of news beats. This yields a considerable amount of news. But many times the public—and investigative journalists—are interested in an overall situation, not just the obtrusive events that are the latest aspect of the larger situation.

The news about the rapid growth of Austin, Texas, is more than the latest zoning controversy or the month-long detours on the interstate highway. These are small bits in the larger mosaic of urban growth. On a broader scale, the information collected in the national census every 10 years provides a wealth of news stories that detail not just how many of us there are in the United States, in each state, and in each community, but what kinds of people live in what kinds of homes and how all this differs from 10 years earlier.

This is one example of news stories about who we are and how we live our lives. There are many others that present the full picture, not just the obtrusive events. Our stratified samples of life in the world around us need to encompass general situations as well as obtrusive events.

These stratified samples of events and situations also need to extend beyond the traditional journalistic strata of government, sports, finance and entertainment. Even in the unfamiliar language of sampling theory, the names of these strata sound familiar because these are the typical sections and topics of most daily newspapers.

Those are the strata routinely sampled each day by journalists. But there are many other strata that could be sampled to provide the public with news that it finds newsworthy and relevant.

Until very recently, religion was one of those strata defined out of the news picture. Some years ago, a public opinion survey asked Maryland residents in the area adjacent to Washington, D. C., who were the important community leaders in their area. This roster of leaders was compared with the sources quoted in the Maryland section of the *Washington Post.* You can guess the results. Clergy were high on the public's list of leaders, but seldom quoted in the newspaper. There were numerous other disparities. Many strata of activities that are relevant and interesting to the public are ignored by most news organizations.

STRATIFIED SAMPLES OF REALITY

Because the tradition of news beats and news values is so familiar and so entrenched in the thinking of journalists and because the concept of stratified sampling is so unfamiliar, we review the basic outlines of the idea of stratified sampling before discussing some creative ways to apply this idea to gathering the news. Pollsters divide people into groups—in other words, they stratify society into two or more groups—for two basic reasons.

One of the reasons already mentioned is that it makes no sense to interview certain kinds of people. In an election poll, only the opinions of persons eligible to vote are meaningful. In a survey of what people watch on cable TV or how people use the Internet, only the responses of those who actually subscribe to cable or who have access to a computer and use the Internet are meaningful. Stratification is used on many occasions to exclude some people and narrow the focus to others whose behaviour is more relevant.

At other times, the reason for stratification is to emphasize the focus on certain kinds of people, usually people characterized by some relatively rare trait or pattern of behaviour.

If you want an accurate assessment of the political views of American Indians in North Carolina or of persons who contribute money to political candidates, a stratified sample is needed to find enough of these people who are relatively rare in the population in order to make any accurate assessment of their views or behaviour.

In sum, we as journalists stratify to sharpen our focus, sometimes to exclude those in whom we are not interested so we can attend to the others, sometimes to ensure that we have an accurate picture of an important group. Sampling people, even in strata that are defined by some very rare trait, is much simpler than that the task that faces journalists; sampling all the happenings in the world. There are a lot of people in the world, even in the United States or even in a single community. But it is a finite number. In contrast, the number of happenings in the world each day, even the number of happenings in a single community in a single day, is essentially infinite.

There are many, many ways to define and describe the happenings of the day. Identifying the relevant ones—defining and sampling the key strata of happenings—is the creative aspect of journalism.

Of course, journalists have been constructing stratified samples that included some of the happenings of the day for decades. News beats and the various sections of the newspaper are one way of stratifying the happenings of the day. Each is an outcropping of some aspect of life in the nation or community. But the traditional set of news beats and newspaper sections aren't the only—or even the best—way to find news that is meaningful to the public, even with some of the new wrinkles added in recent years such as religion, shopping malls and high-tech.

In the face of yawning disinterest among large segments of the public, especially among young adults, journalists need to understand two fundamental points. First, any plan of news coverage is, in the abstract and of necessity, a stratified sample of the day's happenings.

Most aspects of reality are ignored; a few are heavily sampled. Second, there are many ways to construct a stratified sample of reality, many interesting and useful ways to define the newsworthy strata of your community. Creative journalists will identify these strata in innovative ways to produce stories that an audience will consider as important news, something that involves more of their life than just passing the time.

There are no fixed or magic answers to the question of how to sample the day's happenings. But there are some very familiar starting points for thinking creatively about how to sample the important realities of everyday life and how to develop new kinds of content and insight to the public.

Probably near you at this moment is a highly detailed catalog of the activities in your city that occupy a substantial part of everyone's time every day—the yellow pages. All those classifications tell you how most people spend most of their week, either as the providers of those different kinds of goods and services or as the consumers of them.

To sharpen the focus on what is important to people in your city, compare the yellow pages in your town with those of other cities and towns. Social scientists have done that as a way of profiling the differences among communities. You also can compare the current yellow pages with editions from previous years to track key changes in the community.

In Austin, Texas, the yellow pages reveal that there is not a major bank in town today with the same name as any bank doing business here a decade ago.

What are the implications of this upheaval in the financial community? At the same time, the continuing growth of the metropolitan area is indexed by a significant increase in the number of retail outlets listed for the two major grocery chains and two major drugstores, a quick indicator of how much growth there has been and in which parts of town the growth has occurred.

For another slice of daily life in Austin (pun intended), the four largest pizza companies now have more than 60 locations spread across the metropolitan area. Even a yellow pages-based stratified sample can provide insight into a community's dynamics and suggest trends that can be pursued with more detailed reporting.

OTHER GUIDES TO IMPORTANT ACTIVITIES

There are many other readily available guides to the activities that engage major segments of people's lives every day and thus provide clues about their interests.

These range from time-use studies on how people carve up each 24 hours into a variety of activities to the economic analyses of each state's gross domestic product, the total dollar value of the goods and services produced.

Of course, at the individual level there also are numerous analyses of how consumers spend their money. In the hands of creative journalists, these statistics become the indicators and the foundation for news stories that address key aspects of daily life, news stories that will resonate with readers and viewers because they describe and explain important parts of people's lives.

Another key indicator of events and situations that resonate with the public because they impact daily life are occupational surveys, both those indicating major shifts and those indicating stagnation. A computer company that didn't exist 20 years ago now employs 21,000 people in central Texas. Investigating and explaining the implications of that for life in that metropolitan area—daily life for everyone, not just those 21,000—can keep a newsroom full of journalists busy for years.

At the other end of the spectrum, there also are major implications for daily life in communities where the mix of occupations shows little change over time. This situation often indicates current or impending economic and civic stagnation.

And, of course, in both changing and unchanging situations, there is likely to be major news about the dominant occupational groups in the community, whether they are government workers, low-level service providers or high-profile professionals. What people do for a living tells you a lot about a community and can be important clues to news about the activities that engage people every day.

In a similar fashion, the way that land is used—and how that may have changed over the past decade—also tells a lot about a community and points the way to news that resonates with the public. Nearly half of the land in downtown Los Angeles is dedicated to automobiles in the form of streets and parking facilities and about half of the land in downtown Syracuse, N. Y., is tax exempt because it is the site of various governmental and religious facilities.

These facts are the opening gambit to major analyses about life in these cities. Every county has extensive property tax records, most urban areas have detailed zoning maps, and many areas have extensive urban development plans. These lead to news stories ranging from the fifth generation family farm about to become part of the new expressway to how much money people pay—and are likely to pay in the future—in property taxes.

CURIOSITY AND UNDERSTANDING

If telephone books, compilations of economic statistics, and zoning maps seem mundane, it is because they are. These are the detailed maps of everyday life in the community, the state, and the nation, much of which is mundane and ordinary. But there are leads to many fascinating individual stories in these sources, and in the aggregate they trace the trends that impact people's lives in very significant ways every day.

These trends are the stuff of compelling news stories that resonate with readers and viewers and engage their close attention. To characterize these sources and many similar ones as unproductive lodes of journalistic ore is to commit two fallacies.

The first fallacy, which already has been discussed, is to miss the opportunity to broaden the sampling of events and situations in the local community and to retreat into narrow, shopworn definitions of news that engage fewer and fewer members of the public each year. The second fallacy is to miss the critical distinction between curiosity and understanding. Both are innate, embedded psychological characteristics.

Most people are curious, and most people seek to understand significant segments of the world around them. Last year, the short three-block-long street that loops into our immediate neighbourhood from the main thoroughfare suddenly filled with fire trucks and police cars, lights flashing and sirens blaring. About as many neighbours turned out on the street that evening as turn out for the annual neighbourhood picnic. People were very curious about what emergency might account for the sudden appearance of all these vehicles.

The explanation—a high intensity lamp had overturned and set a rug on fire in the living room of a neighbour's home—satisfied their curiosity. The crowd quickly melted away, and the incident was largely forgotten.

Do a simple experiment. Park a police car, or some other emergency vehicle with flashing lights on top, in front of some commercial establishment.

A crowd is likely to quickly gather. People are curious. There are many journalistic examples, of course, and the most famous of recent times may be the OJ. Simpson "chase" in Los Angeles in which TV news helicopters followed O. J. and his friend for miles as they drove along the freeways.

In subsequent weeks, both television and newspapers continued to feed this curiosity with dozens and dozens of news reports. People are curious and these kinds of news reports do draw an audience. But in the long run, do people really care? People slow down to stare at automobile accidents along the highway.

They are curious, but this is not an endorsement for more automobile accidents or more coverage of fender benders. People are curious about many things, but most of these are not things that they really desire to understand. Why? Because these things have little or no bearing on their personal lives.

For a brief time, people were curious about Monica Lewinsky. Her misadventures had all the elements of superlative gossip. But most people quickly grasped the essentials, including the fact that this sex scandal had little or nothing to do with President Clinton's governance of our nation. The press' persistent salacious framing of the scandal guaranteed both its short-term appeal to curiosity and the lack of any long-term link with the need to understand the political environment.

Many topics can briefly arouse people's curiosity, but individuals are highly selective about the topics that they seek to understand. This desire to understand significant aspects of the surrounding environment is innate within humans—and is quite distinct from mere curiosity. But unless the content of the news media satisfies this basic need for orientation, these audiences will continue to shrink.

The news media are frequently described as people's windows on the world. But to what extent does the view through this window provide personally relevant surveillance of the world around us? This is a key ethical question and organizing principle for journalists' techniques of sampling the news.

Beyond this question about the topics that the news media offer for public attention and scrutiny, there is the critical follow-up question of how well the public understands these topics. Recall that attention and comprehension are the two aspects of the communication process involved in the agenda-setting role of the news media. In this chapter, we have talked about focusing journalists' attention on topics that the public finds relevant. Extending this discussion to comprehension, we talk about framing news stories in ways that engage and inform citizens.

UNWRITEABLE DISCOURSE AND INTERPRETIVE PRACTICE

In most of this literature journalists serve either as channels through which interested institutions speak or as agents whose actions are overdetermined by institutional constraints. Whether one regards them as vehicles which provide "officials a place to elaborate interpretive webs as part of a negotiating and signaling process" or as relatively unconscious agents of the "everyday practices of domination", analysts taking such views effectively erase the agency of journalists as social actors and interpreters.

Journalistic accounts of journalism, on the other hand, portray journalists as almost entirely free agents. In its most extreme articulations this journalistic self-representation takes the form of reports of often epic proportions, in which journalists draw from an American cultural metanarrative of "the fiercely independent, intelligent, and brave male, who by virtue of those qualities is able to overcome insurmountable obstacles" to construct themselves as flawed but persistent heroes (or, alternatively, as trickster figures) on a quest for truth in a landscape of obstructions, illusions and dangers?

A phenomenological account of journalists, describing the world from "the native's point of view" would describe journalists are relatively free agents who struggle against institutional authority, sometimes reluctantly compromising with but never giving in to, hegemony.

One of the ways to deal with this structure/ agency problem is to see journalism as a form of language-in-use. To the understanding of journalism as a socially structured practice and a view of journalism as a struggle to represent social dynamics existing "out there," a structure-in-use approach adds a further insight: journalism embodies social creativity. It is an interpretive practice.

Journalists interpret the social world in the act of representing it and they do this by interpreting the social contexts through which they apprehend the world they are representing.

Furthermore, this interpretive creativity is not random but both constituted by and constitutive of social epistemologies. Finally, it is out of these interpretive practices that the regularities perceived by media sociology as structures, emerge.

Journalism as interpretive practice can be viewed as supplementing or, perhaps, even bridging, other perspectives on the press as a social institution. Certainly there are social dynamics that structure the ways in which the work of journalism is done and which thus contribute to the reproduction of social formations.

At the same time, journalism makes truth claims that are read as such and evaluated as such according to widely-accepted cultural epistemologies which belong not only to a journalistic subculture but reflect widely shared American cultural knowledge about the referential nature of true statements.

In this chapter I offer a view of journalism as interpretive practice by focusing on the series of speech acts by which news stories are constructed. In particular, I examine off-the-record discourse, as a particular site where accounts of social dynamics are contested and negotiated between journalists and their sources and institutional agents (such as editors) before written representations are generated.

OFF-THE-RECORD

"Off-the-record" is a domain of discourse between newsmakers and their sources in which public disclosure of what is said is ethically forbidden. The overt purpose of off-the-record communication is to enable journalists to learn information which will help the journalists to contextualize a story. It is also used as a means of supplying journalists with information that, if sourced, might cause problems for the source.

The ethical taboo on mimetic reproduction of off-the-record discourse allows responsibility for the content of what is said to be deferred. It therefore serves not only as a safe site for the disclosure of "sensitive" information, as journalists themselves tend to see it but is even more important as a discursive space in which sources can try-out different explanatory scenarios as part of the rhetorical process of "getting to the story."

Off-the-record messages are frequently clearly delineated by a marker: "this is off the record," "this is just for background," or "this isn't for publication." Either the source or the journalist may initiate such discourse (as when a journalist asks, "look, off the record, what's really going on here?")

In interaction, off-the-record discourse is frequently coded by intimacy markers. These include the use of first names by both parties, a softer more intimate (or perhaps conspiratorial) tone of voice and mutual courtesies: "I've been very impressed with your work, you've written a couple of good stories, I wouldn't want you to get this wrong . . . " and "Look, you've always been straight with me . . . .

The utility of off-the-record discourse is linked to the complex construction of authority, responsibility and voice in American newspaper writing. American journalism is mimetic; it seeks to represent the world by iconically reproducing it, using propositional descriptions and quotations.

These constitute "facts" about the event-object being represented. Journalistic authority is established through sourcing, the verbal representation of indexical relations between facts and the people and events from which these facts are drawn. The byline serves as a master trope that names the journalist who uncovered and arranged these facts for us. Journalists thus do not take responsibility for the truth of the facts they represent; they take responsibility for the accuracy of the mimetic reproduction: getting the names right, having the events accurately described and so forth. The responsibility for truth about the world lies in the object world itself, including the social actors in that world (like Congressional staffers) who serve as sources.

Because these actors have interests which lead them to privilege certain facts and interpretations, truth is never completed in journalism but must ever be (re)represented. Off-the-record discourse allows the sources an opportunity to enter the privileged world of the reporter and editors, that is, to speak outside of representation. To speak off the-record is to have the opportunity to speak without being discursively responsible for the truthfulness of one's words.

Professional sources like those hired by congressmen to represent them to the press are quick to make use of off-the-record discourse as a strategic resource. Going off the record encourages breaches in the normal processes of turn-taking and narration. Since responsibility for the truth of the content is deferred, off-the-record discourse offers a means to transform normal journalistic interview procedures and shift them to processes of co-narration.

Ochs and others have argued that co-narration of events leads to significant cognitive reframings in adultchild relationships. My sense is that among professional sources it is employed towards a similar effect, but often as a specific rhetorical strategy, one in which journalists, because of their need to "get to the story" are complicit. At the very least, going off the record undermines the journalist's ability to use the power of the question-andanswer format to structure the interactions.

Journalists commonly speak of two levels of off-the-record discourse: "off the record" and "deep background." The distinction involves issues of sourcing. Normal off-the-record discourse allows attribution but at a remove from the individual making the statements. This is textually marked by phrases like, "sources close to the President said . . ...Background means the journalist may use the material to understand what's going on but cannot attribute it, even generally. In my experience these distinctions are negotiated rather than constituting clearly marked frames.

The general rules for off-the-record discourse are well understood by newsmakers, both journalists and their professional sources. Messages disclosed may not be broadcast, published or otherwise recorded. They may, however, be gossiped about. A good deal of the conversation of reporters meeting at the press club over drinks is a sharing of off-the record information.

This exchange is understood to be part of how reporters stay current on what .is going on "behind the scenes." Thus I refer to off-therecord discourse as unwriteable rather than unspeakable; it can be gossiped, shared and debated but never mimetically recorded and attributed. Indeed, when off-the-record discourse is mimetically reproduced orally as gossip, it retains this essential feature. Going off-the-record thus protects sources from the consequences of mimetic reproduction of their words as they seek to define and interpret facts and events in order to produce coherent representations for public consumption.

NEGOTIATING THE NEWS: A CASE STUDY

He handed me a packet of materials including copies of two bills introduced by Republican Congressman Alpha, two press releases from Democratic

Congressman Beta (of the same state) criticizing one of the bills (HROO01) and endorsing the other (HR002), and a press release from Alpha's office listing supporters and cosponsors for the first bill. My editor said he'd intended to write the story himself but to his unspecialized eye, both bills looked exactly the same. He'd called Alpha's office but no one there had been able to explain the difference between the two bills. Since I had previously covered stories on the political issue concerned, and knew both Congressmen, he asked me to "see what the story is."

After reviewing the materials, I went back to my editor and told him that on the surface it appeared that Congressman Alpha had introduced a bill, Congressman Beta had attacked it in the home state papers and the next day Congressman Alpha had introduced a revised version of the bill. We agreed that such a story would make good copy and since the attack was detailed in the press releases, I estimated I could complete the story by the 3-hour deadline if I could get Congressman Alpha's "side of the story"-that is, his response to Beta's attacks. The editor-in-chief called me into his office to provide "some additional background: Alpha was running for governor of an East Coast state and Beta considering running against him. He urged me to keep this in mind as a possible angle. I called Alpha's office but his press secretary was not in.

The chief legislative aide was also out and no one else in the office could explain the differences between the two bills. More importantly, no one in the office was authorized to speak for the congressman. I warned the secretary again that I was under deadline and that the office needed to call me back as I had strong statements from Congressman Beta and I wanted to give Alpha the opportunity to respond. I spoke with my editors, telling them it looked to me as if Beta's criticisms might be justified.

After all, how could a Congressman create a bill and almost no one in his staff know what it is about? How could a congressman introduce two different bills on the same issue? I began sketching out the body of the story, using Beta's press release and incorporating background on Alpha from the morgue (the newspaper's archive of previous stories, clippings, and press releases).

Bert said he was glad he'd reached me because my angle was "all wrong." He explained that Alpha had written and introduced the first bill and that he was actively seeking cosponsorship and support for it. He introduced the second bill to get the chief lobbying organization's position into Congress, not as a result of the criticisms by Beta, which he claimed not to have heard. I read him the strongest language by Beta (accusations of political one-upmanship) and got back even stronger language (Congressman Alpha has forgotten more about this issue than Beta ever knew). I led my story with the "fact" of Congressman Alpha having introduced two bills with different legislative intents, described the bills and their current status in the calendar, then introduced Beta's criticisms and Alpha's office's rebuttal.

The story was read and passed without further changes by my editor and the editor-in-chief and ran on the front page the next day. Brinkmanship, after all, can go on indefinitely. Ernie insisted that I needed more "background," and that Alpha's office was not telling the truth. I suggested that if he would give me details we might consider a follow up story.

Ernie went off the record and made a number of accusations, specifically that: 1) Alpha had introduced two contrary bills so he could claim support from both sides of the issue; and 2) Alpha lied about his second bill (HROO02) being supported by the chief lobbying group for this issue. He suggested I call the lobbying group for "verification," that is, for on-the-record support of his off-the-record allegations.

The spokesperson for the lobbying group provided a different story. She said that her group did support HROO02, but that they had they had not written the bill and that it did not contain their preferred language. They had, however, provided input to Congressman Gamma, who, she said, had actually written the bill, even though Alpha had introduced it. She added that they had not been asked to support the bill until after it had been introduced. Dropping off the record, the spokeswoman told me that in fact Alpha had stolen the bill from Gamma and that Gamma's office would confirm this. She said that this "theft" had prevented the lobbying group from building broad support for the bill before it was introduced.

Gamma's office did not confirm this. The spokesperson said that while Congressman Gamma did write HROO02, he had cosponsored it with Alpha "in a move of bipartisan support" on this issue. Asked to comment specifically on why Alpha had introduced a bill Gamma had written, the spokesperson merely said that "everything moved very quickly." Off the record, he said that Gamma had been working with the lobbying group to create a bill acceptable both to the Congressional leadership and to the lobbyists. Gamma's office appraised Alpha because he was the minority leader of the committee that the bill would be reported to. After Alpha read the bill, it was introduced a day later. This had taken Gamma's office by surprise as they had planned to slowly build support before introducing it.

On the face of it, this story seemed to support Beta's allegations of political brinkmanship by Alpha, but since no one in Gamma's office would say so on the record, it was not a writeable story.

I called the lobbying group again, and this time spoke "on background" to an official with whom I had a long-term relationship. She repeated what her colleague had said and told me I could quote her as a source within the lobbying group but could not print her name or title. I called back Ernie and told him that the story he'd fed me didn't pan out. He asked me if I would talk to Congressman Beta when he returned to Washington that evening. I asked what more the congressman could add, but Ernie was evasive. We scheduled a time for the congressman to call me at my home that evening. My editor was out, so I spoke to the editor-in chief and told him what was going on. He reminded me about the state political angle and suggested I see if I could get Beta to admit on the record that he was going to run for governor.

Beta called me at home that evening and I brought up the political angle suggested by my editor. Beta told me for the record that he would run for governor and called this introduction of two opposing bills "a symbolic move" by Alpha that showed "lack of real concern" for the issue.

The next morning I called Alpha's office and offered Bert Beta's charges that Alpha was playing politics. From Bert I again obtained dramatic quotes for the record, and allegations of political chicanery off the record.

The story generated from these interactions was passed by the editor without further changes and appeared on page three as a "news analysis."

JOURNALISM IN THE SUBJUNCTIVE MODE

To analyse this series of interactions I want to treat each interaction between a set of participants as a separate speech act with its own set of messages, goals and outcomes and media of transmission. Cumulatively, these acts form a speech event that culminates in the production of a written text, a news story. In this case, reactions to the first news story generated a second speech event culminating in the production of a second news story. Space precludes a detailed analysis of each of the twenty acts that comprise these two speech events.

What I will focus on here are the epistemologies and heuristics that give order to the process. In the first speech event, I was, as the journalist, charged with the project of "seeing what the story is." This project emphasizes several of the points of the underlying epistemology of journalism: that there is an object world that can be represented verbally, that the object world is constituted by social events and that previously-inscribed discourses (press releases, bills introduced) constitute events in this object world. Most importantly, the use of the definite article points up a central assumption of journalistic practice: that there is a best possible account and that the production of this best account is the project of journalism.

"Getting the story" thus involves recovering, or uncovering, referential meaning. This search for truths, however, is only the first step; truthful reports must be further organized around the truth, a main point that can serve as an "angle," or master frame, for construction of a story.

This distinction between reports and story draws on the insights of Livya Polanyi, who defines a story as a narrative in which a teller describes events which took place in one specific past time world in order to make some sort of point about the world which teller and recipients share. Reports on the other hand, are not supposed to be trying to make a point but rather to recount past, present or future events in a more-or-less non-evaluative way. Reports are usually elicited by the recipients or in response to circumstances that require an accounting of what went on. It is the context of reporting that supplies the framework in which the relevance of the states and events being reported can be ascertained.

In fact, the recipients may even apply relevance to very specific pieces of information whose importance escapes the narrator. The burden of assigning differential weighting to the various narrated propositions thus falls on the receiver of the report. The reporter himself may implicitly tell the elicitor, "O.K., you wanted to know. You figure out what it means".

News stories clearly lie in between these two genres, as is suggested by the terminology used by journalists: reporting is what journalists do, but stories are what they write. A news story is like a report in that it is not written—or, at least, it is not supposed to be written-specifically to make a point. Instead, it is supposed to be a non-evaluative recapitulation of events whose meaning is inherent in the events themselves.

The choice of what is reported is not supposed to be actively chosen by the reporter; rather it is dictated by circumstances. Some things are news, and some are not. But a news story is a story in that these events must be organized and arranged according to their relevance, that is, their point. For example, although bounded by specific time lines, news stories are rarely told in chronological order. News stories seek to open (or lead) with the most "relevant" information, which may or may not coincide with the most recent information.

In reporting, the facts are seen as lying within the sources and the goal of the reporter is to extract these from him or her as directly as possible.

The truth value of the source's statement is measured according to its correspondence to the real object out there in the real world of objects. However, the interaction is complicated by two problems.

First, the journalist usually does not have direct access to the event-as-object being represented but can only get to it through the discourse of his or her sources. He or she cannot check what a source has said directly against the phenomenological world but only against other sources. Second, all these sources are known to have "interests" which will bias their subjective (that is, emotional and mental) attitude towards the objects and so shape the representations the source offers the reporter. This problem, that the truth is out there and is writeable but the people who know the truth have reasons for not telling it to you accurately, is the paradox that drives the journalistic enterprise.

A central problem of interpretive practice for journalists, then, is handling the polyvocality of multiple reports to produce a coherent story. To handle this, journalists treat the event-object of their representation as something to be uncovered so that it can be represented. Sources are treated as people who know about the event-object but for various reasons of their own (including simple misunderstanding) seek to obscure or mask that knowledge. "Getting to the story" is largely a process of sifting through reports to see what's "really going on" so that it can be represented.

My own efforts to get to the story involved both interpreting the written documents according to my own competence and in seeking sources who could explain them. This is typical of political journalism in Washington where it concerns actions of the legislature. As one colleague told me, "the bill isn't the story.

The story is what I find out about the bill on the phone after I get back [from the press conference where the bill was introduced]." Beginning with a set of faxed press releases and copies of the actual bills (brought in by newspaper staff from the Government Printing Office downtown) I began not by simply reporting the two newly introduced bills but by looking for the story behind the bills.

This story came to me couched by my editor as a puzzle. Normally, we would expect to see two conflicting bills on the same subject by two rival Congressmen, a situation for which there are standard story frames. Here we had two different bills on the same subject written by the same Congressman. The press release criticizing the first bill from the rival Congressman offered a clue for interpreting these bills: Perhaps Alpha introduced the second bill in response to the criticisms made by Beta as described in Beta's press release.

This interpretation is a transformation of the existing interpretive frame and "makes sense" given the assumptions of that frame. It was endorsed tentatively by my editors but we agreed that in order to present it as a story, that is, as a statement of referential truth, it needed to be confirmed by Alpha's office. At least, Alpha's "side of the story" would need to be included in our representation.

Bert was able to use my effort to "balance" the news to go off the record and offer me an entirely different frame, one that would entirely exclude Beta and his allegations. My final story positions these two frames in tension, describing Alpha's actions, offering Ernie's/Beta's interpretation of them and concluding with Bert's/Alpha's rejoinder.

Had I not been working under such a tight deadline, a call to a political scientist as to how common the strategy of introducing two bills on the same topic is, a call to some other lobbyists and perhaps an academic expert on the topic of the bills might have fleshed out the story. As it was, the lead was rather prosaic-it was the dramatic exchange of insults in the fifth and sixth paragraphs on a slow news day that made the editors consider the story for the front page.

There are several anomalous elements to the first speech event, not the least of which is the fact that the story was given to me by my editor as a story.

In the normal course of events a reporter is expected to handle his own beat, uncover and recognize stories as they arise, and keep the editor informed of what he is working on. The abnormal number of editorial conferences in the first speech event reflects the odd genesis of the bill, although it seemed natural at the time. The second story is a more reflective of routine processes of newsmaking. In the initial telephone call, Ernie attempts to hook me by suggesting my published story is wrong or incomplete.

Such conversation is de facto off the record since he can be certain a reporter will not make use of such casual criticisms. He goes formally off the record in order to offer a new interpretation of what is going on and offers me a suggestion as to where I can get this confirmed.

This leads to a sequence of interactions in which I seek to discover the "true" state of affairs. Each source has an official statement to offer me "for the record" and an interpretation of or claim about the events to offer off the record. The official statements are insufficiently newsworthy to justify a new story but any of the off-the-record allegations would, if true, make a good story. In the end, I called Bert to tell him there's no story not simply as a courtesy but in an attempt to coerce him into saying something interesting for the record.

This led to my conversation with Congressman Beta and his allegations that Alpha's actions were simply political machinations. Yet Beta's allegations were not sufficient to justify running the story as "hard news." In the end, the story that ran as a "news analysis" mimetically reproduced this bickering to highlight the theme (denied by both Congressmen as applying to themselves) that political rivalries over gubernatorial and other stakes can impact federal legislation on issues largely unrelated to those stakes.

One of the most interesting aspects of both series of speech acts is that each act is contingent. Each speech act has a dynamic of its own driven by the need of the participants to negotiate a frame, the relations between speech acts, and the dynamic of their constitution as a speech event which produces a written text.

The journalist seeks continually to discover a story that can be the story, that is, which can be understood as true by reference to the objective world. The journalist abrogates to himself the right to determine which story, or synthesis of stories is the story, but only through reference to prior representations offered by sources, whether documentary or oral. As a result, each speech act produces an interpretation of events whose validity as the story is held in check while the reporter pursues additional sources, which lead to additional interpretations.

These interactions also expose the degree to which the interpretive practices of journalists are social and how much of what they write as having been uncovered is in fact negotiated. These negotiations are excluded from the written news story" yet they are an essential part of interpretive practice. In order to arrange for such negotiations, journalists and their sources, particularly professional sources, recognize off-the-record discourse as a special register of talk specifically used for such negotiation.

Off-the-record discourse offers a site within which journalists and sources can handle polyvocality by trying out different explanatory scenarios.

In setting out to get to the story, the journalist is engaging in a series of encounters that take place within a structured "field" of journalism, "a microcosm which has its own rules, which is constituted autonomously and which cannot be understood from external factors".

To understand what a journalist writes, it is necessary to understand his or her place in the journalistic fieldthe status of the newspaper for which the journalist writes (and hence the authority with which he or she speaks and asks questions), the journalist's specific competence in the writing technologies privileged within the field, the position of the journalist within the sets of roles within the newspaper, and the history of the journalist's prior relations with the social actors he or she is constituting as sources.

The journalistic field is in turn bordered by other fields; the problematic overlap between these fields is also a necessary context for understanding interpretive practice. Each of the twenty interaction/ negotiations described above, then, can be more thickly described in terms of situated interests within overlapping social fields.10 From the journalist's perspective, much of the story lies in interaclions taking place in these fields-in this case, particularly, the political.

Perhaps more importantly, the engine that powers these interactions derives from the fact that the representations ultimately fixed in textual form constitute a form of capital in these overlapping fields. For the journalist, the story becomes part of a portfolio that may be used in seeking promotions or new jobs or simply increased status within the field. For professional sources like Ernie and Bert, these texts, if they can be framed as supportive of the politicians and their agendas, are likewise sources of economic and social advancement.

In talking about the negotiations of the story in off-the-record discourse it seems to me that neither structural/institutional nor free-agent theories are useful, as both obscure elements of this process. Negotiations take place as a result of interests on the part of various social actors within structurally constrained fields.

The interpretive practice of journalists is further affected by the fact that they are not seeking to write against normative frames of understanding. They instead offer accounts of the world that can be read by their audiences as natural, that is, according to the "common sense" frames of interpretation in circulation in the society for which the accounts are intended." These practices are largely unreflexive. One way to articulate this is with Bourdieu's term habitus, which he has defined in one place as an "art of inventing." Life is a series of confrontations between the social actor and situations; habitus makes it possible to produce an infinite number of practices, each situational and thus "relatively unpredictable" but also "limited in their diversity".

Habitus is the product of our prior encounters with the world, our successes (positively sanctioned behaviors) and our failures (negatively sanctioned behaviors) and hence it "tends to generate all the `reasonable,' `common-sense,' behaviors (and only these) Which are possible within the limits" of the regularities of our life experiences.

Practices-like the practice of journalism-are the outcome of an encounter between one's professional habitus and a particular social field:

The Kabyle woman setting up her loom is not performing an act of cosmogony; she is simply setting up her loom to weave cloth intended to serve a technical function. It so happens that, given the symbolic equipment available to her for practically thinking her own practice-in particular her language which constantly refers her back to the logic of plowing-she can only think what she is doing in the enchanted, that is to say, mystified, form . . ..

Similarly, the journalist, sitting down with her computer and telephone, is not engaging in a process of cultural reproduction or of resistance; she is trying to write a story about people and events that her readers, as she imagines them, will read and understand.

The symbolic equipment available to the journalist for making sense of the world in order to define and get at the story is much the same as other members of her cultural background, including her sources, and in the U.S. constantly refers her back to the logic of the market, of free choices and rational calculation.

The professional habitus that informs her writing practices, the language in which she commits her story to words, is further organized by a particular cultural logic: a logic of objectivity.

To understand what a journalist writes, it is necessary to understand his or her place in the journalistic fieldthe status of the newspaper for which the journalist writes (and hence the authority with which he or she speaks and asks questions), the journalist's specific competence in the writing technologies privileged within the field, the position of the journalist within the sets of roles within the newspaper, and the history of the journalist's prior relations with the social actors he or she is constituting as sources.

The journalistic field is in turn bordered by other fields; the problematic overlap between these fields is also a necessary context for understanding interpretive practice. Each of the twenty interaction/ negotiations described above, then, can be more thickly described in terms of situated interests within overlapping social fields.10 From the journalist's perspective, much of the story lies in interaclions taking place in these fields-in this case, particularly, the political.

Perhaps more importantly, the engine that powers these interactions derives from the fact that the representations ultimately fixed in textual form constitute a form of capital in these overlapping fields. For the journalist, the story becomes part of a portfolio that may be used in seeking promotions or new jobs or simply increased status within the field. For professional sources like Ernie and Bert, these texts, if they can be framed as supportive of the politicians and their agendas, are likewise sources of economic and social advancement.

In talking about the negotiations of the story in off-the-record discourse it seems to me that neither structural/institutional nor free-agent theories are useful, as both obscure elements of this process. Negotiations take place as a result of interests on the part of various social actors within structurally constrained fields.

The interpretive practice of journalists is further affected by the fact that they are not seeking to write against normative frames of understanding. They instead offer accounts of the world that can be read by their audiences as natural, that is, according to the "common sense" frames of interpretation in circulation in the society for which the accounts are intended." These practices are largely unreflexive.

One way to articulate this is with Bourdieu's term habitus, which he has defined in one place as an "art of inventing." Life is a series of confrontations between the social actor and situations; habitus makes it possible to produce an infinite number of practices, each situational and thus "relatively unpredictable" but also "limited in their diversity". Habitus is the product of our prior encounters with the world, our successes (positively sanctioned behaviors) and our failures (negatively sanctioned behaviors) and hence it "tends to generate all the `reasonable,' `common-sense,' behaviors (and only these) Which are possible within the limits" of the regularities of our life experiences.

Practices-like the practice of journalism-are the outcome of an encounter between one's professional habitus and a particular social field:

The Kabyle woman setting up her loom is not performing an act of cosmogony; she is simply setting up her loom to weave cloth intended to serve a technical function. It so happens that, given the symbolic equipment available to her for practically thinking her own practice-in particular her language which constantly refers her back to the logic of plowing-she can only think what she is doing in the enchanted, that is to say, mystified, form . . ..

Similarly, the journalist, sitting down with her computer and telephone, is not engaging in a process of cultural reproduction or of resistance; she is trying to write a story about people and events that her readers, as she imagines them, will read and understand.

The symbolic equipment available to the journalist for making sense of the world in order to define and get at the story is much the same as other members of her cultural background, including her sources, and in the U.S. constantly refers her back to the logic of the market, of free choices and rational calculation. The professional habitus that informs her writing practices, the language in which she commits her story to words, is further organized by a particular cultural logic: a logic of objectivity.

My final story positions these two frames in tension, describing Alpha's actions, offering Ernie's/Beta's interpretation of them and concluding with Bert's/Alpha's rejoinder. Had I not been working under such a tight deadline, a call to a political scientist as to how common the strategy of introducing two bills on the same topic is, a call to some other lobbyists and perhaps an academic expert on the topic of the bills might have fleshed out the story. As it was, the lead was rather prosaic-it was the dramatic exchange of insults in the fiJournalists are not entirely unaware of their epistemological dilemmas. Commentary on these issues constitutes a heterodox zone within journalism, sometimes characterized as "the new journalism." Most journalists run up against situations that expose these dilemmas at some time in their careers. In stories they tell, reporters attempt to speak as direct observers about matters of empirical fact and are squelched by editors, who as gatekeepers of journalistic objectivity, are quick to suppress such behaviour.

Unexamined by journalism is the possibility that the object world perhaps cannot be neutrally represented or that journalism is a particular form of knowledge whose truthfulness lies not so much in its reference to the object-world as in the mode of production which engenders it.

The importance of objectivity as a conceptual framework is marked by every ethnographer who examines the American press. The problem is the relationship of objectivity to journalistic practice. Tuchman has looked at objectivity as a "ritual practice," a repetitive series of actions through which journalism is produced. Iyengar has presented objectivity as a system of frames.

Both these concepts largely ignore the creative, performative and negotiated aspects of journalism, particularly since Iyengar's notion of frames is a cognitive one quite different from the attention given to the ongoing negotiation of framing activity proposed by the originators of the term. More recently, Pedelty has offered the notion of objectivity as a "disciplinary apparatus," one of several which organize the social fields in which journalism takes place.

This is a useful notion, particularly since it draws attention not only to constraints but to the pleasures-"pay, promotion, notoriety, identity, fantasy"- that draw journalists towards the reproduction of cultural forms favored by institutions.

However, it tends to draw attention to the structure of the field in which practices take place rather than the unfolding of the action. My own effort here is to draw attention to the links between epistemologies and the heuristics that social actors use it interpreting situations so that they can act in them. For this reason, I am here considering objectivity as a practical logic.

A "practical logic," Bourdieu says, "understands only in order to act". Faced with the subjunctive, contingent nature of reporting, a reporter finds that objectivity provides a generative logic that can produce a universe of action without reporters being under the burden of carrying about an imaginary "file of prefabricated representations". Off-the-record discourse offers a privileged and perhaps necessary site for much of this action to take place. Faced with the unsubstantiated but attractive claims offered by sources (and editors) off the record, the logic of objectivity allows the reporter to act creatively in order to bring negotiations around to a writeable story.

3

Changing the Newsroom Culture

Nearly all editors who have involved their newsrooms in change initiatives have suggested the key to making change work is to create a new culture. Weaver said changing the newsroom culture requires "getting the staff to think of the whole paper, as opposed to their own story or small piece they contributed." She said that reporters need to be trained to work in a new system, as many lack the editing, headline writing, and design skills required in the team structure.

Managers, too, have more pressure, as the staff is often competing for the attention of fewer bosses. And, because of the changing nature of journalism work, job performance evaluations need revision to reflect the standards and goals of a new system. She admits that "newsroom stars" under the old system often fool stifled by the team structure. Teams require a "new breed" of journalist with different personality traits and skills than the "lone wolf" who worked well alone and often produced breakthrough stories.

Sue Deans, editor of The (Myrtle Beach, S.C.) Sun News, said for change initiatives to work staff members need to understand that change is a constant; it will not go away after a short time or a few experiments. The two "core issues" of change are continuous product improvement, and keeping aware of what readers want and the market demands. She said changing the newsroom culture requires emphasizing "passion" for the newspaper business and:

- Impressing on people who do not want change that they must change or leave;
- Eliminating "silo" thinking by creating cross-departmental approaches to work and evaluating work quality;
- Staying focused on strategy and on the market.

Campbell, who resigned in April 2000 as Si. Louis Post-Dispatch editor after a stormy 3 1/2 years, had embarked on an ambitious attempt at "cultural transformation" at the paper. He claims the existing newsroom "judgmental culture" is part of the problem with American journalism, and he attempted to change the Post-Dispatch's culture from one based on "judgmentalism" to one based on "collaboration."

By the millennium, the ideas for change that began in a couple dozen newsrooms in the mid-1990s were becoming the industry norm. Stepp (2000) wrote:

"From civic journalism to New Directions for News, from credibility reforms to the Committee of Concerned Journalists, a host of foundations, trade groups and other forces have been pouring millions of dollars into attempts to remodel how journalists think and act".

IMPACT OF CHANGE ON MORALE

Change initiatives have required journalists to rethink some fundamental principles of their work: their sense of news, audience, organization, and even the purpose of journalism. Signs of eroding morale were present before change began in the mid-1990s, and morale problems in relation to change initiatives have been reported in trade journals.

Columbia Journalism Review, in a 2001 cover story, reported that its national survey found 84 per cent of the responding journalists indicate that low morale is widespread in their newsrooms. This finding is supported by a 2001 ASNE study that found 54 per cent of the respondents saying they weren't sure if they would remain in the newspaper business.

Among the reasons for low morale: ineffective leadership, management and editors who don't listen, not enough opportunity to be creative, and increasing budget pressures that arise from the drive to maintain high profits.

Underwood wrote that the mid-1990s layoffs and a widespread belief that management used downsizing as a way of getting rid of unhappy journalists - many of whom were aggressive, good journalists in a traditional sense - have left "a deep and growing cultural divide between newsroom managers and their reporters".

Many veteran reporters think that change initiatives - and associated reader-driven, marketing consciousness - made newspapers look needlessly desperate in the late 1990s when newspaper companies were posting record profits.

Stepp wrote that changes in management goals may mark a historic period of journalism. Journalists always considered themselves bestowed by the First Amendment with special status, feeling they were public servants who value social responsibility; however, he writes, "You feel it in virtually every newsroom, the sag, the deflation, the suspicion that a special way of life is teetering".

The frustration is not limited to rank-and-file, but includes editors who face the challenge of leading changes they may not understand or support.

Stepp (2000) wrote that editors are no longer seen by their staffs as in control of the newsroom, as publishers look for top editors who understand "a different approach" based on what the market needs and the reader wants.

This leaves editors less time to focus on journalism and interact with their staffs, further widening the gulf between managers leading change and rank-and-file.

The Newspaper Association of America surveyed more than 2,600 newspaper journalists who left their jobs in the mid-1990s, trying to find the factors that caused journalists to leave the profession.

The NAA found, beyond the expected reasons of stress and long hours, that people left newspapers because of low morale, lack of advancement, and perceived inequities in pay and promotions. The authors conclude all of these reasons are issues that management can control.

ORGANIZATIONAL NEWSPAPER RESEARCH

In the past half-decade, a line of organizational newspaper research has looked at the impact of public ownership (companies that publicly trade stocks) on corporate goals and identifying the level of newspapers' market orientation. This section reviews three areas of research that were relevant to the conception of this study: early organizational studies, the recent profit and market-orientation research, and the few attempts in recent years to study the process of managing change in the nation's newsrooms.

Breed and Argyris (1974) were pioneers in newspaper industry organizational research. Breed, a sociologist, suggested that role theory provides a model that explains the organizational relationships in newsrooms. he asserted that all newspapers, whether management and journalists admit it or not, operate under the influence of a publisher policy.

The publisher, as a representative of ownership, has the authority to set and enforce the policy. Journalists learn the policy, which is often covert because it betrays journalistic values, through experience and observation. The social norms and conventions of the newsroom teach journalists how and when to conform or deviate from the policy. Breed concluded:

Thus the cultural patterns of the newsroom produce results insufficient for wider democratic needs. Any important change towards a more 'free and responsible press' must stem from the various pressures on the publisher, who epitomizes the policy making and coordinating role.

Argyris, an organizational development scholar, studied one of the nation's largest newspapers for 3 1/2 years, exploring the paper's internal dynamics and how they related to problems of press credibility. he also provided the paper an organizational development programme and advised during its implementation. In his book, Behind the Front Page, he concluded the internal system at the paper helped create policy clashes, one-upmanship among reporters, and fear of authoritarian bosses. He found the greatest resistance to new ideas came from mid-level editors and managers, who, despite acknowledging the need to change, would not participate in organizational efforts at change. Discussing his frustration about why the problems his systems analysis identified were not addressed, he wrote: The reason is not (italics Argyris) a lack of motivation to solve them on the part of top management. The problems will not be solved because the individuals and groups behave in ways that create a living system which teaches them (they become acculturated) to be hard of hearing, to be unable and unwilling to take action on threatening issues.

Gassaway used observation and survey to study the social construction of a journalist's reality. he found news judgement decisions were most often the result of "preordained news," determined by coverage beats and how editors decide to use their resources. Editors and reporters struggle for control of information because they often disagree on what should be communicated to the public. Editors' authority is derived from organizational hierarchies, but reporters can deny editors' authority by controlling information obtained in iiewsgathoriiig. Gassaway concluded editors and reporters negotiate for control to prevent confrontations and reduce resorting to power.

Jeffers and Lewis studied organizational communication at a midsized newspaper and found rank-and-file journalists perceived their communication with their immediate supervisor and publisher as poor. They suggested the organizational climate could be improved by increasing the amount and frequency of communication at all levels. The authors concluded their study supported the findings of Pincuss, Knipp, and Rayfield, who found rank-and-file employees' communication relationship with their immediate supervisor is a predictor of job satisfaction; however, employees' sense of having meaningful communication with top-level managers was as strong a predictor of satisfaction as immediate-supervisor communication.

In the mid-1990s, several scholars began to assess organizational structure and goals, often considering profit motive and its impact on normative journalism values. Deniers integrated organizational and economic theory in his book, The Menace of the Corporate Newspaper: Fact or Fiction?, to define the corporate newspaper, its characteristics, and organizational dynamics. Demers asserted that corporate newspapers are complex bureaucracies controlled by trained managers, not owners. These managers are best understood as innovative professionals or "technocrats" who are morn interested in professional, organizational, and technical goals than profit goals.

Demers juxtaposed the roles of managers to those of owners, defining the latter as "capitalists" most interested in returns on their investments. In the 20th century, managers replaced owners as the driving force; in corporations because llie organizations had become complex bureaucracies that required professional management.

Further aiding the transition was the death of the original owners, whose influence was dispersed over time and divided among heirs. Deniers wrote the result is that corporate newspapers are efficiently managed and structured to maximize profits, but they place less emphasis on profit than non-corporate newspapers, which tend to be family-owned, less bureaucratic organizations. In two studies, his results indicate that newspapers become more rigorous editorially as they become larger, more complex organizations.

In studies that both support and refute Deniers' work, Beam studied the conditions that influence newspapers' market orientation and whether market orientation affects content. To define and measure market orientation, Beam explored the extent that newspapers:

- Have one or more departments active in understanding customer needs and the factors affecting the needs,
- Share this information across departments,
- Have various departments engaged in meeting select customer needs.

He found that ownership by a large group is the most important predictor of a newspaper's market orientation, suggesting the corporate parent may not be involved in specific content decisions but is more likely to require certain general processes be followed in making content decisions. he concluded that traditional journalistic values are important at market-oriented papers, and while more market-oriented newsrooms are more committed to special interest and visual content, they are not less committed to traditional content, including public affairs.

Beam (2000) has also found that newspapers that are part of privately owned companies are more market oriented than those of public companies.

Using his survey data, Beam (2001) then chose 10 newspapers for a content analysis - 5 papers with strong market orientation and 5 papers with weak market orientation. he found the majority of items on page one of both orientations was "public sphere" content, which includes government affairs; however, the percentage of public sphere items on page one for weak market orientation newspapers was significantly higher (65.6 per cent) than for strong market orientation papers (54.9 per cent).

Overall, Beam analysed the display pages (section front or topic lead page) and found papers with strong market orientation have proportionately more items devoted to private life, coping, and sports, while proportionately fewer items about government and public life.

Martin (1998) compared profits earned by 15 public newspaper companies to profits of publishing companies and yields from corporate and government bonds over an 11-year period. For the entire period, newspaper profits averaged 90 per cent higher than publishing companies, 78 per cent higher than government bond yields, and 54 per cent higher than interest payments from corporate bonds.

Using a scale created by an economist that labels profits 50 per cent above those of comparable measures as "excessive," Martin found that in 23 of 33 annual comparative indices (70 per cent) the newspaper companies in the sample earned excessive profits. In some cases, these excessive comparative profits occurred in the early 1990s during what an analyst called "the biggest advertising recession since World War II".

After newspapers embarked on broad, and in some cases bold, change initiatives in the 1990s, a few researchers began to study these initiatives through the lens of organizational development. Gentry observed while a small California daily embarked on several change initiatives aimed at better aligning its content with community interests.

The year-long efforts, orchestrated by New Directions for News, led Gentry to conclude the following elements were essential for successful newspaper organizational change:

- Strong leadership;
- Management communication about: why change is needed, management's vision, and new performance standards;
- Staff involvement in the change process;
- Management rewarding correct behaviour and extinguishing improper behaviour;
- Anticipating problems of acceptance and implementation.

Working a few years later with the American Press Institute, Gentry developed a model he calls "A Roadmap for Change" that added several variables, including:

- Prechange analysis of the current culture to determine the extent and types of changes needed;
- Use of mission statements to clarify core values for employees;
- Flexible management strategies and putting people in the proper roles to execute them;
- Enabling structures, such as job training;
- Creating visible symbols of the new culture.

Testing the model, Gentry surveyed management and rank-and-file at six newspapers and found management thought it was doing a better job than the staff thought it was doing on all 10 elements of change the study addressed.

In a longitudinal case study, Gade and Perry measured newsroom employees' perceptions of change initiatives led by editor Cole Campbell from 1996-2000 at the Si. LOUJS Post-Dispatch. Over 4 years, Campbell, known as an industry innovator, had some success making news values more reader driven, but the 1999 reorganization of newsroom coverage from beats to teams left much of the staff confused about their roles and job responsibilities.

Campbell's embrace of public journalism did not resonate with a majority of the staff. Morale declined and was lowest among respondents with management duties. Respondents consistently indicated they wern open minded towards change until after reorganization, which apparently was the last straw in a series of changes that underscored Campbell's tenure as editor (he resigned under pressure in April 2000). Over the course of the study, respondents consistently indicated that they failed to see how change initiatives contributed to better journalism.

At a time when cross-departmental teams were still new to the industry, Sylvie studied how department heads of news, advertising, and circulation perceived their identity and ability to cooperate with each other. News managers named advertising as the most difficult department, while the advertising directors named the news editors as least cooperative.

News editors showed a significantly greater tendency to say more cooperation between departments is needed. Sylvie concluded the news managers exhibit a "surprising sensitivity" to market-oriented concepts, which gives credibility to journalists' anecdotal claims that the newspaper industry is moving towards a greater market orientation.

A meagre amount of research exists on newspaper team performance. Russial studied changes in health and science content at The Oregonian after that paper created a Health and Science team. He found that the team produced more coverage that received better play (Al or Metro section front) than before the team was created. Russial suggested that although his study did not measure coverage quality, the creation of a team-based system represents a realignment in the use of newsroom resources that may have important consequences on news content.

Neuzil, Hansen, and Ward surveyed Minneapolis Star Tribune and St. Paul Pioneer Press journalists working in teams and found most thought they had less authority and less success getting story ideas in the paper than before teams were created. Those who thought they had less authority also said they were unsure of the chain of command, worked on larger teams, and wore reporters more than editors. The researchers concluded if a goal of team work was to "empower" journalists by granting them more autonomy to be innovative, this goal was not being met.

In sum, trade journals and a developing body of research provide evidence that newspapers are changing in some fundamental ways: flattening organizational structures, replacing traditional beats with teams, revising job descriptions and required skills, rethinking organizational values, and redefining news judgement.

USING ORGANIZATIONAL THEORY TO MAKE SENSE OF CHANGE

The study of "organizations" is a relatively new discipline. Drucker wrote that "no one in the United States - or anyplace else - talked of Organizations' until after World War?" Drucker said that the modern idea of an organization - as a purposely designed and specialized entity that is defined by its task and is distinct from society's other institutions - emerged in the second half of the

20th century with what he calls the "management revolution." Initial theoretical assumptions of this revolution were largely shaped by turn-of-the-century scholars: Taylor's views on "scientific management" and Weber's ideas on the rational and specialized bureaucracy. This organizational model is characterized by a hierarchical division of labour where managers are the "thinkers" and laborers are the "doers". Employees develop highly specialized skills that increase performance and productivity, while management's job is to ensure the conditions exist for the organizational "machine" to run smoothly.

Recognizing that organizations must evolve and adapt to survive in changing environments, Lewin suggested a "natural" (as opposed to mechanical) metaphor to explain organizational dynamics; change, he wrote, can be best understood and managed through a process of "unfreeze, change, refreeze." These early attempts to understand organizations and their dynamics prepared the intellectual soil for the growth of organizational development, which attracted the interest of U.S. scholars and corporate managers in the last quarter of the 20th century as the changing global marketplace threatened U.S. dominance. Although Taylor's and Weber's (and to a lesser extent Lewin's) ideas are considered outdated, they have proven resilient and modest adaptations of them are still very much alive in both theory and practice. Bergquist wrote that most organizational theorists have conceived organizations as pendulum-like mechanisms, which value "simplicity in motion" and homeostasis. When organizations experience turbulent times, they tend to seek equilibrium by returning to their previous form and function.

However, the structured and predictable environment in which U.S. companies once thrived no longer exists, and Bergquist contends a more accurate metaphor in the postmodern world is that of the organization as a liquid, "poised on the edge of order and chaos". The liquid system, he wrote, contains at the same time both elements of stability and change, especially along the edges, or shifting boundaries.

In an organizational sense, it is the shifting boundaries that offer potential for understanding the change process. It is these places on the "edge" where innovation occurs and where organizational traits such as mission, communication, and leadership become integral to success.

In perhaps the seminal book on organizational change and development, Kanter wrote American companies that value "innovation" are better placed to use their employees' creative capacities and stay ahead in changing environments. Interviews with 65 corporate executives led Kanter to conclude the innovative companies are integrated (my italics); they grant power to individuals to encourage fresh thinking and create opportunities for new ideas to cross organizational boundaries.

She juxtaposed integrated companies with "segmented" companies, which are characterized by an "ovorspecification" of resources and consider themselves successful when every segment works well independently, without much need for communication. Segmented companies, Kanter wrote, seek stasis, because they are constantly looking to the past to define the future; accordingly, habits and routines that maintain the course are valued.

Kanter identified five major building blocks in change initiatives that increase the company's capacity to meet new challenges:

- *Departures from tradition*: Activities or ideas that require the organization to think and behave in new ways.
- *Crisis or galvanizing event*: A critical event that cannot be solved by traditional means. This allows a non-traditional idea to be pushed forward.
- *Strategic decisions*: The opportunity for management to create a vision by articulating a deliberate and conscious direction.
- *Individual "prime movers"*: People who push the innovative strategy through the organization by communicating strategic decisions and manipulating the symbols of the organizational culture towards the direction of change.
- *Action vehicles*: Mechanisms that allow new action. These include training programmes, successful results for people using new practices, new organizational rewards that support new practices, and ongoing messages of the benefits experienced by individuals using the now practices.

Kanter wrote that managers need three new sets of skills to operate effectively in integrated, innovative environments: "power skills" used to persuade others to invest in new initiatives; ability to manage problems associated with teams and greater employee participation; and understanding of how organizational change is designed and constructed. She concluded that "the art and architecture of change" requires managers to abandon their reliance on traditional analytical tools, which measure what already exists or has occurred.

"Change efforts have to mobilize people around what is not yet known, not yet experienced... they require a leap of faith that cannot be eliminated by presentation of all the forecasts, figures, and advance guarantees that can be accumulated". Accordingly, the paradox of managing changes, she wrote, is "there needs to be a plan, and the plan has to acknowledge that it will be departed from".

Most attempts at organizational development involve efforts to transform an organization's culture. Schneider, Brief, and Guzzo wrote that the values and beliefs that are the foundation of an organization's culture can be changed by focusing on the tangible things - such as practices, policies, and procedures - that define daily life in the organization. It is these tangible phenomena that comprise an organization's climate, and for real cultural change to occur, management must change the climate in which the employees exist. The authors contend that many efforts at cultural change are focused on "macro" issues such as values and beliefs, while overlooking the more tangible issues that create the organizational climate in which employees experience everyday life. They wrote: "Sustainable organizational change is most assured when both the climate - what the organization's members experience - and the culture - what the members believe the organization values - change".

Successful companies have increasingly educated workforces, and they are creating cultures that are more innovative and flexible. The new, desired culture is one in which power and accountability are shared between managers and employees in a manner that allows companies to respond quickly to challenges and opportunities. The goal of these efforts is to unleash and channel the power of employees' knowledge in an organizational "culture of contribution."

Fisher acknowledges that this is a major cultural shift for most U.S. companies because - unlike the Japanese, whose collective society adapted easily to a team-building, egalitarian corporate model - "America's professional workers value their individualism and often express it in counterproductive ways". Corporate America also clings to some values that work against creating a culture of contribution; most prominent among these, Fisher wrote, is the corporate view on job attachment.

Workers are expected to accept such surprises as downsizing, job reclassification, or relocation with quiet stoicism, which contradicts companies' claims they are striving to empower employees as co-partners with management. Fisher contends that U.S. managers need to be aware that there is no single ideal corporate culture; rather, corporate culture is better understood as a combination of macro and micro cultures.

Many senior managers claim to embrace a culture of contribution, but Fisher contends that few have ideas about how to put a programme or process in place to let the transformation occur. On the other hand, the changing nature of professional work, driven by new technology, has organizations acting as though they are horizontally constructed even though most corporate organizational charts still reflect a vertical hierarchy.

If management is to be successful creating the culture of contribution, it must cede some of its "span of control" and forge a "span of relationships," with workers and managers acting more as "learners than knowers, listeners than tellers, partners than adversaries". Fisher cautions that management should not be too optimistic that a reorganization into teams will solve the ills of the company; rather, a culture of contribution is more likely to develop in a climate where workers are trusted and have the freedom to think and act like owners.

At the core of many organizational development efforts over the past two decades has been the restructuring of organizations from vertical hierarchies into more horizontal, "flattened" designs where most of the work is done by self-directed teams. In theory, teams "empower" employees by giving team members more decision-making authority and eliminating vertical chains of command.

However, empowerment efforts not only require management to share power, they also demand that individual team members think differently about the nature of work. Labianca, Gray, and Brass (2000) found that empowerment efforts require a change in "schemas" - cognitive frameworks that give meaning to experience - for both management and lower level employees. The authors analysed a 2-year organizational development project involving team building and increased participation of lower level employees in decision making.

Before the project, the "schema-in-use" for organizational decision making was that management should maintain control of events and decision making, and this schema was understood by both management and employees. The expected new schema for management included: making the organization more team oriented and collaborative, empowering lower level employees, aligning organizational structure effectively, and keeping current workers.

For the ruiik-aiid-filu, the expected new schema was characterized by working on team building, creating more avenues of communication, and encouraging employees to air their "beefs." The authors found: a great amount of employee skepticism at the outset about the likelihood of real change; despite a series of organization-wide meetings, interviews revealed both managers and non-managers were unclear about the project's goals; resistance was heightened when managerial behaviour failed to conform with its stated expectations; and management incorrectly assumed that employees would postpone judgement of the reorganization plan until after it was implemented. The authors concluded that employees' resistance to the empowerment plan was motivated less by intentional self-interest than by constraints of well-established, ingrained schema.

Randolph (2000) wrote that few managers or employees fully understand how empowerment affects traditional patterns of corporate hierarchy and behaviour. Management confuses empowerment as "giving people the power to make decisions," and this perception misses the essential notion of empowerment, that a great amount of power already exists in employees' knowledge, experience, and motivation.

Rank-and-file perceive empowerment to mean they will be given the freedom to make all major decisions about their jobs. Randolph wrote that empowerment efforts do require a cultural shift; however, the shift is from one person making decisions to team-based shared decision making. he asserts that empowerment makes employees more accountable than the older, hierarchical culture, and it is best understood as a strange combination of opportunity and risk.

An organization moves towards team-based empowered culture through three stages:

- Starting and orienting the process of change,
- Making changes and dealing with discouragement,
- Adopting and refining empowerment to fit the organization.

Each stage utilizes three "interlocking tools" - sharing information, creating autonomy through boundaries, and replacing the hierarchy with self-directed teams.

Hirschhorn, a management scholar whose work focuses on team-based organizations, wrote that the entire philosophy of management is changing as corporations flatten hierarchies and adopt new team environments. Successful managers develop roles for team members and "manage the boundary," communicating the company's needs to the team and the team's needs to the company. Managers lead by creating a structure in which the team can be successful and by positioning themselves to defend the team's efforts.

Managers must realise they are both cause of and solution to many team problems. To be successful, managers must show their vulnerability (a traditional management faux pas) and willingness to learn from team members. Exhibiting these traits shows that managers are open to new ways to solve problems and encourages team members to respond to challenges that can enhance team performance.

Although development efforts are characterized by dispersing power throughout an organization, management's ability to provide leadership remains a key to organizational success. Kets de Vries, a psychologist who focuses on the "psychodynamics of organizations," wrote that organizational culture depends on the psychological contract that exists between its leaders and followers. Effective leaders need to: articulate a vision of the future; create symbolic impressions to communicate the vision; build networks; empower followers; make choices (often painful ones); and keep perspectives of the followers based in reality.

He wrote that the leader/follower relationship a process of social comparison that involves power, authority, hero worship, flattery, ambition, and attention seeking - provides tremendous opportunities for distorted management reasoning. The key is for managers to "preserve their hold on reality."

Trust is essential for a healthy organization, and trust is dependent upon communication, support, respect, fairness, competence, and consistency on the part of the leaders. he concluded, "In order for the leader to understand the meaning of these words, it is important that he or she realise what it means to be a follower, how it feels to be in that position".

The importance of communication in organizations, especially during times of change, has spawned its own discipline of study. Lewis wrote that a growing body of empirical research indicates that the communication process and organizational change efforts are "inextricably linked processes".

Communication plays an important role in several aspects of the change process, including: creating and articulating a vision; soliciting input and channeling feedback to and from all levels of the organizational hierarchy; and propelling and altering the paths of change. The organizational communication literature reveals that communication has been shown to reduce uncertainty associated with change efforts, increase accuracy in perceptions about the reasons and goals of change, and increase willingness to participate in planned change.

Studying the methods and channels organizations use to communicate change, Lewis found change agents consider themselves to be the primary sources of change-related information, and they solicit input much less frequently than they disseminate information. She suggests that management's lack of use of channels of communication, especially upward channels, limits feedback from lower level employees who do the work of the organization.

This approach can affect the success of change efforts, as "changes in status, reward structures, job descriptions, roles, work methods, work relationships, and procedures bring significant organizational issues to the surface" that increase rank-and-file employees' need to communicate with their supervisors.

There is a small body of literature; on organizational attempts to initiate market-oriented cultural change. Narver and Slater described a market-oriented culture as one that most effectively and efficiently creates superior customer value. Harris defined a market-oriented culture as "the dominant, dynamic segment of an organization whoso orientation, attitudes and actions are geared towards the market". Harris contends that most reseachers err when they assume an organization has a single, unitary culture. This approach ignores the dynamic interaction of many aspects of an organization's culture and denies the possibility of the existence of multiple cultures.

Generally, developing a market-oriented culture can be understood as a means to improve organizational efficiency and effectiveness. However, Piercy maintains the success of developing such a culture is largely dependent on internal power relationships and organizational politics, which - at least in the short term - do not necessarily lead to high levels of organization-wide motivation, commitment, or satisfaction.

When understood in this context, developing a market-oriented culture can be seen as one of many ways that an organization can impose cultural control over the attitudes, actions, and behaviours of its members. Overall, Harris and Ogbonna (2000) wrote that the literature on the effects of developing market-oriented cultures is inconsistent, with some studies suggesting that the new culture improves employee satisfaction and commitment and others indicating this is not the case.

However, researchers tend to agree that the success of any attempt at creating a market-oriented culture is contingent on employees who have to implement it. In nearly all cases, this is the front-line employees who are the primary link between an organization and its customers.

The authors also contend that developing a market-oriented culture should be concerned with the long-term generation of values, attitudes, and behaviours, but the underlying assumption of the market culture is continuing responsiveness to customer needs.

The dilemma for organizations is how they can craft short-term responses to "increasingly fickle" customer needs in a manner that does not conflict with long-term organizational objectives. Harris and Ogbonna concluded that this condition is "a contradiction yet to be resolved or fully understood".

Change, because it requires giving up what is known and routine for something new that may not be understood, is often met with resistance.

De Jager wrote that many managers perceive employees who resist change as a problem. He contends this short-sighted view that fundamentally misunderstands the causes of resistance and the potential benefits resistance can exert on an organization. De Jager wrote that businesses today acknowledge the need to change, but there is so much change that employees become confused and see themselves pushed in conflicting directions.

Management is wise to understand that resistance to change is a tool that can be used to guide an organization. "Another way of looking at resistance is as a gateway or filter. Resistance to change helps us select from all possible changes the one that is most appropriate to the current situation". Because change involves replacing old organizational routines and values with new ones, managers must be able to provide answers for employees to some fundamental questions:

- Why is the old status quo no longer sufficient?
- What will it cost to make the transition from the old to new ways of doing things? De Jager identified several likely costs: disruption of routines, training, temporary low morale, new hires, people leaving, and the emotional cost of destroying what was.
- Is the cost of change justified by the incremental benefits of the change proposed?
- Does the proposed change support and reinforce existing core values?

As the millennium approached, the newspaper industry faced imposing, concurrent challenges on several fronts: stagnant circulation and a slowly dwindling base of readers; a fragmenting mass modin market; new electronic media that are changing the way people access and use information; threats to traditional sources of advertising; and unpredictable but rising costs of production. In the wake of a mid-1990s recession that saw significant cutbacks, layoffs, and downsizings, newsrooms were restructured and reorganized.

Hierarchical newsroom designs were flattened, and the beat system of coverage centered on social institutions was replaced by a team system that defined coverage areas by topics believed of greater interest to readers and consumers. What becomes apparent from the industry trade journals is that"change" became the guiding light of the industry in the late 1990s.

Feeling out of step with the social patterns and interests of the public, the industry questioned its news values and management has focused on changing the culture of the newsroom to include greater marketing awareness and knowledge. Editors are increasingly taking on marketing duties, working in cross-departmental teams with advertising, circulation, and marketing directors to create strategies to attract readers, often in specific demographic groups that advertisers are willing to pay to reach.

Rank-and-file journalists are expected to accept restructuring, redefined news values, and a greater sensitivity to marketing as part of a larger cultural change process that is redefining their jobs and norms as journalists. Organizational theory suggests that integrated organizations are more innovative and flexible and respond more quickly to opportunities and challenges.

The basis of power and decision making in integrated organizations shifts from being solely in the hands of management to a shared arrangement that empowers employees to use their knowledge and skills in team-based systems. Teams, and their individual members, respond to more decision-making power and autonomy by taking more responsibility for the quality of their work and becoming more productive.

Organizational change and development is understood as a process with several stages, including planning, executing, and monitoring the progress and results.

Because organizations have different values and goals, the study of OD has usually focused on one organization at a time, identifying the impact of site-specific variables on organizational development.

This approach, while making theory building more difficult, has, however, led to researchers identifying several variables that impact the success of OD efforts.

These variables include an organization having a clear mission, employees who understand the mission and organization's core values, effective organizational communi-cation, employee participation in Grafting and implementing change initiatives, strong leadership, trust, flexibility, and mechanisms that monitor the progress of change initiatives and reward desired behaviour.

The effect of successful OD efforts should be empowered employees who, in self-directed work teams, are more motivated, productive, and responsible for their work. In theory, at least, successful OD efforts should in the long term improve employee morale.

However, change is also understood as a difficult and risky process. It requires employees (both management and rank-and-file) to embrace new values, to alter routines, and to think differently about their organizational roles and the nature of their work. It requires greater accountability from empowered rank-and-file and a new, less autocratic style from management. Accordingly, resistance to change should be expected, and in some cases is rational.

For management, successful OD includes understanding the reasons for resistance and having the flexibility to find ways of working through resistance. In short, the challenge of conceiving and leading change falls on management, while rank-and-file are expected to enact and embrace change initiatives that affect many of their conventions and values.

Management perceives it is initiating change in the best interests of the organization and industry, while rank-and-file ponder the reasons for change and are sensitive to how it is implemented. Organizational theory and change models provide conceptual guidelines that should help predict effective organizational development (OD) initiatives.

Given the vast amount of change in the newspaper industry and the relative dearth of research studying these OD initiatives, this study of top newsroom managers and rank-and-file journalists at newspapers leading industry change explores the following research questions and tests three hypotheses.

*RQ*l: What are the attitudes and opinions of management and rank-and-file journalists towards organizational change?

*RQ*2: How do management and rank-and-file perceive the change process in relation to organizational development theory?

*RQ*3: How do management and rank-and-file perceive organizational change in relation to the normative values of journalism and marketing?

*RQ*4: Have change efforts affected rank-and-file perceptions of news values and organizational structure?

*RQ*5: Have change efforts affected rank-and-file morale?

*RQ*6: Does organization size (measured by circulation) affect how rank-and-file perceive change?

*H*1: Management will perceive it has done significantly better at organizational development than rank-and-file.

*H*2: Morale among rank-and-file will be low.

*H*3: Rank-and-file perceptions of organizational develop-ment will predict morale.

METHODS

This study used two survey instruments: a 62-statement survey sent to a sample of rank-and-file at 17 newspapers that have been engaged in change initiatives and a 20-statement survey sent to a census of top newsroom managers at the same papers. The rank-and-file survey was designed to explore respondents' attitudes towards concepts important to all newspapers experimenting with change: news values, organizational structure, and morale.

The survey included statements that allowed measuring the degree to which the newsroom change process has adhered to organizational development theory. There were also statements asking rank-and-file to assess the relationship of change with journalistic and marketing goals.

The 20-statement management survey focused primarily on issues of organizational development, asking managers to assess the change process and their leadership of it. These 20 statements also appeared on the rank-and-file survey, allowing for a comparison between managers and rank-and-file on issues important to successful organization development. On both surveys, respondents were asked to record their level of agreement or disagreement to stimulus statements along a 5-point Likert-like intensity scale.

Choosing the Newspapers. The intent was to generate a large enough number of respondents from abroad enough sample of newspapers (in terms of size, geographic location, types of ownership, and experience with change) to have results that are generalizable to newspapers implementing change. To ensure the newspapers in the sample were among those most experienced in change initiatives, the 1997 ASNE Change Committee annual report was used to draw a purposive sample. These newspapers had top managers who were members of the 1997 Change Committee, or the newspapers' experiments with change were discussed in the committee's annual report.

The publisher or a top news executive of all 17 U.S. newspapers active on the committee was contacted by telephone. Only two Change Committee papers declined involvement in the study: Chattanooga (Tenn.) Times and Charlotte (N.C.) Observer.

It should be noted that the Columbia Missourian is staffed by students in the University of Missouri School of Journalism, and the rank-and-file from this newspaper - because they are not professional journalists - were not included in the sample.

Three newspapers were added to the study: Si. Louis Post-Dispatch; Kansas City Star; and The Los Angeles Times. The Post-Dispatch was chosen because its editor at the time, Cole Campbell, instituted sweeping changes focused on issues relevant to this study. The Kansas City Star was chosen because that paper was sold and restructured in the years immediately preceding the study, and its publisher, Arthur Brisbane, was the chair of the 1998 Change Committee.

The Los Angeles Times was chosen because of its self-proclaimed desire to set an industry example of how to restructure a news organization into cross-departmental teams that are more marketing conscious. The additions created a sample of 18 newspapers with a circulation range from about 5,000 (Columbia Missourian) to more than 1 million (The Los Angeles Times). The papers come from 14 states, representing every major geographic region of the nation. At the time of the survey, newspapers from 11 companies were in the sample, including 9 newspaper groups or chains and 2 family-owned papers. Thirteen of tho papers were owned by public companies (those that offer public stock), and 4 were private.

CREATING THE SAMPLE

Sixteen of the papers supplied the researcher with a list of newsroom employees. At the remaining paper, the San Jose Mercury News, a contact person worked with the researcher to identify top newsroom managers and draw a random sample of rank-and-file. To ensure a response from managers that would be large enough to allow for statistical comparison with rank-and-file data, a census of the top newsroom managers at each paper was included in the overall sample.

Each paper was asked to identify its top newsroom managers or those people at the rank of department head, section editor, or team leader and above. These managers were chosen because they are responsible for creating or implementing and overseeing newsroom policies and procedures. At several papers, there were as few as a half-dozen people at these ranks or higher, and at some of the larger papers, there were more than a dozen managers in these positions.

The rank-and-file sample was determined by newspaper size. The first consideration was to have enough responses from the smaller papers for statistical analysis by organizational size. Accordingly, all rank-and-file at the four smaller papers (less than 50,000 circulation) were included in the sample (n=137).

Overall, a sample was sought that would enable an approximate proportional representation of journalists for all three circulation strata. From the seven papers between 50,000 and 250,000 (the actual range is 71,000 to 156,000), a random sample of 1 of 3 newsroom employees was drawn from each newspaper (n=259); from the six papers with more than 250,000 circulation, 1 of 5 newsroom employees was randomly selected (n=313), except for The Los Angeles Times, where 1 of 10 employees was randomly selected (n=98).

A total of 989 surveys - 182 to top managers and 807 to rank-and-file - was mailed in May 1998. Following closely Dillman's Total Design Method (1978), a postcard was sent as a reminder to non-respondents about 10 days after the first mailing; a complete survey packet was sent to non-respondents about 3 weeks after the first mailing.

Of 807 surveys sent to rank-and-file, 457 were completed and returned, a response rate of 56.6 per cent. The 182 surveys sent to top managers yielded 68 responses, or 3 7.3 per cent. The instrument sent to management had 20 statements, mostly about organizational development, that were also on the rank-and-file survey. This approach allowed for a comparison of management and rank-and-file responses. The lower response rate for management can be partially explained by the instrument; beyond the 20-statement survey, management was asked to complete a Q study (not reported in this monograph). Comparative results are reported first, followed by rank-and-file data.

Management respondents' demographics:

- 26 women, 42 men;
- 1 African-American, 2 Asian-Americans, 2 Hispanics, 62 whites, and 1 indicated othor;
- Ages ranged from 26 to 59, with a mean of 44.5;
- Experience ranged from 3 to 38 years, with the mean 22.0 years.

Rank-and-filo respondents' demographics:

- 177 females, 274 males, and 6 did not respond;
- 25 African-Americans, 19 Asian-Americans, 9 Hispanics, 2 Native Americans, 382 whites, and 20 indicated other or did not respond;
- Ages ranged from 22 to 77, with the mean 41.98;
- Experience ranged from 1 to 60 years, with the mean 17.72 years;
- 272 indicated they had "no managerial duties," 181 said they had "some managerial duties," and 4 did not respond.

Variable Measures. Most of the 62 rank-and-file survey statements were written to probe change initiatives in relation to news values, organizational structure, organizational development, and morale.

The statements exploring news values incorporate ideas from trade journals about the changing nature of news, but also reflect norms articulated in the Libertarian and Social Responsibility theories of the press.

The statements that construct the organizational structure variable were taken from trade journal and organizational development literature.

The statements in the organizational development construct were all derived from the OD literature. Morale statements were written to explore both individual respondents' attitudes about their own morale and their perceptions of morale in the newsroom.

Factor analysis of the rank-and-file data assisted construction of the four concepts: 14 statements measure news values; 12 statements measure organizational structure; 14 statements measure organizational development; 6 statements measure morale.

Statement responses - on a 5-point scale with 1 strongly agree, 5 strongly disagree, and 3 neutral - were coded so that a positive response indicated support for the concept (*i.e.*, positive response indicated high morale). Conceptual quotients were created by calculating the mean response to the set of statements measuring the concepts. Accordingly, a quotient significantly below 3.0 (the assumed population mean on the 5-point scale) indicates positive agreement with the concept, and a quotient significantly above 3.0 indicates that respondents disagree with the concept (*i.e.*, disagree with statements suggesting high morale).

INFORMATION TECHNOLOGY USES IN THE NEWSROOM

A small number of editors and reporters at *The Chronicle* in Muskegon, Michigan, use a range of computer tools and databases more often associated with larger news organizations in the Great Lakes region. However, small news organizations can also successfully use CAR. In recent years, the 55,000 evening circulation newspaper has developed local stories from information in numerous public databases obtained from state, county, and city government agencies through open records laws.

Among them are the Michigan Department of Corrections Inmates database, bench warrants issued by area courts obtained from the sheriffs department, community service case tracking from the local courts, school district employee data, and Western Michigan firefighters data.

"I started building my own databases," *Chronicle* reporter Michael G. Walsh, who has headed his newspaper's movement towards CAR, explained. Walsh said he would often approach individuals in the court system, such as bailiffs, who would provide him with copies of documents he needed for his databases. He entered cases as they occurred over a period of time and, of course, the databases grew into a usable form. He said his newspaper also bought public databases whenever possible. "We bought databases from the Department of Corrections, for example.... One lesson that I have learned from all this is that all data are cumulative.... I never throw anything out."

The Chronicle, a Newhouse newspaper, serves the Western Michigan area about 100 miles west of Lansing. The newsroom maintains a set of databases for regular use by reporters, librarians, and editors. Among the databases are drunken driving cases, sentencing data involving convicted criminals in local courts, and all published pending criminal complaints. The Chronicle's editors encourage staff members to take classes that focus on use of individual software products as well as to attend CAR seminars. However, in the beginning, because of limited resources, the CAR effort has been small.

"We are not there yet, but we now have four other people with laptop computers in the newsroom. But there are still a larger number of people in our newsroom who do reporting with the tools of the 1970s," Walsh stated."I am pretty much the one person using CAR now. But those four others are hitting at it. We have much more administrative support now than we had a year ago. We have a lot of new hardware and software and it (CAR) is coming fast for us."

Walsh, who specializes in covering courts and conducting investigations, works with an editor on CAR-based projects. Walsh has used both a mainframe and PCs for his projects. In 1995, the newspaper was using a 486 desktop and

Walsh used his own 486 notebook system. The computers were part of a network with a 1 GB server in the newsroom and a 500 MB drive on the desktop PC. Microsoft Works, a package of office-oriented products, provided a basic spreadsheet for simpler and smaller projects. Walsh also used Microsoft Office and Access for larger database reporting. Digital tape was the major storage medium used. Although these may not be the ideal configurations, these tools were more than enough for Walsh to work with local databases.

"Most of the circuit court records data was small enough for Works to accommodate my needs," Walsh, explained. All I needed was a flatfile programme for the regular, routine projects."

The newspaper was spending about $2,000 a year in 1995 to make available such services as America Online, PACER, DataTimes, FedWorld, various government BBSs, and the Internet. The Internet and PACER, a federal courts database, were the most used services at The Chronicle in 1995."Our ability to pull into deadline stories data that used to be days away, if reachable at all, has been our biggest success with online tools," Walsh, his newsroom's spreadsheet expert, stated."Spending too much as we learned how to use them is our biggest failure."

Chronicle reporters also use online services to report. Walsh likes to use the Internet and individual services aimed at journalists, such as ProfNet, for example, to find experts outside of the Western Michigan region.

Walsh explained that, like many other journalists in the mid-1990s, he has begun to use the Internet extensively in his reporting."My wife is an educator and, through a state network, I have my own Internet account which gives me unlimited access for very little money each month," Walsh explained."The paper will pay my expenses if I ask for it."

Walsh has completed numerous CAR stories since 1992. He has written about jail overcrowding and early releases to reduce the inmate population problem, drunken driving cases, drunken driving sentencing trends, and child abuser sentencing patterns.

One example of Walsh's work, a routine story about jail crowding. In the story, Walsh used a locally obtained courts database and his spreadsheet software for the analysis and supplemented that work with some routine interviewing.

"That story is an example of something you can do very quickly. It shows quick and dirty stories that you can do with very little time and money.

Editors usually think that to do CAR stories, you need to take a long period of time. This shows how you can give a routine story more with some data and a spreadsheet," Walsh stated."If you do these sorts of daily stories often enough, then editors start to expect it."

Walsh has also used CAR for more lighthearted feature stories about popular pet names using pet license data and the most popular namesakes --

such as celebrities, historically known individuals, and political figures -- whose names are found on lists of individuals in trouble in the Muskegon County courts.

LOOKING AT THE POWERFUL PEOPLE OF TUCSON

Nashville Tennessean business reporter Heather Newman was a reporter for the Tucson Citizen when she examined the most powerful people in town for a project for the medium-sized Arizona daily newspaper. Newman described her work with desktop computers to complete the project: We had looked at the influential folks in Tucson five years ago in less depth, and decided that it was time to revisit the concept.

We sent out hundreds of surveys to everyone we could think of and solicited reader comment to come up with some idea of who to include.

In the end, we had profiles of the top five and one man who had burst onto the power scene; individual biographies of forty-six other powerful folks, including separate lists of ten women and ten minorities who did not appear elsewhere: stories on how women, minorities and public officials stacked up; a board game featuring the characteristics our powerful folks had in common; a"Where are They Now?" section for the people we listed five years ago; a main story on the nature of power; an issues story that pointed out areas of concern for the next five years and who might take the helm; a story about the lack of leadership training in town; and a list of everyone who was mentioned at least three times, including their titles and job descriptions. There may even have been a couple other stories -- I've been trying to forget.

The project took six months and had one reporter (me) and one photographer. It ran thirty-two pages. Here's the computer-assisted end of things: Before we even started the project, I sent out a general call on CompuServe and the Internet to other journalists around the country.

In response, I got more than fifty usable suggestions on trends to watch for and places to look when putting the project together. I also got about a dozen copies of projects from other newspapers that had done similar analyses. That gave me a place to start when suggesting stories and gave our design person examples to look at for graphics and layout purposes.

As a result of that contact, we also received a copy of asksam, a specialized database programme, for one-third its retail price (still in the original shrink-wrap) from a database editor online who heard of our project. When we first decided to send out questionnaires, I created a database of names and addresses for who we would send them to using Paradox.

I also used Paradox to retrieve addresses for people we wanted to mail to from my Rolodex, which was already set up as a computerized database. Finally, Paradox enabled me to quickly select a variety of neighbourhood representatives from neighbourhood associations around town, ensuring that we had good coverage of the city for average folks.

Once we had mailed out the surveys and started getting some back in (including reader and staff comments), I set up another database. This one recorded every vote, what type of person the vote came from (based on codes written on the surveys) and what "position" the person was suggesting someone for (top ten, up and comers, etcetera). I also entered more than 1,000 names from non-profit boards and committees around town into a separate Paradox database.

When everything had been entered, we ended up with about 5,000 lines of names and votes. I used Paradox to sort them by name, search for and replace any inconsistencies caused by using nicknames, and count them for us. We ended up with more than 950 individuals, many of whom were named once. I used Paradox to start ranking them in the orders you saw on your reports: who had the most mentions, who was mentioned the most for each category, who had the most "points" if we weighted what they were mentioned for, etcetera.

Once we decided who was going to be on our top lists, I put Paradox to work pulling out the names and phone numbers of people who served on groups or committees with the folks we had selected. When I began doing the actual interviews, I used a word processor (Word for Windows) to enter the notes. When I was ready to write a story, all I had to do was bring all my interview notes together with another database programme — askSam — and ask it to select out the paragraphs that referred to a particular topic.

For example, when I was writing the profile of Jim Click, all I had to do was tell asksam to get me every paragraph that mentioned his name. The programme printed me out a list of all of my notes, paraphrases and quotes, along with who had said what. That enabled me to track more than a hundred interviews without having to flip through hundreds of sheets of note paper, and it took just seconds when I was ready to pull out notes on a particular topic.

I used asksam in the same way for our issue and trend stories in the tab, asking it to give me every paragraph that mentioned "minorities" and so on. We used Paradox to alphabetize everyone that had been nominated for the project and cut out those people who had not gotten three votes, giving us our back page list. It also generated a list of everyone who had been mentioned three times that also had at least one nomination for a "women" or "minority" position, giving us a place to start on those lists.

For graphics, we used a spreadsheet programme (1-2-3 for Windows) of mine to analyse affirmative action, city and board statistics to generate the numbers for the pie charts and bar graphs that appear next to the women and minorities stories. Once I did the legwork through our clips, that programme also enabled us to generate the statistics on women in elections that we used in the story and in graphic form. And finally, I used a computerized project manager of mine (Lotus Organizer for Windows) to plot each part of the project and estimate the time to completion.

USING PERSONAL COMPUTERS IN NEWSROOMS

Computer users come in all "sizes" in terms of their expertise. Some are very experienced, whereas others are not at all experienced. Most users fall somewhere between the two extremes. Similarly, there is an equally wide range in the types of computers used by journalists in the newsroom. There are some news organizations that use mainframe computers for data analysis and others than use the tiniest of portable personal computers for their database-oriented reporting. In short, there is no single model for the types of hardware and software used for CAR.

Throughout the 1980s, a shift began to occur in computing. Not only did the use of mainframe computers slowly begin to be reduced because of the growth of other types of computing systems, such as more powerful minicomputers and desktop computers, but there was significant growth in access to online services as modems became faster and more locations with modems became available.

Furthermore, a shift from stand-alone computers on desktops to networked client-server systems began to occur in the workplace. Personal computers, originally used on their own, were gradually linked into local area networks and wide area networks for various group computing purposes, such as sharing software and database resources.

Neill Borowski, director of CAR for *The Philadelphia Inquirer,* began using computers in his business reporting in the early 1980s, but he began thinking about computer applications to his work even before PCs were developed. "My first job was covering city hall in 1975. I did a calculator and legal pad analysis of taxes and caused a taxpayer rebellion," recalled Borowski:

I have realized that you have to make a distinction between data and the computer. It was the data that were powerful, not the computer. The computer just gives us the ability to do more with the data. My first real CAR project was probably back in 1983-1984 when I was covering the break-up of ATandT. All the newspapers around the country were taking six or seven typical long distance phone calls giving them to ATandT, MCI, Sprint, and the others at that time, and asking 'What's the cost of this phone call?' and putting the cost in chart form. It dawned on me that there are data behind that to compute this, so I built a spreadsheet in DOS Lotus and put all the rate schedules in it. It enabled us to compute our own rates. We put out sections, one every quarter. We took a full page. People could sit down and figure out who would be the least expensive long distance carrier.

Changes in use of computers have come, but sometimes very slowly, to news companies in the 1980s and in the first half of this decade. However, these changes did not occur at all types of news organizations at the same time. In some cases, smaller newspapers and other news companies were able to make the change to PCs faster because of the lower costs involved. But in many cases, these applications were solely for production and did not, or rarely, involved CAR applications such as online services or database building and analysis. Size is clearly a distinction in general use of computers among daily newspapers in 1995. Large dailies, those with circulation over 52,800 in the University of Miami survey, clearly use computing tools for CAR more than small dailies. Overall, more than 70 per cent of newspapers use computers in newsgathering, but larger newspapers (93 per cent) nearly double the smaller ones (48 per cent) in proportion of use.

Table. Use of Computers in Newsgathering, 1995

Computer Use of	Large Dadiesa		Small Dailiesb		Totals	
Some Type						
Yes	132	93.0%	68	7.9%	200	70.4%
No	10	7.0	74	52.1	84	29.6
Totals	142	50.0	142	50.0	284	100.0

Note: n = 287; missing observations = 3.
[a]Circulation over 52,800. bCirculation under 52,800.

Table. Use of Computers In Newagathering, 1904-1995

Computer Use	1994		1995		Percentage
Some Type					Change
Yes	138	66.3%	200	69.7%	+3.4%
No	67	32.2	84	29.3	-2.9
Missing	3	1.4	3	1.0	-0.4
Totals	208	100.0	287	100.0	

Table. Use of Mainframe Computers, 1995

Use of Mainframe	Large Dailiesa		Small Dailiesb		Totals	
Computers						
Yes	35	25.9%	12	12.4%	47	20.3%
No	99	73.3	83	85.6	182	78.4
Don't know	1	0.7	2	2.1	3	1.3
Totals	135	58.2	97	41.8	232	100.0

Note: n = 287; missing observations = 55.
[a]Circulation over 52,800. [b]Circulation under 52,800.

The comparison is similar in terms of use of mainframe systems. An often overlooked category of computers is the minicomputer. These systems were developed in the 1980s for heavy power and widespread use, but these systems did not have the size or power of mainframe systems. Still, they became popular at some newspapers as the workhorses of the production systems. Because of this, some newsrooms put these systems to work in the same manner as they might have used mainframes. A total of one quarter of the newspapers responding in the 1995 study reported used minicomputers in newsgathering. However, size is not a significant factor when discussing minicomputers.

How does a news organization integrate CAR into its newsgathering? The idea was introduced that there are two main approaches to bringing CAR to newsrooms. One suggests the need to set up a special team of newsroom CAR experts. The other advocates bringing CAR to the entire newsroom. Because of the unique nature of CAR, some news organizations have set up desks

Table. Use of Minicomputers, 1995

Use of Minicomputers	Large Dailies[a]		Small Dailies[b]		Totals	
Yes	38	29.0%	18	19.8%	56	25.2%
No	88	67.2	70	76.9	158	71.2
Don't know	5	3.8	3	3.3	8	3.6
Totals	131	59.0	91	41.0	222	100.0

Note: n = 287; missing observations = 65.

[a]Circulation over 52,800. [b]Circulation under 52,800.

as a work centre for reporters and editors using CAR in their daily stories and special projects. Yet, as noted, other news organizations have taken a different route by integrating CAR into the entire newsroom through comprehensive training and complete access to resources and tools needed for CAR. Paul McElroy, systems editor for the Seattle Post-Intelligencer, feels CAR desks are not needed:

This concept can give rise to the misconception that CAR projects must always be lengthy and complicated. In many, many cases, CAR is useful even when writing on deadline. Several of our reporters regularly dial into our state and federal court systems for online record searches.

A few are also quick to turn to a spreadsheet to crunch numbers for budget or election stories. Having said all that, a formal CAR desk can be useful if the resources are available to create one. Reporters can concentrate on reporting while we systems editor types handle the technical infrastructure of getting data into usable forms.

A CAR desk can also serve as a common meeting ground for discussing problems, techniques, ideas, and so on.

Neil Reisner, training director for NICAR and former database editor for The Bergen Record, also believes that existence of a CAR desk does not encourage widespread use of CAR tools in newsrooms:

But that seems to cut against what much of the industry is doing. I believe that CAR is merely another arrow in the quiver of journalism's armaments.

Everyone should use CAR techniques when appropriate, just as everyone uses the telephone or a newsroom writing terminal.

There is no part of journalism to which CAR does not have some application, be it the municipal reporter analyzing a town budget, the feature writer analyzing census data for a lifestyle or trend story, or the sports writer using a spreadsheet to compile team statistics.

I believe concentrating the technology at a special CAR desk mitigates against these sorts of uses and promotes creation of a CAR elite. That's" not the most effective use of the tool.

A total of 44 per cent of newspapers responding in 1995 used some form of a CAR desk to coordinate and conduct computer-assisted newsgathering. A total of 47 per cent of the newspapers in the 1994 study had created CAR desks, and 21 per cent reported plans to add a CAR desk or project team. In the 1995 survey, the proportion of newsrooms with CAR desks dropped slightly to 43 per cent. Of the 55 per cent that did not have desks, 56 per cent reported plans to add one within a year.

Newsroom individuals in charge of CAR have a wide range of titles and responsibilities. Many are called directors, supervisors, or coordinators. But their duties remain similar despite the variation in titles.

The typical CAR manager coordinates use of the computing resources, acquires databases, often oversees use of online services, trains other reporters, and serves as a liaison with upper level newsroom management. At some larger newspapers, a CAR supervisor

Table. Car Desks, 1995

CAR Desk of Some Type in Place	Large Dailiesa		Small Dailiesb		Totals	
Yes	93	66.4%	30	21.1%	123	43.6%
No	46	32.9	112	78.9	158	56.0
Don't know	1	0.7	0	0.0	1	0.4
Totals	140	49.6	142	50.4	282	100.0

Note: n = 287; missing observations = 5.
[a]Circulation over 52,800. bCirculation under 52,800.

Table. Car Desks, 1994-1995

Car Desk of Some Type in Place	1994		1995		Percentage Change
Yes	98	47.1%	123	42.9%	-4.2%
No	104	50.0	158	55.1	-5.1
Don't know/	6	2.9	6	2.0	-0.9
Totals	208	100.0%	287	100.0%	

may be database oriented only, leaving supervision of online resources and research to the news research or news library director or editor.

The number of individuals involved in CAR in newsrooms is increasing even if the proportion of desks is decreasing.

The mean number of persons involved in CAR in 1995 was reported to be 4.74 per newspaper, with numerous newspapers reporting none and one reporting as many as 75 persons. In 1994, the number involved in CAR was 3.54 persons. It makes sense to anticipate continued growth in the number of individuals involved in CAR in 1996 and beyond as more and more newsrooms take a full saturation approach.

PRINCIPLES IN THE BASIC NEWS REPORTING CLASSROOM

Basic news reporting classes offer us an excellent opportunity to alert future journalists to important aspects of human perception such as those studied in the field of general semantics. Reporting required identifying and discovering enormously complex events and responsibly representing them in summary form. Even the most energetic and capable reporter, however, cannot discover all the complexity and detail available in a single observation of a single event, and describe it while still meeting deadlines. Scholars in the field of general semantics have made the study of perception central to their discipline, and acquainting novice reporting students with some of their findings can help students understand the role perception plays in reporting.

Journalism scholarship includes perception among its many areas of investigation, but the articles that focuc on perception tend to primarily identify examples of differences in the way people perceive and how these differences contribute to interpretation of events.

Eberhard demonstrates that "news value" treatments differ among newswriting texts; Van Ommeren shows that knowing reporters' backgrounds changed student views about published stories; McAdams examines relationships between psycholinguistics and perception; Allen shows that journalists often do not explain how disparate pieces of information fit together; Stocking and Gross establish that people make errors in assessing risks; and Abbott and Slattery explore topics like "intuitive goods ears." Journalism scholarship does not appear to have directly focused on examining and explaining human perception as it relates to observing and interpreting human behaviors and world events.

Allen perhaps comes closer to recognizing a need for specific focus on perception than most scholars when she observes that we need to be "...more aware of culture as a blueprint for perception..." and suggests "But neither anthropologists nor journalists nor educators nor anyone else is assuming the responsibility for sharing the contextual frameword necessary for interpreting this morass of data..." Stocking and Gross suggest we may be "unknowingly failing our students and profession" not only in failing to point out common perception errors, but also in not developing exercises that "...will provide opportunities for learning about cognitive distortions without sacrificing the basics." We propose the field of general semantics and specific focus on human perception as one contribution to meeting Stocking and Gross' requesting.

If you ask basic news reporting students (or even experienced reporters for that matter) if their stories accurately represent what actually happened in a given instance, they are likely to say yes. They are used to relying on the fact that as humans they have sophisticated powers of observation and are able to quickly process large amounts of stimuli. They might readily accept the analogy that they record events much like a camera.

Korzybski, the founder of the general semantics movement, suggested even the mosot careful observer is unable to observe all stimuli within range. Bois offered an extension of Korzybski's work in a somewhat more understandable form. Both authors offered models that explained how perception necessarily differs from a given stimulus field. The models also show how perception may even result in reports that add up to more, or in some cases less, than the sum of the stimuli observed. Russell has adapted these earlier perception models and added to their range. This modified model may help basic news writing students understand that, much like a camera, their perception is limited and subject to distortion.

AVAILABLE STIMULI

This human perception model illustrates how perception is incomplete and how it always differs from the observed stimulus field. The open-sided box on the left represents the infinite stimulus field containing all individual stimuli potentially observable (dots). Some of the stimuli are in free space and others are within contained areas labeled Remembered Past, Attended to Present and Anticipated Future.

The Remembered Past box represents our ability to recall some, but not all, of the events from our past. We can recall events in varying degrees of completeness, but never completely. Our recall of these events can serve as a filter of present and future events. For example, previous deception by an assumed reputable source can influence belief in a present source.

The Attended to Present box represents stimuli available for detection in the present. Again, these stimuli are not all of the stimuli available. Fewer stimuli are attended to than are available. Psychological experiments show only a few of any available stimuli may be attended to by the senses and consciously registered at any one time. Magicians and three-card monte players know this principle well, as do sources who mislead by answering with an avalanche of irrelevant facts instead of those few facts which would answer a question.

The Anticipated Future box represents stimuli thought to be probable in the future. Those things, which are inconceivable to the subject simply do not exist in this perceptual frame. But items in an anticipated future can filter both present and remembered stimuli. For example, suddenly realizing that a source, caught in a compromising position, plans to lie to protect his reputation, could contribute to reconsideration of his previous comments and also the conclusion that his present comments may be untrue.

The model presumes a balanced individual in whom the Attended to Present is larger than the other two areas. Healthy observers pay more attention to the present than to their Remembered Past or Anticipated Future. This apparent contradiction must be perplexing and difficult for newsroom managers. There is some evidence in the data that managers are a bit frustrated, placing the "blame" for a lack of success on rank-and-file, who are perceived as close minded and resistant to change.

However, the results from the rank-and-file survey suggest it is not accurate to simply dismiss journalists as resistant to change. Rank-and-file indicate they accept change as a part of work and are personally committed to their paper's change efforts. They credit their managers for taking leadership roles and being committed to change. However, they question the factors motivating change and are able to distinguish between intentions and results. In brief, while management says it has articulated a vision, included employees in creating changes, been flexible, and sought feedback about the change process, rank-and-file respond that they are confused about the vision, fool loft out of the process, and perceive their managers as inflexible.

Rank-and-file also sense management's vulnerability and frustration in leading change, showing strong agreement that change is ego driven by inflexible managers who, refusing to recognize its lack of success, resort to authoritarian measures to counter pockets of resistance. Rank-and-file's perception that management has failed at nearly every step of the process, combined with their sense that profit is increasingly important to newsroom managers, further explains the low level of trust rank-and-file express towards their managers. Numerous scholars cite trust as a prerequisite condition for successful OD initiatives. Thus, despite management's general optimism about an improving newsroom culture, the breakdown of trust that both management and rank-and-file acknowledge does not bode well for continuing efforts at change, as theory suggests and common sense reveals that people do not readily accept the ideas of those whom they do not trust.

Beyond the organizational development issues associated with change, rank-and-file's skepticism about change can be understood by an apparent lack of producing successful results. Change initiatives are not only failing to create more efficient, productive, and happier newsrooms, they are also falling short on their stated goals. Journalists don't perceive changes as attracting more readers and advertisers, or helping to produce better newspapers.

Instead, rank-and-file connect change initiatives with fewer resources for journalism in a more market than they disseminate information. She suggests that management's lack of use of channels of communication, especially upward channels, limits feedback from lower level employees who do the work of the organization. This approach can affect the success of change efforts, as "changes in status, reward structures, job descriptions, roles, work methods, work relationships, and procedures bring significant organizational issues to the surface" that increase rank-and-file employees' need to communicate with their supervisors.

Other influences, such as physical condition and competing stimuli can also serve to filter perceptions, of course, but the five offered above can begin to help students in recognizing human perception is more complex than a simple stimulus-response act.

CLASSIFY

This box only has only one dot in it which represents the tendency in human perception to think in terms of classes and thereby reduce something complex into something overly simple. Classification encourage equating the characteristics of new members of a class, with characteristics of established members of the class. Perhaps, the intent is to help understand the world, but the outcome is more often to ignore important differences among members of the class. Making the comparison with known members of the class can contribute to assuming the new member is "exactly like" the known members. For example, knowing that a source is a Catholic could contribute to assuming she is opposed to abortion "because Catholics oppose abortion."

NAME

The box also only has one dot in it to represent yet an additional reduction of stimuli that are attended to. In naming, something complex is overly simplified. For example, a complex and unique individual can be reduced to "politician," or a thousand separate activities can become "war." Names represent on enormous reduction of available and observed stimuli.

MEANING

This box represents an expansion of the reduction process that has occurred in the first three boxes. At this stage of perception, individuals begin to determine the meaning of their experiences. Scholars in the field of general semantics hold that meaning is something created by an interaction between the individual and stimuli. The increased number of dots in the meaning box represents the capacity of expand what was previously reduced.

The additional dots in the box do not mean the available stimuli, or only those attended to have been faithfully reproduced. For example, a police officer could primarily attend to the reflection of light in a suspect's hand, and conclude the reflecting object is a gun. The officer may then assign this perceived stimuli to mean danger and that he must therefore protect himself. Meaning is a very private construct and the meanings of stimuli are not necessarily universally shared. Assuming they are may lead to misunderstanding. Determining that a public official is acting out of caution or weakness can be as much the consequence o the observer's assigning meaning as the official's actions.

The final box represents an additional reduction inthe perception process. The fewer dots in this box compared to the meaning box suggests we are unable to share all of our private meanings. This is particularly important for reporters since time and space constraints alone will always limit their ability to offer all that they know.

The lines going out of the What We Can Share box enter the available stimuli for others. This area is represented by a question mark because we have no way to be sure what others do with our stimuli. The number and nature of dots in their perceptual field is subject to their control and limits, not to the journalist's.

As a result of long experience in assigning meaning in particular situations, a reporter may understand the implications in a political candidate's refusing to debate an oppenent. Merely reporting the action, however, does not mean the reader will automatically grasp these implications.

Exposing news reporting students to the models of human perception suggested by general semanticists may help students appreciate what Harrison Salisbury (1988) recognized after many years of reporting.

[The war in Vietnam] was the first of the separating images which, as time went on, showed me that in war, as in the simplest things in life, truth is multifaceted, a crystal that refracts light in many forms and many shapes, the quicksilver of the mind.

Basic news reporting students who can understand and appreciate that human preception is not a simple stimulus-response act, and is always incomplete can perhaps begin to demonstrate what has been called maturity and good news judgement. If they can be taught their observations are by definition incomplete, perhaps they will learn to ask even more questions and search for more sources and vantage points before concluding they have observed and reported everything.

Admission criteria for journalism and mass communications programmes vary, ranging from a GPA requirement, to satisfactory completion of an introductory course, to use of language skills examinations. Concerns about admission requirements surfaced in the mid-1970s when enrollment growth began to exceed programme resources and was accompanied by a decline in scores on national standardized college entrance tests, especially in verbal scores reflecting writing achievement. Results of a 2003 ACT National Curriculum Survey of high school and college instructors found that while college instructors believe grammar and usage skills are important skills for entering college students, high school teachers ranked these skills as least important. However, writing for the National Review Online, Ridgley (2003) laid the blame for declining writing skills on universities that fail to teach writing basics and place a misdirected focus on "strange literary theories."

Ridgley, a former executive director of the Collegiate Network, a national association of college newspapers, and a Duke University instructor, lamented that too many college students graduate "without the ability to express themselves with the written word".

For graduates of mass communications programmes, such inability threatens the very core of a profession that depends upon communications skills. This concern about students' weak writing skills has been echoed by many, including Maxwell (2002), who in an article in the Alameda Times-Star wrote: "They [students] need to learn the craft and art of writing.

Unfortunately, most writing-across-the-curriculum programmes are too hit-and-miss to inculcate a love of writing or even an attitude of appreciating the importance of writing".

This chapter examines one department of journalism's efforts to identify, address, and correct basic writing deficiencies for students seeking a journalism degree with a concentration in news-editorial, broadcast, or public relations.

Northwestern State University's (NSU) Department of Journalism, located in a mid-sized, open-admissions university in the rural South, initiated a writing diagnostic test as a prerequisite for admission to the gateway media writing course required of all majors. To assist students failing the test, the department created a new elective course, "Literacy Skills for Journalists".

This preliminary report presents the findings and discussion based on initial data collection and instructor observations.

These results provided a platform for discussing the efficacy of requiring diagnostic writing tests for admission into a journalism programme and the most effective methods to remediate poor writing, to teach writing basics, to focus students' attention on the importance of good writing, and, ultimately, to develop writing skills acceptable for entry-level mass communications positions.

Bissell and Collins found in their research that writing deficiencies have not gone unnoticed at the college level. However, the issue remains: what are universities doing to correct students' writing deficiencies?

For journalism programmes, corrective action is critical because writing remains at the profession's core. Kunkel, dean of the Merrill College of Journalism at the University of Maryland, stated succinctly, "Writing instructors are obligated to teach the fundamentals of media writing". Calling journalism writing "part skill, part craft and part art" he said that students should have a solid foundation in reporting, writing, and editing.

The LSDT was administered to 175 students between spring 2001 and 2003. While some quantitative figures for the LSDT pass-fail rates and for successful completion of the basic media writing course were identified, both the data and faculty member observations, at this point, are more qualitative in nature. The database used for this study includes LSDT test data, ACT scores, and grades in prerequisite English and journalism courses. Additionally, identification of effective methods for data collection and analysis are ongoing. The initial findings and conclusions presented in this chapter represent efforts to address a curriculum problem through an action research project.

The Unit's diagnostic assessment and foundations course were created with the following beliefs:

1. Many students enter the programme with weak writing skills;
2. The results of the LSDT will alert students and faculty to writing deficiencies;
3. Poor writing skills can be improved with added emphasis and through curriculum offerings;
4. Students who pass the LSDT and the literacy skills course will successfully complete the basic media writing course; and
5. A writing diagnostic requirement will emphasize the importance of writing skills for journalism majors.

THE FINDINGS

Data for this study were gathered over five fall and spring semesters during the 2001-2003 academic years. Basic descriptive statistics were calculated based on this data. Since the initial data were sparse, findings are reported below as frequencies and as percentages.

1. As of spring 2003, 175 students have taken the LSDT. Of these, 100 students (57 per cent) failed to perform at the expected level.
2. Of those who took the LSDT, 29 students (91 per cent) having ACT-English scores requiring a developmental English placement (ACT 0-17) did not meet minimum scores on the LSDT. Of those students having ACT-English scores not requiring a developmental placement (ACT 18-27), 66 students (49 per cent) failed to meet the minimum score requirement on the LSDT.
3. All students who initially did not meet minimum scores on the LSDT, took the JOUR 1010, and afterwards met minimum score requirements on the LSDT earned average final grades of"B" and "C" in the gateway media writing course (JOUR 2510). None, however, earned a final grade of "A."
4. Of those 100 students who did not meet minimum scores on the LSDT, 55 students (55 per cent) have not yet taken JOUR 1010 and have not been admitted to the gateway course;

5. Students who took the gateway course after successfully completing the remedial course and passing the LSDT (38) earned grades of "B" and "C" in the gateway course.
6. An analysis of English course placement indicated that 19 students (21 per cent) who obtained three hours of credit in freshman English (ENGL 1010) based on ACT scores (28-31) passed the LSDT. All seven students who received six hours of credit in freshman English (ENGL 1010, 1020) based on ACT scores (32 and higher) passed the LSDT.
7. Not enough evidence was available to determine the significant effects of successful completion of ENGL 1010 and 1020 on the pass rate of the LSDT. However, an analysis of grades in freshman English reveals that students who received a grade of "C" or higher in the prerequisite freshman English courses experienced equal success in the gateway media writing course.

Since the implementation of the prerequisite diagnostic test, faculty members have noted three major outcomes: (1) more instruction and activities have focused on media writing principles and techniques, rather than writing remediation; (2) grades averages have improved; and (3) students' confidence in their writing abilities and awareness of the importance of these skills for the profession have lessened the complaints (whining) about instructor emphasis on correct language usage.

Students' increased confidence correlates to the importance of student self-efficacy in a media writing course, as described by Collins and Bissell (2002).

This study, based on a pilot diagnostic and basic writing skills course, validated faculty members' beliefs and the literature that addresses poor preparation for college-level writing. Specifically, findings from this study indicated that a majority (57 per cent) of those students taking the LSDT did not meet minimum requirements for success. Of this group, those having developmental English placements based on ACT-English test scores constituted the largest non-success rate on the LSDT (91 per cent). Of note, however, is the significant number of students with no developmental English course placements (49 per cent) who failed to meet the minimum score requirement on the LSDT.

One of the more important findings was that all students who initially did not meet minimum score requirements on the LSDT, who successfully completed JOUR 1010, and afterwards passed the LSDT earned passing grades in the gateway media writing course.

The study also found that earned credit in the first English course only does not provide the adequate preparation needed to meet the requirements of the LSDT. However, credit in both ENGL 1010 and 1020 yielded a 100 per cent pass rate.

Lack of sufficient evidence precludes determining the significant effects of successful completion of ENGL 1010 and 1020 on the pass rate of the LSDT as well as precluding determining the significant effect of "C" or higher grades in the prerequisite freshman English courses on success in the gateway media writing course.

The findings, though sketchy, warrant future investigation into the efficacy of diagnostic tests likes the LSDT and basic writing skills coursework for journalism majors.

Continued collection of data will allow for more significant data interpretation. Additionally, a more in-depth look at the basic writing skills course and its effect on improved writing skills is needed. non-etheless, the findings to date have validated the need for assessing writing skills and providing corrective programmes.

Faculty members in this department have commented on students' general poor preparation for college-level writing and the lack of student interest or motivation to write well and often, or both.

Writing, like any skill, takes practice. The best can take that skill from a craft to an art. One challenge is to have journalism majors meet basic skill requirements and be able to advance academically and professionally based on their studies, talents, and desires. The second challenge will be to better understand how best to teach writing and motivate students. The LSDT and literacy skills course are efforts to remediate weak writing and position students for curriculum and career success.

EMPOWERMENT THROUGH NEWSROOM TRAINING

Most newsroom managers feel that computer-based analysis of public and private records in the form of electronic databases is important and will grow in importance for the rest of this decade. That will require a lot of veteran journalists to learn a lot about computing in a very short amount of time. The training "gold rush" is on. The prize for the "prospectors" is computer literacy and full use of CAR's capabilities.

However, training is a sore spot for many working reporters and editors. It should be a major tool towards success in using computers in the newsroom, most computing experts believe. Many working professional journalists want training, professional development, or some sort of continuing education while they work because they simply cannot stop working, return to school, and earn a graduate degree or a second bachelor's degree. Many journalists feel it is part of their employer's responsibilities to employees to extend their education while working to permit personal career growth and improved overall performance.

Barbara Hijek, assistant library director in the Tampa bureau of the *St. Petersburg Times*, feels the need for training has modified the role of online news researchers: The role of the news librarian has changed. As reporters gain more access to databases (especially the lower-cost government access ones and the Internet as opposed to the more expensive boutique databases like Nexis), the news librarian is emerging more as an information coach -- directing reporters to sources, guiding them through the maze of appropriate databases to use and cautioning them about the pitfalls of online information.

Many times I tell our reporters -- consider this information as a good tip sheet -- check it out and verify the info. Databases provide info-rich background on individuals. WDIA often lists an individual's employer. This is often valuable. For example, after the Oklahoma City bombing the media became obsessed about citizen militias.

We decided to look into the activity level of our local militias. We found the leader of the 77th regiment of Pinellas County. The militias are united through their very basic belief that the federal government has gone haywire. They tend to have a deep distrust of the government. Well, our local militia leader would not disclose where he worked -- only that he has a day job"enforcing contracts." Well, WDIA revealed that he worked for the local county in a permit office. Some anti-government minuteman!

A CRITICAL NEED FOR CONTINUING EDUCATION

Kathleen Hansen is an associate professor and online research expert in the School of Journalism and Mass Communication at the University of Minnesota. A former librarian at the University of Wisconsin-Milwaukee and at the University of Wisconsin-Madison, she feels that continuing education is the single most important way to succeed with CAR in the newsroom:

Training, Training, Training

Unfortunately, news organizations are among the most stingy groups on the planet when it comes to furthering the education of their workforce. But I have gone to meeting after workshop after conference with journalists who are desperate to upgrade their skills, including CAR skills. Some even go so far as to pay their own way during their vacation times to get to IRE workshops or special training sessions offered by some local or regional group.

The obvious way to keep CAR going in the newsroom is to have a variety of types of folks who have"bought in" to the system and who understand how CAR can be useful in everyday reporting and editing.

The worst strategy, in my view, is to designate some kind of CAR guru, the keeper of the secrets, the computer, and the database access codes.

Spread it around, let everyone who's interested see how the skills and techniques can make their jobs easier, more interesting, more challenging, of better service to the community.

This training should be done in-house as much as possible, with occasional"inspirational" visits by leading experts who come in to cheer on the crowd and keep interest high.

Newspapers have a variety of ways to bring training to newsrooms. At The Philadelphia Inquirer, for example,"Bit-by-Bit University" has been created to train reporters and editors how to use spreadsheets, World Wide Web browsers and Internet resources, and other CAR tools.

The programme consists of a series of classes held:

- In-house classes
- Individual tutoring or coaching
- Local workshops or classes
- National or regional conferences and seminars
- Supplemental publications

in a small room just a few steps away from the newsroom. The classroom is equipped with personal computers, online connections, and software. It is used by news staffers, advertising staffers, and other employees of Philadelphia Newspapers, Inc., which also publishes the Philadelphia Daily News.

"Training is mandatory in my view. People must know the ins and outs of the software they are using, and the ups and downs of using numbers. Using computers to analyse data, for instance, opens up a whole new way to mess up our facts and maybe not even notice until it is too late," stated Carol Napolitano, a member of the public affairs team of the *Omaha World-Herald* and a CAR specialist. She had been in charge of CAR training when she was on the staff of *The Times* in Munster, Indiana.

"We began by individually working with the people most interested. Then we held training sessions, each three days long, nine hours a day.

We covered the basics of personal computers, DOS, Windows, statistics and math, database managers, spreadsheets, graphing, mapping, and Internet use over those twentyseven hours. Classes were small, three to five people per session. It was pretty successful."

FIGHTING COMPLACENCY IN NEWSROOMS

Despite the interest to be trained and to offer training in some newsrooms, some editors report that their staff members are complacent and have no desire to grow beyond their current skills. CAR is one such area for improving reporting skills. Some editors say their staffs have no interest in learning CAR. They say they are quite perplexed by the seeming lack of interest in computing shown by younger reporters.

One editor criticized colleges for not providing the computing background for graduates. "I am surprised by the lack of interest in CAR manifest in my reporting and editing staff of eighty-seven people. And these are young people!" exclaimed Managing Editor Paul Jagnow, who selects, buys, supports, and develops CAR for the 95,000-circulation *Vindicator* in Youngstown, Ohio.

"I'm not sure the 20- to 35-year-old group received enough computer training in college. They don't seem to be interested in, or committed to, computers, except to learn enough about them to input copy, write heads, and so forth."

Some small news organizations are using unique arrangements to bring CAR into their newsrooms and to facilitate CAR training. In Oshkosh, Wisconsin, for example, the 26,000-daily circulation *Oshkosh Northwestern* could not afford its own training programme, so it became part of a programme funded by a grant that brought an outside expert to the newspaper for part of a year.

With funding from the Knight Institute for Journalism Excellence, the American Society of Newspaper Editors, and the Knight Foundation, Executive Editor Thomas P. Lee was able to invite Arizona State University Journalism Professor Ed Sylvester for a summer to help set up the equipment and facilities, within the newspaper's limited resources, and to teach CAR skills to staff members for 6 weeks on site.

The Palm Beach Post's Mary Kate Leming offered an argument for investing in training, whether staff members seek it or not: "A big problem with CAR is, since not enough training is done and reporters are not given time away from their daily beat, that it is often done sloppily. There's a real risk there. I've seen computer projects happen where you get to the day before publication and somebody goes, 'I don't know how I got that number. How did I get that number?' and they can't go back and replicate what they did. That's very scary."

Arkansas Democrat-Gazette CAR Editor Bob Dunn agreed, saying CAR needs to be taught at journalism schools as well as on the job to working journalists: "Reporters need to learn how to use computers, databases, and spreadsheets. Journalism schools need to make that part of the curriculum."

Laura Frank is a former CAR team leader and reporter for Gannett's Rochester newspapers, the *Democrat and Chronicle* and *Times-Union*, who moved to the Nashville Tennessean in mid-1995. She emphasizes training in her role of "assisting reporters in using CAR for every-day stories." Frank explained the importance of learning CAR: "CAR is a powerful tool. Training is essential — any mistakes made with CAR are magnified by its power".

Nieman Fellow Brad Goldstein, computer-assisted reporting editor for the *St. Petersburg Times*, was previously a reporter for *The Eagle Tribune* in Lawrence, Massachusetts. He supervises CAR for *The Times*. Goldstein was not satisfied with the Lawrence newspaper's approach to CAR: "Despite all of the successes, The Eagle Tribune staff does not see the light in terms of allocating resources, or even training, reporters to use their tools," he noted. "They (the managers) want it done on personal time, not company time. And they manage from editors down."

Many news organizations expect their staff members to learn CAR on their own. *Fresno Bee* reporter Russell Clemings explained: "Our management has historically failed to encourage or support computer use, other than for production (*e.g.*, Leafdesk and remote filing of stories). Those who have developed those skills have mainly done so on their own."

SUPPLEMENTING TRAINING WITH PUBLICATIONS

The Hartford Courant is typical of many news organizations trying to supplement training with locally produced publications. *The Courant's* Computer Reporting Centre publishes a monthly report for news staffers called *dataBasics.* Larry Roberts, projects editor, organizes articles about databases, files, coverage ideas, analysis of data, new tools for staff, and plenty of how-to tips and ideas.

Similarly, Deborah Wolfe produces *Tech Talk* for newsroom staffers of the *St. Petersburg Times*. Wolfe, newsroom technology training coordinator, began the bimonthly in-house publication. Like dataBasics, Wolfe's newsletter runs 8 to 12 pages and covers a wide range of subjects such as newsroom information gathering technology, Internet ideas and tricks, upcoming in-house training classes, hardware and software advice, using the newsroom's Coyote system more effectively, accessing and using electronic public records, e-mail, and use of statistics.

Computer-assisted reporting skills are rapidly becoming the cutoff point in determining who makes the "employed list" or "preferred reporting team" and who does not in many newsrooms. At professional meetings, editors often discuss the need for employees to have CAR skills. Reporters know it. Students are beginning to seek them as an edge in the job application race.

"The candidates with computer-assisted reporting skills stay. All those without those skills are eliminated. The candidates with on-line searching experience stay. All those without that experience are eliminated," observed *Waterbury Republican-American* systems editor Christopher Feola and San Francisco State University Journalism Professor Tom Johnson. Feola and Johnson talked with consultants and newsroom managers.

From their discussions, they concluded that reporters need CAR skills, particularly the ability to use spreadsheets, use data on nine-track tape, conduct online research, and the ability to manage new media such as electronic newspapers or the World Wide Web.

A NOW ROLE FOR NEWS RESEARCHERS

Leading newsroom researchers agree that there needs to be more training and many argue that the individuals to do that training are news librarians.

Some, such as the Poynter Institute's online authority, Nora Paul, believe that news librarians should become the trainers of newsroom personnel in the area of computer use, especially online services. In some newsrooms, training responsibilities have begun to fall into the news library's domain.

At several newspapers, such as the *Raleigh News and Observer* and the *St. Petersburg Times*, news researchers have been tapped as full-time newsroom computer trainers. However, some news organizations depend on part-time in-house training provided by the existing CAR newsroom staff.

The types of training offered also vary. More and more, in-house classes are becoming common at larger newspapers. However, smaller news organizations must go outside for training, bring in temporary experts for special in-house classes, or send selected employees to workshops and seminars offered by outside experts, such as local computing companies or schools or Journalism organizations such as the NICAR at the University of Missouri.

"I've taught some classes for our newsroom and I was encouraged by how much interest there was. The problem is that after the class, everybody goes back to their daily beat and very few make any use of it. Their skills atrophy and, by the time they're ready to do something CAR-related, they have to be taught all over again," observed Ray Robinson, projects editor at The Press of Atlantic City:

I'm coming around to the idea that the best kind of training, at least in the beginning, is that which emphasizes possibilities rather than the nuts and bolts technical aspects. Instead of drowning them in how-to stuff that they're going to forget, dazzle them with what can be done using CAR. Then, when they're ready to tackle a project, you can teach the hard part to them on a more individualized basis.

Some papers are expecting all of their staffers to learn CAR and even tackle at least one CAR project. I don't like that approach. In any newsroom there are going to be some people who have a gift for this kind of work and some that don't. Those that don't should be allowed to use whatever other talents they have. Newsrooms are wonderfully diverse places, and we should encourage that, not try to turn every staffer into a database editor. Using a PC isn't such a vital skill that everyone should be required to learn it as a condition of their employment, at least not yet.

Neill Borowski, CAR director at The Philadelphia Inquirer, likes to use a"spider plant" model to teach CAR in his newsroom. He starts with his two-person CAR leadership team."Like a spider plant, you have a CAR core.

Like the plant, the core sends off chutes. And the chutes send off more chutes. There are generations of chutes and you eventually have a lush plant," Borowski explained.

TRAINING REMAINS A LOW PRIORITY

Minnesota's Hansen, a national authority in information technology, the sociology of news work, and related issues, sees in-house or localized computer services and databases training as much too low on the priority list in most newsrooms: It is the rare newsroom or publishing hierarchy that sees fit to train their news workers.

Therefore, the professional organizations are crucial for the educational function. I haven't thought much about their role for setting standards -- I suppose they do that, but in a more informal way. My own knowledge and level of comfort with all of this has been greatly enhanced by my participation at IRE, Poynter, AP, and other types of professional workshops and conferences.

Lack of resources is one barrier to CAR training as well as CAR itself in many newsrooms, but training has been an even more severe problem for some news organizations wanting to begin CAR.

If a desktop computer or several computers exist in a newsroom for part-time or full-time use for CAR, there may be such demand for use for the PC that training time takes a back seat.Because responsible and accurate use of computers in reporting requires considerable computer literacy, some sort of on-the-job training has become an important issue in almost all newsrooms.

Although some recent entry-level journalists may be learning CAR in some colleges, most journalists must learn CAR while at work.

DEPENDENCE ON EXTERNAL TRAINING PROGRAMMES

News organizations without their own CAR training programmes are dependent on outside programmes such as those offered by the IRE and NICAR.

There are several journalism organizations that offer training on a regular basis. By far, the leader has been NICAR. Both IRE and NICAR have taken their CAR classes on the road since 1994, but learning opportunities are still rare for most journalists.

The alternative, in-house training, is coming along slowly. However, the 1995 data, show 44 per cent reported some form of CAR-related training. Larger dailies (66 per cent) use some type of training three times more frequently than smaller dailies (21 per cent).

In 1995, 11 per cent more newspapers offered some form of training than did in 1994. In 1994, only 30 per cent of newspapers responding reported

Table. Car Training Programmes, 1995

Training programs of Some Type in Place	Large Dailiesa		Small Dailiesb		Totals	
Yes	90	66.2%	28	21.4%	118	44.2%
No	46	33.6	103	78.6	149	55.8
Totals	136	50.9	131	49.1	267	100.0

Note: n = 287; missing observations = 20.

[a]Circulation over 52,800. bCirculation under 52,800.

Table. Car Training Programmes, 1994-1995

Car Desk of Some Type in Place	1994		1995		Percentage Change
Yes	62	29.8%	118	41.1%	+11.3%
No	117	56.3	149	51.9	-4.4
Missing	29	13.9	20	7.0	-6.9
Totals	208	100.0%	287	100.0%	

in-house CAR training of any type, but the figure was up to 41 per cent of the responding newspapers in the 1995 study. This indicates more concern about training and investment in it by newsroom managers.

Without careful planning, training can go wrong. Editors who are unable to offer newsroom-wide training must make decisions about who to train and how to train the selected individuals.

This is typical of the problems facing small newspapers with limited resources. "One thing you have to be careful about as an editor is training. You have to figure out who you are going to send to seminars," stated Thomas P. Lee, executive editor of the Northwestern in Oshkosh, Wisconsin. I wasted some money big time last year sending some people to seminars.

They came back with nothing: The training, the encouragement — everything we could do and it just didn't happen. You send the right people and it's going to pay off. My advice is to make a list of the people who are going to do really well at a seminar and then throw in a couple of others and hope, through osmosis, it is going to happen."

Table. Training Programme Types, 1995

Type of Training	Large Dadiesa		Small Dailiesb		Totals	
Program						
In-house classes	52	58.4%	10	33.3%	62	52.1%
In-house tutoring	15	16.9	3	10.0	18	15.1
Outside workshops	13	14.6	5	16.7	18	15.1
Informal or ad hoc	7	7.9	4	13.3	11	9.2
Just beginning	1	1.1	6	20.0	7	5.9
CAR						
Newsletter or	1	1.1	1	3.3	2	1.7
handouts						
Committee work	0	0.0	1	3:3	1	0.8

Totals 89 74.8 30 25.2 119 100.0

Note: n = 287; missing observation = 168.

[a]Circulation over 52,800. [b]Ciculation under 52,800.

A closer look at training at the newspapers in 1995, shows most training to be in-house classes or seminars (52 per cent of those offering any training) or in-house tutoring (15 per cent). Providing outside training opportunities, such as workshops and seminars, is also popular (15 per cent). Another substantial number used ad hoc or informal training programmes (9 per cent). As with training in general, there are significant differences in large and small newspapers and the type of training they offer to staff members. Larger newspapers tend to offer more structured training programmes than do smaller dailies. Larger newspaper programmes are more often class oriented, whereas smaller newspapers use ad hoc or one-on-one training when it is available at all.

4

Values and Roles of Modern Journalism

While Weaver and Wilhoit and others have identified the various roles that journalists perceive themselves as performing, social psychology research suggests that individual value systems may determine how journalists perceive different roles. Moreover, it provides a basis from which to explore why journalists embrace particular roles over others. Personal values and demographic factors contribute to a web of context through which journalists view their roles and make decisions about which functions they feel are central.

The values that we hold, or the philosophical principles on which we base our reasons for doing things-claims to truth, social justice, fairness-constitute the engine that drives many discussions about the behaviour of media practitioners. Individual values, conceptually more fundamental than the roles we see for ourselves in society, inform as well as lend context to the functions journalists undertake. This study seeks to examine how incorporating value-theory research might expand our understanding of journalistic role conceptions established by the studies of Weaver and Wilhoit, Voakes, and others.

There is little question over whether ethical frameworks are used in journalistic decision making. The most substantive discussions revolve around the factors that influence that process or the philosophical underpinnings of a democratic free press.

Others have sought to explore the journalistic applications of particular philosophical approaches. This study explores the suggestion that the conventional applications of philosophical approaches alone do not adequately explain journalistic behaviour and the roles embraced by journalists on a daily basis.

VALUE THEORY RESEARCH

Research into values has an extensive history in sociology and social psychology and has culminated in a body of theory that suggests individuals conduct their social lives according to a "value system"-"a hierarchical arrangement of values, a rank-ordering of values along a continuum of importance." Research also has produced sophisticated assessment instruments used in value analysis, most notably the Rokeach Value Survey that has been widely used since the early 1970s.

The Rokeach Value Survey, which assesses the respondent's rankordering of eighteen values in two categories, has been independently validated and used extensively to compare value systems of individuals as well as diverse cultures.

Rokeach's definition of value has informed much contemporary value analysis: "More formally, to say that a person 'has a value' is to say that he has an enduring belief that a particular mode of conduct or that a particular end-state of existence is personally and socially preferable to alternative modes of conduct or end-states of existence." Values, research suggests, are relatively stable over time for members within a given group. Ranked values obtained by individuals and groups also have been directly linked to behaviour.

Using the Rokeach Value Survey, researchers have examined the influence of values on television viewing behaviour, the value systems of city planners and managers, and how values guide the ideological outlooks of social workers. The value survey also has been used to examine how specific instrumental values and internalized messages work together when individuals self-assess their behaviour. The value-theory research of sociologists has not been widely utilized by media theorists, who have largely focused their work on cognitive psychology and on normative frameworks drawn from philosophical approaches.

Black and colleagues examined how the content of an ethics course alters the value systems of journalism students. Viall proposed applying a modified Rokeach survey to explore journalistic values, but only in a notably constricted approach.

Other researchers using the Rokeach Value Survey have noted that the value list does not adequately represent "basic human rights" such as dignity, privacy, and protection from harm. This study adds six values to the list of eighteen instrumental values included in the Rokeach Value Survey. Values added to the instrument for this study should help to close that "basic human rights" gap.

CONCEPTIONS OF JOURNALISTIC ROLES

Much media research has implicitly depended on assumptions about journalistic values, but has stopped short of analyzing how a value theory might be at work. The landmark studies by Johnstone and colleagues, Culbertson, and Weaver and Wilhoit examine the professional roles-what could be referred to as the generally held teleology, or end purpose, of journalism.

In their 1992 study, for example, Weaver and Wilhoit categorized survey responses as reflecting how journalists assessed their professional roles based on "interpretive," "disseminator," or "adversarial" values. This study focuses on the dynamic of interaction between those professional roles and the motives behind them. Journalists were asked to rate the importance of various media roles-for example, to "investigate government claims," to "avoid stories with unverified content," to "let people express views"-as well as to rank a set of values according to their perceived importance to journalistic work.

In an earlier study that visited the issue of professional roles, Janowitz found that, over time, people working in journalism changed their perceptions of the role of journalism in society from one of strict neutrality to one that attempts to explain the news by putting it in a broader context. Echoing Lippmann, Janowitz wrote that earlier models had journalists adhering to a role that emphasizes objectivity to provide verifiable information to the public.

"The model was reinforced in part by the increased prestige of the academic social researcher, and it assumed that, through the application of intellectually based techniques, objective and valid results could be obtained." In time, the model evolved from one of detachment to one of involvement, giving prominence to the role of the interpretive or advocate journalist.

The philosophical values on which these journalistic roles are based are conceptually more fundamental than the roles themselves; the three previously mentioned survey items related to the work of Weaver and Wilhoit-to "investigate government claims," to "avoid stories with unverified content," to "let people express views"-can be considered to refer to the principles of truth, justice, and equality.

Consequently, it is not unreasonable to expect that perceived roles and underlying principles correlate with one another-not only in the sense that journalists endorse various media roles and corresponding values, but that values, even potentially conflicting ones, are held simultaneously.

Such pluralism was a key finding in Weaver and Wilhoit's 1992 survey of journalists: "[M]ost journalists strongly endorsed a combination of two, and sometimes three, core roles. At least superficially, then, most journalists saw themselves as serving seemingly contradictory functions" [authors' emphasis]. Preliminary findings of the 2002 survey update by Weaver, Beam, and colleagues suggest similar pluralistic role conceptions.

RESEARCH QUESTIONS

Measuring individuals' value systems and examining how certain values are given more weight than others offers direct insights into the motivations of behaviour-including the decision-making process. This study is motivated by the following research questions:

RQ1: What are the value systems of journalists?

RQ2: What is the relationship between the values that journalists rank highly and the roles that they embrace?

RQ3: What are the relationships between the roles that journalists embrace, the values that they rank highly and demographic factors such as age, length of time in their position, length of time in the profession, and length of time spent in a community?

Because the link between personal values and professional roles is such an intuitive one, bodies of research on both topics have remained distinct, and the relationship between the two has not been explored in a systematic way.

The literature and reflections of individual journalists are filled with anecdotal references suggesting the two are related. Shoemaker and Reese, while arguing that the individual journalist has less of an influence on news content than do organizations or social systems, non-etheless note that an individual journalist's characteristics can shape what that reporter thinks is important and that reporter's definition of news.

Journalists regularly note how their personal values and outlooks are brought to bear in their professional lives.

Journalists' perceptions about what is news are influenced as much by their personal experiences as by their training and newsroom socialization. In this sense, news content can be highly individualized. "Reporters bring their own expertise to bear-their environment, their heredity, their biases. If you have all males on the campaign, there won't be any questions about abortion rights.

If you have no people of colour, you may not get a question about reaction to the beating of Mr. Byrd in Jasper," said Ann Scales, an African-American reporter for the Boston Globe who covered the Gore campaign during the 2002 presidential election.

While Scales points out how who she is affects how she does her job, Louise Knott Ahern, the education reporter at the Riverside, California, Press-Enterprise, suggests that core personal values are intrinsically tied to her professional behaviour. "...[I]f you're not going to be an ethical person in your life, you're not going to be an ethical journalist. Do you cheat on your taxes repeatedly? Do you find kids smoking pot, and say, 'Way to go, Johnny'? You know? You're not going to be an ethical journalist. If you're not that way in life, you're not going to be that way in your reporting."

The approach that a reporter takes to a story and the series of decisions she makes regarding what facts are newsworthy and what facts can be ignored-her "bias," some would say-are "the inevitable consequence of the combinations of one's experience and inbred nature."

HYPOTHESES

While much research has been conducted independently on value theory and on the roles that journalists see for themselves in society, few efforts have been made to explore the link between the two. However, both bodies of research represent different ways of examining the internal forces that drive reporters and editors.

Social psychology research suggests that media practitioners operate by constantly reassessing the primacy and relevancy of each within a set of fixed, so-called instrumental values as they are applied to diverse questions. We also can, based on the assumptions about journalistic values that fill the literature of media ethics theory, hypothesize the following:

H1: Newspaper journalists who rank the values "Courageous," "Independent," and "Just" highly will endorse an adversarial function of the press.

Based on research that establishes a relationship between values and behaviour, the value systems of journalists help shape how they perceive their function in society. The nature of the adversarial role as defined by Weaver and Wilhoit represents strong support for the watch-dog responsibility of journalism and a "skeptical" outlook, both of which suggest the values of "Courageous" and "Just."

Weaver and Wilhoit also concluded that so-called adversarialist journalists placed great value on job autonomy-which, of course, corresponds with the value of "Independence."

H2: Newspaper journalists who rank the values "Minimizing harm," "Fair," and "Self-controlled" highly will endorse a disseminator function of the press.

Defining the disseminator role, Weaver and Wilhoit characterized journalists who embraced it as "audience-oriented" and "cautious," which corresponds with the values of "Minimizing harm" and "Self-controlled." The authors also described disseminators as "considerably less accepting of controversial reporting practices, such as posing as someone else or using unauthorized documents," which also suggests the value of "Fair."

H3: Newspaper journalists who rank the values "Civic-minded," "Imaginative," and "Capable" highly will endorse an interpretive function of the press.

While Weaver and Wilhoit are less precise in their description of the interpretive role, they suggest that journalists embracing this role express strong support for the concept of the press as a public service, which corresponds with the value "Civic-minded."

The interpretive role also presumes a more active approach to the news that calls for a greater use of individual creativity. This suggests that the values of "Imaginative" and "Capable" rank highly for journalists embracing the interpretive role.

METHOD

This project is based on a nationwide random-sample mail survey, stratified by state, of 600 newspaper journalists conducted in early 2002. The individual journalists constitute two groups: newspaper reporters and newspaper editors, with one of each drawn from each newspaper in a process of stratified random selection.

The number of newspapers needed from each state for proportional representation was calculated, with a target total of 300.

A table of random numbers was then used to select the established number of newspapers.

To prevent the large number of small daily newspapers from being overrepresented, major metro dailies with circulations of 150,000 or more were weighted by assigning each of them two consecutive numbers instead of one, thereby doubling their chances for selection.

A single editor (team editor, metro editor, city editor, managing editor, etc.) and a single reporter were selected using a table of random numbers applied to each group on each newspaper's staff list.

These staff lists are commonly available on newspaper Web sites. Phone calls were made to verify the presence of each selected journalist when necessary. The initial mailing was in mid-January 2002, the second mailing was during the third week of January, and a third wave was during the first week of February.

Respondents were presented with a sheet of movable adhesive tabs, each listing one of the 24 values. They were asked to rank them in importance by placing each tab next to one of the printed numbers between 1 and 24. The overall value hierarchy was derived by obtaining the average ranking for each value.

The brief descriptors that Rokeach originally used to present each value were retained. To assess respondent positions regarding journalistic roles, reporters and editors were asked to respond to 14 statements on a 5-point Likert scale, with 5 = extremely important, 3 = neither important nor unimportant, and 1 = extremely unimportant.

RESULTS

The survey elicited 355 usable responses from journalists at 239 newspapers, representing a response rate of 59 per cent. Respondents ranged from neo-phyte reporters just on the job at small rural papers for a few months to veteran executive and managing editors at some of the country's largest metro dailies.

With one exception, the demographic makeup of this study's respondents does not deviate dramatically from what Voakes found in 1997 and Weaver and Wilhoit found in 1994.

Women made up 48.7 per cent of respondents in this study, compared with 37 per cent for Voakes and 34 per cent for Weaver and Wilhoit. Whites made up 94 per cent of the respondents, while Blacks constituted 3.2 per cent and Hispanics 1.4 per cent.

PRAGMATIST ETHICAL THEORY FOR MODERN JOURNALISM

What philosophical foundations can the ethics of journalism rest on, if not on the doctrines of objectivity, neutrality, and the centrality of information? The answer may lie in the American philosophical tradition of pragmatism and in the work of John Dewey on problems of truth, communications, and society.

John Dewey was one of Walter Lippmann's chief intellectual adversaries during the 1920s, when Lippmann was propounding his theory of democracy. Dewey did not disagree that individual citizens were on the whole poorly prepared to play an active role in democratic life, but he was far more optimistic than Lippmann about the potential of the public.

Moreover, he argued, the government by experts that Lippmann proposed, with the public relegated to ratifying expert opinions, could never "be anything but an oligarchy managed in the interests of the few." Only the public can truly say what the public good is, and that can only be discovered through public participation in an ongoing conversation.

Because communication was so central to Dewey's theory of democracy, he was keenly interested in the role of the press. When Dewey speaks of a public, he means a group of people who are affected by the indirect consequences of the actions of others. Government arises out of the need to control those consequences in order to protect the public's interests. In a democracy, the members of the public participate to the fullest extent of their capacity in self-governance.

America's democratic institutions are the legacies of a less complex era. But unlike Lippmann, Dewey did not feel that the complexity of modern society made it necessary to abandon the ideal of participatory democracy. Rather, he believed that new forms of communication must be developed to make democratic participation possible in a more complex society.

"Without such communication," Dewey wrote, "the public will remain shadowy and formless, seeking spasmodically for itself, but seizing and holding its shadow rather than its substance. Till the Great Society is converted into a Great Community, the public will remain in eclipse. Communication can alone create a great community."

Dewey's philosophy seems particularly timely and relevant for journalism today. The vitality of public life was a major concern of Dewey's writing, and today it has become a central issue for many journalists.

NEW JOURNALISM

New Journalism was a style of 1960s and 1970s news writing and journalism which used literary techniques deemed unconventional at the time. The term was codified with its current meaning by Tom Wolfe in a 1973 collection of journalism articles he published as *The New Journalism*, which included works by himself, Truman Capote, Hunter S. Thompson, Norman Mailer, Joan Didion, Robert Christgau, and others.

Articles in the New Journalism style tended not to be found in newspapers, but rather in magazines such as *The Atlantic Monthly*, *CoEvolution Quarterly*, *Esquire Magazine*, *New York*, *The New Yorker*, *Rolling Stone*, and for a short while in the early 1970s, *Scanlan's Monthly*.

Various trends and tendencies throughout the history of American Journalism have been labeled "new journalism." Robert E. Park, for instance, in his *Natural History of the Newspaper,* referred to the advent of the penny press in the 1830s as "new journalism."

Likewise, the appearance of the yellow press, papers such as Joseph Pulitzer's *New York World* in the 1880s, led journalists and historians to proclaim that a "New Journalism" had been created. Ault and Emery, for instance, said "Industrialization and urbanization changed the face of American during the latter half of the Nineteenth century, and its newspapers entered an era known as that of the 'New Journalism.'

"In 1960 John Hohenberg, in *The Professional Journalist*, called the interpretive reporting which developed after World War II a "new journalism which not only seeks to explain as well as to inform; it even dares to teach, to measure, to evaluate."

During the sixties and seventies the term enjoyed widespread popularity, often with meanings bearing manifestly little or no connection with one another. Although James E. Murphy noted that '"...most user of the term seem to refer to something more specific than vague new directions in journalism" Curtis D. MacDougal devoted the Preface of the Sixth Edition of his *Interpretative Reporting* to New Journalism and cataloged many of the contemporary definitions: "Activist, advocacy, participatory, tell-it-as-you-see-it, sensitivity, investigative, saturation, humanistic, reformist and a few more."

The Magic Writing Machine—Student Probes of the New Journalism, a collection edited and introduced by Everette E. Dennis, came up with six categories, labelled new non-fiction (reportage), alternative journalism ("modern muckraking"), advocacy journalism, underground journalism and precision journalism. Michael Johnson's *The New Journalism* addresses itself to three phenomena: the underground press, the artists of non-fiction, and changes in the established media.

Journalists recognized as using the style include Norman Mailer, Joan Didion, Truman Capote, P. J. O'Rourke, George Plimpton, Terry Southern, and Gay Talese. Hunter S. Thompson was a major practitioner of new journalism and gonzo journalism, his own particular style.

Thompson's first book, *Hell's Angels: The Strange and Terrible Saga of the Outlaw Motorcycle Gangs*, is a more conventional piece, and shows the beginnings of a more memoir-based approach to reportage. Gay Talese's 1966 article for Esquire, *Frank Sinatra Has a Cold*, was an influential piece of new journalism that gave a detailed portrait of Frank Sinatra without ever interviewing him.

New journalism writers brought new approaches to areas already covered by the mainstream press. The psychedelic movement was something that many of the writers of the period covered, such as in Tom Wolfe's *The Electric Kool-Aid Acid Test.* The Vietnam War was another common topic, as was the political turmoil on the homefront. Terry Southern's Grooving in Chi documented the 1968 Chicago National Democratic Convention for Esquire Magazine in new journalism manner.

New journalism's techniques were also applied to less obvious subjects, such as financial markets (by George Goodman under the pseudonym Adam Smith, in essays originally published in New York Magazine and later collected in a book called *The Money Game*.)

Some authors of conventional fiction switched to writing in the style of new journalism, such as Truman Capote's *In Cold Blood*, and Norman Mailer's *Armies of the Night*. However, neither author ever agreed to their style's comparison to Wolfe's school of narration, nor did many others who have been retrospectively promoted as being members and therein associated. Much to the contrary, many of these writers would deny that their work was generically relevant to other new journalists at the time.

EARLY DEVELOPMENT, THE SIXTIES

How and when the term New Journalism began to refer to a genre has not been clear. Tom Wolfe, a practitioner and principal advocate of the form, wrote in at least two articles in 1972 that he had no idea of where it began.

Trying to shed light on the matter, literary critic Seymour Krim, offered his explanation in 1973. I'm certain that [Pete] Hamill first used the expression. In about April of 1965 he called me at *Nugget* Magazine, where I was editorial director, and told me he wanted to write an article about new New Journalism.

It was to be about about the exciting things being done in the old reporting genre by Talese, Wolfe and Breslin. He never wrote the piece, so far as I know, but I began using the expression in conversation and writing. It was picked up and stuck. But wherever and whenever the term arose, there is evidence of some literary experimentation in the early 1960s, as when Norman Mailer broke away from fiction to write *Superman Comes to the Supermarket* A report of John F. Kennedy's nomination that year, the piece established a precedent which Mailer would later build on in his 1968 convention coverage (*Miami and the Siege of Chicago*) and in other non-fiction as well.

Wolfe wrote that his first acquaintance with a new style of reporting came in a 1962 *Esquire* article about Joe Louis by Gay Talese. "'Joe Louis at Fifty' wasn't like a magazine article at all. It was like a short story. It began with a scene, an intimate confrontation between Loius and his third wife..." Wolfe said Talese was the first to apply fiction techniques to reporting.

Esquire claimed credit as the seedbed for these new techniques. *Esquire* editor Harold Hayes later wrote that "in the Sixties, events seemed to move too swiftly to allow the osmotic process of art to keep abreast, and when we found a good novelist we immediately sought to seduce him with the sweet mysteries of current events." Soon others, notably *New York,* followed *Esquire's* lead, and the style eventually infected other magazines and then books.

THE SEVENTIES

Much of the criticism favorable to this New Journalism came from the writers themselves. Talese and Wolfe, in a panel discussion cited earlier, asserted that, although what they wrote may look like fiction, it was indeed reporting: "Fact reporting, leg work." Talese called it.

Wolfe, in *Esquire* for December, 1972, hailed the replacement of the novel by the New Journalism as literature's "main event" and detailed the points of similarity and contrast between the New Journalism and the novel. The four techniques of realism that he and the other New Journalists employed, he wrote, had been the sole province of novelists and other *literati.*

They are scene-by-scene construction, full record of dialogue, third-person point of view and the manifold incidental details to round out character (*i.e.*, descriptive incidentals). the result... is a form that is not merely like a *novel.* It consumes devices that happen to have originated with the novel and mixes them with every other device known to prose. And all the while, quite beyond matters of technique, it enjoys an advantage so obvious, so built-in, one almost forgets what power it has': the simple fact that the reader knows *all this actually happened.* The disclaimers have been erased. The screen is gone. The writer is one step closer to the absolute involvement of the reader that Henry James and James Joyce dreamed of but never achieved.

The essential difference between the new non-fiction and conventional reporting is, he said, that the basic unit of reporting was no longer the datum or piece of information but the scene. Scene is what underlies "the sophisticated strategies of prose." The first of the new breed of nonfiction writers to receive wide notoriety was Truman Capote, whose 1965 best-seller, *In Cold Blood,* was a detailed narrative of the murder of a Kansas farm family. Capote culled material from some 6000 pages of notes.

The book brought its author instant celebrity. Capote announced that he had created a new art form which he labelled the "nonfiction novel." I've always had the theory that reportage is the great unexplored art form... I've had this theory that a factual piece of work could explore whole new dimensions in writing that would have a double effect fiction does not have—the every fact of its being true, every word of its true, would add a double contribution of strength and impact. Capote continued to stress that he was a literary artist, not a journalist, but critics hailed the book as a classic example of New Journalism.

Wolfe's *The Kandy-Kolored Tangerine-Flake Streamline Baby,* whose introduction and title story, according to James E. Murphy, "emerged as a manifest of sorts for the nonfiction genre," was published the same year. In his introduction Wolfe wrote that he encountered trouble fashioning an *Esquire* article out of material on a custom car extravaganza in Los Angeles, in 1963. Finding he could not do justice to the subject in magazine article format, he wrote a letter to his editor, Byron Dobell, which grew into a 49-page report detailing the custom car world, complete with scene construction, dialogue and flamboyant description. *Esquire* ran the letter, striking out "Dear Byron." and it became Wolfe's maiden effort as a New Journalist. In an article entitled "The Personal Voice and the Impersonal Eye," Dan Wakefield acclaimed the nonfiction of Capote and Wolfe as elevating reporting to the level of literature, terming that work and some of Norman Mailer's nonfiction a journalistic breakthrough: reporting "charged with the energy of art"

A review by Jack Newfield of Dick Schaap's *Turned On* saw the book as a good example of budding tradition in American journalism which rejected many of the constraints of conventional reporting: This new genre defines itself by claiming many of the techniques that were once the unchalanged terrain of the novelist: tension, symbol, cadence, irony, prosody, imagination. A 1968 review of Wolfe's *The Pump House Gang* and *The Electric Kool-Aid Acid Test* said Wolfe and Mailer were applying "the imaginative resources of fiction" to the world around them and termed such creative journalism "hystory" to connote their involvement in what they reported.

Talese in 1970, in his Author's Note to *Fame and Obscurity,* a collection of his pieces from the 1960s, wrote:

The new journalism, though often reading like fiction, is not fiction. It is, or should be, more reliable as the most reliable reportage although it seeks a larger truth than is possible through the mere compilation of verifiable facts, the use of direct quotations, and adherence to the rigid organizational style of the older form.

Seymour Krim's *Shake It for the World, Smartass* which appeared in 1970, contained "An Open Letter to Norman Mailer" which defined New Journalism as "a free nonfictional prose that uses every resource of the best fiction." And in "The Newspaper As Literature/Literature As Leadership" he called journalism the *de facto* literature of the majority, a synthesis of journalism and literature that the book's postscript called "journalit."

In 1972, in "An Enemy of the Novel" Krim identified his own fictional roots and declared that the needs of the time compelled him to move beyond fiction to a more "direct" communication to which he promised to bring all of fiction's resources.

David McHam, in an article titled "The Authentic New Journalists," distinguished the nonfiction reportage of Capote, Wolfe and others from other, more generic interpretations of New Journalism. Also in 1971, William L. Rivers disparaged the former and embraced the latter, concluding, "In some hands, they add a flavour and a humanity to journalistic writing that push it into the realm of art."

Charles Brown in 1972 reviewed much that had been written as New Journalism and about New Journalism by Capote, Wolfe, Mailer and others and labelled the genre "New Art Journalism," which allowed him to test it both as art and as journalism. He concluded that the new literary form was useful only in the hands of literary artists of great talent.

In the first of two pieces by Wolfe in *New York* detailing the growth of the new nonfiction and its techniques. Wolfe returned to the fortuitous circumstances surrounding the construction of *Kandy-Kolored* and added:

Its virtue was precisely in showing me the possibility of there being something "new" in journalism.

What interested me was not simply the discovery that it was possible to write accurate nonfiction with techniques usually associated with novels and short stories.

It was that—plus. It was the discovery that it was possible in nonfiction, in journalism, to use any literary device, from the traditional dialogisms of the essay to stream-of-consciousness...

THE EIGHTIES

In the Eighties the use of New Journalism saw a decline, several of the old trailblazers still used fiction techniques in their nonfiction books. But younger writers in *Esquire* and *Rolling Stone,* where the style had flourished in the two earlier decades, shifted away from the New Journalism. Fiction techniques had not been abandoned by these writers, but they were used sparingly and less flamboyantly.

"Whatever happened to the New Journalism?" wondered Thomas Powers in a 1975 issue of *Commonweal*. In 1981, Joe Nocera published a postmortem in the *Washington Monthly* blaming its demise on the journalistic liberties taken by Hunter S. Thompson. Regardless of the culprit, less than a decade after Tom Wolfe's 1973 New Journalism anthology, the consensus was that New Journalism was dead.

CHARACTERISTICS

As a literary genre, New Journalism has certain technical characteristics. It is an artistic, creative, literary reporting form with three basic traits: dramatic literary techniques; intensive reporting; and reporting of generally acknowledged subjectivity.

AS SUBJECTIVE JOURNALISM

Pervading many of the specific interpretations of New Journalism is a posture of subjectivity. Subjectivism is thus a common element among many (though not all) of its definitions. In contrast to a conventional journalistic striving for an objectivity, subjective journalism allows for the writer's opinion, ideas or involvement to creep into his story.

Much of the critical literature concerns itself with a strain of subjectivism which may be called activism in news reporting. In 1970 Gerald Grant wrote disparagingly in *Columbia Journalism Review* of a "New Journalism of passion and advocacy" and in the *Saturday Review* Hohenberg discussed "The Journalist As Missionary" For Masterson in 1971, "The New Journalism" provided a forum for discussion of journalistic and social activism. In another 1971 article under the same title Ridgeway called the counter-culture magazines such as *The New Republic* and *Ramparts* and the American underground press New Journalism.

Another version of subjectivism in reporting is what is sometimes called participatory reporting. Robert Stein, in *Media Power,* defines New Journalism as "A form of participatory reporting that evolved in parallel with participatory politics..."

AS FORM AND TECHNIQUE

The above interpretations of New Journalism view it as an attitude towards the practice of journalism. But a significant portion of the critical literature deals with form and technique.

Critical comment dealing with New Journalism as a literary-journalistic genre (a distinct type of category of literary work grouped according to similar and technical characteristics) treats it as the *new nonfiction*. Its traits are extracted from the criticism written by those who claim to practice it and by others. Admittedly it is hard to isolate from a number of the more generic meanings The new nonfiction where sometimes taken for advocacy of subjective journalism. A 1972 article by Dennis Chase defines New Journalism as a subjective journalism emphasizing "truth" over "facts" but uses major nonfiction stylists as its example.

AS INTENSIVE REPORTAGE

Although much of the critical literature discussed the use of literary or fictional techniques as the basis for a New Journalism, critics also referred to the form as stemming from intensive reporting. Stein, for instance, found the key to New Journalism not its fictionlike form but the "saturation reporting" which precedes it, the result of the writer's immersion in his subject. Consequently, Stein concluded, the writer is as much part of his story as is the subject and he thus linked saturation reporting with subjectivity. For him New Journalism is inconsistent with objectivity or accuracy. But other have argued that total immersion enhances accuracy. *As Wolfe put the case*: I am the first to agree that the New Journalism should be as accurate as traditional journalism. In fact my claims for the New Journalism, and my demands upon it, go far beyond that. I contend that it has already proven itself *more* accurate than traditional journalism—which unfortunately i saying but so much... Wolfe coined "saturation reporting" in his *Bulletin of the American Society of Newspaper Editors* article. After citing the opening paragraphs of Talese's Joe Louis piece, he confessed believing that Talese had "piped" or faked the story, only later to be convinced, after learning that Talese so deeply delved into the subject, that he could report entire scenes and dialogues.

The basic units of reporting are no longer who-what-when-where-how and why but whole scenes and stretches of dialogue. The New Journalism involves a depth of reporting and an attention to the most minute facts and details that most newspapermen, even the most experienced, have never dreamed of.

In his "Birth of the New Journalism" in *New York,* Wolfe returned to the subject, which he here described as a depth of information never before demanded in newspaper work. The New Journalist, he said, must stay with his subject for days and weeks at a stretch. In Wolfe's *Esquire* piece saturation became the "Locker Room Genre" of intensive digging into the lives and personalities of one's subject, in contrast to the aloof and genteel tradition of the essayists and "The Literary Gentlemen in the Grandstand." For Talese, intensive reportage took the form of interior monologue to discover from his subjects what they were thinking, not, he said in a panel discussion reported in *Writer's Digest,* merely reporting what people did and said.

Wolfe identified the four main devices New Journalists borrowed from literary fiction:

- Telling the story using scenes rather than historical narrative as much as possible
- Dialogue in full (Conversational speech rather than quotations and statements)
- Point-of-view (present every scene through the eyes of a particular character)
- Recording everyday details such as behaviour, possessions, friends and family (which indicate the "status life" of the character)

Despite these elements, New Journalism is not fiction. It maintains elements of reporting including strict adherence to factual accuracy and the writer being the primary source. To get "inside the head" of a character, the journalist asks the subject what they were thinking or how they felt.

PRACTITIONERS AND WRITERS

Which writer who are New Journalists is hard to define. In *The New Journalism: A Critical Perspective* Murphy writes, "A a literary genre, New

Journalism [...] involves a more or less well defined group of writers [...]. Each is stylistically unique, but all sharing common formal elements." Among the most prominenet writers of New Journalism, Murphy lists: Jimmy Breslin, Truman Capote, Joan Didion, David Halberstam, Pete Hamill, Larry King, Norman Mailer, Joe McGinniss, Rex Reed, Mike Royko, John Sack, Dick Schaap, Terry Southern, Gail Sheehy, Gay Talese, Hunter S.

Thompson, Dan Wakefield, and Tom Wolfe. In *The New Journalism,* Johnson and Wolfe, also includes George Plimpton for his *Paper Lion*, *Life* writer James Mills, Robert Christgau and a few others. Christgau, however, stated in an 2001 interview that he did not see himself as a New Journalist.

CRITICISM

While many praised the New Journalist's style of writing, Wolfe et al., also received severe criticism from contemporary journalists and writers. Essentially two different charges were leveled against New Journalism: criticism against it as a *distinct genre* and criticism against it as a *new* form.

Robert Stein believed that "In the New Journalism the eye of the beholder is all—or almost all," and in 1971 Philip M. Howard, wrote that the new nonfiction writers rejected objectivity in favour of a more personal, subjective reportage. This parallels much of what Wakefield said in his 1966 *Atlantic* article.

The important and interesting and hopeful trend to me in the new journalism is its personal nature—not in the sense of personal attacks, but in the presence of the reporter himself and the significance of his own involvement.

This is sometimes felt to be egotistical, and the frank identification of the author, especially as the "I" instead of merely the impersonal "eye" is often frowned upon and taken as proof of "subjectivity," which is the opposite of the usual journalistic pretense.

And in spite of the fact that Capote believed in the objective accuracy of *In Cold Blood* and strove to keep himself totally out of the narrative, one reviewer founf in the book the "tendency among writers to resort to subjective sociology, on the other hand, or to super-creative reportage, on the other." Charles Self termed this characteristic of New Journalism as "admitted" subjectivity, whether first-person or third-person, and acknowledged the subjectivity inherent in his account.

Lester Markel polemically criticized New Journalism in the *Bulletin of the American Society of Newspaper Editors,* he rejected the claim to greater in-depth reporting and labelled the writers "factual fictionists" and "deep-see reporters." He feared they were performing as sociologists and psychoanalysts rather than as journalists.

More reasoned, though still essentially negative, Arlen in his 1972 "Notes on the New Journalism," put the New Journalism into a larger socio-historical perspective by tracing the techniques from earlier writers and from the constraints and opportunities of the current age. But much of the more routine New Journalism "consists in exercises by writer... in gripping and controlling and confronting a subject within the journalist's own temperament. Presumably, " he wrote, "this is the 'novelistic technique.' " But he conceded that the best of this work had "considerably expanded the possibilities of journalism."

Much negative criticism of New Journalism were directed at individual writers For example, Cynthia Ozick asserted in *The New Republic,* that Capote in *In Cold Blood* was doing little more than trying to devise a form: "One more esthetic manipulation." Sheed offered, in "A Fun-House Mirror," a witty refutation of Wolfe's claim that he takes on the expression and the guise of whomever he is writing about. "The Truman Capotes may hold up a tolerably clear glass to nature," he wrote, "but Wolfe holds up a fun-house mirror, and I for one don't give a hoot whether he calls the reflection fact or fiction."

"PARAJOURNALISM" AND THE NEW YORKER AFFAIR

Among the hostile critics of the New Journalism were Dwight MacDonald, whose most vocal criticism compromised a chapter in what became known as "the *New Yorker* affair" of 1965. Wolfe had written a two-part semi-fictional parody in *New York* of the *New Yorker* and its editor, William Shawn.

Reaction notably from *New Yorker* writers, was loud and prolonged, but the most significant reaction came from MacDonald, who counterattacked in two articles in the *New York Review of Books* In the first, MacDonald termed Wolfe's approach "parajournalism" and applied it to all similar styles. "Parajournalism," MacDonald wrote... seems to be journalism—"the collection and dissemination of current news"—but the appearance is deceptive. It is a bastard form, having it both ways, exploiting the factual authority of journalism and the atmospheric license of fiction.

The *New Yorker* parody, he added, "... revealed the ugly side of Parajournalism when it tries to be serious."

In his second article, MacDonald addressed himself to the accuracy of Wolfe's report. He charged that Wolfe "takes a middle course, shifting gears between fact and fantasy, spoof and reportage, until nobody knows which end is, at the moment, up" *New Yorker* writers Renata Adler and Gerald Jonas joined the fray in the Winter 1966 issue of *Columbia Journalism Review.* Wolfe himself returned to the affair a full seven years later., devoting the second of his two February *New York* articles (1972) to his detractors but not to dispute their attack on his factual accuracy. He argued that most of the contentions arose because for traditional *literati* nonfiction should not succeed—which his nonfiction obviously had.

Gail Sheehy and "Redpants"

In *The New Journalism: A Critical Perspective* Murphy writes, "Partly because Wolfe took liberties with the facts in his *New Yorker* parody, New Journalism began to get a reputation for juggling the facts in the search for truth, fictionalizing some details to get a larger 'reality.'

"Widely criticized was the technique of the composite character, the most notorious example of which was "Redpants," a presumed prostitute whom Gail Sheehy wrote about in *New York* in a series on that city's sexual subculture.

When it later became known that the character was distilled from a number of prostitutes, there was an outcry against Sheehy's method and, by extension, to the credibility of all of New Journalism. In the *Wall Street Journal,* one critic wrote: It's all part of the New Journalism, or the Now Journalism, and it's practiced widely these days. Some editors and reporters vigorously defend it. Others just as vigorously attack it. No one has polled the reader, but whether he approves or disapproves, it's getting harder and harder for him to know what he can believe. *Newsweek* reported that critics felt Sheehy's energies were better suited to fiction than fact John Tebbel in an article in *Saturday Review*, although treating New Journalism in its more generic sense as new a trend, chided it for the fictional technique of narrative leads which the new nonfiction writers had introduced into journalism and deplored its use in newspapers.

CRITICISM AGAINST NEW JOURNALISM AS A DISTINCT GENRE

Newfield, in 1972, changed his attitude since his earlier, 1967, review of Wolfe. "New Journalism does not exist," the later article titled "Is there a 'new journalism'?" says. "It is a false category. There is only good writing and bad writing, smart ideas and dumb ideas, hard work and laziness." While the practice of journalism had improved during the past fifteen years, he argued, it was because of an influx of good writers notable for unique styles, not because they belonged to any school or movement.

DEMOCRACY AND PUBLIC PARTICIPATION

Dewey's concept of public opinion is rooted in an intellectual tradition that can be traced back to Montesquieu. In this tradition of thought, public opinion is understood as a body of shared beliefs and attitudes that emerged within the public sphere. With the decline of absolutism in the Renaissance, there emerged an independent social sphere, dominated by neither church nor monarch, in which an educated class was able to meet, to exchange ideas, and to formulate improved, shared concepts to benefit society as a whole.

The venues for this discourse were neither churches nor the royal courts, but salons, coffee houses, and the pages of the early newspapers, which offered both a forum for ideas and a stimulus for face-to face discussion. The public itself can thus be seen as in some sense a product of the media. It was the early newspapers that provided a common body of knowledge and ideas among urban residents who were not connected by face-to-face relationships.

The participants in this discourse saw themselves as citizens, not merely giving expression to private interests, but rather participating as representatives of the larger society.

Public opinion, as understood in this tradition, was the social consensus that emerged as the result of dialogue. Juergen Habermas traces the decline of the public sphere to the middle of the last century, prompted by, among other factors, the transformation of newspapers from political journals into commercial enterprises, and the development of a broader, more heterogeneous audience.

A great deal has been written about the decline of the public and the decline of community. Both issues are complex, but they are distinct. What is meant by community seems generally to be small groups "bound together by history, faith, and fellowship." The notion of a public, by contrast, is that of private individuals, who do not necessarily share a common history, faith, or fellowship, but who come together to participate in critical rational discourse about common concerns on the basis of common knowledge—a common knowledge provided by shared sources of information.

The concern with revitalizing the public sphere goes back at least to the 1920s, when John Dewey worried, in *The Public and Its Problems*, about the eclipse of the public. Recently, there has been a major upsurge of interest in revitalizing the public sphere, evidenced by such works as *The Good Society* by Robert Bellah, Richard Madsen, William Sullivan, Ann Swidler, and Steven Tipton; Benjamin Barber's *Strong Democracy*; and such civic enterprises as Harry Boyte's *Project Public Life* and Frances Moore Lappe's *Centre for Living Democracy*, as well as the writings of Jay Rosen, James Carey, Noam Chomsky, and Douglas Kellner.

Any defender of participatory democracy must address the objection that, as Benjamin Barber phrases it, "popular government carries within it the seeds of a totalitarian despotism." John Dewey's answer is, in part, that if the people cannot be trusted to take an active role in governing themselves, then it is not plausible to imagine that they can play a meaningful role as watchdogs over their leaders either. The real alternative, in this view, is not elite democracy, but oligarchy.

And, argues Dewey, "the world has suffered more from leaders and authorities than from the masses." Dewey was prepared to acknowledge that the average citizen, considered as an individual, does lack the knowledge necessary to play an effective role in governing. But for Dewey, it was not the individual in isolation who was to play an active role in self-governance; it was the individual as the member of a community and as a participant in the processes of debate and discussion who had the ability to draw on the knowledge of others and participate in the formation of a public will.

Nonetheless, our collective memory is haunted by images of masses out of control: lynchings and pogroms and the mass terrorism of a Kristallnacht. But are these really examples of publics that have become overly active, as social conservatives and political realists would argue, or masses of individuals who have become overly passive, as advocates of participatory democracy maintain? Barber argues that "thin democracy has itself nourished some of the pathologies that it has attributed to direct democracy and . . . strong democracy may offer remedies for the very diseases it has been thought to occasion."

The frenzied masses feared by democratic realists are most frequently seen in totalitarian or oligarchic societies, and their participants typically have little access to effective mechanisms of democratic participation. By contrast, the very culture of democratic participation fosters a climate of rationality, deliberation, and respect for persons. In participatory democracies, by definition, power and decision-making authority is decentralized and diffused throughout the society. The capacity for collective willformation at the smallest levels of organization is enhanced, but the capacity for the formation of a mass will is diminished.

In the past few years, the theoretical debate between democratic realists and advocates of strong or participatory democracy has been overtaken by events. There has been a devolution of power from the federal to the state and local levels, and a scaling back of our national commitment to provide, through the mechanisms of government, basic social guarantees in the areas of education, housing, welfare, and other social services.

The responsibility for addressing these needs is being shifted to communities and individuals. With a change in the political reality of who must govern and solve problems comes a change in the institutional definitions of who and what is newsworthy.

The Lippmann model of the citizen as interested spectator must be abandoned as citizens become the key players in the social drama.

Some social critics, such as British sociologist John Thompson, question the viability of participatory democracy in a mass media age. The arguments raised by Thompson against the ideal of public participation have less to do with a distrust of the public than with considerations related to technology and scale. Thompson argues that "the idea of the public sphere is largely inapplicable to the circumstances of the late twentieth century," and he offers two arguments for this claim:

- The development of technical media has dramatically altered the nature of mass communications and the conditions under which it takes place, so much so that the original idea of the public sphere could not simply be reactivated on a new footing. The media of print have increasingly given way to electronically mediated forms of mass communication, and especially television, and these new media have transformed the very conditions of interaction, communication and information diffusion in modern societies.

- The second reason why the idea of the public sphere is of limited relevance today is that the idea is linked fundamentally to a notion of participatory opinion formation. The idea of the public sphere assumes that the personal opinions of individuals will become *public opinion* through, and only through participation in a free and equal debate which is open in principle to all. But this assumption, whatever relevance it may have had to eighteenth-century political life (and this may have been considerably less than Habermas suggests) is far removed from the political realities and possibilities of the twentieth century. . . . We live in a world today in which the sheer scale and complexity of decision-making processes limits the extent to which they can be organized in a participatory way. Hence the original idea of the public sphere, in so far as it is linked to the idea of participatory opinion formation, is of limited relevance today.

Neither of these objections seems fatal. If we understand the public sphere as an ideal, realized only in a very partial way even in the Enlightenment, then the prospect of even a partial realization of this ideal in our own era may seem like a partial victory worth striving for, rather than a dream impossible to achieve. The emergence of new media makes participation more, rather than less possible. It is not face-to-face participation that matters, but rather participation in dialogue, and new technologies have broadened the possibilities for public participation.

However imperfectly realized, such new forms of media as talk radio and electronic bulletin boards offer new forums for public dialogue.

Their potential to serve the common good can only increase if civility is acknowledged as a core value for public communicators. Public access channels on cable television are as yet little used, but they too represent a space in which public dialogue can take place. Although it is true that some decision-making takes place on a scale that makes public participation difficult or impossible, that would seem to constitute an argument for, rather than against, political decentralization.

Even though some decisionmaking must take place on a regional, national, or even international scale, there is also a great deal of decision-making that takes place on a local scale and can be opened up to much greater participation.

OUTLINES OF AN ETHICAL THEORY

An ethical theory grounded in the philosophical tradition of pragmatism offers the news media a much more promising means of fulfilling the social role envisioned for them by democratic theory, that is, enabling citizens to play an active role in self-governance. Ultimately, these principles and practices may also provide a way for journalists to find in daily practice a fulfillment of the ideals of public service that attracted many of them to journalism.

It may be helpful to summarize the key elements of the realist/objectivist view embodied in traditional journalism ethics and then contrast them with the pragmatist view.

ONTOLOGY

In the traditional realist view, the world exists independently of our knowledge of it, and there are facts about the world that are true, independent of any human knowledge of them. In the pragmatist view, reality is socially constructed, emerging out of the human activity of creating words and concepts as tools to meet human needs.

The concepts and categories through which we try to understand and manipulate our environment emerge historically as the products of human interaction with each other and with our environment. As we transform our social reality through our productive activity, we continuously transform our language and the concepts and categories through which we see the world.

EPISTEMOLOGY

In the realist view, truth consists in a correspondence between a statement and an external reality. By the use of scientific methods—or the scientifically based methods of journalistic objectivity—trained observers can come to have knowledge of the world that is objectively true. Expressions of fact must be clearly distinguished from expressions of opinion, which convey beliefs about facts for which we lack sufficient evidence, and from expressions of value, which state attitudes towards the facts.

The current role of the news media is to disseminate the vocabulary and the point of view of those segments of society that are recognized as authorized knowers. Insofar as the ethic of objectivity explicitly defined the news media as a medium for the transmission of an expert discourse, the structure of journalistic communication is designed to guarantee that the flow of vocabulary is overwhelmingly one-way. Journalists interview experts and then transmit their views to the public, but journalists generally do not disseminate "uninformed" public opinion.

In the pragmatist view, by contrast, a statement is true when its truth conditions are satisfied, but what these truth conditions may be is established through human activity. This conception of truth was expressed by William James when he defined truth as "what it is good for us to believe." What it is good for us to believe is established experientially: the criteria for what it is good for us to believe about how to bake bread bear no direct logical relation to what it is good for us to believe about the existence of an afterlife. The procedures known as "scientific method" or "journalistic objectivity" are just particular ways of interpreting the world; any special claim that they confer to epistemic authority must rest on their usefulness to particular human ends. Standards of truth and falsity are always internal to a domain of activity.

Some have suggested that this notion of truth invites relativism or even nihilism. Christopher Norris, for example, bitterly attacks the neo-pragmatism of Richard Rorty, Stanley Fish, and others as leading to a moral bankruptcy that easily rationalizes accommodation to power.

This consequence would indeed seem to follow from a notion that holds that multiple domains of activity (or communities of interpretation) entail multiple truths. But within the pragmatist conception, truth is always provisional, subject to revision in the light of new experience, changing values, or the encounter with other communities of interpretation.

If we wish to imagine a kind of truth that is not provisional, it could reside only in the kind of knowledge that would emerge at the end of all such experiments and encounters. Thus, C. S. Peirce describes truth as "the opinion which is fated to be ultimately agreed to by all who investigate."

This notion of ultimate truth seems problematic; why suppose that all who investigate will ever reach agreement? Even if one remains agnostic about whether such ultimate consensus is possible, Peirce's description points to several features of a pragmatist conception of truth that are more widely shared: understanding truth as a product of human activity, and specifically, as the product of a social, rather than individual process of inquiry.

This pragmatist notion of truth seems to be compatible with Habermas' notion that universal consensus under ideal conditions is the criterion of defensible truth claims. The ideal conditions that Habermas envisions are characterized by uncoerced and equal participation in public discourse.

What are the practical implications of the rejection of journalistic objectivity? The rejection of objectivity consists not merely in the assertion that the news media fail to provide an objective picture of reality, or even that objectivity is impossible in practice, but rather that it is impossible even in theory.

There is no neutral standpoint from which we can give an account of reality that is a-perspectival. Denying that there is such a thing as objective truth is not denying that there is such a thing as truth; nor is it saying that all truth claims are of equivalent value. Rather, it is to say that propositions are always true or false relative to some standard that is internal to a theory, language game, or system of beliefs.

One implication of this conceptualization is that journalists should continuously try to explore and to disclose the frame of reference and the conscious and hidden assumptions from within which they and their sources operate. This is a responsibility for journalists to a far greater degree than for practitioners of other disciplines or professions precisely because journalism is not a discipline in which standards of truth and fundamental premises are established by convention and are relatively stable.

Journalism operates in a public sphere in which multiple standards and interpretations come into conflict. Another implication is that the provisional and contestable character of truth claims should be emphasized; where there is significant disagreement, the media should be made accessible to and should disseminate the widest possible range of viewpoints.

SOCIAL ROLE

In the realist view, the primary social function of the news media is the collecting, organizing, and disseminating of information. In order to perform these functions effectively (as observer, gatekeeper, and messenger), the news media must maintain a stance of neutrality and avoid becoming instigators or participants in the events that they cover.

In the pragmatist view, the media of mass communications are one of the most important institutions through which we come to know ourselves as individuals and as members of society. Our common language and values are circulated by the mass media; within the mass media, the news media play a particular role in defining the set of common understandings and values that sustain the social order. The challenge is to perform that role fairly, in a way that addresses not merely individual interests, but also the common interest that defines us as a public.

ETHICS

In the realist view, the primary duty of the news media is to give a true picture of the world that can serve as the basis for political participation. Within this view, theorists disagree about the degree of public participation that is possible or desirable. Whereas social responsibility theorists, such as the authors of the Hutchins Commission report, envision active participation in self-governance, democratic realists like Lippmann favour a more limited role for the public—namely the ratification of expert decisions.

From this ontology, epistemology, and conception of the social roles of the news media is derived the set of values previously discussed: accuracy, fairness, objectivity, truth-telling, avoidance of conflict of interest, and so on. We have seen, though, that this derivation is powerfully influenced by the relations of power within the news media.

In the pragmatist view—or at least in this version of pragmatism-there can be no such thing as the one true picture of the world. Rather, we are all continuously in the process of constructing and modifying our pictures in light of new experiences and changing objectives. As individuals, we have the capacity to make use of the experiences of others in modifying our pictures of reality and redefining our objectives. As members of communities, we operate most successfully when a broad range of perceptions and values enters into our deliberations.

From this pragmatist perspective, the proper role of the news media is to facilitate the operation of communities as contexts for democratic decision-making. This means that journalism must serve as a medium for the public exchange of ideas and for the exchange of competing views of reality and the public good; in addition, it should facilitate the formation of public consensus.

The arguments that follow rest upon a view of the ideal social order as one in which all citizens participate, to the limits of their abilities, in determining the course of their common life. Towards that end, the key values of the news media must include accessibility, respect for persons, fairness, interpretation, and skepticism.

PROFESSIONAL PRINCIPLES

It probably would not be helpful to propose a revised code of ethics for journalists. Traditionally, at least, such codes are part of the ideology of professionalism and have sustained the idea that journalism is properly the domain of a specialized class. What is needed instead is to open up the process of news making and to create new forms of partnership between news producers and news consumers. This does not mean a wholesale abandonment of the principles expressed in current codes of professional ethics.

Objectivity, both as a procedural norm and as an epistemological objective, must be rejected, but such values as accuracy, fairness, and the injunction to avoid sensationalism remain important. The injunction to avoid conflict of interest gives way to an obligation to fully disclose interests and to give access to a broad spectrum of interests. All of these values become subject to reinterpretation in the context of a pragmatist conception of the role of the news media in public life.

As with the prevailing liberal/realist model, a pragmatist theory of journalistic responsibility would take as its foundation a commitment to enable citizens to participate in democratic life, though with a much more robust conception of what participation means. But a pragmatist account would regard not the transmission of information, but rather the creation and sustaining of a public sphere as the most important role of journalism in a democratic society.

This difference in conception of the social role of the news media implies a different set of professional principles:

- *Diversity and Accessibility*: Democracy is equated with the widest possible participation of citizens in public life, and thus one of the foundational professional commitments must be to diversity and accessibility. Journalists must actively seek to make sure that the widest possible range of viewpoints is represented in public debate.

- *Civility*: Another core value in the promotion of civic life must be civility, a set of behavioral norms built around the idea of respect for persons. The media are the most important sources for the ideas the public has about how conflicts, and especially conflicts between strangers, are resolved. Since the media have traditionally placed a priority on dramatically charged images of conflict and confrontation, there has been little symbolic representation of how peace-making, reconciliation, and compromise are achieved.
- *Debate and Dialogue*: Since facts are understood not as accurate representations of reality, but rather as interpretations of reality from a point of view, the greatest emphasis must be given to those issues in public life where there are significant divergences of interpretation. Specifically, the news media ought to serve as a forum for debate and dialogue. Whether there was an earthquake in Azerbaijan is not a matter over which there is much divergence in interpretation, nor is it a matter of much immediate consequence for the lives of most American news consumers; by contrast, whether the United States should give large-scale foreign aid to the states that made up the former Soviet Union is a matter of far greater consequence to American citizens and a subject over which there is much greater disagreement.

With the acknowledgment that the news media do make the news and are inevitably major players on the social stage, the news media can begin to openly engage the question of how their social responsibilities are to be fulfilled. The pragmatist conception of the social responsibility of the news media understands participation and democracy in much more robust terms than does the objectivist account.

Democracy, in a Deweyan view, requires the active participation of all citizens, to the limits of their ability, in determining the course of the common life. This concept of democracy extends its meaning beyond the political sphere to the workplace, home, and school. Participation means that each individual has an opportunity not merely to give assent, but to be heard.

This conception of democracy poses a problem of scale: although the New England town meeting was small enough that each citizen could be heard, the modern city is far too large to accommodate such forms of direct democracy. The solution is, at least in part, that the citizen can participate through a variety of mediating institutions, such as precinct caucuses, block clubs, parent teacher associations, unions, or worker management committees.

The role of the media in this expanded conception of democratic life is to facilitate and to model such participation. The media must serve as a forum for dialogue, not simply between individuals, but also between communities within a larger society. More fundamentally, they can enable individuals to find an identity as members of communities, to help members of communities communicate amongst themselves, to facilitate communication between communities, and to help communities find commonalities that link them as members of a greater community.

In practical terms, this expanded role can take a variety of forms, all of which suggest a redefinition of what counts as newsworthy. One form entails a greatly increased emphasis on the bulletin-board function: a great deal more space could be given over to announcements of meeting times, places, and agendas of civic organizations.

The news media must also en sure that the citizen exists in the symbolic universe that it projects. The forms and norms of citizen participation can be modeled and communicated by the media, for example, in debates and discussions and in coverage of demonstrations or other forms of symbolic expression that emphasizes explanation.

The exclusion of the public from public debate that resulted from the rise of objectivity has had an impact on how individual citizens perceive themselves and their abilities. In large part, they do not perceive themselves as citizens at all, and they have little experience in the civic arts of debate. Moreover, they often do not perceive themselves as legitimate participants in public discourse.

Beyond the implications these perceptions have for the larger society, on an individual level it reflects how establishing an expert discourse in the news media has resulted in a diminished selfhood for news consumers. Whatever we want to see as a dynamic element of social reality must also have symbolic existence in the representation of reality constructed by news media. This implies a commitment to representing not only all communities within society, but also all of the occupations.

The invisibility of, for example, service occupations in the mass media is a form of symbolic annihilation that devalues and demeans caretaking work and the people who perform it. If this society values the necessary work of teaching, childcare, nursing, and farming, the only meaningful expression of that value is in assuring that the symbolic representation of those activities reflects that valuation.

Moreover, many consumers of news media turn to newspapers and especially to television for the sense of belonging or community that the media create. This is often a false sense of community, argues Elayne Rapping, created by "happy family" news teams. But there is no reason to believe that many viewers would not be receptive to a more substantial concept of community.

The dogma of objectivity, or representation, privileges overt events at the expense of ideas, debates, or other forms of communication. A rejection of objectivity frees the news media from the commitment to the primacy of "news" and opens the door to other forms of journalism. A parents' guide to getting the most out of the public schools or an article on how to be a citizen-lobbyist do not qualify as news under any traditional definition, but they are examples of ways in which journalists can facilitate public participation.

A PROFILE OF JOURNALISTIC VALUES

The profile of journalists' instrumental values that emerges from the survey places a strong emphasis on a mix of competency-based and morality-oriented concepts, much of which would be expected to describe the professional outlook of journalists. Three respondents did not rank the values but completed other sections of the survey, giving the value rankings a total of 352 valid responses.

An analysis of this journalistic value hierarchy has been reported elsewhere; this study, however, focuses on the value rankings as they are related to journalistic role conceptions. "Honest" was ranked the most important value by far by most journalists; more than one-third of all journalists ranked it first, and another sixty-two journalists ranked it second.

More journalists ranked "Honest" in either one of those positions than all other positions combined. "Honest" was followed by "Fair." Roughly half of all journalists placed this value in one of the top three spots. Those two morally oriented values were followed by two values that Rokeach related to the concept of competency: "Responsible" and "Capable." Nearly one-half of the journalists ranked "Responsible" at positions two through five.

When testing his original list of instrumental values on different populations, Rokeach said the average intercorrelation among the rankings for all the instrumental values was -.06, which suggested that each of the values could be considered discrete, valid measures for different concepts. While several of the original values do significantly correlate with each other due to an intrinsic parallelism of the concepts involved (*i.e.*, "Responsible" and "Self-controlled"), the intercorrelations for the rankings of the original values by journalists in this project mirror intercorrelations that Rokeach found in his general-population studies.

To Rokeach's 18 values, 6 others were added for this study to reflect the most predominant values commonly found in the media ethics literature: "Fair," "Just," "Aboveboard," "Empathetic," "Minimizing harm," and "Civic-minded."

The journalistic-oriented values added by this project also show negligible intercorrelations, with averages ranging from -.03 to -.059, suggesting that each of the added values is in fact measuring additional concepts and not simply other dimensions of values already listed. Among the 18 instrumental values, the highest negative intercorrelation Rokeach found was -.38.

Roles Embraced by Journalists. Responses to 14 journalistic "function" statements generally correspond to what Weaver and Wilhoit found in their survey ten years ago, with some notable differences that may be due to changes in cultural and professional emphases over that time period. The response rate for this final section of the instrument was slightly lower, at 53 per cent (N = 328). Most of the role-conception items were from Weaver and Wilhoit and can be grouped into the authors' factors of the predominant "interpretive," "disseminator," and "adversarial" functions. Journalists gave "Get information to the public quickly" the highest overall average.

They gave "be less critical of officials during national crisis" the lowest, at 2.3, closely followed by "set the political agenda" at 2.6. This study's three hypotheses predicted that journalists who rank particular values as highly salient also would embrace certain journalistic role conceptions over others. Specifically, Hl predicted that journalists ranking "Courageous," "Independent," and "Just" highly would endorse an adversarial role; H2 predicted that those ranking "Minimizing harm," "Fair," and "Self-controlled" high would endorse a disseminator function; and H3 predicted that those ranking "Civic-minded," "Imaginative," and "Capable" high would endorse an interpretive role.

The predicted relationships did not produce significant Spearman's rho correlations, so data analysis did not show support for Hl and H2. Spearman's correlations also did not appear to provide immediate support for H3.

While the survey included several statements used by Weaver and Wilhoit as indicators of the degree to which journalists embraced the adversarial, disseminator, and interpretive functions of the press, only the two statements associated with the adversarial role ("Be skeptical of public officials" and "Be skeptical of corporations") produced a Cronbach's alpha strong enough to constitute an index.

A linear regression model showed some support for H3 when accounting for the demographic variables. H3 hypothesized that journalists who ranked the values "Civic-minded," "Imaginative," and "Capable" highly also would be more likely to embrace the interpretive function of the press.

In the regression model, the individual values served as the predictor variables and the role-conception statements served as the dependent variables.

For one of the interpretive-function statements, "Influencing public opinion," the value "Civic-minded" proved to be a significant predictor of some of the variance, with a modest yet significant change in the r-square.

Years spent in journalism also were a good predictor in explaining some of the variance in the extent to which journalists embraced the statement, "Influencing public opinion."

The longer journalists were in the profession, the more likely they were to support that statement.

The models also showed that the same demographic variables of age and years in journalism produced significant r-square changes for two of the four statements associated with the interpretive function: "Providing analysis and interpretation of complex problems", and "Discussing national policy while it is still being developed".

DISCUSSION

The journalism ethics literature is rich with speculation on the values of journalists, both what people believe they are and what they ought to be; the results of this survey provide a quantitative profile of journalists' actual value systems, which offers a more solid ground on which to theorize about how journalists should conduct themselves. The profile simultaneously points to areas where the theory of media ethics and the practice of newspaper journalism converge as well as to wide gulfs between the hierarchy of values that journalists have and the approach that ethicists say journalists ought to take to their jobs.

Several patterns emerge between the values and journalists' assessments of various roles and functions. The two statements that constitute the adversarial role ("Being constantly skeptical of actions taken by public officials" and "Being constantly skeptical of actions by businesses and corporations") are both positively correlated with "Above-board" and "Broadminded," and negatively correlated with "Polite."

Again, this indicates the immense importance placed on the need for credibility (though not necessarily civility) among those journalists who take the watchdog role as their primary function. A third statement that could be considered a measure of the adversarial-oriented role, "Being less critical of public officials during a national crisis," was negatively correlated with "Fair," "Imaginative," and "Independent," and positively correlated with "Responsible."

The more that journalists indicated that government should be supported in times of national crisis, the less highly they ranked the values of "Fair" and "Independent." While the correlations are relatively weak, they are significant, indicating some relationship.

At the same time, journalists who ranked "Responsible"-as well as "Obedient"-highly appeared to indicate that being less critical during crises was part of what it means to be a responsible journalist. Only one of the two statements ("Getting information to the public quickly") associated with the disseminator role was significantly correlated with any of the values.

Journalists appear to hold a deep ambivalence towards the so-called interpretive function of the press. While the values such as "Broadminded" and "Courageous" are positively correlated with several of the statements ("Providing analysis and interpretation of complex problems" and "Investigating claims and statements made by the government"), "Responsible" is negatively correlated with the first statement, suggesting that journalists remain uncomfortable with being perceived in any way as activists.

In addition to these three journalistic role conceptions, the 1992 survey data by Weaver and Wilhoit as well as the 2002 survey data by Weaver, Beam, and colleagues suggested the emergence of a fourth role-that of "populist mobilizer," which "developed and channeled" the public's interest in intellectual and cultural issues after grabbing audience attention.

Several statements served to assess support for this role, including "Setting the public agenda," "Developing intellectual and cultural interests of the public," and "Giving ordinary people a chance to express their views on public affairs." Weaver and Wilhoit concluded that the support among journalists for these statements was "tantalizing evidence that the spirit of the 'public journalism' movement may have established a foothold."

Correlations between the mobilizer statements and the value rankings in this project seem to provide qualified confirmation of this. The value "Civic-minded" is positively correlated with the statement, "Developing intellectual and cultural interests of the public."

However, even here journalists appear to shy away from any behaviour that might smack of advocacy: The value "Fair" was negatively correlated with another mobilizer statement, "Setting the public agenda," and none of the values was correlated with a third statement, "Giving ordinary people a chance to express their views on public affairs."

While results yielded little support for the study's specific hypotheses, the data clearly suggest some connection between journalists' value hierarchies and the roles that they embrace. The results also suggest that these two overlapping realms require further research.

The survey instrument used here could be applied to broadcast and Internet-based journalists as well, providing potentially valuable comparative profiles. Similar comparisons can be explored regarding journalistic role conceptions among different groups of journalists as well as differences in how these roles are perceived by journalists and the general public.

Several suggestive relationships between journalistic values and roles emerge from this study. But given the research that has explored at length the forces of newsroom socialization, the relationships are surprisingly weak ones.

While previous research has suggested that social control in the newsroom is a strong shaper both of the values that guide their work and how journalists perceive their function in society, this study suggests that newsroom socialization does not exert a strong influence on general values, or vice versa, given the weak correlations between role priorities and the value rankings.

Rather than consider values-whether general or specifically journalistic-as products of a singular newsroom socialization dynamic, research may need to differentiate the various "environments" in which particular values and role conceptions are formed. Values, beliefs, and behaviour interact, as Voakes suggests, in "a dynamic swirl of social factors."

It seems likely that journalistic role priorities are influenced more by the newsroom environment and professional socialization, whereas more general values are shaped by family, religious, and cultural environments. Also, while the value profile of newspaper journalists that emerges is valuable and suggests many different applications, this study also illustrates the difficulty in assigning such broad, generalized values to specific behaviors. Several associations that emerge in this study are worth considering. The value profile established in this study elaborates upon-and in some cases contradicts-what journalists have reported regarding self-perceptions of their professional roles. Weaver and Wilhoit concluded in their 1992 study that 51 per cent of journalists reported that the disseminator role was "very important," 63 per cent reported that the interpretive role was "very important," and 18 per cent placed a similarly high priority on the adversarial role.

However, just as interesting is the finding that the data showed more correlations among the top six values and the two statements associated with the adversarial role-being skeptical of government and being skeptical of business-than with any other set of role conception statements. And in all, the adversarial role statements were correlated to ten of the values ranked by journalists.

While these correlations are somewhat weak by objective standards, they are among the stronger correlations in the data, and they are statistically significant. They also may reflect the recent findings by Weaver, Beam, and colleagues that more journalists placed importance on the watchdog function of the press in 2002 than in 1992.

The emphasis on the adversarial role also is underscored by the frequency with which five values in particular - "Broadminded," "Fair," "Courageous," "Imaginative," and "Independent" - correlate with various role statements that suggest a watchdog function.

Two of those values rank among the top six. In fact, among the entire list of twenty-four values, the adversarial role is linked to more values than any other role, based on correlations between these values and the two role statements that indicate support for the watchdog function. In total, the adversarial role is linked to five values, while the disseminator role is linked to only three ("Capable," "Fair," and "Responsible").

The interpretive role, which Weaver and Wilhoit found to be most widely endorsed by journalists, is linked to only two values ("Broadminded" and "Courageous"), and both of those are values where the adversarial role also shows strength. In other words, journalists may disavow the public notion of an over-aggressive journalist, yet they consider such a watch-dog function as critical to what constitutes being a credible journalist. However, like the research by Weaver and Wilhoit, this study finds those sometimes contradictory roles that journalists endorse-and the underlying values that are their foundations-can be held simultaneously.

The role conceptions research and this value profile both speak to the internal forces that drive journalists. This study reveals some intriguing links between the two approaches. What remains unclear is how the two interact, and to what extent journalists' values and role perceptions influence how they go about the daily job of reporting and presenting the news. Clarifying these relationships in future research will require revisiting some theoretical constructs used in this study to represent values and roles. It is obvious, for instance, that the "Civic-minded" value triggered possibly negative associations with public journalism in the minds of some journalists, rather than the idea that journalists have a role in the cultivation and maintenance of community.

Additionally, the theoretical linkages between some of the findings that were not initially hypothesized should be put to test in future studies. More importantly, however, this study points up the need for more research that brings to bear value theory and social psychology on the profession of journalism and the journalists themselves.

5

Civic Journalism on Newspaper Journalists

There seems to be a shared wisdom among observers of civic (or public) journalism that the most vociferous critics of this emerging movement are the journalists themselves. While public journalism ultimately depends on the "publics" it is attempting to engage, journalists' attitudes are obviously critical to the fate of this movement. Jay Rosen and Davis Merritt, the two principal founders and leading evangelists of civic journalism, have each stated that this new approach to covering communities can succeed only if journalists internalize its values and participate in its evolving definition. Anderson, Dardenne, and Killenberg add that this will require substantial rethinking of traditional journalistic values and the learning of new skills such as listening and mediating.

How can journalists take on such responsibilities if they're opposed to the idea of civic journalism in the first place? Perhaps they're not. This study takes a systematic look at the assumption that most journalists reject the practice of civic journalism. These are the results of a 1996 survey of more than 1,000 newspaper journalists. The study's purpose is to offer a fully explicated definition of the concept of civic journalism, to gauge journalists' support for practices associated with this concept, and to explore possible antecedents of acceptance of these practices.

One reason for the contention over the merits of civic journalism is the absence of a universally accepted definition. In a published debate with Merritt, Paul McMasters rhetorically asked for guidance as to whether civic journalism is "a technique, a theory, a practice, or a philosophy, a new method or a new order, an elaboration on what already exists, or a radical revolution." The most appropriate response would be that civic journalism is some quantity of all of the above. Even Rosen has acknowledged that the term's definition is still in development. Fouhy and Schaffer, fortunately, have offered a simple working definition: It is a set of journalistic "initiatives which make a deliberate attempt to reach out to citizens, to listen to them, and to have citizens listen and talk to each other."

"Initiatives," of course, could refer to intellectual or philosophical innovation or to a pragmatic plan of activity in conjunction with a short-term news project. Merritt and Rosen argue for the former understanding; in fact, Merritt claims that many of those who deride civic journalism are observing only its most superficial manifestations, without attempting to understand its philosophical roots. The two fundamental axioms of civic journalism (in Merritt's conception) are that journalism is inextricably bound up with the public life of a community, whether its practitioners acknowledge it or not, and whether its practitioners like it or not; and that journalists have an obligation to engage citizens with their communities.

Rosen adds that because most American citizens have become disengaged from the public life (which includes political decision making), some institution or institutions must step forward to reconnect people to the public processes that can revitalize democracy. Civic journalists see journalism as an appropriate institution. In this conception, however, the successful public life extends beyond specific political events, such as informing the electorate before an election in order to improve voter turnout. Rosen often cites John Dewey's formulation of democracy not as a form of government but as a way of life.

In order for journalists to serve as the catalyst for such invigoration, Merritt warns, they must set aside a few of the "journalistic reflexes" that traditional journalism has instilled. Such reflexes include placing a premium on conflict; framing issues at their extreme positions (rather than also reporting complex "gray" areas or areas of agreement); adopting "adversary" positions towards those in authority; conceiving of readers and viewers as spectators and not potential participants; and assuming that an attitude of "detached objectivity" will lead to credibility for the journalism. Merritt proposes instead that journalists seek out the concerns of a wide variety of citizens and, through their journalistic practice, motivate them to become involved in solving civic problems.

This notion emerged in the form of experiments at a few different newspapers in the late 1980s, and it attained some national notice when Merritt's own Wichita Eagle and its parent company, Knight-Ridden embraced civic journalism in the early 1990s. But it began to resemble a national movement in journalism in 1993, when the Pew Charitable Trusts hired a staff to develop public-journalism strategies and began funding projects in several cities across the country. Since that time Pew has funded dozens of projects, many of them joint ventures involving newspapers, radio stations, and television stations in the same community.

As Merritt could have predicted, journalists have often framed the controversy over civic journalism in accordance with extreme positions, and those who harbor serious objections to the movement have been given ample voice in the trade press. Consequently, tales of failed attempts at civic journalism have traveled widely. For example, after a project in North Carolina in which several media revised their political campaign coverage in ways that focused on issues of citizen concern, several politicians observed that the new approach had not improved the electoral process.

Editors in the elite media accused their North Carolina colleagues of abdicating their news judgement in order to follow an agenda set by public opinion polls. In California, a paper hosted a town meeting involving an ongoing dispute over building codes, which turned into a brawl. The editors of the paper reportedly recast the originally embarrassing story into a positive account. A Connecticut paper sent reporters out in vans on weekends to give away merchandise and to engage citizens in public conversation on community issues, but the reporters said the citizenry, in a hurry to finish shopping, were not interested in conversing.

Merritt's general response to such stories of misguided efforts, or disingenuous reporting of efforts, is twofold: Many newspaper editors attempt public journalism without understanding its underlying philosophy, and those who understand its philosophy should realise that the results of any one project are unimportant. Civic journalism is not a marketing device or a commitment to report only "positive" news. It is a partnership between journalists and their community, and if it is not undertaken as a long-term commitment it is likely to fail.

The stories of civic-journalism-gone-wrong have also raised deeper concerns, about the movement's philosophy. Some critics worry about its self-conscious rejection of the notion of detachment. McMasters argues that journalists must be dispassionate and detached in their coverage of news in the same way physicians are detached in dealing with patients' medical problems. Too much involvement in community issues compromises their professional competence. Friedland responds that a rejection of detachment does not imply taking sides or reporting with a bias towards a particular group or position. If there is bias, civic journalists assert, it is bias in favour of a smoothly functioning democratic process. Kruh states that the civic journalist's bias should be no more offensive to traditional journalism than the medical writer's bias towards the eradication of disease.

Another concern is a perceived loss of the "watchdog" role of journalism that is strongly implied in the First Amendment. Stepp notes that when journalism commits itself so fully to solutions it inevitably associates itself with the public policymakers who are leading the planning and implementation of a solution. This constricts the journalists' time-honored (though much debated in academic circles) freedom to criticize governmental officials and policy. Some practitioners respond that they publicly monitor officials' responsiveness to public concerns in a manner resembling traditional "watchdog" journalism.

Some say they have experienced quite the opposite of boosterism. Editors at the Charlotte Observer have reported that during their civic journalism projects they were publicly monitoring local officials' responsiveness to citizens' concerns and that "we told the community hard truths about itself." A third undercurrent of philosophical discomfort involves journalistic pandering. Critics worry that in responding too eagerly to citizens' views, journalism will become little more than market research. Polls and focus groups will replace professional news judgement; that is, news media content will reflect what audience members want to consume, rather than what journalists think their audiences need to know.

Merritt has responded that public journalism is ultimately more concerned with public Life than it is with journalism.23 Journalists who are intent on improving public discourse will not be content to feed their audience inane (but popular) pabulum, regardless of what a focus group may indicate.

As his responses in the foregoing paragraphs indicate, Merritt seems to believe that much of the criticism of civic journalism is rooted in misunderstanding. He readily acknowledges his critics' "angry dismisiveness." It is entirely possible, however, that if civic journalism were defined in a way that reflected its philosophical tenets (as put forth by Merritt, Rosen, and other early advocates of the movement), journalists might react differently than with dismissive heuristics such as "boosterism," "focus-group pandering," "loss of objectivity" and "same old same old." This study's empirical inquiry, therefore, begins with an explication of civic journalism.

DIMENSIONS OF CIVIC JOURNALISM

The foregoing review of the literature and controversy concerning civic journalism displays recurrent themes that can be aptly transferred into dimensions of the variable concept "approval of civic journalism."

As we have seen, civic journalism involves journalistic initiative rather than reactive coverage; it involves an interest in moving towards solutions to community problems that takes journalism far beyond the detached reporting of the problems; it involves ongoing, long-term commitment to the betterment of the public life; and it involves not only the reporting of important public issues but also nonpublished efforts to probe citizens' concerns and engage them in the public life.

With the help of Ed Fouhy, former executive director of the Pew Centre for Civic Journalism, the research team for this project developed the following dimensions and indicators of civic journalism.

1. Enterprise. In the view of Merritt, Rosen, and others, civic journalism starts with the initiative of the journalists in reinvigorating the public life. It is rooted in the belief that journalists have a stake in the health of a community's public life, and that journalism stands uniquely poised to engage citizens. This enterprise not only discovers problems of common concern but continues to motivate citizens to seek out solutions. This is one of the aspects of civic journalism that has

prompted the observation that it is no different from traditional enterprise reporting. That is true to some extent, but it is different in two basic ways: It begins with a consideration of what will improve the public life, rather than what will make a good story, and it implies a commitment to solving community problems beyond the publication of one story or series.

2. Information for Decision Making. This dimension speaks to the development of what Charity has termed "public judgement. A principal role for the civic journalist is to enable citizens not only to communicate in a public arena but to be able to work towards solutions without necessarily being led by institutional policymakers. It requires journalists not only to listen to and synthesize public commentary but to present independent research on alternative public views, so that citizens can be informed in their public judgement. This also involves the journalists' close monitoring of official responses to the various alternatives. The effect, Charity states, is that the reporting can "foster a sense of drama and possibility" in the community.

Merritt also sees in this dimension an obligation of the civic journalist to identify shared ideas he calls "core values," to which all participants in the public discussion would adhere. The recognition of core values is often the critical first step in the assessment of alternative solutions.

3. Facilitation of Discourse. Critical to the success of public deliberation is that citizens feel they have an opportunity to discuss issues and concerns themselves in a public forum -not merely to read about them in the news media. The civic journalist does what is necessary to begin and sustain this public deliberation, even if it means taking nontraditional steps to convene participants. The most common practice in this dimension is the news media's hosting a "town meeting," usually to discuss a particular issue. Anderson, Dardenne, and Killenberg and Charity have written extensively about the news media's suitability for such a role, as they comprise one of the few institutions in American communities that regularly address a wide range of issues across economic, racial, and social boundaries. Public agencies and other private organizations have convened innumerable meetings, of course, but civic-journalism proponents cite the failure of current public life generally as an indication of the more traditional institutions' inability to kindle true public discourse.
4. Attention to Citizens' Concerns. This dimension of civic journalism refers to the rejection of agendas set by those in political and economic authority and the substitution of a citizens' agenda. Charity believes

this aspect to be so strange to traditional journalists that retraining is needed, to enable them to elicit, understand, and represent the concerns of ordinary, unaffiliated speakers and to accord those concerns at least as much credulity as they do the concerns of those wielding power.

This dimension is the source of the critique that civic journalism relies mindlessly on focus groups and market research. Merritt and others respond that if such research is truly oriented towards news-consuming preferences, then it is indeed inappropriate as a tool of civic journalism. The value of seeking out public opinion is in setting an agenda for public discourse that reflects popular concerns regardless of political leaders' priorities. This understanding of public opinion resonates with the recent work of political scientist James Fishkin, who urges that public opinion research take place among small, representative groups of citizens who have been carefully informed of the issues under discussion.

The results would represent not an aggregation of individual Americans' uninformed hunches and heuristics but instead the "considered judgments of the public," which would elevate the utility of public opinion. Fishkin observes that this idea "builds on the movement towards public journalism."

As the final stage of the explication, indicators of each dimension were written for inclusion in the survey instrument. Respondents were asked "How do you feel about the following approaches to journalism?" The dimensions were represented by the following sentences:

1. (Enterprise) "A newspaper develops enterprise stories, supported with editorials, to focus public attention on a community problem and tries to help the community move towards a solution."
2. (Information for Decision Making) "A newspaper reports on alternative solutions to community problems, pointing out trade-offs that may be involved."
3. (Facilitation of Discourse) "A newspaper conducts town meetings to discover key issues in the community and follows up with stories focusing on these issues and some possible solutions."
4. (Attention to Citizens' Concerns) A newspaper polls the public to determine the most pressing community issues, then tries to get the candidates to focus on these issues."

While all four dimensions are meant to reflect basic conceptual changes in the way a news organization covers a community, the indicators represent two distinct degrees of departure from current norms. The Enterprise and Information dimensions' indicators represent modest departures from current reporting and editing practices, while the Discourse and Citizens' Concerns indicators represent bolder departures. The indicators were grouped as such in part of the data analysis.

EMPIRICAL RESEARCH ON CIVIC JOURNALISM

Because civic journalism is a relatively recent phenomenon, what little scholarly work has been done on the movement has been mostly evaluative and prescriptive, rather than empirical. Most of the empirical work has been concerned with the impact of civic journalism projects on political participation and community awareness.

For example, in a comprehensive, Pew— funded study of civic-journalism projects in four cities in 1996, Thorson et al. found that awareness of civic journalism projects was positively associated with citizens' attitudes that are known to bring about political participation.

Their overall conclusion was that civic journalism helps reconnect citizens to public life. In Pew's own report of the same study, 40 per cent of those surveyed in the four cities said the project had made them think more positively about their community.

Less work has been done about the journalists' attitudes and reactions to civic journalism. In a content analysis of the coverage of "The People Project" at Merritt's Wichita Eagle, Riede found that the journalists broke away from only a few traditional routines. He saw a reduction in the political reporting that focuses on personality and political strategy and an increase in substantive reporting of issues. He also noted an increase in stories that encouraged readers to become involved in community organizations and debates. He noted a tone of increased "engagement" and activism, as distinct from detached objectivity.

But he still saw widespread allegiance to experts and politically important people as sources for stories. Voices of "the people" were published more often, but usually superficially and episodically, in ways that could not facilitate discourse. "In fact, the project's doggedly nonadversarial stance, its avoidance of negativism and conflict and its faith in the efficacy of compromise and orderly voluntarism gave it a profoundly conservative tone."

In the Pew Center's own report of the four-city research project in 1996, reporters at the conclusion of the projects were portrayed generally as unimpressed with what they had done. Some thought their stories had been boring and had been read by only a few; others thought their work, focusing in-depth on a single issue, quickly had become repetitive. The Pew evaluators seemed to think that newsroom executives and middle managers were most supportive of the projects, and rank-and-file newsroom employees least supportive.

Webster University researchers surveyed editors and journalism educators to gauge levels of support for various aspects of civic journalism. They found that about half the editors approved the use of polls and focus groups to determine what stories the press should cover.

Majorities of the sample of editors also approved of the notions that journalists should see people not as news consumers but as players in the democratic process; that journalists should devote more attention to what affects ordinary citizens and less on the "major news events of the day;" and that political coverage should include more issue analysis and less "horse race" analysis.

The Webster project does offer a strong indication, however, that civic journalism is not as reviled as the popular, anecdotal accounts would have us believe. But the project surveyed only editors and educators, not rank-and file reporters, photographers, or copy editors-the foot soldiers of this campaign.

The most theoretically provocative finding is found in the most recent study of American journalists by Weaver and Wilhoit. In a replication of earlier analyses, the researchers used factor analysis to identify three "ideal types" of roles for journalism in society. In the analysis of their 1992 survey data, they found renewed evidence of identification with the roles of "disseminator" (whose priority is to deliver information factually and quickly); "interpreter" (whose priority is to provide analysis of complex problems), and "watchdog" (whose priority is to serve as adversary of government and business).

The analysis, however, also revealed a fourth, puzzling factor: journalists who identified with developing the cultural interests of the public, providing entertainment and relaxation, setting the political agenda, and letting ordinary people express their views.

The last item suggested a dimension of civic journalism to the extent that Weaver and Wilhoit labeled this factor "populist mobilizer." Unfortunately, the "ordinary people" item had the weakest loading in the factor, but it obviously intrigued the researchers: "If our analysis is right, the new role ('populist mobilizer') is tantalizing evidence that the spirit of the 'public journalism' movement may have established a foothold among the core values of a tiny minority of journalists."

What sorts of journalists might embrace civic journalism? Another important goal of the current study was to develop a rough profile of the journalist who seems supportive of the indicators of civic journalism, based on a host of independent variables. In this regard the recent research literature provides some guidance. The Pew project's authors found qualitative evidence that younger journalists were less enthusiastic about what they were involved in, which the authors attributed to a sense of professional transience and a lack of commitment to the communities in which they worked.

The size and type of the news organization also may be a factor. In their investigation of the "populist mobilizer factor, Weaver and Wilhoit cautiously suggested that small-market journalists may have more favorable attitudes towards civic journalism than their metro-market counterparts. They found greater resonance for that factor-especially for the item "allowing ordinary people to express their views"-among journalists at radio stations, weekly newspapers, and small-sized dailies.

This is hardly surprising if civic journalism involves a commitment to local issues and community discourse-which are more likely staples in the news diet of small-market media.

From the explication of the term civic journalism and from the suggestions of previous research, a set of hypotheses was developed:

H1: Majorities of the newspaper journalists will approve of each of the four indicators of civic journalism.

One goal of this project was to gauge journalists' approval of civic journalism without explicitly introducing the terms civic journalism or public journalism, thus keeping at bay the generally negative reaction that those terms seems to elicit, and thus keeping the focus of the survey on the concepts and practices of civic journalism rather than on labels. The expectation of approval stems from the findings of the Webster and Pew studies (in which editors, at least, approved of many aspects of civic journalism).

H2a: The smaller the journalist's newspaper, the more accepting he or she will be of these civic-journalism approaches.

This would verify the finding of Weaver and Wilhoit that the "populist mobilizers," few though they were, were more often in small-market media.

H2b: Newsroom managers will be more accepting of civic journalism approaches than will rank-and-file journalists such as reporters, copy editors, and photographers.

This would reflect the general sense of the Pew investigators who detailed the complaints of some of the reporters involved in civic journalism projects. It would also reflect Merritt's contention that support of civic journalism results from an understanding of its philosophical underpinnings. Because top editors are the most likely staff members to introduce and assign a civic journalism project, they are the journalists also most likely to have read and thought about civic journalism's purpose.

H2c: The younger the newspaper journalist the less accepting he or she will be of civic journalism approaches.

This last control variable would reflect the Pew authors' impression that younger journalists were less sympathetic to their projects' goals and practices.

H3: The association between identification with the "interpreter role of the media and approval of civic journalism will be stronger than the association between civic journalism and the "disseminator" and "watchdog" roles.

The disseminator and watchdog roles represent two traditional attitudes that Merritt and Rosen find somewhat incompatible with civic journalism.

The disseminator role implies a telling of the news without context or understanding, but rather a detached forwarding of information. The watchdog role implies a state of "adversariness" that delights in conflict and news that splits groups apart in a community. Rosen maintains that civic journalists constantly challenge elected leaders to heed the public discourse, but that bringing down public officials is not a goal of civic journalism. H4: The stronger the feeling of the importance of neighbourhood and community news, the stronger the approval of civic journalism.

Civic journalism focuses on the concept of community, and because community in journalism is often defined as a geographic community, it seems likely that civic journalism-friendly news people will also be highly interested in issues of local communities. Respondents were asked to rate the importance of "a number of things that newspapers the size of the one you work for do, or try to do, today," which included the item, "Cover community and neighbourhood news." Respondents could choose a response from a fourpart scale ranging from "Extremely Important" to "Not Very Important."

H5a: Journalists who approve of a top editor's involvement in local civic organizations will be more likely to accept civic journalism than will journalists who disapprove of such activity.

H5b: Journalists who approve of rank-and-file staff members' joining civic organizations will be more likely to approve of civic journalism than will journalists who disapprove of such activity.

This set of hypotheses attempts to bring to a personal level the civic journalism tenet of involvement in one's community. One measure of a journalist's rejection of the traditional detachment from the people and issues that one covers would be the attitude towards personal involvement of the journalist in the community-not involvement in a particular faction or political cause, but in a nonpolitical civic organization.

If a journalist feels favorable towards making at least that modest personal connection to the community, he or she will endorse the connection for both the top editors and for rank-and-file staff members. In the same vein, we might also expect journalists who themselves felt involved in their local communities-actually, not hypothetically-to share that attitude.

H5c: Journalists who describe themselves as involved in their local communities will be more likely to approve of civic journalism than will journalists who describe themselves as uninvolved.

The final set of hypotheses examines attitudes about the current state of journalism at one's newspaper. Proponents and observers alike seem to agree that civic journalism has grown out of a dissatisfaction with the role journalism has played lately, especially with journalism's inability to connect to citizens, and its inability to connect citizens to one another.

H6a: Journalists who feel their own papers do not connect well with readers will be more likely to approve of civic journalism than will those who feel well connected with readers.

H6b: Journalists who feel their own papers are getting worse in quality will be more likely to approve of civic journalism than will those who feel their paper is improving.

THE SURVEY METHOD

The survey was conducted in the fall of 1996 under the auspices of the Human Resources Committee of the American Society of Newspaper Editors. A stratified probability sample of newspaper employees was constructed. From a list of the 1,487 newspapers in the United States, 61 were randomly selected, after measures had been taken to ensure proportionate representation from eight circulation categories. Three of the newspapers in the original group of 61 declined to participate; in these cases the research team randomly chose substitute newspapers from the same circulation groups.

The directing editor of each selected paper was asked to select randomly a sample of journalists from his or her staff. Only full-time employees who fit the categories of reporter, copy editor, photographer, artist, supervisor, or editorial writer were to be included. The number of participating employees depended on the size of the paper, again in order to maintain the validity of the stratified probability sampling procedure.

Each employee participating received a survey packet, which included the questionnaire with instructions and a computer-scannable answer sheet. Participants were assured, both in the written instructions and by the on-site survey coordinator, that responses would be entirely confidential. If an employee declined to participate, a substitute was to be chosen by use of the same "nth name" random process. Editors were asked to give the employees three days in which to complete and return the questionnaire, which in a pre-test in August 1996 had taken respondents about 30 minutes to complete.

Of the 61 newspapers that eventually agreed to participate, only 3 failed to return their questionnaires by the 15 October 1996 deadline. All 3 of these were below 25,000 in circulation. Thus of the 1,191 questionnaires sent, 1,037 were returned, for a response rate of 87.1 per cent.

The four indicators resulting from the explication of civic journalism appeared as closed-ended items in the survey; respondents could choose the degree to which they approved or disapproved of each.

The two "modest" approaches to civic journalism appear first, and more than 90 per cent of the respondents expressed some level of approval. The two "bolder" approaches, involving the polling of readers and the town meeting, appear next, each garnering more than 70 per cent approval. The mean approval for all four measures is 81 per cent, with only 19 per cent on average expressing some degree of disapproval.

It cannot be known what the approval ratings would have been if this section of the instrument had been labeled "civic journalism," but clearly without the labeling these journalists seem to be comfortable with the approaches described in the four items.

It should also be noted that none of the four items cited any of the more controversial or radical examples of civic journalism, such as training editorial employees in mediation and conflict resolution, or having staff members register citizens to vote. This, of course, was in keeping with the explication of the concept, which was based in large measure on the work of the movement's two theoretical founders, Merritt and Rosen.

The "strongly approve" rating for the modest approaches was, predictably, different from the "strongly approve" results for the two bolder measures: a mean of 60 per cent compared to a mean of 28 per cent. The results for "somewhat approve" were 10 percentage points higher for the bolder approaches, however.

The journalists seem to be implying support for town meetings and polling the public for agenda issues, but not as enthusiastically as doing enterprise stories and providing information on alternative solutions.

Survey respondents were asked to attach comments whenever they felt moved to supplement their closed-ended responses, and a few of these were directed to the items on civic journalism.

A staff member at a large East Coast paper wrote, again without using terms like "civic journalism," an eloquent explanation of the movement's rejection of detached objectivity: "Many papers, while remaining objective, led in some way the struggle for civil rights. Now, we do not lead as much as we try simply to report... Unless newspapers make people in their communities feel a part of them, as if they have a stake in them, they will disappear. Papers cannot be observers and reporters of a community. People no longer want to be merely observed. People want to be cared about."

A few others, however, voiced caution about the direction civic journalism may be taking. A journalist at a small paper in New England stated that there is only one place to be a catalyst for community discourse: "A newspaper and the stories it reports should reflect its surrounding communities and should always seek out the input of its readers. It is not a paper's role to 'lead' its readers, but to listen to its readers. There is plenty of room for our own agenda and suggestions of alternative solutions via the editorial and op-ed pages."

To test the remaining hypotheses, an index was created with the four civic journalism measures (Cronbach's alpha =.61) that enabled correlation and regression analysis using "civic journalism approval" as a dependent variable 46.

H2a is supported: the smaller the newspaper, the greater the support for the index of the four civic-journalism approaches. This association was especially pronounced for the two "bolder" forms of civic journalism. The influence of newspaper size remains significant throughout a multiple regression involving the variables with the strongest bivariate associations with the dependent variable.

Newsroom managers did indeed seem more receptive to civic journalism approaches than rank-and-file employees did (H2b), but the strength of this factor pales in the course of the regression. Age appears not to be a predictor of support for civic journalism. While it is likely that older, higher-ranking journalists may be the initiators of a civic journalism project at a paper, a three-way crosstab analysis also revealed that older reporters and copy editors are among the most skeptical about civic journalism.

A few other personal variables were examined for possible correlations with support for civic journalism. Education seemed to make no difference, and while women seemed to approve of civic journalism more often than men do, the difference was never statistically significant.

The third hypothesis sought to learn whether conceptions of journalism's roles have any influence on attitudes towards civic journalism. But the connections seem flimsy.

The "interpreters" were neither less nor more supportive of civic journalism than others; the "watchdogs" and "disseminators" held no significant association with civic journalism either. H3 thus gets no support. It is worth noting, however, that "watchdogs" and "interpreters" both significantly influence approval of the "modest" approaches to civic journalism, but not the "bolder" approaches. Even that influence, however, lost its significance in a regression.

H4 predicted that journalists who accord respect to neighbourhood and community news would applaud civic journalism approaches, and the data support the hypothesis. The influence is particularly strong when the two bolder approaches are considered.

Neighborhood and community news is one of the few independent variables to hold its influence throughout the regression. In a regression on only the bolder approaches, this variable had a higher beta coefficient than any other variable in the equation.

It was also predicted that journalists who were comfortable with their bosses' and colleagues' involvement with civic organizations would approve of civic journalism techniques, as would journalists who themselves felt "more involved than others" in the community. H5a and HSb, posing the hypothetical questions about staff involvement, both enjoyed strong positive correlations with civic-journalism support. The data suggest that those who approve of these civic-journalism approaches are also likely to approve of journalists at any level becoming personally involved in community organizations.

That approval does not extend to the respondents' personal lives, apparently. H5c enjoyed no support. Whether the respondents were involved in community activities themselves seemed not to make a difference in the attitude on civic journalism. This may suggest that journalists are more open to the personal dynamics of civic journalism in theory, but that there is no connection, at least not yet, between their own actual community involvement and their support for civic journalism. Perhaps they see journalists' personal lives as simply detached from whatever professional values they espouse. The sixth set of hypotheses examined measures of dissatisfaction with the current state of journalism, but the data did not support either H6a or H6b. Whether the journalist felt his or her paper was connecting with readers was irrelevant to his or her feelings about civic journalism. The evaluation of the journalist's own paper, in fact, was significant in the direction opposite that of the hypothesis. It was expected that those who feel their own papers are deteriorating in quality would look to civic journalism as a means of rescue.

However, the data indicate that the higher the journalist's rating of his or her own paper, the more positive the reaction to civic journalism. And this influence held its significance throughout the regression. Apparently those who see their newspapers' quality eroding have no faith that civic journalism is the answer, and those who embrace civic journalism are journalists who think their paper is improving. Perhaps civic journalism will require a sense of collective confidence in the enterprise before it can win newsroom adherents.

Thus only a few independent variables remained, after a four-step regression, as significant influences on a journalist's approval of these four approaches to civic journalism: The smaller the newspaper, the greater the attention to neighbourhood and community news, the greater the approval of journalists' joining community organizations, and the greater the sense that one's own paper is improving, then the more likely the approval of civic journalism.

It must be noted, however, that the regression equation accounted for only 14 per cent of the variance of the dependent variable. Clearly other factors, not explored in this survey, also influence support for civic journalism.

One final piece of analysis was conducted: a factor analysis to follow up on Weaver and Wilhoit's earlier discovery of the "populist mobilizer." The data in the present study were gathered more than four years after the Weaver-Wilhoit survey.

Weaver and Wilhoit had included only one item that could be clearly identified as an indicator of civic journalism ("letting ordinary people express their views"). In a factor analysis of the present data, with a full mix of professional-role items including disseminator, interpreter and watchdog, the four civic-journalism items loaded onto their own separate factor (eigenvalue 1.88).

As the discussion above indicated, approval of civic journalism is correlated with some of the other, older role conceptions, but not robustly so. It could very well be that a new understanding of journalism's role in society has indeed begun to emerge, as Weaver and Wilhoit speculated in 1996, in which a newspaper's commitment to the public life, for at least some journalists in some situations, takes precedence over obligations of disseminating information quickly, analyzing events, or serving as adversary to powerful institutions.

Whether or not newspaper journalists scoff at the term "civic journalism," this much is clear: Many of them seem to approve of four specific manifestations of the movement's guiding principles. It would be inappropriate, however, to draw overarching conclusions about the future of civic journalism on the basis of this study alone. The survey's four approaches to civic journalism were referents of pillars of the movement's philosophical foundation, and while they represented a fundamentally different approach to journalism, not even the two "bolder" approaches seem revolutionary in form.

In fact, it might be argued that the two "modest" items are quite similar to longstanding normative understandings of strong local news coverage. Further research on journalists' conceptions of civic journalism is warranted, and it might begin with a broader selection of approaches and strategies, to see where journalists might finally "draw the line" and begin objecting to certain approaches. Because civic journalism projects increasingly involve broadcast and online media, further studies should include more than newspaper journalists. Rosen has stated that the definition of civic journalism is phenomenological: Ultimately, it will be whatever journalists say it is.

For this reason it is important to measure not only what journalists think of a Merritt-Rosen— derived definition of civic journalism, as this study has done, but also to measure how journalists themselves would define the term.

If their definition emerges as similar to the explication of this study, then the future of civic journalism is more promising than even this study suggests. If, however, journalists define it in ways that cause Merritt, Rosen, Charity and others to howl with exasperation, it's more likely that the journalists will also disapprove. Then proponents of civic journalism will truly have their evangelistic work cut out for them.

The most influential independent variables have created a profile of sorts of the pro-civic-journalism practitioner. It suggests that civic journalism may enjoy greater success in smaller communities and in media outlets that are seen by their employees as improving.

But here, too, further inquiry is needed. In carefully steering away from respondents' preconceived notions of civic journalism, the survey instrument did not measure whether the respondent had read or discussed any materials regarding civic journalism, or had participated personally in a civic journalism project. These factors could be expected to influence a journalist's opinion of the movement and its practices.

Even with this early indication that a large proportion of the newspaper workforce seems poised to approve of (at least this conception of) civic journalism, it is still unclear whether this will create any deep changes in journalism, or in the quality of civic life.

Riede's study of Merritt's own paper suggested that journalistic routines are extremely difficult to alter even in one of the pantheons of the movement.

Some scholars question whether civic journalism can survive within a liberal-economic media model like the United States'. Glasser and Craft, for example, suggest that civic journalism, if implemented consistently and seriously, might either risk losing its ratings appeal among advertisers or would challenge power structures in a way that would anger advertisers.

Rosen and Merritt, predictably, have pondered this concern and responded, but with different views. Rosen asserts that civic journalism, properly executed, can draw in a large audience of citizen— participants and thus more advertising revenue.

Merritt acknowledges that civic-journalism content may not compete for audience with the crossword puzzle or "Seinfeld" but that it doesn't have to. As long as it enjoys a permanent place in the mix of programming or editorial features that maximize an audience, it can continue to uplift the public life.

Judgement on the viability and desirability of civic journalism is beyond the scope of this study. Such considerations assume, of course, that civic journalism will indeed catch on among the majority of journalists.

This study suggests that at least one aspect of Weaver and Wilhoit's earlier notion of a "populist mobilizer" attitude towards journalism has taken hold among newspaper journalists.

There may still be only a few journalists actually waving "civic journalism" banners, but in terms of four specific activities that stem directly from the movement's philosophical roots, the movement is quietly finding acceptability. Civic journalism's ultimate reformative power— especially its ability to challenge powerful institutions on behalf of the public and "the public life"-will only be as strong as its support among its practitioners. That support seems to have made important initial strides.

UNMAKING OF CIVIC JOURNALISTS

Perhaps more than any other profession, journalism grapples with an apparent contradiction between autonomy and public service. Sociologists define professional autonomy as wide latitude of judgement in executing occupational duties.' Autonomy provides discretion in the application of techniques and separation from influences that threaten a professional's ability to apply expertise in service to the public. Thus, practitioners adhere to norms of public service even as the lay public itself is excluded from formal decision making. This conception of autonomy becomes problematic when applied to the press, according to advocates of civic (or public) journalism.

This reform movement is based on the premise that news media should go beyond the mere reporting of information to act as a catalyst and as a forum for the revitalization of democracy. But according to civic journalism opponents, these goals threaten the institutional independence of the press and thereby jeopardize journalistic autonomy. Under the traditional view of journalism, autonomy allows the press to cover public affairs with some protection against partisan bias and other corrupting influences.

If civic journalism is to succeed in the long run as a reform movement, it must meet head on the tension between the profession's autonomous identity and its role in democracy. Civic journalism has focused on the implementation and consequences of professional values, but it has been less concerned about understanding the origins of these values as a function of professional socialization. The purpose of this study is to model the process by which professional socialization predisposes college students to reject or embrace civic journalism.

We will first assess the extent of support for various dimensions of civic journalism within two groups: journalism students and professional journalists living in the same community. Our general expectation is that students will be relatively supportive of civic journalism while professionals will express reservations in light of their commitment to autonomy. We will then consider college experiences that might help to explain when and why this gap emerges.'

Our intent is not to argue for the merits of civic journalism, but to provide insight into why support for it might erode as a consequence of professional socialization. For those who do support civic journalism, this line of inquiry could suggest implications for curriculum reform geared towards enhancing-or preventing the erosion of-civic journalism support.

This approach will also allow us to make an empirical contribution to the ongoing debate as to whether civic and traditional journalism principles coexist in harmony, or whether the two perspectives necessarily conflict as values take shape during professional socialization.

Why Autonomy Is Important to Journalists. While autonomy for all professions is ostensibly a mechanism of public service, it also accommodates the psychological needs of the practitioners. Autonomy contributes to group identification-the perception of belonging to a particular human group. Cheney and Tompkins observed that identification helps to sustain "an individual's or a group's 'sameness' or 'substance' against a backdrop of change and 'out side' elements." Prior research shows autonomy strongly correlated with both professional identification of journalists and job satisfaction.

Management trends in news media have increased the need for autonomy in recent decades. Comparison of the findings of Johnstone, Slawski, and Bowman in 1976 with those of Weaver and Wilhoit for 1986 and 1996 reveals that perceived autonomy declined. As Johnstone, Slawski, and Bowman surmised, the bureaucratization of media organizations diminishes the sense of autonomy among rank-and-file reporters. In the first two surveys, 60 per cent of respondents reported they were almost entirely free to select the material on which they worked; this dropped to 51 per cent in the third study.

Potential threats to autonomy include increased corporate chain ownership, the crumbling of the metaphorical wall between business and editorial, competition from Internet sources of news and entertainment, and the blurring of editorial and business functions in news organizations. With an erosion of perceived autonomy, and without the organizational protection and academic credentials of other professions, journalists are likely to feel vulnerable in the face of structural changes.

This probably accounts for some of the defensiveness, if not outright hostility, many prominent journalists express towards civic journalism, a reform movement that is itself an explicit challenge to traditional notions of autonomy.

CIVIC JOURNALISM GOALS

The press traditionally understands its role as a disseminator of accurate information that allows individuals to participate as competent citizens. This requires neutrality in the coverage of political actors, institutions, and issues. By contrast, civic journalists argue that news media should not be neutral about the quality of civic participation in their communities.

We asked respondents to assess their support for two goals associated with civic journalism: going beyond the mere transmission of information to increase political participation, and focusing on news that helps a community to solve problems.

While these goals are potentially problematic in light of the norm of detachment, they are described at a fairly abstract level, with the threat to autonomy more implicit than explicit. Thus, we again propose a research question instead of a hypothesis:

RQ2: In comparison with professionals, will students express stronger support for civic journalism goals?

CIVIC JOURNALISM PRACTICES

We do anticipate differences between professionals and students in the evaluation of practices that might jeopardize autonomy. For example, we asked respondents to assess their support for news media sponsoring meetings to address local problems.

According to professional critics, such events cripple the ability of journalists to remain critical of the favored policies.

We also asked respondents to evaluate the use of polls to help journalists decide what should be covered. Critics have dismissed this technique as another manifestation of how marketing has intruded into the newsroom. Handing news judgement over to the public directly violates the profession's traditional understanding of autonomy.

H1: In comparison with professionals, students will express stronger support for practices associated with civic journalism.

ANTECEDENTS OF SUPPORT FOR CIVIC JOURNALISM

A review of prior literature suggests that college experiences and attitudes adopted during professional socialization will influence students' acceptance of civic journalism. Potential predictors of civic journalism support include the amount of college instruction, anticipatory socialization as a psychological construct, working for a campus paper, and support for traditional roles of the press.

FORMAL INSTRUCTION

Participation in a college journalism curriculum should influence the likelihood of students adopting values similar to those of professionals. Weaver and Wilhoit reported that alumni of journalism programmes expressed a connection between their formal education and their current news values. Students are likely to adopt a commitment to professional autonomy-and consequently a reticence about civic journalism-to the extent that instruction emphasizes the conventional understanding of professional detachment and neutrality. Prior participation in a civic journalism project should also predict support, but we did not include this variable because of the minimal presence of civic journalism in the journalism programme where we recruited respondents. The programme had provided only one civic journalism class (in 1998), with an enrollment of eleven students.

ANTICIPATORY SOCIALIZATION

Individuals typically view themselves as members of a profession long before they join a specific organization. "Anticipatory professional socialization" represents the extent to which an individual has thought seriously about a particular career. An important dimension of this process is "identification," or the perception of belonging to a particular group. This need for professional membership and acceptance might predispose students to reject civic journalism.

A central argument of civic journalism is that news media should display their inner workings, thereby becoming more accountable to the public. But if students begin to value an insider's perspective on newsroom culture, this group identification could evoke an aversion to the civic journalism critique.

WORKING FOR A COLLEGE NEWSPAPER

While these two factors should facilitate the adoption of traditional values, neither duplicates the degree of autonomy experienced by professionals. Working for an independent college newspaper, however, might represent an indelible socializing experience that produces a resistance to civic journalism. Campus newspapers vary in their degree of independence from journalism departments and university administrations, but a tradition of American universities is that student newspapers should maintain substantial institutional independence.

The experience of working for a campus newspaper-including the sense of empowerment gained from reporting and editing with little or no instructor supervision— should instill an appreciation for autonomy that cannot be duplicated in the classroom.

Theorists of human development have observed that a young person's identification with an occupation or profession facilitates a realization of self identity, and thus many students might become attracted to journalism precisely because it allows them to express independence and personal identity through their writing and news judgement.

H2: Students with campus newspaper experience will be less supportive of civic journalism compared to other students.

SUPPORT FOR TRADITIONAL ROLES

Civic journalism opponents argue that its goals and practices are not compatible with the traditional mission of the press as an institution that relies on autonomy to provide accurate and balanced information. In the case of journalism training, the question is whether the formation of a professional identity will allow for not only multiple role conceptions among students, but for acceptance of roles that are potentially incompatible. Prior surveys of professionals provide evidence that journalists do identify with more than one role.

Weaver and Wilhoit identified three highly correlated but distinct attitudes about professional purpose: interpretation, dissemination, and adversary orientations." The interpretive function resonates with a recommendation of the Commission on Freedom of the Press-that journalists should investigate the truth about facts while providing a context that gives them meaning.

The disseminator function highlights the need for the press to transmit information that is useful to a large audience, while the adversary function reflects the importance of acting as a "watchdog" of government.

In a survey of newspaper staff members, Arant and Meyer concluded that the majority of journalists do not support practices that violate professional autonomy, but those who did also supported traditional roles of news media. In the context of this study, we anticipate that students would support the traditional roles. But with relatively little concern about journalistic autonomy, measures of traditional values might correlate strongly with civic journalism support among the students, given that the overarching commitment to public service is reflected in all of these role conceptions. We propose the following research question:

RQ3: Will support for the dissemination, interpretive, and adversary roles predict students' support for civic journalism?

The student respondents attended the University of New Mexico (Albuquerque), and the professional journalists were recruited from two daily newspapers published in the same city. While the restriction of respondents to one community in the Southwest limits the external validity of findings, the design eliminates regional factors as alternative explanations for possible differences between students and professionals.

SAMPLING

We used a purposive sample of students in courses taught within the university's Communication and Journalism Department. The intent was to include a large percentage of students who identified to some degree with journalism as a profession. During April of 1999, we administered questionnaires to classes that contained students in four undergraduate major tracks: print journalism, broadcast journalism, public relations, and advertising. We would expect that some students would be sharply focused on journalism, with some fully involved in internships and writing for the campus paper (the Daily Lobo).

Other students, however, would have little or no interest in journalism as a career, but they would have at least some knowledge of news media as an academic topic. This diversity of student background creates the possibility for variance within the variables used to predict civic journalism support.

The sampling frame for the professional journalists was defined as all reporters and editors on the staffs of the Albuquerque Journal and the Albuquerque Tribune. The family-owned Journal represents the largest newspaper in New Mexico with a circulation of approximately 121,000. The Tribune is delivered in the afternoon to about 16,000 subscribers, the vast majority of whom live in Albuquerque. It is owned by Scripps Howard.

We were given permission to distribute questionnaires during the same time period in which we sought responses from the students. The staff list for the Journal included 144 reporters and editors while the list for the Tribune totaled 56.

Interviewing. Questionnaire items for students and professional journalists were identical in every respect practical.

We used paper-andpencil, self-administered questionnaires for both groups. The availability of students in classroom settings allowed us to directly distribute and administer their questionnaires (N=317 respondents), but this degree of supervision was not practical for the professionals' questionnaires.

In both newsrooms, we requested that an administrative assistant place a questionnaire, cover letter, and return envelope in the mail slots of all reporters and editors. Two weeks after the questionnaires were distributed, we distributed a reminder letter to coax potential respondents who had failed to complete a questionnaire.

This procedure produced a response rate of 59 per cent for the Journal and 57 per cent for the Tribune. These can be considered relatively high response rates given that the interviews were voluntary and unsupervised. The final sample consists of N=117 professional journalists.

DESCRIPTION OF SAMPLES

Descriptive statistics reveal a range of interest within the student sample regarding journalism as a career goal. When asked if they plan to pursue a career in journalism, 55 per cent disagreed or strongly disagreed, 16 per cent indicated they were not sure, and 29 per cent agreed or strongly agreed.

For the sample of professional journalists, we sought to gather data reflecting variance in newsroom status among reporters and editors.

When asked how many years they had worked in journalism, 42 per cent indicated 1 to 10 years, 26 per cent indicated 11-20 years, and 32 per cent reported more than 20 years.

CIVIC JOURNALISM MEASURES

One question asked explicitly about civic journalism:

"Several newspapers in recent years have initiated projects known as 'civic journalism.' Indicate the extent to which you agree with the goals of civic journalism."

Respondents were asked to answer using a 1-5 scale for each question, with 1 meaning "strongly disagree" and 5 indicating "strongly agree." No answer (NA) was coded as 3.

Two items described goals:

"Local media should focus on news that directly helps a community solve its problems."

"Local media should go beyond simply reporting news in efforts to increase public participation."

Two items described practices:

"Local media should sponsor community meetings to help citizens solve problems."

"Reader or viewer interest polls should be used to help journalists decide what should be covered."

Predictors of Support for Civic Journalism. Variables used to predict students' support for civic journalism include journalism experiences in college and support for traditional media roles.

College Journalism Instruction. A summed two-item scale (r=.40) assessed the extent of formal instruction:

"Are you a major in the UNM Department of Communication and Journalism?"

"How many news writing courses have you taken at the college level? Include any courses taken this semester." Career Anticipation. A summed 6-

item scale (alpha=.85) measured the extent to which students had anticipated a career in journalism. Responses to the first two questions were coded as yes=2; no, NA=1.

"Do you plan to write news for the Daily Lobo?"

"Do you plan to undertake a news writing or editing internship?"

For the remaining questions, respondents used a 1-5 scale with 1 meaning "strongly disagree" and 5 "strongly agree."

"I plan to pursue a career in journalism."

"I hope to work in a newsroom."

"My interest in a news-related career is growing stronger.

"I have always wanted to be a journalist."

College Newsroom Experience. A summed two-item scale (r=.38) assessed the extent of involvement with the university newspaper.

"Have you been a news writer for the Daily Lobo?"

"Have you worked as an editor for the Daily Lobo?"

Dissemination Role. A single item measured support for the role of news media in disseminating information. Respondents used a 1-5 scale, with 1 meaning "not important" and 5 indicating "extremely important."

"How important is it for the media to concentrate on news that is of interest to the widest possible public?" Interpretive Role. A single item scale measured support for the interpretive role of news media in covering public affairs.

"How important is it for the media to provide analysis and interpretation of complex problems?"

Adversary Role. A summed two-item scale (r=.18) measured support for the role of the media in acting as an adversary of government.

"How important is it for the media to be an adversary of public officials by being constantly skeptical of their decisions?"

"How important is it for the media to investigate claims and statements made by government?"

The five civic journalism measures were first entered together in a one-way repeated-measures multivariate analysis of variance (MANOVA), with journalism experience (student without newsroom experience, student with newsroom experience, professional) as the independent variable. Using all four algorithms, the analysis showed a significant effect for the dependent variables considered together.

When the civic journalism measures were subjected to separate one-way ANOVAs, significant effects were obtained for the following items: local media should go beyond reporting news to increase participation, local media should sponsor meetings, and polls should be used to help journalists decide on news coverage.

With respect to the premise that news media should attempt to increase participation, there was not a significant difference between students with newsroom experience and professionals-both expressed significantly less support for this goal compared to the students without newsroom experience. The same pattern occurred with the practice of local media sponsoring meetings. These results suggest that students with newsroom experience were becoming more like professionals and less like their fellow students in their evaluations of civic journalism.

Finally, the professionals expressed significantly less support, in comparison to both groups of students, for the use of polls to help journalists decide on coverage. Collectively, the three cases show a clear pattern of decreasing support for civic journalism as the respondents gain experience via newsroom participation.

The first research question asks whether college students, in comparison to professionals, express stronger support for the attitudinal item that explicitly mentions "civic journalism" as a reform movement. No significant difference was found.

RQ2 addresses whether college students express stronger support for civic journalism goals. The means for students and professionals are nearly identical with respect to the premise that local media should focus on news that helps a community to solve problems. But in the comparison between students without newsroom experience and professionals, a statistically significant difference exists for the item that concerns media going beyond reporting to increase public participation.

While the first goal describes an agenda-setting function that facilitates a community response to a problem, it apparently does not evoke suspicion among the professionals to the extent of the second goal. To "go beyond" the reporting of news might have suggested a kind of advocacy journalism to the professional respondents.

Hi states that the students will express stronger support for practices associated with civic journalism. Both measures generated significant differences between the student and professional respondents, in support of Hl. The second practice in particular (use of polls) would challenge autonomy if respondents interpreted it as diminishing the importance of professional expertise.

In the interpretation of these results, it is useful to consider that civic journalism has existed for only about ten years, and consequently the older professional respondents would not have been exposed to it while in college. Meanwhile, neither of the Albuquerque papers had conducted projects identified as civic journalism. As for the students' exposure, their journalism programme had not adopted civic journalism as a regular component of the curriculum. Thus, we urge caution in making inferences that would generalize these results.

For example, Arant and Meyer found that the amount of civic journalism support was related to whether a newspaper had previously conducted a project.

H2 proposes that students with campus newspaper experience will be less supportive of civic journalism compared to other students. Lending support to H2, students with newsroom experience were less supportive of the goal in which media go beyond reporting to increase participation. This is also the case for the practice of news media sponsoring meetings.

We consider next the importance of campus newspaper experience in relation to other experiences that might explain the erosion of civic journalism support. We decided to examine this deterioration of support with respect to a civic journalism practice in light of our theoretical argument that specific techniques, rather than abstract goals, would more likely generate opposition as professional socialization proceeds.

The largest variance in student responses occurred with the item that advocates media sponsorship of meetings. This variable was used as the dependent variable in a multiple regression model in which the three indicators of educational experiences are entered as an initial block of independent variables. The second block includes the measures of support for traditional media roles.

In the first equation, only newspaper experience accounted for a significant amount of variance. The beta is negative, demonstrating that writing and editing for a campus newspaper diminish potential support for civic journalism. The second equation addresses RQ3: Will support for traditional media roles predict support for civic journalism?

The attitudinal measure for the interpretive role did account for significant incremental variance, but support for the dissemination and adversary roles did not. All of the betas were positive, however. While these results do not provide overwhelming support in favour of RQ3, they certainly do not suggest a scenario in which the adoption of civic journalism values is accompanied by a rejection of the traditional roles for news media.

This study represents the first empirical effort to model the origins of civic journalism values as a function of professional socialization during the college years. The results confirmed that students tended to be more supportive of civic journalism in comparison to professionals who work in the same community. Gaps between the student and professional respondents emerged when questionnaire items described specific practices that violate the norm of detachment, such as news media promotion of town hall meetings.

A subsequent analysis of factors that might explain these results suggests a scenario of professional socialization that begins with students predisposed to support civic journalism. Acquisition of these values during the college years, meanwhile, is not associated with an erosion of commitment to traditional roles. However, in leaving the classroom for the newsroom, the unmaking of civic journalists might occur as reporters and editors develop a stronger sense of autonomy. One experience in particular— working for the campus paper-appears to instill a sense of autonomy that diminishes acceptance of civic journalism.

A BROADER VIEW OF AUTONOMY

College instruction would ideally promote an open-minded orientation to journalistic roles and an appreciation for both the limitations of routine reporting and the potential for innovation. But those who would reform the curriculum to promote civic journalism must acknowledge the inherent need for increased autonomy during the beginning stages of professional socialization. The desire for autonomy is an inevitable outcome of the process by which students identify with the profession. Journalistic autonomy, consequently, should be appreciated not as a fixed disposition but as a developmental process.

From the perspective of civic journalism advocates, the results of this study highlight the need for college instruction to encourage a broader conception of journalistic autonomy. However, would-be reformers should acknowledge the importance of autonomy for students and for professionals rather than issuing a wholesale attack on editorial detachment. The irony of professional autonomy is that it is the best hope for implementing reform even as editorial detachment appears to preclude civic journalism. Civic journalism can challenge students and professionals to reconceptualize autonomy as the independence to transcend conventional practices that would otherwise limit the contribution of the press to democratic life.

The results of this chapter are based on a single study in one community, thus restricting any inferential claims based on an assumption of external validity. But the findings reflect a certain degree of construct validity given our emphasis on autonomy as a professional value that should dampen support for civic journalism.

Students who work for a campus newspaper should be moving closer to professionals and away from fellow students; the data consistently fit this pattern across various measures of civic journalism support.

Future research would ideally incorporate a panel design of at least two years' duration, with a larger and broader sample of respondents, to track the development of journalistic values as students enter the initial stage of their professional careers. Studies should also incorporate direct attitudinal measures of autonomy as a professional value to supplement the attitudinal and experiential measures used in this study.

We suggest a framework for field research based on the development of operational measures that represent the twentieth-century ethos of professional journalism (*e.g.*, detachment, free press, watchdog role, people's right to know, criticizing institutions) alongside the civic journalism approach (*e.g.*, social responsibility, community building, self-criticizing press institutions, problem-solving). This approach might generate insight that can be used for the reform of journalism instruction as educators promote autonomy in service to democracy.

In the first equation, only newspaper experience accounted for a significant amount of variance. The beta is negative, demonstrating that writing and editing for a campus newspaper diminish potential support for civic journalism. The second equation addresses RQ3: Will support for traditional media roles predict support for civic journalism?

The attitudinal measure for the interpretive role did account for significant incremental variance, but support for the dissemination and adversary roles did not. All of the betas were positive, however. While these results do not provide overwhelming support in favour of RQ3, they certainly do not suggest a scenario in which the adoption of civic journalism values is accompanied by a rejection of the traditional roles for news media.

This study represents the first empirical effort to model the origins of civic journalism values as a function of professional socialization during the college years. The results confirmed that students tended to be more supportive of civic journalism in comparThis debate has been fueled by the lack of a clear definition. Although respected academics and editors have thrown their support behind the movement, Rosen conceded in 1994 that "we're still inventing it. And because we're still inventing it, we don't really know what `it' is." In more recent writings, Rosen has distinguished civic journalism from traditional journalism, suggesting that informing the public and acting as a watchdog are not enough. "The times demand something additional: Journalists should try to strengthen the political community's capacity to recognize itself, converse well, and make choices" (Rosen's italics).

Scholar Philip Meyer writes the failure of civic journalists to define what they are doing has caused two problems: critics can build straw men to attack instead of finding fault with the real thing; and supporters have an automatic defence to critics by claiming the civic journalism that is drawing criticism is not the same civic journalism that supporters embrace.

Merritt writes mat me media's attempt to actively help citizens participate in the political process is a departure from traditional journalistic detachment. It is this departure that has critics of the movement worried that civic journalism is embarking on a slippery slope into advocacy journalism, a move they perceive threatens to destroy objectivity, and in the process, credibility. Some critics, such as Max Frankel of the New York Times and Leonard Downie of the Washington Post, argue that journalism must remain detached.

To focus on "solutions and [community] connections will inevitably distort the news agenda, devalue problems for which no easy remedy is apparent, and end up compromising the paper's independence." Other critics charge that civic journalism panders to the public and advertisers, becoming more a marketing ploy than a journalistic endeavor. Merritt has voiced his frustration that the substance of the civic journalism debate is being lost in a firestorm of "angry dismissiveness" that is based on faulty assumptions.

In a theoretical sense, some scholars believe civic journalism's activism extends social responsibility beyond the recommendations of the Hutchins Commission, calling for a communitarian media that rejects the libertarian ideals espoused by the Enlightenment thinkers who shaped the Constitution and First Amendment. Thomas Jefferson and James Madison, among others, borrowed from the ideas of John Milton and John Locke to create a form of governance that maximized individual freedom, placing the press outside the realm of government with the famous words "Congress shall make no law...."

Contemporary scholar John C. Merrill writes that under this libertarian model freedom was focused on the rights of the press, not on its social or democratic responsibilities. The Hutchins Commission report of 1947 was in response to the media's excessive and irresponsible use of freedom, and it shifted the focus of press freedom from the rights of the press to what the press should do.

Much of the research about how journalists envision their roles in society is framed within the libertarian and social responsibility theories. John Johnstone, Edward Slawski and William Bowman found in the mid-1970s that journalists identified their roles as neutral or participant. Those who adhered to the neutral "nothing-but-the-truth" perspective saw themselves as objective and detached, guided by libertarian principles. The participant perspective was attractive to journalists who saw an obligation to go beyond reporting factual information by providing the interpretation and context necessary to give events meaning. This "whole-truth" perspective parallels social responsibility as defined by the Hutchins Commission.

David H. Weaver and G. Cleveland Wilhoit, using many of the same survey items as Johnstone, Slawski and Bowman, identified three belief systems in 1983 that represent the roles journalists conceive for themselves: interpretive/ investigative, information disseminator and adversarial. The interpretive role, which was the most dominant, closely resembles that of the participant in the Johnstone, Slawski and Bowman model; the disseminator role was adopted by Weaver and Wilhoit to represent the neutral perspective; and the adversarial role emerged after the researchers added questions to probe the depth of the participant role.

John Bare, in a 1994 survey of news staffs at the (Raleigh, N.C.) News and Observer, Omaha World-Herald and Wichita Eagle, expanded the work of Weaver and Wilhoit by adding three types of civic journalism measures: personal public journalism (journalists' attitudes regarding their personal duty to solve community problems); community trust (journalists' faith in community leaders to solve local problems); and institutional public journalism (journalists' attitudes regarding their newspaper's duty to solve community problems).

Bare found that the investigative/interpretive was dominant at the News and Observer and World-Herald, but at the Wichita Eagle, a paper that under Merritt's leadership practiced civic journalism from its inception, the institutional public journalism role was dominant. He concluded that the traditional and civic journalism belief systems coexist; however, because civic journalism at the Eagle had become the dominant institutional belief, when two belief systems are in conflict, the more traditional belief system is less important.

Critics and theorists have voiced their thoughts on civic journalism, but beyond Bare's work very little is known about journalists' attitudes towards this potentially profound change in the role of the media. This research is a step towards addressing this issue by asking journalists at two similarly sized newspapers, the Mobile (Ala.) Register and the Wichita Eagle, to react to a series of statements about the role of the media in society and civic journalism. By examining these journalists' attitudes and beliefs, the researchers hope to clarify what civic journalism means to practitioners and identify how its tenets relate to traditional journalism theory and practice.

The 40 subjects in this Q methodology study sorted opinion statements in January 1997 about the role of journalism in society and civic journalism. The statements were selected from the literature to represent various views about civic journalism and more traditional roles of the news media. Because a variety of definitions of civic journalism exist, participants were left to define the term for themselves. In this way, researchers could explore each journalist's attitudes and beliefs about civic journalism and journalism's societal roles.

The journalists sorted 48 statements according to their degree of agreement or disagreement into a forced distribution grid that resembles a normal bell-shaped curve. Because a vast majority of the statements are created to stimulate a response (they are not neutral), respondents are forced to make subtle differentiations between their extent of agreement and disagreement on the statements. The Q sorts are factor analysed to reveal clusters of opinions. The resulting Q factors are representative of types of people who share similar attitudes and beliefs. The numbers reported parenthetically in this chapter represent the type's overall feeling towards a specific statement along an 11-point intensity scale; a +5 indicates the strongest agreement, -5 indicates the strongest disagreement and 0 indicates neutrality.

Q studies are not intended to indicate how many people in a general population fit within a specific factor or type, rather they present a picture of the types of thinking that exist in relation to a specific issue. The intent of this research was to draw a sample that represents a cross-section of journalists with different levels of exposure to civic journalism. To this end, journalists from two newspapers with different civic journalism experience — the Mobile Register, a mid-size daily that practices mostly traditional journalism, and the

Wichita Eagle, a mid-size daily that has practiced civic journalism since its inception — were asked to participate. A researcher administered the study to 20 volunteers from each newspaper during a one-day newsroom visit.

The demographic spectrum of the journalists in this study includes:

- 23 females and 17 males;
- A range in age from 22 to 60, with 60 per cent of the respondents between the ages of 36 and 55;
- 4 African-Americans, 2 Asian-Americans, 32 Caucasians, 1 Hispanic, 1 other;
- All have some college, 26 have bachelor's degrees, 7 have master's, 1 has a Ph.D.

Because a factor analysis of the Q sorts yields groups of like individuals who share attitudes and beliefs, it is appropriate to think of each group or type as an individual and helpful for the purposes of understanding and clarity to give each type a name. The four types that emerged in this study are Civic Journalist, Concerned Traditionalist, Neutral Observer and Responsible Liberal. Throughout this analysis, the pronoun he or she is used in accordance with the gender composition of each type.

The four factors extracted had eigenvalues greater than 1.7. These factors together explain 57 per cent of the variance, with the Responsible Liberal accounting for 18 per cent; the Neutral Observer, 15 per cent; the Civic Journalist, 13 per cent; and the Concerned Traditionalist, 11 per cent.

THE CIVIC JOURNALIST

The Concerned Traditionalist thinks it is acceptable for journalists to involve themselves in community activities, and seems to consider advocacy when he disagrees with the statement that "mobilizing support for public projects is not the business of journalists" (-3).

It is the role of the media to create forums for dialogue, and the Concerned Traditionalist believes that this includes the media sometimes using their resources as a civic partner. "It is difficult to report on a community you don't love or respect," a respondent writes.

Some activism is approved, but the Concerned Traditionalist strongly disagrees that journalists are responsible for making sure public life goes well (-4). In a traditional sense, he believes the media should be the agenda setters, disagreeing even more strongly with the statement that journalists should set a public agenda based on public demands (-5). "We can't write or not write about something because of anyone's demands," one contends. "The public can't always get what it thinks it wants."

However, the Concerned Traditionalist sees the public as playing a vital role in journalism. He supports the idea that good reporters have always listened to citizens (+4), and wishes journalists were closer to the attitudes and opinions of the public. The Concerned Traditionalist agrees that journalists need to distance themselves from government leaders and get closer to the people they are writing for (+3). "Citizens are still the most important part of journalism. We are not here to serve politicians," one writes. Reporters should develop a sense of what it is like to be poor or a member of a minority group that is severely discriminated against. "Many of the problems we write about as journalists have to do with poor people's issues," another writes. "We need to be closer to those people to accurately reflect their difficulties."

The Concerned Traditionalist is somewhat cynical, though, about some techniques used to reconnect journalists to the public. He does not think public opinion polls, for example, are a good way to find out what the public thinks. "I have seen, time and again, my own newspaper fall on stories when it is too easily influenced by unscientifically conducted polls and anonymous call-in opinion lines.

Such features may entertain and sell but are not serious journalism," one writes. Although a closer relationship with the public is desirable, the Concerned Traditionalist also agrees with the statement that the motive behind the recent "get back to the people" trends at some newsrooms is little more than a commercial response to the declining circulation in the business (+2).

Six of the seven Concerned Traditionalists are male, ranging in age from 26 to 47. The only female has the highest factor loading (.718) of all the members of this type. Two of the four African-Americans in the sample are in this type. Four members say they practice civic journalism and three say they do not. Each paper is about equally represented on this type, with four journalists from Mobile and three from Wichita.

THE NEUTRAL OBSERVER

The Neutral Observer believes that journalists should remain objective, even detached from what they report. She is the only type in this study who is ambivalent about the media's commitment to social responsibility. The Neutral Observer is most skeptical of the ideals and practices of civic journalism, and she believes the democracy will survive whether or not reporters change the way they practice journalism.

The Neutral Observer sees the journalist's central mission as reporting and analyzing the news, not shaping it or directing its outcomes. She agrees with the idea that it is not the journalist's responsibility to fix what's wrong in a community (+4), and strongly disagrees with the statement that the role of journalism is to ensure that public life goes well (-5). "Civic journalism is social engineering. Newspapers have somehow accepted this idea that they have need to shape their communities," one writes. Rather than attempting to solve social problems, the Neutral Observer sees the media's role as revealing them, with the media acting as windows to the world, pointing things out and holding problems up for scrutiny. The Neutral Observer is more comfortable than any other type when the media serve as independent watchdogs over society's institutions.

"Civic journalism is vastly different because it dilutes media independence and integrity, assuming a community consensus as opposed to a separate voice," one writes. She believes the media should provide factual information and let the public decide the truth. She disagrees with the idea that journalists have failed to live up to their responsibilities to inform people about the challenges around them (-2).

For the Neutral Observer, the concept of independence is closely linked with journalistic neutrality and a freedom from social responsibility. She is the only journalist to disagree with the statement that "the media are too powerful to pretend they have nothing to do with social well-being" (-2). Furthermore, the Neutral Observer is the only type that thinks mobilizing support for public projects is not the business of journalists and that subsidizing and promoting events to get citizens involved in civic affairs is not the job of newspapers. And she is the only type in the study to think that the media should refrain from sometimes using their own resources as a civic partner.

The Neutral Observer believes journalists should be able to separate their work from the political process. She disagrees with the statement that journalists should work to improve the way in which they participate in politics instead of denying that such participation exists (-3). The media provide a method in which people in the democracy can share and discuss information, but the Neutral Observer does not think it is the media's responsibility to get people to participate in a democracy. It is, rather, the media's job to provide people with the information they need to take part in one. The Neutral Observer disagrees strongly with the statement that reporters need to change the way they do journalism in order for democracy to survive (-4).

The Neutral Observer sees civic journalism more in economic terms than the other types. She agrees most strongly that the need to "get back to the people" trend in some newsrooms amounts to little more than a commercial response to newspapers' declining market penetration (+5). "If journalists really focused on news rather than wasting resources on "civic" things, newspapers would be better, tighter and more real," one writes. The Neutral Observer is the only group in this study that thinks civic journalism is public relations — what the promotions department does, only with a different name and a fancy evangelistic fervor.

Journalists should not let the public's demands set the news agenda. The Neutral Observer thinks it's lazy journalism when reporters rely on citizen groups to tell them what to write about. She disagrees with the idea that opinion polls are a good way to find out what people think (-3), and with the suggestion that focus groups, town meetings and phone surveys are tools journalists should use regularly (-3). However, her reluctance to follow a public agenda does not mean discounting the value of ordinary citizens as news sources. The Neutral Observer, more than any other type in this study, supports the belief that it is a journalist's responsibility to cover the news from the citizen up, and not from the expert down (+3).

Of the 10 journalists that factor on this type, eight are women. Only one person is from Wichita, the rest from Mobile. Their ages range from 23 to 53. There are seven Caucasians, two African-Americans, and one person who responded "other." Not surprisingly, only one person in this type practices civic journalism.

THE RESPONSIBLE LIBERAL

The Responsible Liberal thinks the ideals of objectivity and social responsibility serve journalism well, but she is open-minded towards civic journalism. She likes the civic journalism ideals of getting closer to the citizens, but is not an activist calling for a new press system. The Responsible Liberal thinks journalists should remain detached, reporting on issues of importance in a healthy democracy to an intelligent, rational audience. The Responsible Liberal also acknowledges that the media's freedom belongs to the people and should be used for the welfare of society. The Responsible Liberal is a practitioner of civic journalism, but she is not a strong supporter of some of movement's core concepts and remains much less pessimistic about the current state of journalism than reformers.

The Responsible Liberal sees the media's role as one of providing a window to the world, pointing out issues and problems for public scrutiny. She agrees that average citizens are intelligent and capable of rational choice if given the opportunity (+4), so the journalist's job is not so much solving social problems as revealing them. A proponent of objectivity, the Responsible Liberal agrees that the journalist's central mission is to report and analyse news, not to shape it or direct outcomes (+3).

One Responsible Liberal writes, "A journalist who thinks it's his or her role to solve problems is a journalist with an agenda. Let's focus on showing the way to solutions." The Responsible Liberal believes good reporters have always listened to citizens. But this does not mean it's the media's responsibility to get people to participate in democracy; providing people with the information to participate is enough. The Responsible Liberal does not see the need for major changes in the practice of journalism, disagreeing with the statement that reporters must change the way they do journalism if democracy is to survive (-3). "(Civic Journalism) is not so new, it's a change in emphasis," one writes. "The goal — to get people talking — has always been the goal."

The media should be responsible, and generally they are, the Responsible Liberal believes. Freedom of the press does not belong to editors and publishers, but to the people (+3), and the media play a role in democracy by sharing information and providing a forum for discussion. The Responsible Liberal believes the media should provide more than just facts, but the media should not be blamed for a lack of public knowledge or interest in civic affairs.

According to one, "Journalism and journalists have not failed — they are doing incredible work every day in communities, large and small. I do not believe the overriding goal of journalism is to make sure "public" life goes well. Sometimes it does not go well — we should not cover that up." The Responsible Liberal disagrees with the ideas that journalists have failed in living up to their responsibilities to inform people about the challenges around them (-4), and that a new kind of press system is needed to refocus the political debate (-3).

Responsible Liberals seem intrigued by some of the ideas behind civic journalism, but are not ready to embrace many of the practices. The Responsible Liberal thinks it's all right for the media to sometimes use their own resources as a civic partner (+2).

Similarly, focus groups, town meetings and surveys are tools journalists should use regularly. The Responsible Liberal implies seeing merit in civic journalism by disagreeing strongly with the idea that civic journalism is public relations (-4). But she is ambivalent towards some civic journalism concepts. She disagrees slightly with the ideas that journalists too often present public life as a depressing spectacle (-2), and that journalism needs a stronger guiding ethical or moral philosophy (-1).

The Responsible Liberal is not attracted at all to some key concepts of the civic journalism movement: the journalist's role is to enrich the civic life of the community (0), and it is the media's role to bring people together to solve society's problems (0). "If they aren't careful, newspapers can get caught up in the gimmicks of civic journalism and unduly shift their focus from excellent day-to-day work to `project journalism,'" one writes. Perhaps most telling is the Responsible Liberal's strong disagreement with the statement that it is journalism's responsibility to make sure public life goes well (-5).

Journalists should not let the public's demands set the news agenda. The Neutral Observer thinks it's lazy journalism when reporters rely on citizen groups to tell them what to write about. She disagrees with the idea that opinion polls are a good way to find out what people think (-3), and with the suggestion that focus groups, town meetings and phone surveys are tools journalists should use regularly (-3). However, her reluctance to follow a public agenda does not mean discounting the value of ordinary citizens as news sources. The Neutral Observer, more than any other type in this study, supports the belief that it is a journalist's responsibility to cover the news from the citizen up, and not from the expert down (+3).

Of the 10 journalists that factor on this type, eight are women. Only one person is from Wichita, the rest from Mobile. Their ages range from 23 to 53.

There are seven Caucasians, two African-Americans, and one person who responded "other." Not surprisingly, only one person in this type practices civic journalism.

CIVIC JOURNALISM IN PRACTICE

There is little doubt that people believe the media are out of touch with the lives of ordinary citizens. A 1994 Times Mirror poll indicated that 71 per cent of Americans believe that the news media hinder efforts to solve society's problems. Recent polls show little change in this public animosity towards the press. The continuing decline in newspaper readership, fewer viewers of television news and a significant drop in voter participation all create what some critics believe is a lethal brew that is threatening not only journalism but democracy.

Studies show that citizens feel that no one is sincerely listening when they express their views and concerns. People are growing more and more isolated from one another and from the public life of their communities. And, despite evidence that people are interested in policy decisions that affect their lives - they no longer know how to access the system or make themselves heard.

As the 50th anniversary of the Hutchins Commission's report draws near, journalists are expanding the commission's concept of social responsibility and enlarging the traditional community journalism paradigm. Civic, or public journalists at some newspapers are attempting to bridge this journalist-citizen communication gap by using a variety of creative methods to systematically listen to citizens - to talk with rather than talk at the people.

This research examines different group-listening endeavors used by four newspapers. These mini-case studies focus on specific listening techniques reporters used to seek information and insights from citizens as they began reporting projects. The newspapers and projects are:

- The Columbia Missourian's School-to-Work project and its Religion in Public Life project.
- The Akron Beacon Journal's - Coming Together, a follow-up project of the newspaper's race relation series A Question of Colour.
- The Wichita Eagle's April 1995 mayoral election coverage and its 1995 neighbourhood conversations project.
- The Tallahassee Democrat's Living Room Conversations method in its Public Agenda Project.

Communication theorists contend that when people hold conversations about topics they believe are important to them and to their families, a number of things happen. First, they begin to feel that their opinions are valued. They gain new insights into the topic by listening to others' opinions, and as they process the information, they start to weigh options. They begin to take ownership of the issues and to assume some responsibility in addressing community concerns.

The media often depend on opinion polls, and while this method has its benefits, it allows for no group interaction. Indeed, some critics argue that polls appear to widen the gap between media and citizens and further distance the people from civic participation.

In Coming to Public Judgement: Making Democracy Work in a Complex World, pollster Daniel Yankelovich argues that polls lack depth and fail to promote public judgement, a deliberative process that leads to problem resolution. Polls tend to define public judgement by adding up the score rather than by the process of thoughtful deliberation.

One of the most important elements in group conversations is the interaction among group members. In fact, researchers gave found that just by participating in the group process itself, group members develop a sense of involvement in the project. Often, the interactive conversation reveals information about issues that had never even occurred to the reporters. One scholar observed that group communication dynamics may "lead us to change the very way that we think about the problems that interest us."

Davis Buzz Merritt, Jr. of the Wichita Eagle, argues that newspapers must find new and innovative ways to listen to citizens. In Public Journalism and Public Life: Why Telling the News is Not Enough, Merritt writes that three elements are necessary for democracy to function: shared, relevant information, a method or place for deliberation about the application of that information and shared values on which to evaluate information and base public decisions. Journalists in these case studies say they are attempting to find ways for citizens to share relevant information with each other and with a wider readership audience.

In each of these case studies, journalists had to confront the aspect of source confidentiality. The usual method is to grant all participants some level of confidentiality. The reporter listens for themes in the conversations and uses the information only as background for subsequent reports. Often the reporter will call the participants back later for more in-depth and on-the-record interviews, but the conversations themselves usually are not reported unless the views, but the reporting staff has decided, with the permission of the participants, to do otherwise.

Although the case studies reveal a variety of listening techniques, most fit into three general categories: Focus groups, resource panels and community conversations. The following is a brief description of each method.

Focus Groups

Focus groups solicit information about citizens' attitudes, beliefs and community concerns. The data then are used to develop news reports. The information received from these discussions helps reporters focus on the topic issues and provide them with new perspectives. Communication scholars argue that focus groups enable researchers to better understand people's views of reality.

It is important to keep in mind, however, that just any group is not a focus group. Traditional focus groups are highly structured and follow specific procedures and methodology. Also, focus groups are not the answer for every reporting project. For example, they are not used to debate or grapple with issues or to recommend solutions, such as in a public forum. Nor can they be used like a survey to generalize results to a larger population. A focus group yields qualitative, not quantitative data.

RESOURCE PANELS

In some instances, when journalists need specialty information, they call upon experts in the community to share their knowledge with the reporting staff. The expert or resource panel is one of many ways in which journalists attempt to gain understanding and broaden their perspectives when writing about complex and unfamiliar topics. The resource panel is a less structured method than a focus group, and it has a different research purpose. Resource panelists are chosen for their knowledge and expertise relating to a defined topic. While both focus groups and resource panels assist the journalist in gaining new insights from people in the community, the information core is different. A focus group is used to refine the questions. A resource panel is used to define the questions themselves.

When journalists decide to convene focus groups, they have already investigated the topic. They have a good idea about general issues, problems or concerns within the topic area. On the other hand, resource panels are used as a primary information source to define the topic itself. A resource panel is convened when the topic is complex and reporters have such limited knowledge they are uncertain how to even approach the coverage.

Unlike focus groups or community conversations, resource panels are created for audience interaction as well as interaction among panelists. The audience has an opportunity to ask questions of the panelists, which in turn usually generates more conversation among the panelists and then sparks additional questions from the audience. This double-level interactivity is one of the benefits of resource panels, and is especially valuable for reporters, who have the opportunity to learn from experts.

COMMUNITY CONVERSATIONS

This technique is the most fluid of the information newsgathering methods and allows a great deal of versatility and creativity. The process of creating a community conversation depends upon the target population and what the research question is: what information the journalist is seeking from the citizens. Reporters target specific groups, neighbourhoods, or demographic characteristics. Participants are selected in a variety of ways, and meetings are arranged to suit the project, but they are usually held at comfortable and informal sites. The purpose of creating these community conversations is specifically to listen to citizens talk about an identified issue. Although it may seem similar to group interview techniques, there is one big difference. The focus is not on the reporter and his or her questions. The focus is on reporters listening to the citizens' conversations. While the reporter or the moderator leads the group and asks an opening question, the purpose of the community conversations is to listen, not to interview.

CASE STUDY: THE COLUMBIA MISSOURIAN - FOCUS GROUPS

In May 1995, the University of Missouri School of journalism undertook a civic journalism project with its daily and Sunday newspaper. The paper created a series of four focus groups in a reporting project called School-to-Work, which investigated the problems high school graduates were experiencing in obtaining employment after graduation, and whether the public school system was addressing the needs of non-college bound students.

Four focus groups were convened targeting four populations: employers, teachers, students and parents. Jennifer LaFleur, a trained focus group moderator, served as the key resource person. Ideally, the reporting staff should be able to get initial story ideas from focus group conversations. In this case, the focus groups were held after the first series, Making Education Work, had been published April 30-June 4, 1995.

LaFleur cited several difficulties in this project. The first problem was in the timing. According to focus group methodology, the focus groups should have been held early in the planning stages of the project rather than after the series was published. Second, resources were limited, which forced the focus groups to be held in a classroom rather than in a neutral place. This gave participants the impression that the school had some stake in the results of the project. Also, there were no financial incentives offered, and some groups (students, parents) drew fewer than five participants. Third, only one set of focus groups was held with each of the four target populations. LaFleur prefers to hold at least two sets of focus groups, in this instance she would have preferred to hold eight, to elicit a wider spectrum of opinion.

Although LaFleur was no longer involved in the process, the taped focus group sessions were analysed later, and the Columbia Missourian staff did follow through in October 1995 with another series on the School-to-Work topic. Thus the focus group data was utilized as it should have been, as a source for story ideas prior to the reporting project. The second series, A Look Beyond the Classroom, was published November 11-16, 1995.

CASE STUDY: THE COLUMBIA MISSOURIAN - RESOURCE PANELS

The Columbia Missourian staff first used the resource panel concept during its 1994 reporting project on health care. Because of the complexity of the topic, reporters and editors knew they would need some help in understanding the issues.

Journalism techniques such as focus groups, polls or surveys, did not seem to fit the research need. The newspaper staff needed insights from experts in the field. It was decided to convene a panel of health care experts so that students could gain knowledge and ask questions about the proposed reporting assignment. George Kennedy, a faculty member overseeing the project, explained the process.

"In that project we were overwhelmed with the scope and complexity of the issue and the gap in the knowledge level we knew was needed. We put it (the resource panel) together out of desperation, and it turned out to be more useful than any of us had ever imagined it to be."

The resource panel served two purposes, Kennedy said. First, the panelists were able to raise the knowledge level of the reporting staff "so we at least knew what the questions were." Second, the panel presentation helped build the reporting team by creating a shared experience among the staff.

For its 1995-96 reporting project, the journalism school decided to focus on the topic of religion and its relationship to public fife, and again decided to use resource panels. Although the topic of religion is of growing interest within the media, studies have shown that journalists are ignorant about it and uncertain about how to cover it. Professors and editors saw resource panels as a way to confront this lack of knowledge among journalism students, editors and professors.

Three separate resource panels were convened in October and November 1995, with panelists grouped according to specific criteria. The first panel was composed of four religion scholars.

Members of the second panel were clergy, and the third panel was composed of four former or current politicians who spoke on religion and politics. These sessions were held in a conference-classroom, ran approximately two hours each and were videotaped. Student reporters attending were able to question the panelists during the final portion of the sessions.

The panels served to not only expose the students and faculty to new information about religion, but also provided students with new sources to tap for story information. The project had an additional, hidden benefit, as well. Panelists said the experience not only added to their own knowledge about other faith groups in the community, but also helped them better understand reporters' perspectives. Several panelists voiced interest in being kept informed about the project and suggested that more such discussions be held. In this sense the group process appeared to help promote good will between the newspaper and the panelists. It also created a learning environment for the panelists as well as for the students and faculty.

CASE STUDY: THE COLUMBIA MISSOURIAN - COMMUNITY CONVERSATIONS

The community conversations experiment was a follow-up to the religion resource panels. To seek views about religion and public life from different faith traditions, the students and faculty decided to hold a series of community conversations. These were created within a two-week time frame during which the target communities were contacted, individuals found to participate and meeting places and times arranged. The specific groups included members from the Jewish faith, Evangelical churches, the Interfaith Council, the ecumenical youth group, Church Women United, the Catholic faith, African-American churches and clergy.

Each community conversation was attended by a reporter representing the school's three media: newspaper, television and radio. Their primary role was to listen to the group discuss their faith and how they saw it interacting with public life in the community. One of the reporters served as moderator of the discussion, while the others took notes. Other than the opening question, reporters asked few questions. Instead they listened to the conversation among group members. After the community conversations were held, the reporting team gathered to discuss and critique its experiences and to create common themes that would be used later for framing the stories. While most of the community conversations went well, some faltered. The most common problem was an insufficient number of participants. Too few participants discouraged interactive discussion.

From these community conversations, the reporting team developed six topic themes on how religion interacts with public life. These were: public policy, race relations among faiths, ecumenism, outreach, youth and the future, women, health. The reporters then used these themes to develop specific story ideas to plan the project. The series was published the first week of June 1996, and the circulation department reported that those issues sold out.

CASE STUDY: THE AKRON BEACON JOURNAL - FOCUS GROUP

Of all the case studies, the Akron Beacon Journal most closely followed the standard focus group procedure in its 1993 Pulitzer-Prize winning race relations series A Question of Colour and its 1994 follow up Coming Together project. The paper has used focus groups for a number of years, said Bob Paynter, the paper's project editor. In this case, the problem confronting reporters was getting people to be candid about the race topic. Editors decided that focus groups, with assurance of confidentiality, would be the best method to use to coax candor about an issue many are unwilling to talk about.

The paper convened one group comprised of white participants and one of black participants for each of the five areas of concern that had been previously identified in a survey. These areas were: Racial attitudes, housing, education, economics and crime. The focus group participants were selected along targeted geographic areas hot bed neighbourhoods as well as along economic and racial lines. The newspaper was able to define the exact population it wanted because it had up-to-date survey data.

Paynter called the focus groups a "wonderful tool" in the 14-month project, but cautioned journalists to remember that "focus groups are not the story. They lead you to the story."

Another benefit of the focus group method in this instance was the creation of the level of trust among participants and towards the media. "The focus groups ended up being ice-breaker sessions about the race issue," Paynter said. "People began to be comfortable in talking about it. They ended up being very informative warm-up sessions for great interviews later."

The newspaper added another dimension in this project. In addition to the community focus groups, it also convened an in-staff focus group of reporters and copy editors to explore the staff's views on race relations. This session enhanced reporter sensitivity to the issue.

CASE STUDY: THE WICHITA EAGLE - PSEUDO-FOCUS GROUP

This newspaper has been a leader in the use of polls, focus groups and public forums in civic journalism projects. its two most recent projects have used a variety of techniques to elicit community information, said Jon Roe, election team leader at the paper. While the first project was called a focus group, it was actually a variant of the stringent focus group methodology.

In March 1995, the newspaper ran a classified ad asking for people to contact the paper's research department if they wanted to be involved in a study concerning the city's mayoral election. Citizens' concerns had already been identified from a prior survey. Group participants were chosen from those responding to the classified ad. Attempts were made to create a mixed group composed of an equal number of males and females, blacks and whites, and those in favour of the incumbent and those in favour of the challenger. A dozen people were invited, 10 showed up, Roe said.

The session was held at the newspaper's research facility, and the plan was to have the two mayoral candidates view the discussion from behind the one-way mirror. Group participants would know they were being observed, but would not know who was observing them. The session was video-taped. However, one candidate did not show up, so only the incumbent viewed the session and later joined the group for further discussion. Roe said the process encouraged group participants to go beyond personal attacks on the candidates and to begin to address the issues of the campaign.

Mama Young, a researcher at an independent research centre housed in the newspaper building, noted that, in this situation, the Wichita Eagle did not follow usual focus group procedures. The sample was biased in that it used volunteers rather than a random sample of the population, and the moderator was a journalist who asked questions. When the format is changed, it is no longer a focus group.

CASE STUDY: THE WICHITA EAGLE — NEIGHBOURHOOD CONVERSATIONS

The newspaper worked with the Harwood Group on its neighbourhood conversations project, which involved setting up a number of neighbourhood meetings based on specific group criteria. Project editor Roe said the newspaper saw "five levels of democracy" in its community. It covered the top level, official government sources, and the last level of personal stories fairly well. It was the in-between levels that reporters were failing to tap. These other levels included places such as community civic clubs, churches, bars, restaurants, barber or beauty shops and incidental meeting places such as supermarkets, backyards, shopping centers.

In the first phase, to find out more about the people in these areas, 10 reporters in teams of two or three went out to map seven different neighbourhoods. Offering a small monetary incentive to participants, the paper set up pseudo focus groups in these neighborhoods. Groups of about 10 people were convened in each of the seven neighbourhoods. A reporter served as the moderator, or in this case, interviewer, and the group agreed to have their comments published, if they were identified only by their first names. Roe said that, had just one person not agreed, no names would have been used.

In the second phase of the neighbourhood conversations project, reporters were given an assignment "to find a group of people and go sit and listen to them." The only other requirement was that the group had to be talking about education.

"I ended up talking with ministers and asking them where to find these groups in Wichita, and I found out that the neighbourhoods were the churches," Roe said. He sat in on an adult class at a church where the members' conversation focused on their children who were just starting school. "When you talk about public journalism, you talk about getting into neighbourhoods, you invariably end up at a church. The church is the local activist in many, many ways," he said."

While these neighbourhood conversations are not focus groups, neither are they group interviews. Instead, they illustrate another way in which the reporter seeks insights from people at all levels in the community. The advantages are twofold. The process brings reporters into neighbourhoods and provides them with new perspectives about situations as well as new story ideas. The disadvantages of these efforts are that they are time consuming and use a great amount of staff time without immediate production of stories. "You have to have a whole new breed of editor as well as reporter to do this," Roe said.

CASE STUDY: THE TALLAHASSEE DEMOCRAT — LIVING ROOM CONVERSATIONS

Other variants on the group phenomenon include the living room conversations held by the Harwood Group for the Tallahassee Democrat. These were conducted as part of the newspaper's Public Agenda civic journalism project, underwritten by the Pew Charitable Trust. For the Public Agenda project, the newspaper conducted a survey in 1994 to clarify the important public issues. Later, a public meeting was held to discuss the survey findings. As a follow-up, another survey was planned for 1995. Lou Heldman, executive editor and senior vice president of the paper, said the living room conversations were conducted to frame the questions for that public survey. Twelve groups were created according to standard demographic criteria. The groups were composed of from three to five people, and they met in participants' living rooms. The sessions were conducted by Richard Harwood or his associates within a two- or three-week period in 1995.

Heldman said this research method offered several advantages. The natural environment provided a better comfort level for participants, which encouraged conversation. As Heldman said, "It seemed stripped of techniques. It came across as a conversation, even though the moderator had a clear set of questions and goals. It was moderated without artificiality."

But this technique has its disadvantages as well. First, these groups do not lend themselves to observation. The natural setting means that there are no one-way mirrors to allow for observation, nor is there any video taping. The only documentation is an audio tape. Because there were no observers, there were no opportunities for journalists to ask follow-up questions of the participants, as is sometimes done after a focus group, he said. There were no reporters present in these groups, and the participants were assured of anonymity. In November 1995, the newspaper ran articles on the community concerns identified in these 11 living room conversations.

Virginia Fielder, vice president of research for Knight-Ridder Inc., one of the corporate leaders in the media's use of focus groups in civic journalism projects, cautions journalists not to lose sight of the purpose of these journalistic techniques. The primary purpose is not to define a structured research project as much as it is to encourage public deliberation about issues affecting people's lives. Just the existence of the group interaction and the involvement of the journalist in analyzing the discussion has great value, she said. Fielder said that, at the heart of every civic journalism project is citizen involvement. These mini-case studies serve to identify ways in which newspapers are seeking information from the people in their communities.

The study suggests that group listening techniques are serving as a catalyst for knowledge and discussion, not only among numerous citizen groups but among reporters, editors and students as well. Journalists are finding ways to actively engage citizens in conversations and to systematically listen to citizens' discussions on a number of topics. The journalists interviewed said they maintain their journalistic independence while broadening their own perspectives about the community on which they report, using these techniques to add greater depth to their news reports. In effect, these journalists seem to be creating new paradigms for newsgathering, using a citizen-based informational foundation.

Group processing studies show that group members often develop a sense of involvement in the project just by participating in the group process itself. Group dynamics can create new perspectives among all participants. These case studies suggest that these listening techniques not only may benefit the journalistic endeavor, but also may have positive effects on the citizens who participate. However, journalists interviewed cautioned that the techniques should not be viewed as ends in themselves, but instead as additional research tools when planning reporting projects.

JOURNALISTS AND PUBLIC JOURNALISM

Because a decision to practice public journalism usually rests with a senior editor or producer, Kurpius examined the relationship between management and content. In two separate examinations of local television news, Kurpius found that visionary managers were the key for the civic-model of successful issues coverage at local television stations, but he also discovered that market forces may hinder civic reporting efforts in local media in the long run.

Factors that may influence journalists' attitudes towards public journalism were studied by scholars in New Mexico. After journalists at the Albuquerque Journal and Albuquerque Tribune and journalism students at the University of New Mexico completed self-administered questionnaires as part of a convenience sample, the results showed "a progression of socialization that begins with students supporting civic journalism."

Journalism students without newsroom experience appeared to be more supportive of civic journalism than practicing journalists and journalism students with newsroom experience. The authors suggested that civic journalism appeared to be inconsistent with autonomy, an attribute greatly valued by practicing journalists and journalism students with newsroom experience.

Indiana University scholars asked journalists directly about civic journalism in their most recent national survey. Although their previous national surveys of journalists, which were conducted in 1982 and 1992, had documented the backgrounds, attitudes, and values of journalists, the latest national study represented the first time that specific questions about public or civic journalism practices were asked.

According to "The American Journalist in the 21st Century," 72 per cent of journalists approved of giving ordinary people a chance to express their views on public affairs and 58 per cent endorsed providing possible solutions to society's problems. Only 32 per cent approved of convening meetings to discuss public issues.

EFFECTS OF PUBLIC JOURNALISM ON THE AUDIENCE

The sixteen audience-centreed studies identified in the Massey and Haas review examined the effects of civic journalism on the public rather than the public's expectations of journalism." For example, one study reviewed by Massey and Haas found evidence that public journalism produced positive results.

In a study of broadcast and print media that included Wisconsin Public Television and Radio, WISC-TV, the Wisconsin State Journal, and the Wood Communications Group and their collaborative effort to provide a more civic-oriented approach towards election coverage, Denton and Thorson found respondents in Madison said the project made them more knowledgeable about the election, encouraged them to vote, and gave them useful tools to assess campaign information.

Although the literature found civic journalism practices improved public attitudes and increased knowledge of election issues, overall, the Massey and Haas review of public journalism studies found mixed audience effects. Public journalism was found to both increase and suppress voter turnout, to both increase participation in civic projects and have no impact on civic participation, and to produce both strong and weak agenda-setting effects.

After reviewing forty-seven empirical studies, Massey and Haas criticized the public journalism literature for its lack of methodological rigor and for narrowly focusing on "jewel box" civic journalism projects that were conducted at the Wichita Eagle, Charlotte Observer, and Wisconsin State Journal.

Only one of the authors' six recommendations for future research involved the public and that was to conduct laboratory experiments that "could prove more useful for more convincingly identifying whatever causal factors may be behind any public-journalism influence on news audiences."

Surprisingly, none of the recommendations that resulted from this comprehensive review of public journalism studies focused on the public as an independent, active, and integral component of the communication process with opinions and expectations about a new type of journalism that ventures to re-engage the audience in the civic arena.

RESEARCH QUESTIONS

Although civic journalism has been discussed, practiced, debated, and studied for over a decade and a half, the public's perspective on civic journalism has not been studied empirically. Understanding the public's view of local news and civic journalism is important for the practice and business of journalism as well as society as a whole.

Without an assessment of what the public expects of local news, it will be virtually impossible to identify journalism practices that may help reverse declining attention to news, restore dwindling public trust in news as a whole and journalists in particular, and bring back the vanishing participant in civic affairs.

Unlike much of the research on public journalism, which has focused on the effects of specific public journalism projects on voting rates and other measures of civic participation, this study explores the public's views about journalism as well as the public's expectations of local news and the underlying dimensions of those expectations.

Specifically, the following research questions will be answered:

- *RQ1:* What do survey respondents regard as the important attributes and roles of journalism and how does that compare with the norms of traditional and public journalism?
- *RQ2:* How do survey respondents compare with journalists on the importance of practices and norms associated with traditional and civic journalism?
- *RQ3:* What segments of survey respondents as defined by race or ethnicity, age, income, education, and gender are more likely to endorse civic journalism and traditional journalism norms?
- *RQ4:* What are the underlying dimensions of survey respondents' expectations of local news?

As part of a research project for a local newspaper and local NPR affiliated public radio station that was starting up a local news division to complement the national news broadcast from NPR, the authors worked with the radio station managers to design a research study that would ascertain public opinion about local news. A Pew Centre for Civic Journalism grant provided funding for the audience study. The radio station manager believed that understanding the public's expectations of local news was a prerequisite to building a radio news division that would report local news of importance and meet the public's needs.

The spring 2001 survey, conducted in a southwestern metropolitan area by a professional telephone survey unit, used random digit dialing to select the sample. Interviews were completed with 600 adults, representing a response rate of 62.2 per cent. Calculation of the response rate was based upon the number of completed interviews (n=600) relative to the number of completed interviews plus refusals (n=286), incomplete interviews (n=37), and persons contacted but not interviewed due to illness, language barriers, or other impairments (n=36).

Answers to the four research questions were based on survey respondents' ratings of roles of local news media and characteristics of news coverage. Respondents were asked: What do you think is the most important role of local news media? Rate each on whether you think it's "extremely important," "somewhat important," or "not very important."

The roles were (1) report the widest range of news; (2) concentrate on certain topics; (3) provide a forum for community views; (4) be a watchdog of powerful people and the government; (5) highlight interesting people and groups in the community; and (6) offer solutions to community problems.

Respondents were also asked the following: What is the most important characteristic of news coverage you want? Rate each on whether you think it's "extremely important," "somewhat important," or "not very important." The characteristics were (1) accuracy; (2) rapid reporting; (3) understand the local community; (4) unbiased reporting; (5) care about your community; (6) be inclusive of different points of view; and (7) provide explanation of issues and trends.

To determine how survey respondents compare with journalists, the survey respondents' opinions about practices and norms associated with traditional and civic journalism were matched with journalists' opinions from "The American Journalist in the 21st Century" national survey.

Specifically, the opinions of survey respondents and journalists were compared in four areas: offering solutions, providing a community forum, being a watchdog, and rapid reporting. Although both studies used random sampling and "extremely" on the measurement scale, there were several methodological differences.

The question wording in the national survey of journalists differed on the four opinions that were compared. For offering solutions, the national survey asked journalists how important it was "to point people towards possible solutions to society's problems."

For providing a community forum, the national survey asked journalists how important it was "to convene meetings of citizens and community leaders to discuss public issues." For being a watchdog, the national survey asked how important it was to "investigate claims and statements made by the government."

For rapid reporting, the national survey asked journalists how important it was to "get information to the public quickly." In addition to the difference in wording, the present study relied on a three-point scale to measure opinions about journalistic norms while the national survey of journalists relied on a four-point scale of "extremely," "quite," "somewhat," and "not really important."

The difference in question wording and the number of points on the measurement may have affected the number of respondents that chose "extremely" as an option. The final methodological difference was that the present study was conducted in spring 2001 in one southwestern metropolitan area while the national survey of 1,149 journalists was conducted summer and fall of 2002.

The survey questionnaire also included questions about socio-economic backgrounds and media use. Standard survey questions were asked to ascertain number of years lived in the area, marital status, level of education, income, age, and race or ethnicity. Respondents were also asked if they had children living at home and their gender was recorded.

To establish media use, respondents were asked if they read the primary daily newspaper 4-6 times a week, 1-3 times a week, less frequently, or never. Similarly, respondents were asked if they read the primary Sunday newspaper 3-4 times a month, 1-2 times a month, less frequently, or never. Respondents were also asked how often they heard news on the radio, which TV stations they watched for local news, and how often they obtained local news from the Internet.

Bivariate analyses with appropriate statistics were used to determine if opinions about public and traditional journalism practices and norms differed by race or ethnicity, age, income, education, or gender. A factor analysis was used to identify underlying dimensions of survey respondents' attitudes about the roles and characteristics of public and traditional journalism.

SOCIO-ECONOMIC BACKGROUND AND MEDIA USE

Survey participants had established roots in this southwestern metropolitan area. The median number of years lived in the area was twelve; 55 per cent were married and 42 per cent had children at home. Although education was high, different educational levels were represented: 21 per cent had a high school degree or less, 27 per cent had some college, 28 per cent were college graduates, and 24 per cent completed at least some graduate school.

Different income groups were also represented: 34 per cent had a household income of less than $40,000; 31 per cent had incomes between $40,000 and $69,000, and 35 per cent had incomes of $70,000 or higher. Slightly more than one-third of the respondents were ages 18 to 39; 31 per cent were ages 40 to 69; 35 per cent were 70 years or older.

Respondents were fairly diverse: 68 per cent were white, 19 per cent; were Latino, 7 per cent were African American, and 5 per cent were Asian American or other. The remaining 1 per cent did not specify race or ethnicity. When asked how many times a week they read the primary local newspaper, 30 per cent said never or less frequently than 1-3 times a week, 25 per cent said 1-3 times a week, and 44 per cent said 4-6 times a week. Survey participants were more devoted to the Sunday newspaper with 64 per cent reporting they read it 3-4 times a month. In addition to the newspaper, survey participants relied on other local news sources: 80 per cent watched one of the five local TV news outlets, 59 per cent often heard news on the radio, and 18 per cent often turned to the Internet.

THE PUBLIC'S VIEWS ON JOURNALISTIC NORMS

The overwhelming majorities said that accuracy (94 per cent) and unbiased reporting (84 per cent) are extremely important, but two major tenets of traditional journalism did not receive strong endorsements.

The traditional journalistic norm of being a watchdog of powerful people and the government was supported by only 49 per cent of survey respondents and rapid reporting was endorsed by only 35 per cent.

THE PUBLIC'S VIEWS ON THE ROLE OF LOCAL NEWS

Slightly more than half (51 per cent) said offering solutions to community problems was extremely important, and 49 per cent said providing a forum for community views was extremely important.

To answer RQ2, these views were compared with journalists' views about civic journalism practices.

COMPARING THE PUBLIC AND JOURNALISTS

Although the survey of the public was conducted in a southwestern metropolitan area and the survey of journalists was conducted nationally, results from the two surveys were compared because both studies used random sampling techniques, included similar questions about characteristics of traditional and public journalism, and incorporated "extremely important" on the measurement scale.

A difference in proportions test on independent random samples was used to determine if survey respondents were significantly different from journalists in their endorsement of two civic journalism norms and two traditional journalistic norms. Even though the majority of survey respondents strongly endorsed the fundamental characteristics of journalism, accuracy and unbiased reporting, there was a statistically significant gap between survey respondents and journalists on two roles that are an integral part of traditional journalism: watchdog and rapid reporting.

Only 49 per cent of survey respondents said being a watchdog of powerful people and the government is extremely important, but 70 per cent of journalists said that traditional journalism role is extremely important. Survey respondents were also significantly less likely than journalists to say that rapid reporting was extremely important (35 per cent vs. 59 per cent). The roles and characteristics of traditional and civic journalism displayed were analysed by five socio-economic characteristics (race or ethnicity, age, income, education, and gender) to better understand survey respondents' opinions about traditional and civic journalism roles and characteristics.

Although there was no statistically significant difference between survey respondents and journalists in their endorsement of the civic journalism role of providing solutions to problems, there were significant differences when this civic journalism role was analysed by sub-segments of survey respondents.

SOLUTIONS

African Americans and Hispanics were significantly more likely than whites and Asian Americans to say that the civic journalism role of offering solutions to community problems was extremely important.

Almost three quarters (72 per cent) of African Americans and 64 per cent of Hispanics said offering solutions was extremely important, but only 45 per cent of whites and 47 per cent of Asian Americans said this civic journalism role was extremely important.

Segments of survey respondents that made less money and had less education were more likely than wealthier and more educated segments to say offering solutions to community problems was extremely important. Almost three-fifths (59 per cent) of adults who had incomes of less than $50,000 compared to 44 per cent of adults with incomes of $50,000 or more said offering solutions was extremely important.

This inverse relationship was also apparent when offering solutions to community problems was analysed by education. Adults with a high school education or less (68 per cent) were more likely than adults with some college (54 per cent) and adults with a college degree or higher (42 per cent) to say offering solutions was extremely important.

Females were also more likely than males to attach greater value to the public journalism role of offering solutions with 56 per cent of females compared to 44 per cent of males saying it was extremely important for local news to offer solutions to community problems.

WATCHDOG AND RAPID REPORTING

The traditional journalism characteristics of watchdog and rapid reporting were also analysed by the five socio-economic variables and three were significantly related.

The oldest age group (55+) was more likely than the youngest age groups to value the watchdog role of traditional journalism, with 62 per cent of adults 55 or older compared to 47 per cent of adults 35 to 54 and 45 per cent of adults 18 to 34 saying being a watchdog of powerful people and the government was extremely important. An inverse relationship emerged when the traditional journalistic characteristic of rapid reporting was analysed by education. Among adults with a high school degree or less, 47 per cent said rapid reporting was extremely important; 30 per cent of adults with a college degree or higher said rapid reporting was extremely important.

Females attached greater value to rapid reporting than males. Among females, 40 per cent said rapid reporting was extremely important but only 30 per cent of males said this traditional journalistic practice was extremely important.

The Underlying Dimensions of the Public's Expectations of Local News

To better understand the underlying dimensions of survey respondents' expectations of local news reporting, researchers factor analysed the six roles of local news and seven characteristics of journalism. The good neighbour dimension that emerged included attributes of public journalism: caring about your community, highlighting interesting people and groups in the community, understanding the local community, and offering solutions to community problems.

The watchdog dimension was represented by four roles of local news including being a watchdog of powerful people and the government, concentrating on certain topics, providing a forum for community views, and providing explanations of issues and trends.

The unbiased and accurate reporting dimension was defined by those two traditional characteristics of news; the fast dimension was represented by the traditional news characteristic, rapid reporting. Providing a wide range of news and being inclusive of different points of view did not load high on any one dimension. In fact, the inclusive factor loading was similar for the good neighbour, watchdog, and unbiased and accurate dimensions.

DISCUSSION

Although more than fifty empirical studies have been conducted on public or civic journalism, none of the studies has tried to gauge public opinion about this new approach to journalism practice.

This study provided insight into a journalistic practice that developed over the past decade and a half in response to the vanishing newspaper reader and disappearing participant in civic affairs. Furthermore, this study provided insight into the public's views on traditional journalistic characteristics.

At a time when newspaper readership, participation in civic life, and the credibility of journalism are at all-time lows, this study helped answer broader questions about journalism: Is traditional journalism meeting the public's expectations? Is the civic journalism movement on the right track? The results of this survey suggest that, in many cases, the public and the press, including traditional journalism and the civic journalism movement, are on separate tracks headed in different directions and unless something is done to better meet the public's expectations, civic participation, newspaper readership, and the credibility of the press may continue to decline.

While it is reassuring to know that the survey respondents overwhelmingly endorse accuracy and unbiased reporting, it is important to recognize that these same expectations can cause the public to turn away from the news.

When Jayson Blair fabricates the news at the New York Times or star foreign correspondent Jack Kelley is accused of inventing parts of stories reported by USA Today, the public's trust in the news media is shaken and the reasons for reading the news are threatened.

It is also important to note that long-held norms of traditional journalism, being a watchdog and rapid reporting, are not strongly valued by a majority of the survey respondents. Only 49 per cent said being a watchdog of powerful people and the government was extremely important, and 35 per cent said rapid reporting was extremely important.

But when the survey respondents were analysed by age, the press as watchdog was popular in the oldest age group. Over three-fifths of adults 55 years or older said the news media's traditional role of being a watchdog was extremely important.

Offering solutions to community problems, a characteristic of civic journalism, was strongly endorsed by only half of the survey participants as a whole, but when different segments were analysed, this public journalism practice was found to be more popular than first thought. The popularity of offering solutions is most evident among those who have traditionally been disenfranchised from the power sources of government and business: African Americans, Hispanics, adults with less income and education, and women.

Perhaps these groups are looking to news media as a source for help. Do the public's expectations of local news fit the traditional journalism model, the civic journalism movement, or some other ideal? The factor analysis of thirteen roles and characteristics of journalism revealed four dimensions with being a good neighbour-not watchdog, unbiased and accurate, or fast-representing the dominant expectation.

Being a good neighbour included caring about your community, highlighting interesting people and groups in the community, understanding the local community, and offering solutions to community problems. The expectation that the press should be a good neighbour may be related to declining trust in the news media and declining attention to news.

If the public expects the press to be a good neighbour but the press fails in that role because it sees its professional responsibility as a watchdog, there is clearly a disconnect between the public's expectations and the press' expectations which civic journalism practices may not be able to fix.

Buzz Merritt and Maxwell McCombs argue for an expanded watchdog role of the press that is consonant with the good neighbour perspective: News media need to be creative watchdogs and agenda setters scanning the horizon for the gaps in current public life.

Part of this larger watchdog role is functioning as social radar, not just a chronicler of what government and other institutions are doing right now, whether good or bad. This means discovering the concerns of citizens and defining what the public needs to know in very expansive terms.

But for this expanded watchdog role to resonate with the public, the news media must educate the public and even persuade the public that in the role of watchdog, they are looking out for the public in the same way that a good neighbour would. According to Andrew Kohut, director of the Pew Research Centre for the People and the Press, a decade and a half ago, which was about the time of the first civic journalism projects?

The public thought the press was "too sensational, too pushy, too rude, too uncaring about people and the public." But most people saw journalists as moral, professional and caring about the interests of the country. Today, the public considers the news media even less professional, less accurate, less moral, less helpful to democracy, more sensational, more likely to cover up mistakes and more biased.

These are not exactly attributes of a good neighbour. Because this study represents only one metropolitan area in the Southwest, additional studies should be conducted in other parts of the country.

Because different communities have different characteristics and needs, it is possible that they have different expectations of their local news. It is also possible that even with different community characteristics and needs, the public's expectations of local news are similar, regardless of community size or geographic location.

Only by replicating this study in other communities can the public's expectations of local news be determined. According to a 3 May 2005 New York Times article, the 1.9 per cent drop in daily circulation and 2.5 per cent decline in Sunday circulation reported by the Audit Bureau of Circulations represented the "largest circulation losses for the industry in more than a decade, and indicate an acceleration of the decline."

The magnitude of the circulation decline for 814 daily newspapers suggests that it is imperative that future studies determine how the public's expectations of local news relate to readership of newspapers and use of other news media. Future studies should also determine how participation in civic life is related to the public's expectations of local news. Finally, it is important for future studies to focus on the public's expectations of news with special attention paid to the concept of the press as a good neighbour. By gaining greater insight into the public's expectations of local news, it may be possible to initiate a dialogue between the public and the press. This dialogue may lead to a closing of the gap between the expectations of the public and the press that could, in the long run, reverse declining attention to news and waning participation in civic life.

CIVIC JOURNALISM AS A MULTI-DIMENSIONAL CONCEPT

In efforts to document the amount of support among reporters and editors, researchers have sought to isolate specific values associated with civic journalism. Bare developed a "personal public journalism" scale that formed a continuum from general goals to specific practices.

Support decreased along the scale in the movement from abstract goals to practices that violate professional detachment. One purpose of this study is to identify where students and professionals might depart in their evaluations of specific goals and practices. We will consider first the possible reactions to a questionnaire item that explicitly mentions "civic journalism" as a reform movement.

"CIVIC JOURNALISM" AS A POLITICIZED TERM

Several proponents of civic journalism have lamented that the term itself has become politicized in that it evokes disdain in professional circles instead of contemplation. Consequently, we expect that the professional respondents, and perhaps some students, will react negatively to a question that merely mentions "civic journalism."

Analysis of responses to this item could help us to evaluate responses to the other questionnaire items: if respondents express support for specific goals and practices, yet object to "civic journalism" itself, this would suggest that they are responding to something not captured by the other attitudinal items.

Given the lack of prior research on differences between professionals and students in support for civic journalism, we propose a research question rather than a formal hypothesis: RQ1: In comparison with professionals, will students express stronger support for "civic journalism" as a general description of the reform movement?

CIVIC JOURNALISM GOALS

The press traditionally understands its role as a disseminator of accurate information that allows individuals to participate as competent citizens. This requires neutrality in the coverage of political actors, institutions, and issues. By contrast, civic journalists argue that news media should not be neutral about the quality of civic participation in their communities.

We asked respondents to assess their support for two goals associated with civic journalism: going beyond the mere transmission of information to increase political participation, and focusing on news that helps a community to solve problems. While these goals are potentially problematic in light of the norm of detachment, they are described at a fairly abstract level, with the threat to autonomy more implicit than explicit.

Thus, we again propose a research question instead of a hypothesis: RQ2: In comparison with professionals, will students express stronger support for civic journalism goals? Civic journalism Practices. We do anticipate differences between professionals and students in the evaluation of practices that might jeopardize autonomy.

For example, we asked respondents to assess their support for news media sponsoring meetings to address local problems. According to professional critics, such events cripple the ability of journalists to remain critical of the favored policies. We also asked respondents to evaluate the use of polls to help journalists decide what should be covered.

Critics have dismissed this technique as another manifestation of how marketing has intruded into the newsroom. Handing news judgement over to the public directly violates the profession's traditional understanding of autonomy. H1: In comparison with professionals, students will express stronger support for practices associated with civic journalism.

FORMAL INSTRUCTION

Participation in a college journalism curriculum should influence the likelihood of students adopting values similar to those of professionals. Weaver and Wilhoit reported that alumni of journalism programmes expressed a connection between their formal education and their current news values. Students are likely to adopt a commitment to professional autonomy-and consequently a reticence about civic journalism-to the extent that instruction emphasizes the conventional understanding of professional detachment and neutrality. Prior participation in a civic journalism project should also predict support, but we did not include this variable because of the minimal presence of civic journalism in the journalism programme where we recruited respondents. The programme had provided only one civic journalism class (in 1998), with an enrollment of eleven students.

ANTICIPATORY SOCIALIZATION

Individuals typically view themselves as members of a profession long before they join a specific organization. "Anticipatory professional socialization" represents the extent to which an individual has thought seriously about a particular career. An important dimension of this process is "identification," or the perception of belonging to a particular group.

This need for professional membership and acceptance might predispose students to reject civic journalism. A central argument of civic journalism is that news media should display their inner workings, thereby becoming more accountable to the public.

But if students begin to value an insider's perspective on newsroom culture, this group identification could evoke an aversion to the civic journalism critique.

WORKING FOR A COLLEGE NEWSPAPER

While these two factors should facilitate the adoption of traditional values, neither duplicates the degree of autonomy experienced by professionals. Working for an independent college newspaper, however, might represent an indelible socializing experience that produces a resistance to civic journalism.

Campus newspapers vary in their degree of independence from journalism departments and university administrations, but a tradition of American universities is that student newspapers should maintain substantial institutional independence.

The experience of working for a campus newspaper-including the sense of empowerment gained from reporting and editing with little or no instructor supervision— should instill an appreciation for autonomy that cannot be duplicated in the classroom.

Theorists of human development have observed that a young person's identification with an occupation or profession facilitates a realization of self identity, and thus many students might become attracted to journalism precisely because it allows them to express independence and personal identity through their writing and news judgement.

H2: Students with campus newspaper experience will be less supportive of civic journalism compared to other students.

INTERVIEWING

Questionnaire items for students and professional journalists were identical in every respect practical. We used paper-and pencil, self-administered questionnaires for both groups. The availability of students in classroom settings allowed us to directly distribute and administer their questionnaires (N=317 respondents), but this degree of supervision was not practical for the professionals' questionnaires.

In both newsrooms, we requested that an administrative assistant place a questionnaire, cover letter, and return envelope in the mail slots of all reporters and editors. Two weeks after the questionnaires were distributed, we distributed a reminder letter to coax potential respondents who had failed to complete a questionnaire. This procedure produced a response rate of 59 per cent for the Journal and 57 per cent for the Tribune. These can be considered relatively high response rates given that the interviews were voluntary and unsupervised. The final sample consists of N=117 professional journalists.

DESCRIPTION OF SAMPLES

Descriptive statistics reveal a range of interest within the student sample regarding journalism as a career goal. When asked if they plan to pursue a career in journalism, 55 per cent disagreed or strongly disagreed, 16 per cent indicated they were not sure, and 29 per cent agreed or strongly agreed.

For the sample of professional journalists, we sought to gather data reflecting variance in newsroom status among reporters and editors. When asked how many years they had worked in journalism, 42 per cent indicated 1 to 10 years, 26 per cent indicated 11-20 years, and 32 per cent reported more than 20 years.

CIVIC JOURNALISM MEASURES

One question asked explicitly about civic journalism: "Several newspapers in recent years have initiated projects known as 'civic journalism.'

Indicate the extent to which you agree with the goals of civic journalism." Respondents were asked to answer using a 1-5 scale for each question, with 1 meaning "strongly disagree" and 5 indicating "strongly agree." No answer (NA) was coded as 3.

Two items described goals: "Local media should focus on news that directly helps a community solve its problems." "Local media should go beyond simply reporting news in efforts to increase public participation."

Two items described practices: "Local media should sponsor community meetings to help citizens solve problems." "Reader or viewer interest polls should be used to help journalists decide what should be covered."

Predictors of Support for Civic Journalism. Variables used to predict students' support for civic journalism include journalism experiences in college and support for traditional media roles.

College Journalism Instruction. A summed two-item scale (r=.40) assessed the extent of formal instruction:

"Are you a major in the UNM Department of Communication and Journalism?"

"How many news writing courses have you taken at the college level? Include any courses taken this semester." Career Anticipation. A summed 6-item scale (alpha=.85) measured the extent to which students had anticipated a career in journalism. Responses to the first two questions were coded as yes=2; no, NA=1.

"Do you plan to write news for the Daily Lobo?"

"Do you plan to undertake a news writing or editing internship?"

For the remaining questions, respondents used a 1-5 scale with 1 meaning "strongly disagree" and 5 "strongly agree."

"I plan to pursue a career in journalism."

"I hope to work in a newsroom."

"My interest in a news-related career is growing stronger.

"I have always wanted to be a journalist."

College Newsroom Experience. A summed two-item scale (r=.38) assessed the extent of involvement with the university newspaper.

"Have you been a news writer for the Daily Lobo?"

"Have you worked as an editor for the Daily Lobo?"

Dissemination Role. A single item measured support for the role of news media in disseminating information. Respondents used a 1-5 scale, with 1 meaning "not important" and 5 indicating "extremely important."

"How important is it for the media to concentrate on news that is of interest to the widest possible public?" Interpretive Role. A single item scale measured support for the interpretive role of news media in covering public affairs.

"How important is it for the media to provide analysis and interpretation of complex problems?"

Adversary Role: A summed two-item scale (r=.18) measured support for the role of the media in acting as an adversary of government.

"How important is it for the media to be an adversary of public officials by being constantly skeptical of their decisions?"

"How important is it for the media to investigate claims and statements made by government?"

The five civic journalism measures were first entered together in a one-way repeated-measures multivariate analysis of variance (MANOVA), with journalism experience (student without newsroom experience, student with newsroom experience, professional) as the independent variable. Using all four algorithms, the analysis showed a significant effect for the dependent variables considered together.

When the civic journalism measures were subjected to separate one-way ANOVAs, significant effects were obtained for the following items: local media should go beyond reporting news to increase participation, local media should sponsor meetings, and polls should be used to help journalists decide on news coverage.

With respect to the premise that news media should attempt to increase participation, there was not a significant difference between students with newsroom experience and professionals-both expressed significantly less support for this goal compared to the students without newsroom experience. The same pattern occurred with the practice of local media sponsoring meetings.

These results suggest that students with newsroom experience were becoming more like professionals and less like their fellow students in their evaluations of civic journalism. Finally, the professionals expressed significantly less support, in comparison to both groups of students, for the use of polls to help journalists decide on coverage. Collectively, the three cases show a clear pattern of decreasing support for civic journalism as the respondents gain experience via newsroom participation.

The first research question asks whether college students, in comparison to professionals, express stronger support for the attitudinal item that explicitly mentions "civic journalism" as a reform movement.

No significant difference was found. RQ2 addresses whether college students express stronger support for civic journalism goals. The means for students and professionals are nearly identical with respect to the premise that local media should focus on news that helps a community to solve problems.

But in the comparison between students without newsroom experience and professionals, a statistically significant difference exists for the item that concerns media going beyond reporting to increase public participation. While the first goal describes an agenda-setting function that facilitates a community response to a problem, it apparently does not evoke suspicion among the professionals to the extent of the second goal.

To "go beyond" the reporting of news might have suggested a kind of advocacy journalism to the professional respondents. Hi states that the students will express stronger support for practices associated with civic journalism. Both measures generated significant differences between the student and professional respondents, in support of Hl.

The second practice in particular (use of polls) would challenge autonomy if respondents interpreted it as diminishing the importance of professional expertise. In the interpretation of these results, it is useful to consider that civic journalism has existed for only about ten years, and consequently the older professional respondents would not have been exposed to it while in college.

Meanwhile, neither of the Albuquerque papers had conducted projects identified as civic journalism. As for the students' exposure, their journalism programme had not adopted civic journalism as a regular component of the curriculum.

Thus, we urge caution in making inferences that would generalize these results. For example, Arant and Meyer found that the amount of civic journalism support was related to whether a newspaper had previously conducted a project.

H2 proposes that students with campus newspaper experience will be less supportive of civic journalism compared to other students. Lending support to H2, students with newsroom experience were less supportive of the goal in which media go beyond reporting to increase participation. This is also the case for the practice of news media sponsoring meetings.

We consider next the importance of campus newspaper experience in relation to other experiences that might explain the erosion of civic journalism support. We decided to examine this deterioration of support with respect to a civic journalism practice in light of our theoretical argument that specific techniques, rather than abstract goals, would more likely generate opposition as professional socialization proceeds.

The largest variance in student responses occurred with the item that advocates media sponsorship of meetings. This variable was used as the dependent variable in a multiple regression model in which the three indicators of educational experiences are entered as an initial block of independent variables. The second block includes the measures of support for traditional media roles.

In the first equation, only newspaper experience accounted for a significant amount of variance. The beta is negative, demonstrating that writing and editing for a campus newspaper diminish potential support for civic journalism.

The second equation addresses RQ3: Will support for traditional media roles predict support for civic journalism? The attitudinal measure for the interpretive role did account for significant incremental variance, but support for the dissemination and adversary roles did not.

All of the betas were positive, however. While these results do not provide overwhelming support in favour of RQ3, they certainly do not suggest a scenario in which the adoption of civic journalism values is accompanied by a rejection of the traditional roles for news media. This study represents the first empirical effort to model the origins of civic journalism values as a function of professional socialization during the college years.

The results confirmed that students tended to be more supportive of civic journalism in comparison to professionals who work in the same community. Gaps between the student and professional respondents emerged when questionnaire items described specific practices that violate the norm of detachment, such as news media promotion of town hall meetings. A subsequent analysis of factors that might explain these results suggests a scenario of professional socialization that begins with students predisposed to support civic journalism. Acquisition of these values during the college years, meanwhile, is not associated with an erosion of commitment to traditional roles.

However, in leaving the classroom for the newsroom, the unmaking of civic journalists might occur as reporters and editors develop a stronger sense of autonomy. One experience in particular— working for the campus paper-appears to instill a sense of autonomy that diminishes acceptance of civic journalism.

A BROADER VIEW OF AUTONOMY

College instruction would ideally promote an open-minded orientation to journalistic roles and an appreciation for both the limitations of routine reporting and the potential for innovation. But those who would reform the curriculum to promote civic journalism must acknowledge the inherent need for increased autonomy during the beginning stages of professional socialization.

The desire for autonomy is an inevitable outcome of the process by which students identify with the profession. Journalistic autonomy, consequently, should be appreciated not as a fixed disposition but as a developmental process.

From the perspective of civic journalism advocates, the results of this study highlight the need for college instruction to encourage a broader conception of journalistic autonomy. However, would-be reformers should acknowledge the importance of autonomy for students and for professionals rather than issuing a wholesale attack on editorial detachment.

The irony of professional autonomy is that it is the best hope for implementing reform even as editorial detachment appears to preclude civic journalism. Civic journalism can challenge students and professionals to reconceptualize autonomy as the independence to transcend conventional practices that would otherwise limit the contribution of the press to democratic life.

LIMITATIONS AND FUTURE RESEARCH

The results of this chapter are based on a single study in one community, thus restricting any inferential claims based on an assumption of external validity. But the findings reflect a certain degree of construct validity given our emphasis on autonomy as a professional value that should dampen support for civic journalism.

Students who work for a campus newspaper should be moving closer to professionals and away from fellow students; the data consistently fit this pattern across various measures of civic journalism support.

Future research would ideally incorporate a panel design of at least two years' duration, with a larger and broader sample of respondents, to track the development of journalistic values as students enter the initial stage of their professional careers. Studies should also incorporate direct attitudinal measures of autonomy as a professional value to supplement the attitudinal and experiential measures used in this study.

We suggest a framework for field research based on the development of operational measures that represent the twentieth-century ethos of professional journalism (*e.g.*, detachment, free press, watchdog role, people's right to know, criticizing institutions) alongside the civic journalism approach (*e.g.*, social responsibility, community building, self-criticizing press institutions, problem-solving).

This approach might generate insight that can be used for the reform of journalism instruction as educators promote autonomy in service to democracy. Public journalism began as a series of experiments in the late 1980s and early 1990s, and soon developed into what Schudson has called "the most impressive critique of journalistic practice inside journalism in a generation" and "the best organized social movement inside journalism in the history of the American press."

Also known as civic journalism, the movement arose in response to a perceived crisis in the role of the press in constituting a public sphere in which citizens could understand and engage productively with the issues of the day. During the first decade, the movement generated an array of innovative practices in newsrooms and communities, as well as an extensive network of journalism practitioners and educators committed to reshaping professional and institutional norms.

The primary philosophical emphasis of public journalism, as manifest in the writings of its leading theorists and practitioners, is on the relationship between the practice of journalism and the democratic work of citizens in a self-governing republic, and suggests journalists are ideally suited to help constitute vital "publics" to deliberate complex issues and engage in collective problem-solving activities.

Public journalism, thus, has set out to help members of the public come to see themselves as citizens, and hold them accountable for grappling with the full complexity of issues and become participants in civil society rather than mere spectators of it.

Still, after more than a decade of practice of public journalism, empirical knowledge of whether and how public journalism has met these goals remains largely based on in-depth case studies. Early literature focused on cases generally acknowledged as the seed-beds of the public journalism movement.

Subsequent comparative research examined other best cases, focusing on changes in newsroom reporting and editing practices, community recognition of public journalism efforts, and shifts in community problem-solving and public deliberation. While researchers found positive evidence in each area, elements were not disaggregated and case studies were often idiosyncratic, making it difficult to measure impact or establish clear relationships among elements.

In their critical review of forty-seven evaluative studies of public journalism, Massey and Haas found that public journalism practices have had limited effects on the attitudes, beliefs, and behaviours of news audiences. They criticize existing research for focusing on "a handful of showcase public-journalism news organizations and projects."

In doing so, they highlight the methodological shortcomings of many of the efforts to assess public journalism, and recommend that future research capture a wider array of experiments and trace the effects of these efforts on community life. With prior research lacking a broad, systematic assessment of public journalism efforts, we set out to provide a holistic analysis of the movement, shedding light on participating organizations, practices, and effects.

An inventory of the archives of the Pew Centre for Civic Journalism found 651 public journalism projects conducted from 1994 to 20027 Our research analyses the inventory using hierarchical regression analysis to trace the effects of organizational factors, project features, story frames, and efforts to involve community members and assess public opinion on three civil society goals:

- Improving citizens' civic competencies,
- Influencing policymaking processes, and
- Increasing civic volunteerism.

The literature on public journalism is extensive, but extracting clear empirical propositions is challenging. First, much of the best literature is normative, advocating a role of the press in improving public life, and tends to draw case-based observations about changes public journalism creates in news organizations.

Second, the large body of case literature is very uneven, ranging from anecdotal and polemic to qualitative and comparative case observation. While it is difficult to untangle the effects of public journalism on civil society given these inconsistencies, there are important insights to be gained from the extant research.

Public journalism research has primarily concentrated on several flagship public journalism newsrooms and projects. Additionally, there are numerous case studies of other cities and regions. These cases, however, have not been analysed using a systematic empirical-quantitative framework.

Here, we consider the scholarship in three domains of public journalism:

- Organization of newsrooms and their effects on individual journalists' values, norms, and behaviour;
- Links between public journalism efforts and changes in news content, framing, and sourcing; and
- Public journalism's impact on electoral knowledge and behaviour, and on citizen participation in public life.

MEDIA ORGANIZATIONS AND NEWS VALUES

There are two broad types of newsroom studies: (1) of news organizations; and (2) of journalists' beliefs and attitudes. While there are no inherent methodological contradictions between them, each tends to have its own understandings of how public journalism is established in newsrooms.

Organizational studies see the adoption of public journalism from the top down, with publisher and editor orientations as the important predictors of public journalism practice. An investment by news organizations in public journalism shapes reporting routines and story content, and accounts for the adoption of the practice over longer periods of time.

This approach posits institutionalization as a property of the organization, with organizational decisions molding the actions and routines, if not beliefs, of individuals within them. Evidence suggests that newsrooms institutionalizing public journalism (*i.e.*, commitments to partnerships with other community organizations and lengthy projects) produce stronger public effects.

A second approach looks at the effect of values of journalists on attitudes and behaviour. Here, the adoption of public journalism values is a prerequisite for genuine individual transformation that leads to newsroom change. Proponents of this approach hold that positive attitudes towards public journalism should precede behavioural change."

This values approach, then, sees change in beliefs and attitudes as generating new public reporting behaviour that underlies the transformation of news organizations. From their review of public journalism studies, Massey and Haas found that journalists are most comfortable with the more "traditional" shadings of public journalism, though some support for more "activist" roles exists.

These mixed results indicate traditional and public journalism beliefs seem to coexist in many newsrooms and within individual journalists, suggesting an "occupational pragmatism." Not surprisingly, "mixed-change" characterizes virtually every case of public journalism, positing a kind of "tipping point" within newsrooms and individuals.

If newsrooms have not tipped, public journalism practice should be weak. As this suggests, both the organizational approach and the news values approach ultimately focus on the degree to which newsrooms have adopted and integrated public journalism practices into the newsroom culture, regardless of whether the spur of this transformation is from the top down or the bottom up.

NEWS COVERAGE AND CONTENT

Research on changes in reporting spurred by public journalism is sparse, with little attention to whether certain topics or frames of reporting are particularly suited to public journalism. Although public journalism often implicitly focuses on community, efforts have addressed a plethora of issues confronting localities, including crime, diversity, education, environment, health, poverty, and, of course, elections and government.

Public journalists have utilized a range of issue frames to structure their reporting, from established conflict and human-interest frames to more novel problem-solving and historical frames. However, little is known about the potency of these framing devices for civil society outcomes or whether certain topics lend themselves to successful public journalism as defined by increases in civic competence and volunteerism.

Instead, most coverage studies focus on the type of content and sources used in public journalism stories, with inconsistent evidence. Some indicate little difference in content, while others have found that public journalism efforts have a greater focus on local concerns and help citizens engage in civic activities.

There is also inconsistent evidence on sourcing. Thus, it remains unclear whether certain public journalism tools, such as encouraging citizen involvement or giving citizen voices greater prominence, improves civil society outcomes.

EFFECTS OF PUBLIC JOURNALISM

The evidence for public journalism effects on civic and public life is partial and incomplete. Studies divide broadly into those investigating the effect of public journalism on electoral outcomes and those addressing civic and public problem solving.

First, there is evidence supporting a positive relationship between citizenfocused journalism and knowledge, trust, and civic participation in elections. There is, however, some evidence to the contrary. Thus, on the whole, studies support a moderate effect of civic electoral coverage in the areas of voter awareness of issues and traditional forms of political participation.

Although untangling political cause and effect is difficult, there is a case for public journalism efforts and broader public engagement. Studies have found an increase in political participation. There is also some evidence that public journalism increases public deliberation and civic problem solving. Moreover, Friedland's study of the "We the People" project in Madison, Wisconsin, found project longevity to have substantial cumulative impact on opinion leaders, media cooperation, and institutional effectiveness, with mixed effects on citizen engagement. If there is episodic coverage with little follow-up, however, a project's cumulative problem-solving effects were attenuated.

In sum, the case-based evidence shows effects of increased civic and public problem solving in limited areas. Past theorizing and case studies concerning the practices and effects of public journalism do not present a clear picture of the consequences of this shift in coverage for civil society. Scholars have focused on different levels of analysis-organization, newsroom, story, and citizens-and attended to a wide range of outcome variables.

Results have not been consistent, though this inconsistency may be a function of community and organizational factors that are not the focus of a particular case study. After a decade of broad practice, it is unclear which organizational factors beyond length of adoption and integration of public journalism contribute to the success of public journalism efforts.

Likewise, beyond attention to certain patterns of sourcing and shifts in content, it is not known whether the success of public journalism efforts is connected with attention to certain topics-such as poverty or crime-and particular frames of reference - such as human interest or problem-solving.

On a more basic level, evidence is lacking on whether particular ways of giving voice to the perspectives of citizens improve civil society in the ways that theorists of public journalism attest. Accordingly, we examine here the effects of a wide range of potentially explanatory variables on assessments of the outcomes of a wide cross-section of public journalism efforts between 1994 and 2002. This study attempts to answer how the influence of organizational factors, project features, story frames, and efforts to involve community members and assess public opinion uniquely contribute to three broad goals of public journalism: (1) improving civic skills among citizens; (2) influencing the policymaking process; and (3) increasing levels of civic volunteerism.

Accordingly, we offer the following research questions to guide our analysis:

- RQ1: What features of news organizations involved in public journalism projects appear to influence whether sponsored efforts increase civic skills of citizens, public input on policymaking, and levels of civic volunteerism?

- RQ2: What features of public journalism projects appear to influence whether sponsored efforts increase civic skills of citizens, public input on policymaking, and levels of civic volunteerism?
- RQ3: What types of story frames used by journalists involved in public journalism projects appear to influence whether sponsored efforts increase civic skills of citizens, public input on policymaking, and levels of civic volunteerism?
- RQ4: What types of efforts to involve community members and assess public opinion appear to influence whether sponsored efforts increase civic skills of citizens, public input on policymaking, and levels of civic volunteerism?

METHODS

Data

This study is based on data collected at the University of Wisconsin-Madison from the archives of the Pew Centre for Civic Journalism. During its ten years of operation as the principle incubator for the movement, between 1993 and 2003, the Pew Centre collected examples of public journalism projects submitted by U.S. newsrooms seeking funding, competing for awards, and/or seeking informal recognition and advice.

Between January 2000 and May 2001, this archive was systematically examined for all evidence of public journalism experiments, with the archive structured into a set of cases organized by discrete projects and publication dates.

A qualitative coding scheme was developed to capture a descriptive account of project attributes, including, but not limited to: the news organization (circulation, population served, partnerships); the project (topic, publication dates, presentation format); the news frames, sources, and civic linkages used in news construction; and the civic practices, polls, and public deliberative events used to give citizens a voice.

In addition, outcomes such as improved civic and deliberative skills, increased public funding and volunteerism, and improved public policy processes were gauged from these reports.

A quantitative coding guide was developed so that statistical tools could be used to more systematically analyse these data. The final inventory of the archive contained a total of 651 cases of public journalism completed between 1994 and 2002.

Although the study sample is limited to public journalism projects in the Pew Centre's archive and undercounts the full range of public journalism work conducted by U.S. newsrooms during this period, it captures public journalism as practiced by the most dedicated of self-identified public journalism practitioners.

Thus, the sample, while biased in favour of best practices, provides a solid foundation upon which to assess a broad range of public journalism practices and evaluate the movement's reach and impact on community life.

Measures

Items coded from the public journalism projects were used to operationalize six general clusters of variables: (1) outcomes of the public journalism project, (2) features of the news organization, (3) features of the project, (4) features of the stories, particularly story frames, (5) citizen involvement, and (6) public assessment.

In the analyses reported in this chapter, the outcomes of public journalism were used as dependent variables predicted by the other five sets of variables.

OUTCOMES OF PUBLIC JOURNALISM

Initially, six outcomes of public journalism projects were identified: improved citizenship skills, enhanced public deliberative processes, increased private funding and donations, expanded volunteer efforts, and greater public policy and civic organization responsiveness.

These items were dummy coded with "present" coded as 1, "absent" as O. The six items were then examined through exploratory factor analysis and three factors emerged.

First, improved civic competence is an additive index consisting of two measures of public journalism outcomes: improved citizenship skills and improved public deliberative processes second, improved political process was constructed by adding two items: changes in public policy and the formation of new civic organizations.

Finally, heightened volunteerism is a two-item additive index consisting of measures of raised private funds and donations, and increased level of volunteer efforts.

FEATURES OF THE NEWS ORGANIZATION

For news organizations' publication schedule, daily publication was coded as 1 and all other scheduling formats as zero. Level of circulation was measured using a six-point scale with 1 representing circulations under 50,000 and 6 representing circulations over 5 million.

Type of population served was measured on a four-point scale with 1 for smaller populations and 4 a national audience. Level of involvement in public journalism represents the length of time in years the news organization experimented with these practices.

Partnerships was coded for evidence of other media or civic organizations involved in the project with "none" coded as 0 "either media or civic" as 1, and "both civic and media" as 2.35

FEATURES OF THE PROJECT

Eleven specific categories were identified to code each project according to the primary topic covered, including community, crime, diversity, economy, education, environment, health, poverty, youth, election, and government.

These items were dummy coded with "present" coded as 1, "absent" as 0 Project branding was constructed with three items, each used to develop a unique project identification, including evidence of a formal presentation format, clearly stated aim of the projects, and guide for reader comprehensiveness. Each item was dummy-coded with 1 being "present," O being "absent."

Mobilizing information consisted of two items: empowerment information (to help citizens engage in civic activities) and civic linkages (contact information for public officials and civic leaders). Each item was dummy-coded with "present" coded as 1, "absent" as 0.

STORY FRAMES

Each project was coded according to six frames used in journalistic reporting: investigative frame, conflict frame, issue-oriented frame, problem-solving frame, human-interest frame, and historical frame. These items were dummy-coded with 1 representing a frame being "present," 0 for "absent."

CITIZEN INVOLVEMENT

To measure a project's effort to include citizens' input, each case was coded for evidence of (a) inviting citizens to provide feedback, and (b) giving them a voice in the publication of their community's conversation. These two variables were dummy-coded with 1 for "present," 0 for "absent."

Each project was also coded for evidence of the news organization's effort to assess the climate of opinion on the project and/or issue including (a) survey and (b) focus group research. Surveys could be the organization's own scientific or informal surveys, or surveys provided by other sources. Each was dummy-coded with 1 for "present," 0 for "absent."

RESULTS

In order to examine the relationships between public journalism efforts and their purported impact on civic competence, the political process, and volunteerism, we performed hierarchical multiple regression analyses in which organizational factors, project features, story frames, and efforts to involve community members and assess public opinion served as independent variables predicting the three criterion variables.

Tables are organized in a manner that highlights the order in which the different blocks of independent variables were entered into the regression and indicates the incremental variance in the criterion variable explained by each successive block. We consider how each additional block affects the standardized betas of the variables being considered simultaneously, and focus on the final standardized coefficients for the full model.

IMPROVED CIVIC COMPETENCE

The regression model predicting improved civic competence performed quite well, as it accounted for a total of 52.9 per cent of variance. The features of the news organization were substantial predictors (20.4 per cent of variance), with news organizations that served small or medium communities and that partnered either with civic organizations or other media the most successful.

Improved citizenship was also anchored in the actual features of the public journalism project (16.4 per cent of incremental variance). The focus on certain social problems such as poverty seems well suited for the purpose of improving citizenship. On the other hand a focus on negative or individualized concerns such as crime and health counter this objective. The news frames utilized in public journalism stories accounted for 10.3 per cent of the variance in the model. Among the frames, it seems clear that the problem-solving frame was most closely linked with reported improvement in citizenship. Conversely, the human-interest frame appeared to produce the opposite effects, reducing the perception of an increase in civic skills among the audience exposed to public journalism efforts.

Above and beyond characteristics of the news organization, features of the project, and selection of story frames, enhanced citizenship seemed to be contingent on involving citizens in the process of public journalism. In our model this block accounted for 4.6 per cent of the final variance, with inviting audience/reader feedback and giving citizens an actual voice serving as key contributors.

In addition, administering surveys in the community was also positively related to improving citizenship in the community. In the final model, public journalism's reported ability to improve citizenship was linked

- To news organizations that serve smaller communities and partner with other community organizations,
- To projects that focus on topics such as poverty as opposed to crime or health,
- To reporting that adopted problem-solving story frames over human interest story frames, and
- To project elements that involved citizens through feedback, sourcing, and surveys.

These findings support many of the conclusions drawn from case study analysis, while clarifying how these different factors intersect to shape citizenship.

IMPROVED POLITICAL PROCESS

The regression model used to gauge political process improvements—accounted for 22.6 per cent of the variance. In this model, the features of the news organization were not as critical as in the previous model, accounting for only 4.2 per cent of the total variance explained. In the final model, only a single organizational factor-partnerships with other community or media organizations-was a significant predictor of improvements in the political process.

The features of the project were substantial predictors of an improved political process, with 10.8 per cent of the variance explained by this block. Among this group, community and education topics are positively related with the dependent variable, while concentrating on the poverty topic is negatively related.

This suggests limited responsiveness in terms of process responsiveness when projects address the needs of the underprivileged. The framing of news also explained variation in improving the political process, with the investigative frame as the strongest predictor, followed by a problem-solving frame. Conflict, explanatory, and human-interest frames appear to be irrelevant for this purpose, while the use of a historical frame is negatively related.

This seems to indicate that attention to long-standing community issues is less effective at spurring political responsiveness than focused attention on current problems or scandals. Engaging citizens with the project or seeking their opinion does not seem to be particularly consequential for improvements to the political process.

These two blocks only account for.5 per cent of the incremental variance and yield no significant predictors. In the final model, then, partnerships, reporting on community and education (as opposed to poverty), and investigative and problem-solving (but not historical) story frames appear to spur responsiveness in terms of improvements to the political process.

IMPROVED VOLUNTEERISM

The model predicting levels of volunteerism in the community explained 22.7 per cent of the variance. As was the case for improving the political process, organizational features do not play as large a role as they do in improving citizenship, explaining only 3.1 per cent of the variance in reports of improved volunteerism, whereas project features explained a sizable amount (13.5 per cent) of incremental variance.

Again, establishing a partnership with another news or civic organization is positively related to increased volunteerism, making this a consistent predictor across all three models. Project topics such as community, crime, and education are linked with reports of increased volunteerism.

In terms of news framing, concentrating on human-interest seems to increase civic volunteerism, whereas historical frames have the opposite effect, consistent with the negative association in the model explaining political process improvement. This block explains 5.0 per cent of the incremental variance.

Finally it seems that citizens' engagement with the project and seeking citizens' opinions are not necessary to improve volunteerism. The model shows a small incremental contribution of these two blocks (incremental variance explained 1.1 per cent) with only the use of surveys actually being negatively related to volunteerism.

In sum, partnerships; reporting on community, crime, and education; and human-interest (but not historical) story frames appear to spur reported increases in volunteerism. This study is the first to explore a broad range of public journalism projects, incorporating a near census of the field of efforts between 1994 and 2002 and tracing the reported effects on civil society.

Further, it incorporates multiple levels of specificity, examining the effects of organizational features, particular projects, story frames, and citizen involvement in civic and public life. Our findings, thus, provide the first holistic assessment of the impact of public journalism on U.S. civil society and critical insights for future research and practice. Before we discuss these implications, we first offer an interpretation of these findings and discuss some of their limitations.

Although we find organizational features such as publication schedule, circulation level, and population type are associated with certain civil society goals of public journalism, most of these effects appear to be mediated through the structure of public journalism projects and journalistic framing.

One organizational feature is consistently found to shape the general success of these efforts: partnerships with other organizations. In our final models, partnerships predicted improved citizenship, political processes, and volunteerism, indicating me centrality of organizations' connections for efforts to renew civil society.

This seems most true of efforts to improve citizenship, where institutional connections may provide the basis for civic recruitment and broader project scope. Additionally, a project's focus also appears to be linked to certain civil society outcomes.

A focus on education, community, crime, and poverty were found to relate to the achievement (or failure) of civil society goals. The potency of a particular issue varied across these goals. For example, focusing on community and education was related to positive effects on the political process and civic volunteerism, with projects focusing on crime also linked to volunteerism.

The positive association of the these topics on political process and volunteerism outcomes suggests that projects directed at issues affecting larger cross-sections of the population are particularly effective at improving processes and spurring action. Notably, a negative relationship was detected between a focus on crime and health topics-individualized issues typically directed at those with higher socio-economic status-and the improvement of civic skills, whereas a focus on poverty was found to have a positive effect on the development of civic competencies, as might be expected.

However, a focus on poverty was negatively related to improvements in the political process, suggesting a lack of elite responsiveness to issues affecting the underprivileged. Future research must work to disentangle these effects and identify the types of issues that produce desirable community outcomes.

Particularly notable are the results regarding the emphasis on certain story frames. Our findings suggest that problem-solving frames have the most pronounced effects on efforts to improve citizenship and the political process, and investigative news frames were also positively correlated with improvements in the political process.

In sharp contrast, however, human-interest and historical news frames appeared to generally reduce the success of public journalism efforts at achieving civil society goals, particularly in relation to citizenship. Our results for human-interest frames show a reduction in the development of civic skills, yet an increase in civic volunteerism, which is surprising given past research on episodic framing and the reduction of a sense of shared responsibility.

46 For historical news frames, we observed negative effects on both political process and volunteerism outcomes, suggesting that projects revolving around long-standing issues are less effective at spurring political or public responses. This pattern of results points to the importance of journalistic choices in framing news stories around certain themes and organizing devices.

Investigative and problem-solving frames would appear to spur involvement and action, whereas historical frames, and to a lesser extent human interest frames, appear to reduce responsiveness to community problems. While not invalidating frames that spur long-term reflection on deep-seated problems, these results do question how stories are organized and presented.

Further, it may be that the cross-sectional nature of these case assessments does not allow an observation of the effects of certain story frames over time. Finally, efforts to involve citizens in public journalism-*i.e.*, inviting feedback from citizens, giving them a voice in coverage and their communities, and surveying their attitudes and behaviours-were linked to the improvement of civic competencies.

In total, these results suggest that journalists who understand the perspectives of citizens are more able to construct projects that improve citizens' civic and deliberative skills. It may also be that asking citizens for their perspective and giving them public forums is fundamentally mobilizing, something we might call a type of "civic Hawthorne effect."

This study, while comprehensive, is not without limitations. Most notably, the cases that function as our units of analysis rely on some self assessment of effects by the editors and journalists involved in the projects. This may create some biases. However, these would seem to be equivalent across all news organizations in the study, thereby rendering differences observed meaningful.

Moreover, every effort was made to validate the outcome variables, which were often self-assessed against real world indicators of change. The reliability of these self-assessments was found to be well above the threshold for acceptability, further suggesting the validity of the data. The implications of this study, even with these limitations, are broad-reaching. They can be used to inform the next generation of public journalism efforts and structure research efforts. Future research should consider the longitudinal effects of public journalism projects on civil society. Using small-N comparative historical methods, researchers might more closely explore the precise configurations of organization, project, and story frame that lead to the most effect on civic and public outcomes.

Finally, there are broad theoretical implications of our study. If historical frames are demobilizing, for example, what alternative frames could address long-term, deep-seated community problems addressed by journalists interested in democracy? If problem-solving and investigative frames are mobilizing, what are the specific features of these types of projects that encourage changes in civil society? If certain topics seem to lend themselves to successful public journalism outcomes, how might coverage of other issues be constructed to spur responsiveness on the part of the public and policymakers?

Clearly, there is much that remains to be learned about the effects of public journalism projects on civil society. Nonetheless, if the findings presented here are any indication, the effects of the projects are considerable and broad reaching, and certainly provide empirical support for the normative project of public journalism.

6

News Gathering in Visual Journalism

State political reporter at *The Age,* Richard Baker, was enjoying a drink at the pub one evening when an "older bloke" told him a yarn about the seals in Port Phillip Bay. It seemed the state government had built an expensive covered platform out in the bay for the seals to loll about on. But the seals were unimpressed. They were snubbing the new platform and refusing to budge from an antiquated, tumbledown structure nearby.

The story had several fine elements for a news piece; among them, government extravagance and appealing marine mammals. After a few calls to check it out, and the dispatch of a photographer to provide a visual showing the old and new platforms, with the seals firmly ensconced on the old one, Richard had a front page story.

The next day it was covered widely by radio and television and had become one of Victoria's more memorable human interest stories of the year.

Journalists call the process of finding and developing an original item "breaking a story" and for most reporters it's what journalism is all about. Richard describes breaking news as "the most fun part of the job". It means "doing something no one else is doing and going home at night knowing that tomorrow it is going to be all over the radio and TV and at this stage you're the only person who knows about it". (Interview with Richard Baker.)

This section is about finding and developing news stories, both those initiated by reporters themselves and those assigned by the news desk.

The news day: Every day in every newsroom begins with a series of story possibilities. During the day some of these will become items for publication or broadcast. Extra stories will emerge while some of the original ones will fall out of consideration. The way in which each day's news agenda is developed is complex and, like so many other features of the industry, varies from one medium and one newsroom to the next.For instance, in a large metropolitan newsroom, most of the day's news will fall into one of four categories:

- First, there will be the predicted events, which are known about in advance and filed in the newsroom's diary. These can include sittings of parliament, council meetings and court hearings, media conferences,

the release of official reports, scheduled meetings or negotiations, all sports events, the release of official statistics, regular financial decisions and events, openings, previews and pre-arranged interviews.
- *Then there are watching briefs*: These are the monitoring activities that generate news, including the calls to the emergency services, monitoring other media, stake-outs (at a scene where a newsmaker might appear) and running stories (where new developments are expected in an existing story or where the story can be developed by journalists finding new angles).
- *There are unpredicted events*: These include accidents, fires, natural disasters, attacks; things no one suspected in advance would happen.
- Finally there are stories which might be termed initiated stories. Like the example at the start of this section, they fall outside the routine news cycle and begin with a reporter's observation or a tip-off from a member of the public.

Non-metropolitan newsrooms, and those that don't have a daily output, including suburban papers, metro weeklies and so on, are likely to have a different pattern of gathering news from metro newsrooms. They may place more emphasis on initiated stories and less on events such as stake-outs or daily emergency stories.

Reporters can be given assignments by the chief of staff or editor. But newsrooms also rely on their journalists to generate stories themselves, within the framework of the organisation's specific news agenda. For instance, agency reporters need to be able to think of ways to develop new angles to stories that are already part of the news agenda because news wire services tend to stick closely to the main events and issues of each day.

Television and radio also usually stick closely to the main events of the day. This is because—with the exception of round-the-clock services—broadcast news programmes are of fixed duration. The first priority for a television bulletin is to touch all the main bases of the day's events. There's usually room for one quirky or lighthearted item at the end. Radio's priority is to continually update the main stories of interest to the station's audience.

Reporters who work in radio and TV know their programmes have "no back page"—in other words, there's nowhere to put the stories of minor significance that are useful fillers in newspapers. But because radio is a high rotation medium, it also has some room for stories of limited impact which can be run on a single bulletin.

Online news services have the capacity to run unlimited numbers of stories. But experience suggests that the stories that receive most of the "hits"—that is, the stories accessed by the largest number of readers—are those placed at the top of the story list on the screen and which are therefore deemed to be the most significant stories of the moment.

INITIATING STORIES

At News Ltd in Sydney, pitching stories is seen as fundamental to each reporter's daily routine. If they're not walking in the door and greeting the chief of staff with at least one story idea, the day's already a failure. We tell them, if they're sitting at their desk waiting for the chief of staff to give them a story, they're not a reporter, they're a clever clerk. We expect people to come up with ideas constantly and to follow those ideas through.

One metropolitan newsroom tests its trainees" ability to find news using a series of exercises. In one exercise, they are made to head out onto the streets without their mobile phones and come back with a publishable Covering assigned stories—such as this opening of a public garden—is a standard part of many reporters" work story. What do they find?

One reporter doorknocked nearby brothels for her story. Another went no further than a local lingerie shop for a quirky piece on the most popular item of women's underwear (the thong) and another used her skills of observation to pick up signs of domestic life in a nearby commercial building. Investigating further she found young squatters had turned the top floor into a personal arts commune.

Not all newsrooms require reporters to generate so many of their own stories. Certainly there is an expectation that reporters with their own round will come up with original ideas and break news. But general reporters may be expected to spend most of their time following up story ideas given to them by the assignments desk. Newsrooms with smaller staffs—for instance those in non-metropolitan areas—may need all their journalists to both cover a large number of stories assigned by the chief of staff as well as find their own material.

Covering assigned stories inevitably leaves a journalist with less time to dig up their own material, but it's a truism in journalism that any reporter who can pitch good stories to the chief of staff on a regular basis will be given more time to follow their own leads and will spend less time chasing the chief of staff's ideas.

The story with which we began this section came about because the reporter was an approachable person who was prepared to listen to a stranger's suggestion and check it out. Had the reporter been out sailing in Port Phillip Bay rather than having a drink in the pub, he might have noticed the unused seal platform for himself and generated the same story from observation rather than a tip-off. News stories can come about in many different ways, which are covered in the previous section of this book. But once the original idea is formulated, the process towards publication usually follows the sequence outlined below.

- From story idea to publication
- Research (this can include calls to check the story and finding an angle)

- Story idea
- Publication
- Interviews Writing and checking Sub editing
- The news conference

No matter who initiates the story idea, at some point early on in the process, it will need to be discussed by the reporter and the chief of staff or someone else in the editorial process. The reporter, the chief of staff and the editor all need to have an idea of the direction the story will take so that it can be fitted into the daily news hierarchy which determines where it will run in the paper, programme or site.

Chiefs of staff and news editors take this information to the news conference so that the various stories on offer for that day can be weighed up against each other to work out the final shape of the paper or broadcast.

Most large newspaper and television newsrooms hold at least two news conferences each day. At the morning conference, the editorial staff (which may include the editor, foreign editor, chief of staff and so on, depending on the size of the newsroom) discuss the day's potential stories, how they might be approached, who will be reporting them, any potential problems such as legal ones, and what rival news outlets might be doing. They hold another conference in the afternoon, to review what stories they have and work out a more detailed version of where the various news items will appear in the publication or broadcast.

THE STORY BRIEF

If a story is assigned to a reporter by the news desk, the reporter will be briefed on the way they should approach it. The story brief may include instructions on the kind of finished item that is expected—that is a human interest story, or a hard news item.

The reporter may be given suggestions as to the angle to take and who to interview. Working to a brief means a reporter has far less autonomy about how to prepare and write their stories than those outside the news business might imagine.

But for young reporters it can provide a useful guide to the way the finished story should read. Reporters who fail to follow the initial story brief can find themselves criticised by their news editor if their story is subsequently dropped. Journalists who generate their own stories have more control over the direction their work takes than those working on assigned pieces. They usually have the opportunity to decide how to frame their pieces and who to talk to when gathering the information needed to write them.

Chiefs of staff and editors value reporters with a positive attitude towards assignments—that is, reporters who don't try to talk down or reject the stories they're given. That doesn't mean that all assignments are potentially good stories. It means that chiefs of staff and editors know that the publication or programme has to be filled.

So reporters who want to challenge their assignments will find the process easier if they have better ideas of their own to offer. Reporters who try to "kill" stories to which they're assigned will quickly gain a reputation for negativity and laziness. Assigning editors are more likely to accept a change to the story brief if the reporter offers an alternative way of approaching it.

THE NEW BROADCAST

In the competition to survive, network news has been forced to rethink what it has to offer that rival services, such as cable and local news, do not. The quality and expertise of network news correspondents is one such asset. When documentaries were still allocated exposure on prime time, correspondents could take advantage of the opportunity to show their stuff. Nowadays, the insertion of longer forms of reportage within the daily summary of the news is a way in which to convince viewers to prefer the offerings of one network over that of the other two.

These days, long form survives on the evening news in the truncated version of four-minute segments, which are usually incorporated in the broadcast in between the spot news of the day. Despite all the angst expressed by Washington correspondents, the items reported on any one of the three network evening news programmes do not seem that different to the casual viewer—nor do the respective abilities of the competing correspondent corps.

Van Gordon Sauter, president of Fox News and former president of CBS News, deplored this sameness in the November 1992 issue of *Communicator*, published by the Radio Television News Directors Association: "There is an inhibiting, discouraging sameness to TV news. The journalism schools, consultants, researchers, timid corporate executives, and narrowly targeted audiences have had the impact of reducing TV news to a spongy blur existing in a narrow framework of creativity.... It is as though each city out there had three or five or seven newspapers, and each had the same format, the same target audience, the same editorial attitude, the same photographs."

His boss, Fox chairman Rupert Murdoch, agreed, including local news in the indictment: "I honestly cannot distinguish one programme from another. It's like every news director in the marketplace graduates from the same dumb journalism class." Sauter's attempts to enliven CBS News had included a sharp reduction in the number of stories originating in Washington and a formula that defined story values in terms of "moments" that could capture the audience.

There is, however, no evidence that the audience was enlarged during Sauter's watch. Moreover, his actions generated considerable unhappiness in the ranks of veteran CBS correspondents who had inherited their news-gath ering ideas from Edward R. Murrow, the pioneering newsman who had hired most of the individuals who became the nucleus of the CBS correspondent corps, first in radio and then in television.

The fact remains that it is fairly predictable that the evening news programmes on ABC, CBS, and NBC will each have the same lineup of the day's major developments. They do not even look that different, with computer-driven graphics illustrating the spots introduced by an anchor sitting at a desk. Except for the personalities of their anchors, the main points of difference between these shows are subtleties: the relative competence of reporters covering the same story, the balance of features versus hard news in the coverage of secondary events, and the order in which these events are presented to viewers.

When John Chancellor retired as an editorialist on NBC's *Nightly News* in 1993, it marked the end of an eleven-year tradition on that broadcast, the only one of the three shows to sustain such a feature into recent years. CBS had long since abandoned a similar heritage developed by Eric Sevareid and Bill Moyers.

The changes occurring in evening newscasts coincide with similar changes taking place in magazines and newspapers. Evening newspapers are disappearing from the scene, newspaper circulations have ceased to grow, and weekly newsmagazines such as *Time* and *U.S. News* and *World Report* have recently undergone design changes in the way they present information.

Television is at its best when communicating live images of graphic events-floods along the Mississippi, "ethnic cleansing" in Bosnia, war and famine in Somalia, fires and looting in Los Angeles, hurricanes in Florida, a student uprising in Tiananmen Square, tearing down the Berlin Wall.

Even Washington sometimes provides such opportunities for dramatic, direct coverage, such as the Army-McCarthy hearings, President John E Kennedy's funeral, and the Anita Hill-Clarence Thomas confrontation during the Senate hearings on the latter's nomination to the Supreme Court. But news of this dramatic dimension does not happen every day, and the day-to-day flow of the news from Washington does not usually fit the limited capacities of TV to communicate complex ideas.

It is the job of the network correspondent on the evening news to explain with a very broad brush stroke what has happened in Washington that day, to put what pictures and sound bites are available into intelligible focus, to help the viewer understand what he or she is seeing and hearing when events themselves do not carry their own message.

Moreover, this has to be done in a very short period of time allocated to the spot on the total broadcast, which itself is of very limited duration. The job of the network Washington correspondent is thus both challenging and frustrating.

When the news is exciting and graphic, audiences no longer have to wait until the dinner hour for their first glimpse of daily dramas, which can be seen earlier on CNN or local newscasts.

Having lost their monopoly, the nightly network news programmes thus would have needed to change whether or not there had been a turnover of network ownership or new executive producers in New York. Takeouts on important running topics in the news are one way to add a valuable dimension to the evening news.

One consequence, however, has been that there are fewer minutes available on the broadcast for hard news out of Washington.

Although some Washington correspondents carry out these longer features, such stories generally call for different talents than those possessed by "crash" reporters who scramble to make deadlines on breaking news. And correspondents who work on these longer features have less and less time to cover the general run of Washington news.

The dilemma created by these in-depth segments, now a regular feature of network evening news, is that on the one hand, they provide an opportunity for network correspondents to make use of their expertise on significant areas of the news, such as science, health, and education, but on the other hand, they decrease the resources available for coverage of the daily flow of news.

The model for these longer takeouts is "American Agenda;" the concept developed by Paul Friedman, then executive producer of ABC's *World News Tonight* with Peter Jennings. The idea for doing longer pieces has been around for a long time. Friedman himself had worked on features called "Segment 3" on NBC's *Nightly News* before joining ABC. CBS called them enterprise stories in the sixties, before abandoning them for the time being. But the execution of Friedman's "American Agenda" has accompanied the ascent of *World News Tonight* into the number-one slot in the ratings of network evening news programmes.

CBS's *Evening News* with Dan Rather calls its current version of the long form "Eye on America." NBC's original longer segment, "Daily Difference," on the *Nightly News* with Tom Brokaw—after a period in which it had difficulty defining what its label meant—was renamed "America CloseUp" in imitation of its two network rivals. The general consensus was that NBC's special segments under former executive producer Steve Friedman had tended to feature a softer approach to the news. An old hand from another network thought that this had turned out to be the wrong approach at the wrong time:

When Steve Friedman introduced the "Daily Difference" on *NBC Nightly News* it was a period of international upheaval, overwhelming stories, real tough issues. "Daily Difference" was built around categories labeled by producers with no thought of what, if anything, they might mean to viewers. These special segments have become a code word for the pictorial and frothy items. Education, employment, race-these are the grist of what these longer pieces ought to be about. Done correctly, longer stories on the evening newscast can contribute a lot. But Friedman chose the soft route and NBC is slipping. There was no reason to stay tuned.

Under executive producer Erik Sorenson, the *CBS Evening News* has a tendency towards "user friendly" pieces, such as the best way to buy a used car or how to plan for your retirement. "Eye on America" is supposed to tell the audience what other people are talking about across the country.

ABC's "American Agenda" is more focused, according to two ABC producers: When "American Agenda" started, the ABC evening news was in a rut. There was weakness in the body of the show.

It was foreign-news heavy. Jennings was perceived as a foreigner. He couldn't pronounce "Ohio" the way people from there pronounce it. We wanted to make our coverage of domestic news credible.

So they created these special beats: family, health, education, environment, drugs. Correspondents and producers were assigned full time to each other.

"American Agenda" pieces by definition are supposed to offer a solution to the problem being covered. If not a solution, a point of view. It's easier to make a connection with an audience that way. "Eye on America" doesn't do that. NBC's longer pieces are really more feature-ish than the other two. "American Agenda" is a harder version of special segments. It takes a major commitment of resources to do that. When Jeff Gralnick came over from ABC to become executive producer for NBC's *Nightly News* in the spring of 1993, one of the things he brought with him was the thinking behind "American Agenda." "America CloseUp" almost immediately focused on stories that outlined not only a problem in the news but also a possible solution, one of the guidelines for "American Agenda" pieces on ABC. (Fads have a way of chasing each other on television programming.) Of course, all problems do not have solutions readily at hand, and such segments run the risk of claiming too much for a single local example of an attempt to cope with issues that are national in scope. By coincidence, just as Gralnick was bringing the formula to NBC, Emily Rooney, the new executive producer for ABC's *World News Tonight*, was telling staffers there that the problem-solution approach to "America Agenda" was a hackneyed idea in her opinion, and she proposed abandoning it.

The willingness of ABC to make a major commitment to new ideas is documented by its patience in staying with *Prime Time Live*, with Diane Sawyer and Sam Donaldson, after a rocky start. NBC, by contrast, went through seventeen short-lived magazine shows before its entry *Dateline NBC* went on the air in 1992 with a promise from management to give it time to develop an audience.

The differing approaches of the three major networks to dealing with the crisis involving the future of the evening news have perhaps been influenced by a difference in the commitment of top management to the business of broadcasting over the long term. NBC has been recurrently rumored to be on the auction block.

CBS President Laurence Tisch has been selling off CBS subsidiaries and has supposedly been waiting for the most propitious time to sell his CBS stock holdings. Capital Cities/ABC alone among the three seems to be positioning itself for the future. It has acquired a sports cable network, ESPN, and a share of Arts and Entertainment, another cable programming service. Most interesting, it regards its whole news output as the basis for future expansion.

ABC's "American Agenda" pieces on *World News Tonight*, although subject to some changes in format, are often announced a night in advance. A regular feature of the Friday broadcast is the "Person of the Week," which attempts to provide an upbeat alternative to the sometimes negative flavour of the run of broadcast news. "American Agenda" has been part of a studied effort to keep audiences tuning in just to watch *Work News Tonight*. In the words of one ABC producer: The ABC philosophy on news is called "appointment viewing." "American Agenda" provides the opportunity to promote a piece in advance so viewers will feel they have an appointment to see it. The future is going to be newsmagazine shows in prime time that the viewers will also have an appointment to see. Especially the key demographic groups, such as women aged nineteen to thirty-nine whom advertisers love. It's no accident that "American Agenda" concentrates on family, education, health—things that particularly appeal to women.

Steve Weiswasser [then executive vice-president of ABC News] said in a recent meeting that we are producers of programmes, not just newsgatherers. We have got to learn to package and repackage what we do.

World News Now, the 2 A.M. broadcast, is an example. Weiswasser talked about creating a cable component of all-night news, so that if you missed it, you can still see it. The same with Nightline and "American Agenda." These are programmes with a shelf life, unlike spot news.

ABC owns rights forever to its news products, unlike the first-run-only rights to entertainment shows. A network possesses a library of raw tape. Weiswasser pointed out that Capital Cities/ABC includes a publishing division. Perhaps we can produce something like a printed guide to go along with in-school video.

The emphasis of the new regimes in New York on all three networks is on an evening news broadcast that can hope to attract audiences already beset by viewing options, ranging from local news programmes, to cable services such as CNN and C-SPAN, to a host of syndicated shows—such as *Entertainment Tonight*, *A Current Affair*, and *Hard Copy*—that fuzz the distinction between entertainment and news. Can the audience tell the difference? Does it care as much as professional journalists?

Reporters know from experience that newspaper readers often blame the fact gatherer for opinions expressed on the editorial page; the distinction between news and editorial pages, so frequently cited by journalism professionals, is lost on many in the general audience. Similarly, some tabloid "reality" programmes sold by syndicators to local stations are viewed by the audience in the same continuum as adjacent news programmes, both local and network. Not all viewers are that sensitive as to when one leaves off and the other begins. In the passive environment of television-watching, TV news is sometimes lumped together as an indiscriminate whole. Indeed, the important distinctions between responsible journalism and trash are more difficult to recognize in this most invasive of mass media.

NEWS GATHERING AND PROCESSING THROUGH INFORMATION TECHNOLOGY

Many journalists are just beginning to use computers as tools for newsgathering. How can it be done successfully? Many novices may not be quite sure how the process works. To get things going, let's consider the successful nature of these two case studies. Philadelphia's public schools had been judged by experts in 1994 to be failing their educational mission. But why? And how? Reporters and editors for *The Philadelphia Inquirer* sought to find answers and explanations. The newspaper's team of reporters began by collecting information about the performance of the schools in the School District of Philadelphia.

Staff writers found data and other forms of information in a variety of places. They obtained much of the data from the school district itself, but also found useful information from the Pennsylvania Department of Education, the University of Pittsburgh, the U.S. Department of Education, and a variety of other public sources. Led by Borowski, who is director of computer-assisted reporting (CAR) for his newspaper, the group worked with sociologists and other experts from Temple University to analyse data and uncover trends about the schools and their students.

Borowski (personal communication, November 17, 1995) explained:

Tom Ferrick has been with *The Inquirer* for years. In the early 1980s or late 1970s, he did, in essence, a project just like this with yellow sheets of legal paper and a calculator, books, and he did it by hand. This time, we did it with a computer. The other interesting thing is that the city school district, through the 1980s, would not release a lot of data. They did not want to have their successes or their failures measured in any way. Very, very little data trickled out. They got a new assistant superintendent who came down here with a different attitude. The old administration of the school district left. And they said, "We'll give you whatever you want. We can't give you studentlevel stuff, but we'll give you different groups and things like that."

The result of the investigation and analysis was an eight-page special section entitled, "A District in Distress," that told readers how the problems causing the district's poor performance in educating children were only becoming worse. It described how the city had two school systems: a mostly minority public system and a mostly White private and parochial school system. The reporters pointed to the facts: Students could not complete basic tasks, such as math and reading, and their academic performance was poor when compared to other schools on standardized tests.

Other data showed that students did not attend school and that they did not graduate. The schools were unsafe and remained deeply segregated. The district, overall, was not doing well compared to nearby suburban districts. The project also demonstrated how the public school system was growing after a period of decline, but that funding was dropping. In the end, the team of reporters and editors found some cause for hope in a new superintendent, a court order to restructure the district, and a public focused on seeking change in the schools.

Most of the special section consisted of tables, colour graphs, and charts of data gleaned from the vast collection of sources located by *The Inquirer* staff. These summaries were supplemented with short stories to explain data and photographs to illustrate points. The help the journalists got from experts paid off, Borowski stated:

We got all the data. We got someone from Temple University who was doing research. And we came out with the project. In a newspaper like *The Inquirer* that puts a premium on investigations and nailing the bad guys, it was embarrassing that the school district sent over its congratulations on this project and said they loved it.

We wondered: "What did we do wrong?" We didn't do anything wrong. It was probably the best summary of school district statistics in a decade, something, I'm told, the school board can use as a reference. The project won a National Education Writers award and other recognition from journalists.

CASE STUDY: ST. PETERSBURG TAMPA AREA TRAFFIC ACCIDENTS

Residents of Pinellas and Hillsborough counties in Florida know the safe and not-so-safe places to drive in their area. They have this information because a reporting team from the *St. Petersburg Times* analysed the most dangerous intersections in the two most populated counties in the Tampa Bay area.

The newspaper recently published a major Sunday edition project that outlined the most likely places that drivers would be involved in injury-causing traffic accidents on local and state roads. The newspaper placed the project's lead story on page 1 and included a location map displaying the most likely sites for serious accidents. Inside the front section, the report filled two additional open pages that contained:

- The main story jump from page 1.
- Three sidebars that focused on how to solve traffic problems.
- Sidebar describing a peculiar intersection of odd angles and blind spots.
- Two colour aerial photographs of intersections with text labels to explain problem spots.
- Three informational graphics displaying how to improve intersections and how to change traffic signals.
- Project "How we did it" research methods box and an "About the reporter" background box.

Reporter Bill Adair, who covers the transportation beat for his newspaper, was assisted by researchers Simon Lau and Connie Humburg. The stories Adair produced were based on his review and computer-assisted analysis of more than 10,000 injury accidents in the two counties.

Adair, 32, was a veteran of 5 years at *The Times* at the time he worked on the project. Adair and his research team acquired the data from the St. Petersburg and Tampa police departments. The statistics did not include expressways or interstate highways, nor did it include noninjury accidents because both types of accidents are reported differently by different law enforcement agencies.

Such a project is typical of how news organizations are using computers to enhance reporting in the last half of this decade. The project required some computing power combined with more traditional reporting such as interviews and public document searches and reviews.

The result was a powerful and simple-to-understand report about traffic safety in the region. It demonstrates what contemporary news reporting should be — an effort taking advantage of all the best information gathering and analyzing tools at hand.

SUCCESS IN MERGING JOURNALISM WITH COMPUTING

The process of using computers for newsgathering is dynamic. Computers are now inescapable in newsrooms because of their widespread use in writing, editing, typesetting, page layout, graphics creation and editing, and picture editing.

But computers are quickly becoming tools for information gathering as well and the discussion ahead focuses on ways to succeed in the endeavor. Computing is the new direction of newsgathering in the last half of the 1990s and in the decade to follow.

Computers have become a part of every journalist's professional life. Anyone regularly visiting one variation of the virtual newsroom of the late 1990s, also known as list serves on the Internet, knows the scenario: A new personal computer software product comes onto the market. Soon, the questions begin to appear about the product:

- "Is it a good upgrade? Is it better than...?"
- "How much is it? Should we buy it? Is the cost worthwhile?"
- "What new data massaging tricks can be done with it?"

A similar process occurs when significant new computer hardware appears. *The questions are equally predictable*:

- "Is the extra speed worth the cost?"
- "Is the additional storage (or memory) worth it?"

The exchanges and comments continue for days and even weeks on some of these more technically oriented lists. There is seldom early agreement among the list subscribers, but eventually some sort of consensus is reached.

At some point in the evolution, individuals, as well as the journalists responsible for their news organization's CAR policies, make decisions about the requisite hardware and software and about the databases and online services needed for their work to succeed.

This is the highly informal and often casual nature of the serious computer-oriented journalist. This is how he or she builds the requisite toolbox for computer-assisted reporting, commonly known today as CAR.

Most journalists, however, just use what is available to them. They are not that interested in the details of software and hardware, as long as they get the newsgathering job done.

More and more, it seems, journalists interested in CAR are required to use products someone else chose because of corporate decisions about hardware and software that relate more to what is happening in corporate America than in newsrooms.

These journalists often must use what is provided, regardless of its suitability and the needs of the project. In some cases, journalists have had to acquire their own computing tools at their own expense.

The hardware and software selection process is highly influenced by the computer industry. Like many other businesses, the computer industry puts its products on retail store shelves and news organizations choose from them. Seldom, if ever, do news organizations create their own tools for CAR.

When Microsoft, Computer Associates, Lotus, Packard Bell, Dell, Toshiba, IBM, U.S. Robotics, Hayes, or another computer company introduces a new product, it becomes a potential tool for journalists engaged in this relatively new form of newsgathering that uses computers to collect and often analyse the information. With few, if any, useful tools being developed in the news or information industries, there are not many alternatives. All of these decisions are helping to define success in CAR.

- What tools do journalists use for newsgathering today?
- How are these tools applied to news reporting?

- How do they learn to use them?
- What strategies work best?
- What stories have the most impact and public service?

These are some of the looming questions about uses of computers in journalism. In many ways, they are not very different from the questions asked about computer use in other professional environments. Newsgatherers are adapting the new technology of personal computers to their work. No longer do editors and reporters ask whether computers should be used in reporting. For most news organizations, the decision has been made. Computers do improve reporting and newsgathering. But the next generation of questions centers on different issues, such as those related to the most successful strategies for application of computers in newsgathering. What has the industry learned so far?

DEFINING COMPUTER-ASSISTED REPORTING

Computer-assisted reporting is the use of computers to locate information and retrieve it from other computers and their databases as well as the use of computers to analyse original databases and databases obtained from other sources for news stories. Simply put, CAR is gradually bringing the methodologies and strategies of the social sciences into the newsroom. CAR is sometimes also termed *computer-assisted journalism*, but regardless of its label, CAR is a process of newsgathering that employs the data processing power of both personal and mainframe computers. Thus, computer-assisted reporting is the term widely used to refer to the use of computers:

- To connect with other computers (online).
- To create databases or import existing databases, for analysis of data (databases).

"Computer-assisted reporting techniques allow you to take national datasets, localize them, or replicate stories that other people have done on similar topics with similar data across the country," observed Penny Loeb, a CAR specialist for *U.S. News and World Report*. "Like social scientists, we can now build upon what has been done somewhere else and each time we will expand the knowledge.... The data are much easier to get now and the technology is much easier and cheaper, so we have a responsibility to our profession and to the public to always try to do our work better."

The Philadelphia Inquirer Editor Maxwell King believes CAR offers enhancement of existing strengths to newspaper newsrooms. "CAR is essentially the marriage of technical capacity with the sort of analysis and synthesis that marks strong enterprise and explanatory journalism. We should... aggressively pursue a strong position in this field. It is likely, if we are successful, to reward us with a special expertise, strength, and position in the markets we serve."

Rosemary Armao, IRE executive director, and Brant Houston, NICAR managing director, have cautioned journalists about the limits of CAR: "[R]emember what computer-assisted reporting is not. It is not a different species of investigative reporting. It does not replace intelligence and good instincts. It does not end the need to develop sources or to coax people into revealing interviews. It does not reap award-winning stories out of raw numbers alone. But in the hands of careful and thoughtful reporters, computers can elevate their skills".

COMPUTERS HAVE CHANGED NEWSROOM WORK

The appearance of computers in newsrooms has forever changed the work of journalists just as computers have affected just about every other business and industry worldwide.

With dedicated wordprocessing systems that were introduced to newsrooms in the early 1970s and uses of mainframe computers for polls and surveys and a few other unique investigative projects in the 1960s, journalists have had a generation of reporting, writing, and editing with computers available to them.

Yet the finer applications of personal computers — introduced to the mass market in the early 1980s — have remained new to many newsrooms, even in the late 1990s, nearly two decades after the development of the first PCs. Today, the impact of computing is unmistakable and widely recognized.

"Journalism... has been transformed by computerization," Cole C. Campbell, editor of *The Virginian-Pilot* in Norfolk, recently wrote to his readers. "Computers now shape nearly every aspect of our work."

Utica College Journalism Professor Cecilia Friend feels the use of computers for news reporting is significant: "Computer access to government data and the technique of using a computer programme to analyse them is a dramatic breakthrough for journalists-not only because it allows reporters to dig deeper and faster than before and find patterns not possible by traditional means, but because the tool can be value-neutral."

Friend stated. "It can replace anecdotal tales or interpreted statistics with the record itself. By dealing directly with the unadorned numbers of a database, reporters can bypass the spin doctors and vested interests who previously not only supplied the information but selected and interpreted it as well."

The handful of journalists who have been working with computers for reporting spent the first half of this decade creating and fine-tuning strategies for use of their new tools in the newsroom.

The process is still evolving. How can computer hardware and software be used to enhance news reporting? How can a news organization do a better job in covering its community empowered with CAR resources? These are some of the questions posed and, hopefully, answered in the following pages.

MAKING COMPUTERS WORK FOR JOURNALISTS

The whole point of CAR is to make computers work more efficiently for journalists. If computers did not make work faster, easier, better organized, more systematic, more thorough, or more analytical than that done by hand, there would be no need for computers as news reporting tools.

There would be no need for CAR. But like their academic cousins, social scientists who have used computers to study human behaviour since the machines were first developed, journalists know computers do make a difference in bringing new meaning to information.

Research that has focused on how computers are used in newsrooms has long documented that most journalists are painfully slow in adjusting to new technology. Early studies that looked at the newly appearing computers in newsrooms in the early and mid 1970s found reluctance among journalists to use computers for basic tasks such as writing stories and editing.

Almost a generation of journalists later, research continues to show reluctance on the part of many journalists to take computers beyond writing and editing functions. "So far, it seems, reporters use computers as new tools to do the same old journalism," concluded Carleton University researcher Catherine McKercher. "The fact that reporters are aware of the wider possibilities inherent in computer-assisted reporting but have not made significant steps towards upgrading their own skills suggests that training may be an issue. But it also suggests that many reporters feel they do their jobs well enough with their existing skills, or believe they have little incentive, time, or energy to spend on acquiring new ones."

CAR can be successful at any level. From college campuses, weekly newsrooms, and small-market television stations to the major dailies and news magazines to broadcast networks, CAR has been shown to be effective in improving how a community is covered. Most authorities argue, or preach, some critics say, that CAR works just as effectively and inexpensively for small news organizations as it does for the major dailies and networks.

The Philadelphia Inquirer, highlighted in one of the case studies at the beginning of this chapter, has a two-person team of CAR experts — reporters Neill Borowski and Tom Torok — who lead the newspaper's movement towards complete integration into the newsroom.

The newspaper planned in 1995 and 1996 for a completely renovated newsroom with a PC network to replace an aging Atex editorial system, but it had to make the transition slowly until all reporters and editors are able to work with networked Pentiumgrade PCs capable of running spreadsheets, Internet browsers, and other more common CAR tools. CAR is being brought into the newsroom in several ways, Borowski explained:

Part of it is our Bit by Bit University where we teach spreadsheets, databases, basics of PCs, Windows, and Internet to reporters. It's one way to whet their appetites and get them interested. On the news side, actually applying CAR, it is a two-way process.

Reporters will come to us with databases or reporters will come to us with data questions: "Here's a sheet of data. How do we analyse it?" Or, we are always trolling for data — looking for little gold mines within databases within government reports. Tom visits, every now and then, different county and state offices, engages people and finds out about databases. We then try to sell the concept to a reporter: This is a good story and so forth.

CAR REMAINS A "NOW FRONTIER"

Some of the most experienced CAR journalists in the United States still see their work as taking their colleagues to the new frontier in newsgathering. These individuals, in a sense, have been the explorers and have seen the new promised land, and now these individuals wish to tell others in the newsroom about this new place filled with opportunities.

Rose Ciotta is one of them. Ciotta, who is compute-rassisted CAR editor for *The Buffalo News*, has worked as an investigative specialist before beginning to direct her newspaper's CAR effort. She joined the newspaper in 1977 and has worked on business and finance stories, including award-winning projects about bank lending and home mortgages. I believe CAR is at a new frontier, in other words, facing the challenge of moving from the nerd in the corner to the middle of the newsroom. We all agree that we want this to happen.

The biggest worry is that it won't happen or it won't happen fast enough or as completely as it should. Many people are working on different techniques, such as specialized training, to make this happen. I call it "just-in-time-training."

Get people into classes for overview so that they can understand the tools and appreciate them.

Give them an opportunity to really learn how to use them when they are working on a story or project. I did that recently with a reporter who did a story using census data on in and out county migration. By the end of it, he knew how to use the spreadsheet pretty well.

The other thing happening to insure that CAR moves out there is to use the software available to make it easier for reporters to use online information. Whether it's front-ends, Web sites, networks — anything that takes the computer-ese out of the hunt — will sell CAR. We in the CAR field also all agree that journalists must use these tools, so one of my fears is that not enough people will become believers soon enough. In just the eighteen months or so that I've been at this full-time, I've seen a dramatic change in software, World Wide Web publishing, online information, and so forth.

The rate of change is amazing. The window is open a little still, but journalists can't think they can function in this business and stay out of the computer loop.

I also fear that newspaper owners may not realise that they need to invest and continue to invest in skills training for everyone. There's certainly more training in newsrooms today than ever considering the demand being experienced by IRE/NICAR. We're just scratching the surface on what is needed, especially when you consider that most news organizations are moving to a PC-based operating system for their newsrooms.

FIRST HAND VIEWS: SEEING CAR'S EFFECTIVENESS

Some newsroom experts argue that reporters and editors will use the tools if they can see CAR's effectiveness firsthand."Reporters and editors are very result-oriented. What they're interested in is getting good stories in the paper that have some impact and result in lots of'well dones' from their bosses," noted Ray Robinson, projects editor at The Press of Atlantic City, where he has worked on investigative and computer-assisted stories for 3 years:

As they start seeing more and more CAR stories that have those results, they'll start thinking more about how the computer can help them on their own stories. They'll realise that the copy of the budget they just got from the town they cover was probably prepared using a spreadsheet. And they'll understand that if they can get it on diskette instead of paper, they can pop it into a PC and do some pretty sophisticated analysis. With a little training and encouragement from management, I think CAR will take hold pretty much by itself.

CAR: USE IT FOR DAILY STORIES AND PROJECTS

It is clear that CAR is most successful, newsroom managers and CAR experts both agree, if it is used for projects and for daily news reporting. Brad Weisenstein, a bureau chief and CAR coordinator for the Belleville News-Democrat in Illinois, explained his newspaper's most effective approach:

Our programme has evolved from nine-track tapes and BIG projects only to lots of use on a weekly basis. We're much more spreadsheet oriented and quickly moving into online services. BBSs have been popular with us for some time, though. Our philosophy is to use technology to point out a story angle, but we then turn to very traditional methods -- basic legwork -- to make the story readable, relevant, and interesting.

PROVIDING ADEQUATE ACCESS TO CAR TOOLS

Another strategy is not to isolate the individuals using CAR, but to bring it to everyone in the newsroom by making the resources available on all computer workstations at all times. This is a form of empowerment through access."The tools must be accessible," believes Paul McElroy (personal communication, October 13, 1995), systems editor at the Seattle Post-Intelligencer since 1991. McElroy serves as liaison between the newsroom and the Systems Department and handles most staff computer training.

Here, CAR tools are not available on our mainframe Atex system. We have just had three PCs dedicated to CAR; one is in our library and the other two are in the newsroom. Some reporters are reluctant to use the PCs because it means leaving their desk and risking missed phone calls, among other inconveniences. For newspapers with PCbased systems, I'd hope that Internet access and a few other tools (spreadsheet, database, and so forth) are available from any desk. That will be our goal when we buy our next system.

Bill Casey (personal communication, September 22, 1995), director of CAR for The Washington Post, also feels access to CAR tools is important if CAR is to succeed: Doing CAR right for us is having more than a couple of people who are skilled with computers. That's pretty important. At the same time we do that, we recognize, like Pat Stith (an editor at the Raleigh News and Observer) does, that there is only a small percentage of people, fifteen or twenty years of this has shown us, have an aptitude for it or an interest in it. Achieving a balance between people understanding these tools and people realizing what they don't know is a big issue.

This is the position also held by Jack Lail, assistant managing editor of technology who assists reporters with CAR at the Knoxville News-Sentinel. He is also responsible for developing an online BBS service and Web site and is supervisor for the newspaper library. Lail argues that everyone in the newsroom should be taught the basic tools of CAR."You have to get beat reporters to start doing at least the simple stuff themselves. It's a tool. They don't need to go off to the CAR department to figure out a spreadsheet. They ought to know that themselves and the challenge is to convince them of that and get their buy-in," Lail stated.

NEED FOR WIDESPREAD NEWSROOM INVOLVEMENT

Most individuals supervising or overseeing CAR in newsrooms believe there must be as many individuals as possible involved.

Dave Fallis, assistant city editor for the *Tulsa World,* is one. He strongly supports the philosophy of widespread newsroom involvement. "It is very important to get as many people involved as possible. It has a domino effect. Relying on one person, unless it is a full-time job, is not enough. But start small."

PROVIDING TRAINING AND MOTIVATION

Another newspaper online expert believes success in CAR comes from training and encouragement. "I would like to see editors and reporters become more interested in using the technology available to them," observed *Modesto Bee* Librarian Kate Roberts. "We have the talent to produce quality CAR stories, but I think that being on different computer skill levels and weak communication often blocks us from doing so."

The Washington Post's Casey agrees. Motivating individuals in a newsroom, large ones especially, is critical to succeeding with CAR. "This is a fragile process of cajoling and pushing and pulling, of showing people how it works and how it might apply to their beats. It is not any kind of simple thing. You just don't give classes and then people are all doing it."

Moving CAR fully into the newsroom is, perhaps, a classic case for study of adoption of technological innovation. There may be similarity, some experts feel, in what is happening in newsrooms of the 1990s with CAR and what happened in newsrooms in the 1970s when computers were first introduced for text processing and typesetting.

There is some difficulty on the part of some people to adjust to the new technological tools of newsgathering today. Will it, if the 1970s adjustment period is indicative, take a generation of journalists to adjust to using CAR on a regular basis? "All technological revolutions in the workplace are adopted by a generation that is not present when it is originally introduced," Casey, stated. "There's another generation of people, it might be five years back, or ten years or later, that represent the new technology and use it. And this is exactly what happens in newsrooms, with exceptions."

USE PATIENCE AND UNDERSTANDING

Tom Torok, a member of the CAR team at *The Philadelphia Inquirer*, feels that bringing CAR into a newsroom requires patience and understanding about the individuals who will be using the new approach to their work:

You have to realise that people view the world differently. Where somebody could think in database conceptual terms and others can't. To let those people know the potential, a conversation is not going to do it. You have to show it working, the whistles and bells going off, to sell it. Part of us has to be evangelical about this because — from what we have seen with what we thought was really powerful data, approaching people [on the newspaper's staff) and telling them what we could do — it didn't work. They just didn't get it. But once they saw it, we have more apostles and disciples.

Torok believes it doesn't really matter whether a new CAR user begins with a small project or a large project: The most important thing is to start, wherever the project is and to use CAR as a tool wherever CAR tools are. If you have a story that you're going to get into — whether you use a computer or not — and you can see that the computer would make a much better tool and you are going to have to do this project on a very large scale, I would just say start.

Start big. If you dõn't have anybody with the expertise there, get it. One thing that I think is terrific about newspapers is that CAR has been a grass roots movement where everybody has had to push it. uphill. Even if you are the fiercest competitors, there's always people at another paper willing to help with the strategy of getting it done.

Carol Napolitano, a member of the public affairs reporting team of the *Omaha World-Herald* and former CAR coordinator for *The Times* in Munster, Indiana, offered a networking strategy to get CAR off to a successful start in the newsroom:

I found that starting out by working with individuals who are interested to help them do CAR often resulted in their spreading the good word to others who had no idea CAR was out there, or were ambivalent, or were against it for whatever reason.

Work with those individuals and keep things simple at first. Don't take on huge projects. Have them surf the Internet, or make a ProfNet request, or try some simple spreadsheet work. Additionally, I often suggested to people that CAR might help their story and showed them how. And when I did a story involving CAR, I invited people to peek over my shoulder or sit down next to me and watch and ask questions. By doing that with several people, the word had spread and by the time I offered mass training two years after the first CAR story was done, 90 per cent of the newsroom signed up voluntarily based on what they had seen others do and what they had heard. It worked, I think, because I tried to ease the concept into the newsroom, showing how it could be used on a daily basis. I didn't make it seem so huge and scary and sudden.

John Norton, business editor of The *Pueblo Chieftan* in Colorado, agrees that journalists have to be persuaded that computers can make their reporting and editing work easier: "The biggest hurdle is getting the reporters to learn how to use computers. They are reluctant to take the time and don't see the value."

The managing editor of the 127,000-circulation *Knoxville NewsSentinel*, Vince Vawter, offered a possible explanation: "It's funny," he stated, "that most reporters do not want to do CAR. Perhaps they do not feel confident in their analytical skills."

CREATING EXCITEMENT AND COMMITMENT

Creating excitement is another key to success in using CAR. "The toughest job is teaching the staff and generating enthusiasm," stated Merritt Wallick, assistant city/state editor at the 125,000-circulation *News Journal* in New Castle, Delaware. Wallick supervises training and database story preparation.

"The biggest requirement for being successful is having at least one person who really wants to do CAR and is willing to, unfortunately, invest personal time and probably personal money in the training," believes Steve Doig, Arizona State University professor and former associate editor for research at *The Miami Herald*.

"Most newsrooms are not going to nominate somebody out of the blue, send them to get enough training, and starting doing it. It's a thing that tends to be adopted by some enthusiast who then begins, on his or her own, to produce stuff that finally becomes valuable. The necessary condition is somebody who wants to do it."

COMPETITION AS A MOTIVATING FORCE

Another editor feels that motivation may come from seeing how others have used CAR in a powerful and impressive manner. "Use examples of other reporters' work [in the newsroom].

Nothing gets the competitive juices going faster than showing another reporter an amazing piece of work that someone else did. I hear it all the time," stated James Derk, computer research editor at the *Evansville Courier*.

"How can a computer help me cover city government? The Water Board? Well, whip out three reprints from NICAR and say 'didja ever think of putting the city budget into a spreadsheet and seeing where the money really goes? Where is the city's money invested?' "

On the other hand, success is hindered by a belief within some news organizations that the use of computers in newsgathering is a hurdle too high to clear. Problems such as not having the right tools, or the right people, or the expertise, or the ideas are often cited as barriers to proceed. "We have the technology.

We understand the urgency," stated reporter Dana Nichols, who works in CAR for *The Record*, a 53,000-circulation daily serving Stockton, California. "But we still feel overwhelmed. We need to have someone devoted to developing this."

Bill Kline, managing editor for the *Pocono Record* in Pennsylvania, points to expertise as the central problem at his newspaper. "At small newspapers, CAR is a gray area. We don't understand it — consequently, we're shy to jump into it. We may have to hire someone who, on his or her own, can get us going."

Other small dailies, such as the 43,000-circulation *News and Advance* in Lynchburg, Virginia, must wait to begin using computer tools in their daily and project reporting because of the perceived cost. "We hope to begin in 1995," said Managing Editor Joe Stinnett, "budget permitting." The financial concern among small dailies is echoed by reporter Clint Riley. "Smaller dailies need to find more affordable ways to take advantage of computer research," said Riley, who is leading the *Citrus County Chronicle*, a 21,000-daily in Inverness, Florida, into computerbased newsgathering. "Affordable workshops to set up basic computer options at small newspapers would also be nice."

Amy Kerr, an assistant editor for *The Herald-Dispatch* in Huntington, West Virginia, blames the problem on top managers in newsrooms. "Many upper-level editors who will say they see value in CAR are not interested in committing financial resources to its development."

However, a reporter who specializes in legislative and projects, Kendra Rosencrans, feels most newspapers try to get past the financial pressures.

Rosencrans, who works for the 20,000-daily circulation *Aberdeen American News* in South Dakota, explained: "It's a great tool, but it's a financial challenge to find the money to invest in the necessary software and hardware. We do what we can." Gene Tao, editor of the 20,000-circulation *Hawaii Tribune-Herald* in Hilo, expanded: "We still don't have clear understanding about CAR. Cost is our concern even if the technology is available to us."

Robin Evans, city editor of the *West County Times* in Richmond, California, says that making a transition to use of CAR poses a different set of problems. "We are at the very beginning stages of using computers. Most usage now is only for big projects," Evans explained. "I personally would like my staff to be able to use CAR for a wide range of reporting, from small beat projects to issue-trend stories to big projects."

GROWTH OF COMPUTERS AS NEWS REPORTING TOOLS

Computer-assisted reporting is the newsgathering tool of the decade in the United States, Canada, and, increasingly, elsewhere in the world. Online news research, reporting using online commercial services and the Internet, and news stories based on original database analysis by journalists are no longer ideas of future newsgathering.

As many news librarians and news researchers have known for almost two decades, online tools are here to stay. For a decade or more, reporters and news researchers have not needed to be award-winning investigators at financially successful news companies to access and use online research tools. What has happened in recent years is a broadening base and growing awareness in the industry of the usefulness of these tools.

Similarly, growing use of originally developed databases and use of databases created by outside entities such as government agencies has also become an important part of CAR. Database specialists in circulation and marketing, advertising, and accounting departments of news companies have known the advantages of database tools for more than two decades as well.

In newsrooms, only a handful of journalists used databases on mainframe computers before these powerful tools were introduced to the PC in the early 1980s with products such as dbase and Lotus 1-2-3.

However, some news organizations are still discovering these new tools. There are a growing number of newspapers and television stations and networks — especially larger ones — where CAR is a significant part of daily reporting and is not being reserved just for special projects. For some news organizations, though, CAR is still perceived as a fancy topic for discussion at conferences or as a special projects tool used only by nerdy investigative reporters.

"[T]hese keyed-in reporters find technology a tough sell, despite the fact that in the last six consecutive years. computer-assisted projects won Pulitzer Prizes. The movement occupies a newsroom niche, and its supporters struggle to wrest money from stretched budgets and to convince journalism professors and students that they need to get the religion," stated *Presstime* staff writer Rebecca Ross Albers.

This situation is gradually changing. In the past 2 to 3 years, smaller dailies have begun to use these tools. More are going online each week, and more are beginning to use databases as part of news stories as they discover benefits such as improved reporting.

Carleton University's McKercher studied both the *Montreal Gazette* and *Ottawa Citizen* to learn how computers enhanced newsgathering. She found two main uses: writing and checking electronic libraries, modernized versions of old-fashioned reporting tasks.

McKercher identified computers as useful for communicating, conducting background research, conducting fact-finding research for stories, organizing information related to reporting, and writing.

Most journalists see CAR as a major growth area in newsgathering in the years ahead. In fact, it is hard to find anyone in a newsroom who feels otherwise.

The problem may be that not everyone is doing something about it. "As computers become more common in the workplace and the home, growth can't help but happen. Already the new hires we are getting out of J-schools have had PCs in their dorm rooms.

That's nothing new to them. The first thing they want is a parking space, the second is their free PPP account," stated the *Evansville Courier's* Derk.

"No doubt about it," agreed Atlantic City's Robinson, a veteran reporter who has also reported for the *State Journal* in Lansing, Michigan, and The *Daily Oklahoman* in Oklahoma City. "The use will grow as more reporters and editors become comfortable with computers.

And that'll happen for two reasons:

- More and more journalists these days have PCs at their desks, rather than the single purpose 'dumb' terminals they used to have,
- Computers are penetrating an ever-growing share of the home market, and that includes journalists."

Kathleen A. Hansen, a professor at the University of Minnesota and co-author with Jean Ward of *Search Strategies in Mass Communication*, expects continued growth of computers as reporting tools in the next decade:

If only because news organizations will see themselves competing with other kinds of publications, information services, and highly skilled entrepreneurs who want to horn in on journalists' traditional bailiwick.

In order to keep themselves relevant, informed, and capable of meeting society's needs for high-quality reportage, journalists will have to learn how to make the most of the power of computers as information tools.

You see, unlike many others, I don't think any of this is really about computers (machines). I think all of this is about information (where it comes from, who manipulates it, how it is evaluated and communicated). There is my bias, but so be it. It just so happens that right now, computers are the information tools that are important — in some future scenario, it might be some other form of information device or strategy or process that takes centre stage. It all comes down to how journalists manage and understand information, and communicate that understanding to an audience.

Some news organizations are excited about the new tools and their potential. Robert Long, an investigative reporter for the 50,000circulation *Tribune-Democrat* in Johnstown, Pennsylvania, demonstrates the attitude: "We just purchased a PC for the newsroom dedicated to CAR in November," Long stated. "We anticipate our use and capabilities will grow sharply in the next two years."

INCREASING ROLE OF PROFESSIONAL ORGANIZATIONS

There are a handful of professional organizations that have taken the lead in educating and training journalists and in setting the agenda for CAR in the United States and elsewhere in the world.

Two of these organizations are headquartered in Columbia, Missouri, at the University of Missouri. Founded in 1975 at a meeting in Reston, Virginia, IRE has represented the professional interests of investigative journalism in North America. Originally begun as a separate entity, the Missouri Institute for Computer-Assisted Reporting was organized in 1989 as a focal point for the evolving specialization in reporting.

Renamed in late 1993, funded by a substantial grant from the Freedom Forum, and armed with a new management and training team, NICAR joined with IRE and grew into its CAR leadership role at a national and international level by setting reporting and computing standards, testing new hardware and software products, offering annual conferences, providing training and workshops, giving free technical advice, and gathering public databases.

In 1995, NICAR also began to increase its service as a clearinghouse for government databases. The organization purchases federal and state databases and sells copies to news organizations at a lower price or sells partitions of the databases, such as regions or states, at a reduced cost. The revenue covers costs to acquire the databases.

Among the national databases in the NICAR. library are Federal Election Commission campaign contributions; Federal Aviation Administration airplane and pilot records; Home Mortgage Disclosure Act records; federal procurement data; Alcohol, Tobacco, and Firearms gun dealer records; National Bridge Inventory System data; Federal Bureau of Investigation Uniform Crime Reports; Social Security death records; Occupational Safety and Health Administration violations data; Department of Transportation truck accident and census data; several databases from the Small Business Administration: and Department of Education schools data. A different sort of organization that is making important contributions is the Transactional Records Access Clearinghouse (TRAC) at Syracuse University. Founded in 1989, this organization gathers and develops information about federal agencies.

TRAC focuses on enforcement and regulatory activities of these agencies and serves news organizations by disseminating the information it assembles.

One form of this information is data, but other information is distributed in reports, research studies, and a variety of services provided in offices in both Syracuse, New York, and in Washington, DC. Other nationally oriented professional groups have also begun to offer professional development opportunities in the area of CAR.

Among them are the Society of Professional Journalists (SPJ) at Greencastle, Indiana, the National Institute for Advanced Reporting (NIAR) at Indiana University at Indianapolis, and the Poynter Institute for Media Studies at St. Petersburg, Florida.

The School of Communication at the University of Miami has also contributed to CAR development through its national research project on CAR uses and tools, described later.

"The organizations are extremely important. Look no further than the National Institute for Computer-Assisted Reporting at the University of Missouri," said Ray Robinson. "The whole CAR movement would still be in its infancy if NICAR hadn't worked so hard to promote it and teach the required technical skills."

Evansville's Derk also underlined the value of what IRE and NICAR offer members and other professionals. "Groups like SPJ don't help me much. I read the *Quill,* but it takes hands-on groups like IRE and NICAR to help here.

The week I spent at NICAR's boot camp for reporters, where twelve of us lived and ate CAR, and a conference like the one we had in Raleigh or at San Jose are much more helpful. You get your hands on a PC, you don't read about them."

Seattle's Paul McElroy feels organizations help facilitate information sharing and interaction among people who are doing the same things: Poynter, API, CAR Trek, CARR-L, and such are not absolutely critical for success, but they certainly help. The biggest benefit for me when I attended the annual CAR seminar at Indiana University in 1994, for example, was hearing about the many good projects done by other newspapers.

As a journalist who has since become a "tekkie," I'm comfortable with computers, but I needed a dose of real-world CAR success stories to help inspire reporters at our shop.

I have also found CARR-L to be extremely valuable for general CAR discussion and pointers to Internet sites that are helpful for journalists. One drawback is the periodically low signal-to-noise ratio when a flame war Lensues.

Mary Kate Leming, assistant managing editor at the *Palm Beach Post*, is former head of the News Division of the Special Libraries Association, an international group of news researchers that has about 1,000 members in the division.

Leming is one of a small handful of news librarians who have advanced to newsroom management at the managing editor level. She feel professional groups are important. "There is an educational role for organizations, to let people know CAR is available and how to use it.

They need to work with other organizations, also. It is important to build those ties that help bring more education, more expertise, closer to your members," Leming stated. "For example, we are working very closely with IRE and having joint sessions at our conventions."What do participants gain from attending CAR conferences and training programmes? *The Washington Post's* Casey understands the main benefits:

People hear and see things that are going elsewhere. It's just like having mom and dad talk to them. It's not the same as seeing that your peers are doing things. It's exciting. It definitely has a catalytic effect. That effect is as true for a small or medium paper as it is *The Post*. People get galvanized to see and to hear ideas.

That's the most important part. Skills development means nothing to me at these things.... These classes are consciousness-raising classes. You do not walk out of them thinking you know whatever you are learning.

The idea is that you understand what these tools can do and maybe understand a little about how you can get into trouble, too.

The skills part is not important to me. It is the other people and other papers part of the professional thing that helps people. We can handle the skills ourselves.

Participation in continuing education programmes has made a difference for the *Champaign-Urbana News Gazette* in Illinois. "The newspaper has sent several people over the last twelve to eighteen months to seminars on CAR, specifically IRE and NICAR sessions," said Michael Howie, a reporter and CAR advisor. "Lack of equipment in the newsroom has been our biggest holdup. Several Macs are for graphics first, reporters last. Attitudes about CAR vary widely on our staff, too."

A FORMULA FOR SUCCESSFUL APPROACHES AND STRATEGIES

There are a wide range of ways to succeed with CAR. Examples in the following describe many of the best ideas. There is no sure way to be successful, but it seems that a formula may be evolving.

The elements are rather simplistic:

- A solid story idea.
- Data or information in other forms to be gathered and analysed.

- Willing and motivated journalists.
- Access to appropriate hardware and software tools.
- Proper training to use those tools.
- Newsroom management encouragement.
- Sufficient time.

Add these together, with that elusive element of a newsworthy story or project idea, and a successful project is *likely* to emerge. Likely. Nothing is guaranteed. Besides, what editors and journalists want from their stories will vary considerably depending on the side of the news organization and the original purpose of each story.

"So what makes a great computer-assisted journalism project? If you are a successful journalist, you already know: the same elements that make great stories done without a computer," observes Christopher Feola, news systems editor for the 60,000circulation Waterbury, Connecticut, *Republican-American.*

"In the end, readers don't care if you do a story on a multimillion dollar Cray or a $3.98 calculator — as long as it's interesting. Who wouldn't read a story comparing your school and city bus driver roster with your state's drunk driving conviction lists?"

WINNING STRATEGIES FOR SMALL NEWS ORGANIZATIONS

There are hundreds of small news organizations hoping to use CAR in their newsrooms. However, for one reason or another, they do not. Some of their editors think the costs are too high. Some editors feel there is none of the requisite expertise found in the newsroom.

Others believe there are no hardware and software resources available for such work. These days, however, this is becoming more and more like saying the telephone or fax machine costs too much and cannot be used. Ridiculous? Yes. Are phone bills too expensive? How long did it take individuals to learn to use the new phone system or the new fax machine? Do some people share telephones and desks? If answers to those questions were yes, then it is likely that CAR is a real possibility for even the smallest of newsrooms.

For the 26,000-circulation Oshkosh Northwestern in Wisconsin, the best place to begin CAR was with the newsroom staff, says editor Thomas P. Lee:

The most important part are the people. You have to make it work with people. Still, you have to have someone in charge of the newsroom who has to set the tone and say,"Folks this is the way we are going. Get on the CAR train, get on board, because this is where we are going." You have to get the message out to the troops.

You can have two problems. I suspect the most common problem is editors who aren't excited about it, but the reporters are, and the editors are paranoid about having to spend money. Or, you may have the problem that I had where it was the reporters slaying away from CAR. It takes a special approach in each instance.

Lee recommends that reporters that are not getting support from editors should start quietly on their own. He recommends looking around the building to find resources such as computers and software, even going to other departments. With some success in building resources, he then believes even a single reporter can begin CAR on his or her own: Talk it up quietly, and then start doing some stories. That will cause editors to develop an appetite for it. It will be a drug for them; they will become dependent on it. They will see how the average police story about crime in a neighbourhood can be enhanced when you bring out nut graphs that say,"in this neighbourhood, median income is $35,000, far below the $40,000 median income for the community." If you get into those types of demographic profiles in a regular story, then circle it and show it to the boss. Say,"I used our Mac to do this with census data." Then they will start working on their publishers. If all else fails, work on an editor's appetite to win awards.

When reporters resist, Lee believes, the best strategy is to sit down with each one -- after training has been provided -- and ask why he or she is not trying to integrate it into their work. Provide each resistant staff member with time to do the new type of work on a story, he also advises. When this fails, some people leave.

Lee uses a vacancy as an opportunity to search for CAR-oriented replacements and advises other editors to do the same."Also go by your nearby universities. In some cases, the nearby university may have some people who will be way ahead of the newsroom in this kind of research," Lee stated. John Kohlstrand, a reporter at the 35,000-daily circulation Chronicle-Telegram in Elyria, Ohio, strongly feels that CAR can be a regular part of newsrooms the size of his newspaper, He recommends the following:

- Start small, but work up to higher levels in time.
- Build your own databases and use the graphics tools of the software.
- Brag a little about the"how-to" of CAR stories and projects to your editors.
- Work with government database managers for access and compromises.
- Find allies for projects such as"computer geeks."
- Use the resources of others (such as CD-ROM drives and CD-ROM databases at the local public library).
- Find and use cheap databases (such as the Toxic Release Inventory).

Omaha's Carol Napolitano advocates CAR in newsrooms of all sizes if journalists in smaller newsrooms are willing to make some trade-offs. "CAR can be for the journalistic masses," Napolitano explained. "It takes a little bit of patience, a lot of knowledge about where to find the best buys, and lots of flexibility. Most importantly, though, it means understanding that computerassisted reporting isn't always giant projects and flashy software."

Arizona State University Professor Ed Sylvester, who teaches CAR and who helped the *Oshkosh Northwestern* get its CAR programme going in 1995, believes that small news organizations can find inexpensive ways to begin using CAR on a regular basis. In his view, locating existing hardware and software is the key to beginning with little or no expense in newsrooms with severely limited budgets.

"My rule, basically, is that unless you are really rich in resources, unless you are the MIS person, here's what you've got: It's not only capital intensive to buy these tools, but it takes staff time," Sylvester stated. "There's a lot of virtue in running small and tight on software." Sylvester recommends that small news organizations should try to use software already in the building.

Sylvester also advises editors and reporters working together often on CAR stories. "The computer has allowed us, in some ways, to withdraw from the kinds of casual conversations we used to have more often. That's bad. But it doesn't have to. Editors and reporters need to keep in touch with each other, sort of a running conversation about what they are doing, what they need, what's working, what's not working," he advised.

Sylvester also recommends the U.S. Census databases as perhaps the most valuable database with which a small news organization can start a CAR programme. A moderate investment as databases go, the widespread nature of census data, he says, has applications across the entire company, not just the newsroom. "I can't think of a single database that is more valuable to different departments on a newspaper than the census is," Sylvester stated. "An advertising director wants to know the demographics even more than the newsroom does.

If you can get a number of departments interested, not only to split the costs, you have a unanimity of purpose that the publisher is more likely to go for." Even if a news organization cannot purchase census disks or CDs, Sylvester recommended using local libraries that may serve as repository libraries and have public copies of the census data for use there or for downloading to a diskette for later analysis on a portable or desktop PC. This does not cost the news organization any money at all, he noted.

An ongoing national study of the development and use of CAR has been underway at the School of Communication of the University of Miami in Coral Gables, Florida, since 1993. The foundation of the project is an annual nationwide survey. As this manuscript was prepared, the 1996 study was underway.

To begin in 1993, a national database of newspapers, managing editors, and CAR supervisors was built. From the database, an initial mailing of 514 cover letters, questionnaires, and stamped, self-addressed envelopes was sent to the nation's largest Sunday and daily newspapers in late December 1993.

One follow-up mailing was sent in late January 1994. Using circulation figures from the latest editions of the *Editor and Publisher International Year*

Book in 1994 and 1995, a minimum of 20,000 copies Sunday circulation was used as the cutoff point. In late December 1994, the second data collection wave began with a mailing to 510 Sunday and daily newspapers. Again, a circulation of 20,000 on Sundays was the minimum for inclusion in the population.

Two follow-up mailings were sent. The first follow-up was mailed in early February 1995 and the second follow-up was sent in mid-March 1995.

In 1995, total of 287 responses was received, a response rate of 56.3 per cent. In 1994, total of 208 responses were received, a response rate of 40.5 per cent. Because the two waves of this study involved surveying entire populations, no significance statistics were computed.

Editors of the selected newspapers were asked either to complete the questionnaire themselves or to forward it to the person in charge of online news research and CAR. In some cases, as many as two or three persons completed various portions of the questionnaire related to their newsroom specializations.

Questionnaires used were developed from discussions and interviews during the IRE Conference on Computer-Assisted Reporting at Raleigh, North Carolina, in October 1993 and San Jose, California, in October 1994. The instruments consisted of four sets of questions including institutional and personal information, computer-assisted reporting, online news research, and field reporting use of computers. Respondents were also encouraged to include any additional comments on the subject.

Earlier research on uses of computers in newsrooms has determined that significant differences in computer use exist between large and small newspapers. "Small newspapers lag far behind large and medium-sized ones in newsroom computerization," Brooks and Yang concluded. Because of the wide range of differences, most of the data reported in the 1995 phase of this study are reported by newspaper circulation size.

The median circulation of the 287 newspapers was 52,800 copies. Therefore, small newspapers were categorized as those with circulations less than 52,800 and large newspapers were categorized as those with circulations higher than 52,800. In most cases, variables in the 1995 study phase are reported in contingency tables broken down by circulation size.

Data were processed using programmes from the Statistical Package for the Social Sciences (SPSS) for Windows, Version 6.1.3 and the Microsoft Visual FoxPro relational database system for Windows, Version 3.0.

NEWSROOM CAR USE DEMOGRAPHICS

There was greater participation in 1995 than in 1994, perhaps a reflection of a growing number of newspapers getting involved in some form of CAR and willing to report that fact on a questionnaire. Of those responding, the largest proportion was from the South both years. The mean daily circulation of responding newspapers was slightly over 100,000 both years. In 1994, it was just over 121,000 and it was 113,000 in 1995. The slight drop is likely a reflection of the growing number of smaller dailies becoming involved in one or more types of CAR.

The number of newsroom persons involved in CAR is increasing. In early 1994, the mean was 3.54 persons, and it grew 33.9 per cent to 4.74 in only 1 year, reflecting a growing commitment of resources to CAR in each responding newsroom. Most respondents in the studies each year had CAR supervision (27.4 per cent in 1995 and 26.5 per cent in 1994) or overall supervision (19.5 per cent and 19.6 per cent) roles. Other involvement includes persons responsible for the newsroom computer systems, systems liaison, news projects supervision, training, production, and planning.

7

News Coverage

Studies of framing effects have found that episodic and human interest frames-in which anecdotes are often an element-affect audiences' thinking in important ways. In particular, Iyengar found that episodic framing, focusing news coverage on individuals and events, tends to prompt television news audiences to attribute responsibility for issues to individuals rather than social factors. Valkenburg, Semetko, and de Vreese found that crime stories framed in human interest terms prompted readers to emphasize emotions and implications for individuals more often, and to recall less information about an issue.

The literature on exemplification, because it focuses explicitly on the use and impact of examples, carries particular significance for an ethical analysis of anecdotes. Zillmann and Brosius address the problematic nature of anecdotes in noting that the concept of exemplification calls for the representation of groups of events "by single events that are typical and characteristic of the group. Exemplification by atypical and uncharacteristic events is deemed inappropriate because it fails to provide reliable information about the group." Given the inherent difficulties of accurate representation through anecdotes, the prevalence of anecdotes in journalism stands out as an ethical issue.

Psychological research shows that exemplification can overwhelm the influence of base-rate information-broader figures or statements about the frequency or typicality of an event. In one study, subjects shown an article about a welfare recipient and an interview with a prison guard changed their minds about the population as a whole, regardless of what kind of information they received about how typical the case was. Mass communication researchers have found that different distributions of exemplars have differing effects on audience perception of issues.

Zillmann, Perkins, and Sundar varied the ratio of exemplars to counterexemplars in a story about keeping weight off after dieting. The exemplars either all followed the focus of the story (selective exemplification), or were proportional to the situation in the broader population (representative), or disproportionately favored one side (blended). Audiences' perception of the overall incidence of weight regaining proved most accurate for the representative condition and least accurate for the selective. Likewise, Brosius and Bathelt found that the perception of majority and minority opinions on public issues followed the distribution of exemplars. Zillmann et al. found that changes in the kinds of exemplars used in a news report on the plight of family farmers altered readers' perceptions of the prevalence of family farm failures.

Other research has examined the impact of using examples from extraordinary or highly emotional cases. Gibson and Zillmann found that estimates of the frequency of deaths in carjackings increased as exemplars were tilted more and more towards the unusual case of a fatal carjacking. A study of television news found that exemplification using emotional victims fostered perceptions that food poisoning problems and random violence were more severe than when unemotional or no victim exemplification was used.

Even the use of quotations in exemplars, a conventional journalistic practice, has been found to influence audiences. Gibson and Zillmann found that direct, one-sided personal testimony in print reports changed perceptions of amusement park safety. They also found that personal testimony about the plight of family farmers swayed readers' views. In addition, studies have found effects from the use of both threatening images and innocuous images, for example, changes in perception of risk of skin cancer. Findings about use of images are relevant to the evaluation of anecdotes in broadcast news because of its dependence on images.

Viewed as a body, empirical studies on the power of exemplars indicate a need for careful consideration of the ethical implications of anecdote choice.

ANALYTICAL PERSPECTIVES

Three analytical perspectives are useful tools for assessing these ethical implications because they point both to the potential ethical good and the ethical dangers of anecdote use.

A framework developed previously for studying coverage of news with an ethical dimension involves evaluating stories based on how thoroughly they portray the ethical issues relevant to a topic, the parties connected with those issues, the levels at which the ethical issues play out (individual, organizational/institutional, professional, and social), and the legal backdrop for those issues. Although each story about ethics-laden topics cannot be expected to address all four of these elements comprehensively, coverage that addresses these areas well is considered to be ethical. The normative assumptions about journalism in this framework are in keeping with social responsibility and communitarian press theory, both of which emphasize the importance of not merely reporting events but also serving society.

The attention to levels of analysis reflects the importance of portraying individuals in news coverage. News coverage should include the ways that individuals and families are affected by decisions or events-such as a health maintenance organization's decision about whether to approve or deny coverage for a kind of cancer treatment. Anecdotes shine light on the difficulties that individuals face, and as such they are tools of ethical journalism. The importance of the individual notwithstanding, journalists should go beyond that level to examine issues at the organizational/institutional, professional, and social levels. Attention to only one level of analysis, in an in-depth piece or a body of coverage, falls short of the moral obligation of journalists. In this light, anecdotes are morally a double-edged sword. While they can bring attention to the plight of individuals in riveting fashion, and even place that plight in institutional, professional, and social contexts, the attention remains on a representative, or perhaps unrepresentative, individual or family, as exemplification studies have shown.

Furthermore, previous work suggests that news coverage should include an array of sources, including neither exclusively professionals (such as doctors or businesspeople) or nonprofessionals (patients or customers). Good anecdotes, although they focus on an individual, may point out how that individual interacts with other people, as well as with organizations and institutions. Attention to a range of relevant parties at a variety of levels, both in the anecdote and elsewhere in the story, can mitigate the potential ethical harm from anecdotes' narrow focus. But the exemplification literature suggests that the anecdote still would have power to shape readers' or viewers' perception of the broader issue.

Christians, Ferre, and Fackler's communitarian media ethic also provides ethical justification for using anecdotes to highlight the situations of individuals while it draws attention to the limitations of anecdotes. The idea of mutuality is central to this perspective, which has a variety of intellectual underpinnings including communitarian political theory and theology. Mutuality views humans as having their identity in relation to others and living both for others and themselves. The relationship of persons and communities takes priority over either alone. This ethic is profoundly concerned with both society and the individual. The priority of justice creates a profound interest in the needs of the hurting or marginalized. "A press nurtured by communitarian ethics requires more of itself than fair treatment of events deemed worthy of coverage. Under the notion that justice itself-and not merely haphazard public enlightenment-is a telos of the press, the news-media system stands under obligation to tell the stories that justice requires." Part of telling "the stories that justice requires" involves telling the stories of individuals. This is because justice addresses fair treatment of individuals. One of the most powerful ways, in fact, to draw attention to such individuals is through the telling of their stories, in words and images, in print and broadcast media.

Even as it provides an ethical underpinning for use of anecdotes, communitarian media ethics, with its deeply grounded concern for the good of society, calls into question the structure and choice of anecdotes. Again, this ethic does support the use of compelling individual cases to highlight broader social injustices. However, sloppy use of anecdotes can undermine an effort to portray the broader issue, not simply because of the natural tendency of anecdotes to highlight individuals, but also because the particular choice of individuals can skew understanding towards one side of a controversial issue, resulting potentially in neglect of social justice. The issue is not formulaic balance in news coverage; communitarian ethics calls for more than "fair treatment of events." Consonant with Durham's notion of "strong objectivity," Christians, Ferre, and Fackler call for highlighting the perspectives of the marginalized and, where needed, giving those perspectives attention that is out of balance with the play given to the stories of the powerful. However, since communitarian ethics also implies a concern for faithful portrayal of the whole community, it implies a need to portray the breadth of the community's concern.

Gilligan's feminist ethic of care supports the use of anecdotes because it, too, is concerned with persons in relationships. This perspective, developed out of psychological studies of women's distinctive conceptions of morality, underlines the importance of relationships and responsibilities. Discussing one of her interviewees, Gilligan writes: "Her world is a world of relationships and psychological truths where an awareness of the connection between people gives rise to a recognition of responsibility for one another, a perception of the need for response." Commenting on how another interviewee viewed activities of care, she writes: "The ideal of care is thus an activity of relationship, of seeing and responding to need, taking care of the world by sustaining the web of connection so that no one is left alone." This ethic of care in relationships, however, is not relevant only to women, Gilligan argues. "To admit the truth of the women's perspective to the conception of moral development is to recognize for both sexes the importance throughout life of the connection between self and other, the universality of the need for compassion and care."

Anecdotes are ethically significant in the context of this perspective because they can help to portray the web of personal relationships and responsibilities involved in ethical situations. Anecdotes can dramatically represent the difficulties that individuals, including women facing illnesses such as breast cancer, face in relation to their families and others outside their families, such as physicians. In fact, use of anecdotes is in keeping with the attention to particulars that Gilligan found women bringing to their moral analysis. She discusses what happens when women go beyond hypothetical dilemmas:

However, the reconstruction of the dilemma in its contextual particularity allows the understanding of cause and consequence which engages the compassion and tolerance repeatedly noted to distinguish the moral judgments of women. Only when substance is given to the skeletal lives of hypothetical people is it possible to consider the social injustice that their moral problems may reflect and to imagine the individual suffering their occurrence may signify or their resolution engender.

This passage implies that anecdotes may awaken attention both to the suffering of individuals and the social context of their difficulties. It suggests that, despite the danger of distortion of the broader picture that the exemplification literature suggests, deep concern for the people behind issues that journalists report may arise only through telling the stories of individuals.

Even as it underpins the ethical value of anecdotes, the ethic of care also implies a need for careful attention to what anecdotes are chosen and what they portray. It implies a need for accurate understanding of responsibilities of individuals in the broader context of society, so that the web of relationships and people's responsibilities within them is rightly understood. All three perspectives suggest that anecdotes are best when they situate individuals they mention in the broader context of the issues being discussed. These three perspectives all draw attention to the value of the individual and therefore imply that it is ethically justifiable to use anecdotes to draw attention to the needs and concerns of individuals. The communitarian ethic and the ethic of care complement the ethics coverage framework by emphasizing the individual in relationships. Communitarianism puts priority on the hurting and marginalized. The ethic of care draws attention to the importance of the circumstances of the lives of individuals in prompting a depth of concern for them. Even as they draw attention to the individual, however, all three perspectives emphasize the need to think beyond the individual to the broader contexts of a problem, thereby implying that anecdotes should be carefully chosen for how they may limit or draw attention to these contexts.

Method for Case Analysis

These three analytical perspectives will be applied to three anecdotes taken from larger bodies of stories about human embryo research, physician-assisted suicide, and HMOs, all topics that have received attention from the media and professionals during the past decade. These topics lend themselves to powerful use of anecdotes because of their life-and-death import. Even though both the exemplification literature and the analytical perspectives used here suggest this power may be a mixed blessing, it is appropriate to study these kinds of topics because of the priority that journalists place on powerful, compelling anecdotes.

Stories used here were published or aired during a key period of public discourse on each topic. For human embryo research, this was 1994-1995, amid federal debate on the subject. For physician-assisted suicide, it was 1997-1999, which encompassed a Supreme Court ruling that there is no general constitutional right to assisted suicide, passage of law in Oregon legalizing the practice, and the trial of Dr. Jack Kevorkian for euthanasia. For health maintenance organizations, 1997-1998 was a time of increasing legal and political attention to HMO practices. For each topic, both print and broadcast stories that dealt significantly with the ethical dimension of the issue were examined.

The anecdotes analysed as cases were chosen for their vivid language and emotional power. In these respects, they represent the kinds of anecdotes that journalists strive to include in stories on many topics. Thus, while it is inescapable that they cannot fully represent the range of anecdote use, even in the topics studied, they represent an aspect of standard journalistic usage. They are, therefore, appropriate for ethical analysis of the strong and weak points in this usage. Although space limits consideration to one anecdote from each topic, both print and broadcast cases are included to make the ethical analysis more relevant to both.

Analysis of Cases

George Strait used an anecdote to help illustrate an ABC TV news story about human embryo research, aired just after a federal advisory panel recommended that federal funding be used to pay for research on human embryos. The story outlined arguments for and against human embryo research. This anecdote, shown in the middle of the piece, was the second of two that illustrated potential benefits of human embryo research. The story showed a girl born after genetic testing of her mother's embryos, and Strait talked with the girl's father. Strait described the treatment that enabled this girl to be born, against the backdrop of video that included shots of her:

This research on human embryos has vast potential, from improving fertility and contraceptives to better screening for genetic diseases. Take Brittany Abshire baby is shown wearing a bow on her head and a fancy dress. Her parents, Rene and David Abshire, were afraid they might never have a healthy baby. Their first child, Meaghan face is shown close-up in a still portrait, died of a rare genetic disease called Tay-Sachs. They got help here at the Jones Institute, where doctors recently developed a way to test an embryo for defective genes. Her deformed embryos were discarded; only healthy ones were implanted through in vitro fertilization. The result is Brittany the dressed-up baby is shown again.

By showing compelling video of real people affected by embryo research-especially children-Strait brought home the reality that this ethical topic touches individuals deeply. He thus drew attention to the individual level while remaining consistent with the ethic of care, by showing the web of family relationships in which the individuals are affected profoundly by decisions made about in vitro fertilization. In addition, he used professionals elsewhere in the story to show others involved in these kinds of cases, including a doctor at the institute the Abshires used. He thus represented a range of parties.

In this case, the communitarian ethic does not apply as strongly in the sense that the people involved were not poor or marginalized. But the decisions paralleled those faced by thousands of other families-all of whom, in communitarian terms, should be concerned about people who face similar situations. The story served to highlight the difficulties faced by couples seeking in vitro fertilization, and it pointed appropriately to ethical questions raised about embryo research as well as the benefits.

However, especially given television's ability to use emotional visuals, the use of anecdotes may overshadow broader issues. Strait's anecdote about the Abshire family used a still portrait of their now-deceased child, Meaghan, and shots of dressed-up baby Brittany, born after tests of other embryos for genetic defects and the use of in vitro fertilization. The story also used as sources two doctors, a Catholic leader critical of embryo research, and a member of a National Institutes of Health panel on human embryo research. This sourcing shows that Strait was seeking to place the issue in broader organizational, professional, and social context. But shots of a child who died and of a cute, living baby may overshadow the discussion of the broader context, especially since this and the only other anecdote in the story were used to illustrate potential benefits to individuals.

The second anecdote examined came from an NBC Nightly News story reported by Mike Boettcher. After anchor Brian Williams' introduction, Boettcher opened his reporting this way:

MIKE BOETTCHER reporting: No matter what Barbara Oskamp does, no matter how simple the act, the terminally ill woman writes it down video shows list of simple things she must write down to remember, otherwise she'll forget when she takes a bath, when she washes clothes. A brain tumor slowly is taking her memory as it takes her life, and she wants the option to end her suffering before the pain becomes unbearable close-up of her. She supports Oregon's Death With Dignity Act, the only assisted suicide law in the nation.

Ms. BARBARA OSKAMP: I don't know I'd be brave enough to actually do it. But the feeling that I had a choice, if the pain, maybe, was too awful, just as I said before, gave me a feeling of relief.

The use of this anecdote is commendable from the standpoint of the ethics coverage framework in that it drew attention to the difficulties of the terminally ill at the individual level. From the standpoint of communitarian ethics, with its priority of mutuality and its attention to the marginalized, it amounted to a call for better support-emotional and medical-for this woman and others like her. Similarly, through the lens of the ethic of care, this examination of the particulars of Oskamp's daily life might evoke empathy for her suffering and consideration of the justice of the system of care for her (as well as concern about what seems in this anecdote to be an absence of relationships). However, again these perspectives point to ethical lapses. Oskamp's plight was heart-rending, and it likely would evoke empathy from the audience because she was suffering. However, the very power of this portrayal of suffering may obscure consideration of issues such as, at the professional level, the role of better pain management or counseling, and, at the social level, the implications of legal assisted suicide for people with disabilities and terminally ill individuals who cannot pay for insurance. Social-level issues would be particularly important in the communitarian ethic-which, while supporting the attention to Oskamp and the concerns her situation raised, would also call for more direct attention to these other areas. A doctor was quoted as raising concern about impact on the poor-also important context under the ethic of care -but this professional voice was not as compelling as Oskamp's.

The third anecdote case concerns HMOs, which have become controversial in recent years because of the impact of HMO cost controls on patients. One repeated feature in the HMO stories, particularly the television pieces, was the use of anecdotes that were sympathetic to patients dealing with the fallout of HMO cost controls and related issues. A lengthy story in the Los Angeles Times, part of a series on "The HMO Backlash" in Ventura County, opened with that kind of account:

- Norma Barry had been treated by Simi Valley family doctor Elvin Gaines all her life. She trusted him so much he delivered both of her babies.
- She believed in his judgement to such a degree that she never argued when Gaines prescribed common painkillers after she complained of headaches and dizziness.
- Then, in late 1996, she died at age 26 of a massive brain hemorrhage, and evidence suggests she may have suffered from a series of small brain bleeds.
- "I blame myself so much for not making her go to another doctor," said her husband, Simi Valley truck mechanic Jerome Barry.

Just a few years ago, the Barry case would have represented nothing more than a routine, though tragic, claim of malpractice-a lawsuit not yet resolved in court: Gaines insists he did nothing wrong, and his attorney says medical records do not show a history of chronic headaches.

But in this y ear of HMO reform, it stands as a purported example of how HMO financial incentives to cut costs can interfere with a doctor's treatment of his patients-and as a reason that lawmakers, doctors, and patients are trying to change managed-care medicine.

Jerome Barry claims not only negligence, but that his wife was mistreated by Gaines because an HMO contract required the doctor to pay out of his own pocket for the costly special test the young mother needed, but never got.

This anecdote, too, riveted attention on the plight of an individual, consistent with the three analytical perspectives and especially the ethic of care's concern with the particulars of such a plight. It also placed Norma Barry in the context of her relationship with her husband, who was obviously agonizing over her death, and a relationship of trust with her doctor-in keeping with both the communitarian ethic and the ethic of care. The account also drew readers towards the organizational/ institutional and professional levels because the example was placed in the context of the HMO reform debate that touched on business, medicine, and politics. This paragraph of context also implied concern with the justice of HMO interference in the treatment of patients.

Again, though, there are ethical problems, particularly in the fact that the anecdote, although couched in broader terms, may limit attention at the broader levels. Medical costs must be controlled. Because of the serious nature of medical problems, how costs are to be controlled becomes a profound issue of social ethics. Even though the story pointed to the broader issue of cost-cutting, exemplification research suggests that readers may better remember the individual, tragic case and thus miss the broader attention to economic reality.

Daniel Callahan, a medical ethicist, sees the use of anecdotes as hindering consideration of broader resource questions. His comment regarding use of anecdotes in the assisted-suicide debate is also cautionary regarding HMO coverage and portrayal of other topics that involve social ethics: "I'm endlessly on programmes with people who tell these sad stories, and it's very hard to talk about the larger social dangers of physician-assisted suicide when somebody's got a sad story." The analysis of anecdotes about assisted suicide and HMOs bolsters the argument that anecdotes are ethically problematic if they ignore broader consideration of social-level concerns, such as just treatment of the terminally ill and just allocation of health care resources.

Applying the three analytical vantage points to the three examples suggests the importance of careful consideration of how and when anecdotes are to be used in news stories, especially against the backdrop of the exemplification literature's findings on the influence of exemplars. This section will suggest an approach that adapts the advantages of anecdotes but avoids some of their liabilities.

The suggestions for more critical thinking about choice of anecdotes arise out of an application of David Boeyink's discussion of use of casuistry in journalists' ethical decision making. Casuistry is an appropriate method here because it is case-based, as is anecdote choice. Casuists consider comparison of cases to be highly important in determining whether an action is morally justifiable. The anchor for the comparison and judgement is a paradigm case (or cases), in which the decision made is morally unambiguous. In classical Jesuit casuistry, such a case might involve a clear breach of the biblical command against killing. In terms of journalism ethics, it might mean taking an expensive gift from a news source - or, at the ethical end of the spectrum, accepting a free cup of coffee. In either realm of decision making, ambiguous cases are compared to clear-cut cases before choices are made. The choice of paradigm case thus becomes critical to the decision maker's understanding of the ethical issues at hand.

In situations in which reporters are striving to portray the ethical dimension of a news story, the notion of a paradigm case could be applied in two senses: anecdotes (cases) could be chosen to represent the possible extremes (the clearly ethical and the clearly unethical), or-in a twist on the notion of paradigm case-an anecdote could be chosen to represent the most morally ambiguous situation (as perceived in relationship to clear-cut cases). Without referring to casuistry, many reporters undoubtedly already seek to choose anecdotes that represent the ethical topics they are covering, and they focus on cases that highlight the difficult choices people face. However, the analysis in this chapter suggests that anecdotes could be used more appropriately if more conscious attention were given to how they represent the ethical issues in the situation being covered.

Two examples using stories about the topics discussed above will suggest more concretely how this adaptation of the use of casuistry could refine journalists' choices of anecdotes:

- Use of two anecdotes from "ethical extremes": a story on assisted suicide could use one anecdote that reflects a situation in which both opponents and proponents would come closest to seeing it as ethically unsupportable and one in which they would come closest to agreeing that it was supportable. The writer or TV reporter using this approach need not ignore the ethical concerns of opponents who would object even in this case, but by using this kind of template for choosing anecdotes, the reporter would reflect the breadth of viewpoints more fully. A review of the body of stories on assisted suicide from which the case anecdote was taken did not show any single story with both kinds of anecdotes. However, examples of anecdotes that come close to reflecting both ethical extremes appeared in separate television stories. One depicted Emerson Hoogstraat, whose body was "in excruciating pain from bone cancer" and whose wife said, "He would go to bed at night and say to me, 'I hope I don't wake up in the morning.'" If this pain were too excruciating to be relieved, both sides would be closer to agreement on the appropriateness of assisted suicide than in other cases. Another story had an anecdote that portrayed Karen Mortensen, for whom better pain treatment had made her able to sleep at night and able to think about things other than dying. In this case, both sides might agree that assisted suicide would be inappropriate. Using both these anecdotes in one story would present the viewpoint spectrum. This suggestion is not meant to imply that balance of ethical viewpoints should be the norm for all ethics coverage. In fact, writing which makes explicit a journalist's ethical views may do more for readers' understanding than ethical neutrality. But this suggestion retains the notion that audience understanding is enhanced by exposure to more than one viewpoint.

- Use of one anecdote with maximum moral ambiguity: a story about the practices of health maintenance organizations could use one anecdote that reflected the difficulty of moral choices involved by showing both ethical and unethical sides of HMOs. An ABC story about how to get the care one wants from an HMO focused on Cathy Patti, an Olympic skiing champion who had lost her right leg to cancer at age 9. She was initially denied the kind of prosthetic leg she needed, but eventually the company responded to her research and to her efforts to answer its questions by compromising on price with the prosthetic maker so she could get the leg, at no cost to her. The two sides in this case each individually represent clear-cut cases, but combined in one situation they reflect the ethical tension that arises in connection with HMOs. Although this application of casuistry applies most directly to stories with a clear ethical dimension-such as stories on bioethical topics, or controversial practices in business or government-it also has implications for stories where ethics may not be as prominent. Use of anecdotes reflecting extremes of the positive or negative impact from a public issue, such as a city council decision on subdivision zoning, would help to paint a broad picture for readers or viewers. Similarly, an anecdote that reflected the most mixed impact would, in a different way, represent more than one side of the issue.

Yet another way that journalists can personalize topics while keeping attention to their broadest dimensions is to accompany a broad issue piece with two or three sidebars, each centered on how the issue is playing out in the life of an individual or family. This idea of expanding anecdotes-personal stories-to full sidebars is not unfamiliar to journalists, but the use of more than one person-centered sidebar would broaden reader or viewer understanding of the impact of the issue beyond what might be gained from a single sidebar. In addition, applying the discussion of casuistry above to the choice of these "superanecdotes"-by using the notions of ethical extremes and maximum moral ambiguity-could help make journalistic portrayals more ethically balanced.

These sidebars could be written in third person like conventional news stories, with the sources cited, or they could be first-person pieces by the individuals themselves. In either case, they are consistent in particular with

Gilligan's emphasis on the importance of relationships and voice. This approach can address the relationship dimension better than conventional anecdotes by shedding more detailed light on individuals and how they are wrestling through an issue such as genetic testing for a disease that runs in the family.

A sidebar with an issue piece from the first day of the Los Angeles Times series on HMOs noted earlier provides an excellent example of use of "super-anecdotes." The sidebar, headlined "Faces and Voices," looked at the perspectives on HMOs of ten people including doctors, a nurse, and a hospital administrator.

Each person was introduced in the reporter's voice; then each was quoted directly for several paragraphs, which empirical studies suggest will be more engaging to readers than paraphrasing. In addition, the series that day included a sidebar focusing on one surgeon.

The ten-person sidebar provides one example of "maximum moral ambiguity": a cardiologist cites improvement in the quality of health care and greater accountability for time and resources, but also a deterioration in relationships among doctors and between them and patients as medicine becomes more competitive.

Training readers and viewers to expect anecdotes is problematic if stories without anecdotes are ignored or devalued. But, it is unrealistic to expect journalists to avoid using anecdotes, given their potential power to get the attention of readers and viewers. Thus, both journalists and researchers should think critically about the choice and use of anecdotes.

This analysis suggests that a good anecdote:

- Provides the fullest possible insight not merely about an individual but also about individuals in relationship with one another.
- Provides the fullest possible insight about the broader organizational, professional, and social contexts of a topic.
- Illustrates the tug of different viewpoints within the same situation or works with one or more other anecdotes to reflect multiple viewpoints.
- Is not so highly emotional that it overshadows the broader point of a story.

These criteria suggest lines for further research. Additional studies growing out of this analysis could provide ethical evaluation of the use of anecdotes in larger sets of stories on a variety of topics, with an eye to how well the stories reflect these criteria. This kind of research would further the kind of critical analysis that can help bring readers and viewers stories that have both a powerful personal dimension and the context of social meaning.

The debate rages over why journalists' ethical decision making goes wrong, whether they are capable of doing it well, and how to improve it. Since the 1970s, journalism has been occupied with its own "ethics movement" -media ethics courses have tripled, and ethics is a staple at annual conferences and in academic and professional literature.

Despite this scrutiny, no study has yet examined the ethical reasoning of a large-scale sample of journalists in the objective and quantitative way that other professions have been studied. Instruments that measure moral development have been administered to tens of thousands whose professions require them to make moral choices. Doctors, nurses, dentists, accountants, military personnel, and myriad others have been measured and ranked along a continuum of moral development, but not journalists. This study helps fill that void by gathering baseline data on a national sample of 249 journalists in order to compare journalists to other professionals, to compare subgroups of journalists, and to discover what characteristics of journalists best predict high quality ethical reasoning.

This work is important for understanding how journalists reason about ethical issues and for placing those findings into a larger, professional context. The ethical choices journalists make are crucial to the profession's credibility. By knowing the level that journalists are starting from, we can design better educational and professional efforts to move journalists to higher stages. By expanding on the foundation they have already established, these programmes can address the specific areas where journalists are weak, and build on the strengths they have mastered. With specific information about the influences that significantly predict higher levels of moral development in journalists, we can focus our efforts at those factors for maximum effectiveness.

Literature Review

Classical Ethical Theory and Moral Development. The concept of moral development has roots in classical philosophy. Aristotle believed ethical character was developed through daily living. This concept of virtuous people doing virtuous things was carried forward essentially unchanged until the twentieth century when scholars began to document how the human psyche grows and changes, what psychologists now label "development." Moral development is the change in how people think about ethical issues over time, partly in response to the development of other portions of the individual, for example, the intellect, and partly in response to the environment.

Piaget provided the academic foundation for the field when he studied boys playing marbles and found the way stations of moral growth. As the boys aged, their understanding of rules changed according to a pattern. Younger children were aware of a codified set of rules but played individually. The rules themselves were sacred, emanated from authority figures, lasted forever, and applied to all-absolutely. In later stages, the boys internalized the rules and the reasons for them. They assumed responsibility not only for following the rules but for making sure the spirit of the rule was followed, too. This paralleled

Rawls' concept of distributive justice and its principles of maximizing liberty and protecting weaker parties.

Piaget inaugurated the idea that moral development proceeds in stages and others followed, including Kohlberg, who theorized that people moved through three main stages of moral development, each of which could be subdivided into two parts. The first stage was called the pre-conventional and was defined by simple obedience to the rules, and then the emergence of self interest, in other words, following the rules only when it is in one's own interest. In the latter half of this stage, reciprocity and fairness begin to emerge in a self-serving way. In Kohlberg's second stage, conventional reasoning, the first half was characterized by conformity, or doing what other people expected.

The second half included the notion of social systems, or doing what is expected to maintain social order. Thinking at this stage acknowledged the role of duty. In the final stage of post-conventional reasoning, there was an awareness of the process by which rules are arrived at as well as the content of the rules. In this stage's first half, people are aware of concepts such as a social contract that demands citizens uphold laws even if they are not in an individual's best interest. Thinking at this stage includes understanding that some rights were beyond debate, for example, life and liberty. The second half of the post-conventional stage was characterized by the adoption of universal ethical principles that guided choice even if laws were violated. Those at this stage had internalized such principles and applied them evenhandedly. Kohlberg and others found that most people function in the conventional stage most of the time. This study uses Kohlberg's theory as its foundation.

James Rest made Kohlberg's stages easier to study by developing a quantitative instrument called the Defining Issues Test (DIT), which results in a "P score" measuring the percentage of time that people use universal principles. A P score of 40 means the highest stage is used about 40 per cent of the time, with lower stages being used 60 per cent.

Rest and colleagues also reconceptualized Kohlberg's idea of hard-and-fast stages using schema theory. Schemas, which are expectations about the ways events usually unfold, are developed through previous interactions. People also hold schémas for ethical problems that they use when making decisions about new dilemmas. Rest and colleagues theorized that schemas activate understandings from long-term memory to help people process new information. If a person has acquired a schema for the highest stage of ethical reasoning, statements at that stage on the DIT will activate those schemas; otherwise lower stage schemas are used. Rather than being "in" one discreet stage or another, Rest, Narvaez, Bebeau, and Thoma theorize that people are primarily in one stage, but can use ethical reasoning from lower or higher stages as well. Rather than a staircase with steps, moral development is seen as a shifting distribution.

Journalists' Moral Development. To date, only two small-scale studies have examined journalists' moral development using the theories of Rest et al. and Kohlberg with the DIT. In both, professional journalists showed higher levels of moral development than many other professionals. In one study, sixty-five journalists outscored all but three other groups. All of those-seminarians/ philosophers, physicians, and medical students-had mean education levels higher than the journalists', which is important because education is consistently one of the strongest predictors of moral development. In the other study, seventy-two professional journalists again outscored the same four groups. This study attempts to replicate and broaden these works.

Quantitative studies of journalists' ethical reasoning have primarily sought to identify influences on journalists' ethical decisions. They include external influences such as laws and organizational policies, informal work groups, the newsroom environment, competition, professional values such as codes of ethics, news subjects and sources, advertisers, and the audience. Another important influence was motivation. Singletary and colleagues developed an Ethical Motivation Scale consistent with Kohlberg's stages. External motivators were important, but intrinsic motivations proved more predictive of behaviour. One of the ways to enhance individuals' reliance on intrinsic motivations is to increase their feelings of autonomy, also a crucial variable in Kohlberg's theory; it is important for individuals to feel autonomous to attain the postconventional stage. Other data suggest that choice, a construct related to autonomy, is important in moral growth.

Other variables not studied specifically in journalists but shown to be significant predictors of moral development in other populations include expertise in a particular field. Higher levels of ethical reasoning result when the dilemmas are in the same domain. Religion has been positively correlated with moral development to a point. More fundamental or conservative beliefs are correlated with lower levels of moral development. Some theorize that a higher ethical orientation requires critical reasoning that may be opposed to fundamental religious beliefs. Business research shows managers tend to score lower than nonmanagers and entrepreneurs.

Two other variables-investigative reporting and civic journalism-have been linked to moral development in journalists in qualitative work. This study attempts to test those ideas quantitatively. It has been shown that investigative reporters make moral decisions regarding wrongdoing then abandon objectivity to push for the public good, serve as moral judges, and deal with ethical issues more than other types of reporters.

While no study has yet examined civic journalists' ethical orientation, that orientation has been linked to communi-tarianism and characterized as a higher stage of moral development than libertarianism. Before civic journalism, Culbertson studied activist journalists, to whom civic journalists have been likened, and found they bordered on Kohlberg's highest stage. Age and education are the primary determinants of moral development. Longitudinal studies have found significant changes in DIT scores from high school into adulthood and moral development plateaus when formal education stops. Gender has been studied extensively but with arguable results. A review of DIT studies shows 90 per cent of them find no gender differences, and when they do, the differences are better explained by education. Some studies find women consistently score significantly higher than men.

Guided by the theories of Rest et al. and Kohlberg, and empirical evidence of journalists' ethical reasoning and moral development in other populations, this study asks:

*RQ*1: How do professional journalists score on the DIT, and how do journalists' scores compare with the scores of other professionals? z

Journalists have consistently ranked fourth highest among all professionals tested in two previous studies. However, these two studies used small samples, so we ask a research question designed to gather baseline data.

- *H*1: Journalists will have significantly higher moral development scores for journalism dilemmas than nonjournalism dilemmas.

Past studies that show expertise in a domain leads to better ethical reasoning.

*RQ*2: Are there significant differences between subgroups of journalists, including women and men, managers and nonmanagers, print and broadcast journalists, and civic/ investigative journalists and traditional journalists?

This research question is derived from studies of subgroups. Since Gilligan contested the finding that women scored lower than men on Kohlberg's test, it has become traditional to ask about gender differences, even though no systematic bias has been found with Rest's DIT. The focus on rank in an organization follows studies suggesting that serving in management roles may lead to compromised ethics. The broadcast and print comparison comes from a popular notion in the industry that broadcasters will "stretch the ethical envelope" farther than their print counterparts. The comparison of civic and investigative journalists to traditional journalists arises from qualitative work.

*RQ*3: What best predicts high moral development in journalists? The predictor variables tested included religious beliefs, motivations, job autonomy, investigative and civic journalism experience, age, education, and gender.

This question derived from studies of journalists' ethics showing that motivations matter, and studies that identified religious beliefs, autonomy, age, education, and gender in other populations. The civic and investigative journalism variables are exploratory.

METHOD

Dependent Variable Instrument. Rest's Defining Issues Test, the instrument used to operationally define moral development, has been given to hundreds of populations in its thirty-year history. It poses six ethical dilemmas and asks respondents to rank twelve statements after each dilemma according to how important each was in making a decision (5-point scale, with 1 = "no importance" and 5 = "great importance"). These statements reflect schematic thinking at one of Kohlberg's six stages. For example, "What would most benefit society?" is a universal principle at stage 6. Next, participants rank their top four statements from the twelve. From the ratings and rankings, a P score is calculated that reflects the relative importance the person gave to principled considerations, that is, judgments at Kohlberg's highest stage.

The DIT has been tested for validity in more than 400 studies and can be modified to include two new dilemmas since domain-specific stories can be more predictive of behaviour. This study included two new dilemmas for journalism, one about hidden cameras, the other about whether to run a controversial photo. The four original DIT dilemmas were about whether a high school principal should censor a student newspaper; whether to turn in an escaped prisoner who has led a model life; whether a doctor should help a patient commit suicide; and whether a man should steal a drug to save his ill wife.

Independent Variables. Autonomy and religion questions were from the General Social Survey. Autonomy (Cronbach's alpha =.76) included: "How independent does your job allow you to be?" "How much say to do you have over the assignments you work on?" and "How much are you allowed to take part in making decisions that affect your work?" (1= "none" and 7 = "a lot"). Religiosity was measured with the following: "Would you describe yourself as extremely religious (7) to extremely nonreligious (1)?" and "Where would you place your religious beliefs from extremely fundamentalist (7) to extremely liberal (1)?" ($r = .57$, $p < .01$). Investigative reporting and civic journalism used two questions each (7-point Likert scales) about the journalists' own involvement with and their news organization's commitment to investigative ($r = .53$, $p < .001$) and civic journalism ($r = .60$, $p < .001$).

Participant job titles were dichotomized as management or not management (managers included broadcast news directors and higher, and newspaper managing editors and above).

Sixteen items from the Ethical Motivations Scale asked how important several criteria were when making ethical decisions (1 = "not at all important" and 7 = "very important"). For example, "Whether our competition has the story" and "How my colleagues would handle the same story" were offered as criteria. These were submitted to factor analysis and used to predict level of moral development.

This study sampled 249 journalists chosen with a form of multistage cluster sampling. To determine the proportions of the subsets of the population of U.S. journalists, we used the most recent national, random samples of working journalists as a guide. We initially stratified by geographic region, developing lists of news organizations from the 2001 and 2002 Editor and Publisher and

Broadcasting and Cable yearbooks for the West, South, North, and Midwest. Next, we stratified the news outlets by size in the categories of large (> 100,000), medium (25,000100,000), and small (< 25,000) newspapers.

Letters were written to top managers of news organizations in each size category from each geographic region explaining the study; up to three follow-up phone calls were made asking for participation.

Next, we identified categories shown to be important in moral development or for other variables-age, education, race, gender, and political party-in order to employ stratification techniques at these levels. It proved extremely difficult or impossible to obtain lists of all journalists working in the newsrooms, so we were unable to randomly sample individuals at these levels. Instead, we selected individuals constituting the same proportion of the population on important stratification variables. Babbie says this is "likely to be more representative on a number of variables than would be the case for a simple random sample." We accomplished this by analyzing demographic data after each round of data collection; typically, one to three newsrooms per site were visited with 5 to 20 journalists from each newsroom participating. This allowed us to modify the selection of news organizations for the next wave of data collection in order to conform to the proportions of individuals in the population. For example, if we found we had more journalists age 20 to 24, we would next visit larger news outlets where older journalists were typically found.

We were interested in maintaining proportions at the individual level, not the organizational level, so this modification resulted in a sample that was potentially more in proportion to the population of individual U.S. journalists than a simple random sample of news organizations. For example, Weaver, Beam, Brownlee, Voakes, and Wilhoit found 33 per cent of journalists were women; this sample included 38 per cent women; 90 per cent of the Weaver et al. sample were Caucasian, 89 per cent were Caucasian in this sample; 42 per cent of the national sample of journalists were Democrats, 37 per cent were in this study; 14 per cent were at broadcast outlets in the national sample, 18 per cent were broadcasters in our sample.

Because of the purposive sampling of journalists at the individual level, this was not a probability sample and findings should be considered suggestive rather than definitive; however, that should not discount the importance of the results for several reasons. First, it has been recognized that when probability sampling is not feasible, nonprobability sampling is acceptable. In this study, random sampling was not feasible or even appropriate. The primary ways random samples are collected are by mail and phone; a mail survey would have generated too low a response rate since this survey took forty-five minutes to complete and was on a sensitive topic. A phone survey would have introduced too much random error since the dilemmas require reflection and the ability to consider response choices; having choices read over the phone does not let respondents consider them the way they could if they saw them together and compared their importance. Instead, the surveys were administered in person on site-visits to newsrooms, an approach that almost all DIT studies have followed for more than thirty years.

Second, the purpose of this study is descriptive and explanatory, focusing on gathering baseline data on an unstudied population and understanding relationships between moral development and other variables. Never in the history of moral development research has there been an attempt to generalize to the population in the same way as electoral polls and surveys. Of more than 400 DIT studies, almost none was a random sample, and almost all were administered in person by researchers. Thus, these results are appropriate for comparison with studies of other professional populations.

Furthermore, this study satisfied the three conditions that justify the use of nonprobability sampling. The material being studied was difficult to obtain since ethics is possibly the hardest topic to get journalists, or anyone, to talk about in a revealing way. The ethical quandaries on the DIT do not compare in complexity to the simple demographics or even questions about ethical influences in Weaver and Wilhoit's survey. The ethical questions in this survey reach the depths of a person's core values and beliefs rather than the more simple attitudes and opinions of most surveys. Furthermore, it would have been prohibitively expensive to generate a random sample of the population of journalists by administering surveys in person; it took two years to collect these data in person. Also, this study explored an under-researched but important area; journalists are one of very few professional groups for which baseline ethical data have yet to be collected.

Finally, it is not the intention of this study to generalize to the population in the sense that random sample surveys do; our purpose is to explain relationships and for general comparison, for which Babbie says a nonprobability multistage sample design is sufficient. Science is a cumulative process and consistent results from a number of convenience samples can suggest important questions, to paraphrase one text. This is the third study of journalists, and the three results are consistent. As is traditional with DIT studies, generalizable statements become possible after many smaller studies of different participants from the same profession have been conducted over time. All the populations we compare with our DIT results were collected in this manner, not with large random samples; therefore, the comparisons are fair. As the third such study of journalists, this represents one more step in a cumulative process of knowledge acquisition about journalists' ethical development.

RESULTS

Descriptive Statistics.

In this sample, 62 per cent of the journalists had a bachelor's degree, 13 per cent had some graduate training, 17 per cent had a graduate degree. Only

8 per cent of those taking the DlT had "some college or a high school degree." Of these DlT respondents, 36 per cent were Protestant, 29 per cent Catholic, 4 per cent Jewish, 10 per cent listed other religious preferences, and 21 per cent said they had no religious affiliation. The journalists in this study averaged 14 years in the profession, and were 38 years old oil average. Twenty-eight per cent said they had done civic journalism, 7.2 per cent said they had done investigative reporting, and 46 per cent said they had done both. Thirty-one per cent had management-level job titles. Journalists' autonomy scores ranged from a low of 1 to a high of 7 on a 7-point scale with a mean of 5.3.

The ethical development scores of the journalists in this study were normally distributed. Data fell within a normal curve and rose in a straight line on a normal probability plot. The data met three other tests for normality; the standard deviation was one-fourth or less the value of the mean, and skewness (1.25) and kurtosis (-.75) indicated normality. The sample was statistically normal and met the assumptions for regression analysis.

Journalists in this study scored quite well compared to other professions, mirroring the results of the two smaller studies. This larger sample of journalists again ranked fourth highest of all professionals who had taken this test. The mean moral development score, or P score, was 48.68. These journalists ranked below three professions-all with higher mean education levels than our journalists-and above 14 other groups, including four with higher education levels than journalists.

*H*1: When the P score was broken down into journalism and general dilemmas, journalists in this study did significantly better on dilemmas in their field than other types of ethical problems. The mean P score for the three nonjournalism dilemmas was significantly lower than the mean P score for the three journalism dilemmas, supporting this hypothesis.

*RQ*2. The only significant difference in moral reasoning between subgroups was related to the types of work they did. Journalists who had experience with investigative journalism, civic journalism, or both, scored significantly higher than those who did not do either.

There were no significant differences between men and women, between broadcast and print journalists, or between managers and nonmanagers in this study.

*RQ*3. To discover the predictors of high levels of moral development, a regression model was developed based on factors formed from questions on the Ethical Motivations Scale, religion, type of journalistic work, and autonomy. A factor analysis with varimax rotation resulted in five factors accounting for 57 per cent of the variance. Requirements for factor retention included an eigenvalue of 1.0 and a minimum of two items with a primary loading of at least.30 and no secondary loading as high as.20.

The factors were labeled external motivations, internal motivations, competition, religion, and law. The external motivations factor dealt with influences outside the journalists themselves such as how colleagues would handle the story. The internal motivations factor involved the journalists' ethical values, including their own sense of right and wrong. Religion reflected journalists' religious beliefs. The law factor referred to specific legal constraints such as advice from legal counsel. The competition factor referred to media pressure, both outside the journalist and "within," such as whether the competition had the story.

The five factors and other variables were submitted to a hierarchical regression to find which were predictive of high levels of ethical reasoning. The most parsimonious model was significant ai $p <.001$ and explained about 15 per cent of the variance. The significant factors were religion, internal motivations, autonomy, law, and investigative reporting. Education approached significance at $p =.062$.

Just as in other studies, the religion factor was negatively correlated with these journalists' P scores. For every one-point increase in religiosity, there was nearly a two-point decline in moral development scores. The factor that measured how participants viewed the law and employer rules also was negatively correlated with higher P scores. For every one-point increase in importance of the law, there was nearly a two-point decrease in moral development scores. The internal motivations factor was positively correlated with higher P scores; for every onepoint increase in the importance of internal motives, there was a threeand-a-half-point increase in moral development scores. Journalists in this study who had more autonomy on the job were significantly more likely to have higher P scores; for every one-point increase in autonomy levels, there was a half-point increase in moral development scores. Doing investigative reporting also predicted higher P scores; for every one-point increase in investigative reporting, there was nearly threefourths-of-a-point increase in P scores.

The journalists in this study appear to be strong ethical thinkers. This is the third and largest study to gather data on the moral development of journalists. In the first, journalists' mean P score was 48.1,76 in the second it was 48.17,77 and in this study it was 48.68. While this was not a random sample, the study reported here mirrored the population on important characteristics, and the numerical consistency in the three sets of findings gives us confidence that they are reasonable and may represent something of a larger whole. These journalists appear to have reached a level of moral development that equips them to reason well about ethical problems. In this and three other studies, professional journalists consistently scored higher than adults in general and several professional groups including nurses and orthopedic surgeons, and dental and veterinary students.

When ethical problems are professionally focused, journalists perform even better. This suggests that giving journalists the opportunity to work through more ethical dilemmas, whether they are real, occurring on the job, or hypothetical in seminars and workshops, bodes well for the profession. This also indicates there is a journalistic domain of knowledge and that journalists think even better about ethical problems in that domain than they do about general problems. This evidence of domain expertise adds to the debate over whether journalism should be considered a profession or a craft. This suggests there is more to being a journalist than learning to write in inverted pyramid and mastering nonlinear editing. Thinking like a journalist involves moral reflection, done at a level that in most instances equals or exceeds members of other learned professions.

There is some irony is this result; public opinion would not support such an assessment of journalists as sophisticated moral thinkers. As is frequently the case, conventional wisdom is not always supported by empirical evidence. Professional opinion, the one that holds broadcasters are less ethical than print journalists, also finds no empirical support from this study.

When analyzing these journalists' ranking against other professions, one should note that all the professionals who rank above journalists have more formal education than the bachelor's degree of most journalists. The same is true for dental students, who ranked slightly below journalists. Thus, formal education appears to be influential in how professional groups score on the DIT. Education clearly matters, and, as the demographics indicate, journalists are slowly becoming better educated.

This study also has added empirical evidence to the qualitative work that suggests investigative reporting builds ethical muscles. This correlational study cannot not tell us whether this form of reporting helps create better ethical reasoning or if the journalists practicing it already possess higher ethical development. Previous studies have indicated that investigative reporting entails making moral judgments and that the journalists who do this sort of work wrestle with ethical issues as a part of the reporting process. It makes some sense that journalists whose professional work foregrounds ethical thinking would outscore other professionals because they are regularly practicing and refining their ethical skills. Future research should sort out whether these forms of reporting help build ethical journalists or merely attract them.

This study and others like it using self-reports do not address what participants would actually do in an ethical dilemma. The disconnect between attitudes and behaviour is well documented. Hundreds of studies have looked at the link between moral judgement and behaviour; in general, moral judgement is statistically associated with many different measures of behaviour, but the correlations are not strong. For the DIT in particular, more than sixty studies have found evidence that the hypothetical dilemmas do tap something important to behaviour; there are many links to behaviour measures outside the test such as job performance ratings. Ethical behaviour is determined by several co-acting psychological processes; moral reasoning is only one.

Of course, all these conclusions should be supported with replication, and caution is urged in generalizing these findings. However, the findings of this study suggest that if you give journalists autonomy in the work they attempt, expose them to the rigors of investigative reporting, and moderate the influence of work-based rules and religion, then journalists are capable of high-level ethical thinking.

Just as others have found, the journalists in this study exhibited quality reasoning about their profession. Knowledge about journalism, as a set of practices and as an institution that performs an essential societal role, provided a significant and measurable level of domain expertise. Other studies, using different methods and asking different questions, have uncovered much the same kind of reasoning.

The journalists who participated in the interviews for a 2001 book, Good Work: When Excellence and Ethics Meet, maintained both high professional ideals and the practical knowledge that the economic nature of journalism-as-business represented a corrosive element within the profession. The authors of Good Work characterized these seemingly conflicting understandings as evidence of a profession that is "out of alignment" with some of its more basic understandings. Rather than focusing on the internal cross-signals, the authors suggested that the contradiction itself represented the opportunity for significant professional growth in both an individual and institutional sense. As Kohlberg noted, moving up the stages of moral development often occurs when the conflicts in one stage can be resolved only by a change in thinking. In an institutional sense, journalism as a profession appears to be at the same nexus, one that has potential for development.

AN ORGANIZED CHALLENGE

Two seemingly paradoxical strands of news coverage emerge immediately after Pearl Harbor: the first focused on efforts by Japanese-Americans to show their patriotism and loyalty to the United States and their support of the U.S war effort; the second revolved around glowing reports by journalists on efforts by law enforcement officials to detain Japanese nationals and Japanese-Americans.

Fiske might argue that the competing strands of coverage were a by-product of the "unruly" nature of a story that was still taking shape. Like the law enforcement officials working to develop a policy for dealing with Japanese-Americans, print journalists were trying to make enough sense of events to provide adequate coverage for their readers.

By writing at great length about efforts to detain Japanese-Americans, reporters reminded their readers that local, state, and federal officials still had the ability to "create security systems" - in short, to protect American citizens. Donohue, Tichenor, and Olien note that reporters "are on guard against all intruders so long as the authorities are acting in unison and the power relationships among them are stable".

A cynic might argue that law enforcement officials wanted to create the illusion of instability in order to muster support for their containment efforts. While the threat to national security never existed, there probably was a sincere belief on the part of law enforcement officials that the nation was in danger.

But instead of trying to stem the "confusion about who is running things,", officials, still trying to craft a policy in the wake of Pearl Harbor, decided to put a bit of manufactured "confusion" to work for them in order to sustain their version of stability.

And instead of examining the validity of the government's claims, journalists, who themselves were trying to manage coverage of the story, accepted and disseminated the information. Thus, on December 8, 1941, a page one story in the Los Angeles Times was headlined "Japanese Aliens Roundup Starts." The story, placed next to a story on the reaction of Los Angeles residents to the attack on Pearl Harbor, told of how "a great man hunt was underway," as the FBI sought "300 alien Japanese suspected of subversive activities".

In this story, like many of the others reviewed here, journalists quoted only federal and local law enforcement officials. The reporter described how FBI agents "grabbed" eighteen Japanese-Americans in West Los Angeles and how the "roundup" was the culmination of "months of investigation by FBI agents" led by Special Agent Richard Hood, who had been busy preparing "an index file of suspicious Japanese."

Federal officials, the story said, "planned to hold persons rounded up at various outlying police stations.until a concentration camp is decided upon." Here, the federal government's policy was still forming; nevertheless, journalists showed an early tendency to "sound the alarm" about the as yet unknown threat.

As Donohue, Tichenor, and Olien argue, "[m]aximum uncertainty in the structure occurs when countervailing groups have the capacity to challenge the established power, and thereby raise a realistic possibility that the power relationships may be altered".

But as noted earlier, this threat was manufactured; by reporting what would become an ongoing tally of arrests, reporters allowed federal and state officials to convey the false sense that the nation's position of power was uncertain - that Japanese-Americans living on the West Coast would inevitably alter the nation's power structure.

Thus, even as law enforcement officials were coming to grips with the ramifications of Pearl Harbor, reporters seemed to be creating conditions conducive to an "official version" of events. As we will see, the "intensity" of reporting about the incarceration of Japanese-Americans would increase as days passed.

In addition, the December 8 Times story focused on how the problem of Japanese-Americans living in the area impacted local officials, not JapaneseAmericans themselves or the system of government in place. As Donohue, Tichenor, and Olien note, "guard dog media display a tendency to concentrate on individuals while accepting the structure".

But the December 8 issue of the Times included a page two story that exemplifies the second theme seen in the newspapers reviewed here after the attack on Pearl Harbor: the loyalty and patriotism shown by Japanese American citizens. Under the two-column headline "Japanese-Americans Pledge Loyalty to United States," the story told of how the Japanese American Citizens League (JACL) pledged its "fullest cooperation and its facilities to the United States Government".

In a statement, the JACL deplored the attack, and urged FDR to declare war on Japan. The story quoted Shuji Fujii, editor and publisher of Doho, a Japanese newspaper, as saying that Japanese-Americans would be loyal to the United States. Fujii made his feelings known in a telegram to FDR. Also quoted was Yasuchi Sakimoto, an official with the Japanese Fishermen's Association.

Sakimoto said that his members, many of whom would come under fire as the government began manufacturing a fifth column threat, would "turn to agriculture as a means of support during the present conflict". On the same page, the Times ran a story about an apology from the Japanese consul to Los Angeles, Kenji Nakauchi, for Japan's actions. The reporter referred to Nakauchi as "slight" and "bespectacled" in the second paragraph of the story.

In response to the reporter's question, Nakauchi said 20,000 "Japanese nationals" and the same number of Nisei lived in the Los Angeles area. Under a two-column photo of Nakauchi in the centre of the page reading a copy of the Times with an enormous headline reading "War! Japs Bomb U.S. Base" was a caption that told readers Nakauchi was "surprised and shocked" about the attack.

Internment camps were not necessary, he said, especially since German and Italian Americans living in Vancouver were not interned when war with Germany began. Nakauchi was the subject of a shorter story in the December 9 Times which reported that he was "probably the calmest Japanese in Los Angeles."

A third loyalty-related Times story on December 8 told readers that it was "business as usual" in the Little Tokyo section of Los Angeles. "[T]he Japanese populace went about its ordinary Sunday business with an air of resigned calm" despite a steady, daylong flow of curious sightseers, the reporter wrote. News of the attack "failed-on the surface at least-to create much of a stir," according to the reporter. Japanese-Americans "were discussing the news in little knots on street corners." The story concluded with the news that a Committee of Eleven had formed "to maintain loyalty to the United States on the part of the Japanese population here". Local law enforcement officials did not take Japanese American citizens at their word.

The next day, federal, state, and local officials closed all Japanese-owned businesses in the district. The pejorative language used by Times reporters carried over from the previous day's coverage: "little clusters of Japanese gathered to discuss the wholesale display of American authority". Page five of the December 9 Times featured a five-column photo of seven JACL members and Los Angeles Mayor Bowron.

Ken Matsumoto of the JACL is seen holding the American flag; the photo's heading reads "Citizens Offer Loyalty Pledge to Flag." The accompanying story, headlined "Japanese-Americans Ready to Aid Nation," included a statement from the JACL's Anti-Axis Committee which read in part: "the enemy will try to sabotage our usefulness by inciting race hysteria. Let us be vigilant".

A story on the same page told of efforts by Los Angeles school officials to deal with the antiJapanese sentiment shown by many students. Their plan was a response to rumors circulating about everything from school closures to bombing raids. In a particularly ironic statement, Los Angeles School Superintendent Kersey said "the spreading of inflammatory rumors is a powerful weapon of the adversary to undermine morale".

The article talked about everything but easing the strain felt by Japanese-American students, other than a closing quote from Kersey that a "continuing spirit of tolerance should be shown to all who actively support the ideals we are defending".

It is tempting to applaud journalists for creating a tenor of tolerance in their coverage of events in the days after Pearl Harbor. However, their approach serves an important "guard dog" function: it tries to inspire readers to feel the sense of "local cohesion" that Donohue, Tichenor, and Olien discuss.

Thus, stories about loyalty and patriotism shown by Japanese Americans were in fact a tool used by print journalists to help officials keep order until a policy emerged. As they tried to make sense of Pearl Harbor, officials simply did not need the commotion or controversy-at least not yet.

Like the Times, the Chronicle on December 8 gave a prominent position (the bottom of page one) to a bylined story about Japanese-American attempts to prove loyalty to the United States. The Chronicle article went to greater lengths to show how strenuously Japanese-Americans would back the United States - and how far they had to go to do it. The three-deck headline read: "We Are Loyal Americans - We Must Prove It to All of You".

Ironically, the photo accompanying the story showed Hangiro Fujii, a Japanese national and a local business owner, being led away by San Francisco police officers. Chronicle reporter Milton Silverman led the story with a quote (a rarity in news stories) from JACL President Saburo Kido: "The hour is here. We are Americans!" After delivering his message of patriotism to the fifty-six JACL chapters around the county, Kido "walked away from the radio. He smiled - as he and his people have always smiled when they are tense and worried. He thought of the Japan has never seen".

Kido thought of "the new Japanese-Americans, now, who were born in this country, who are American citizens, who have a new loyalty to face." Silverman assumes, of course, that Japanese-American citizens had to prove their allegiance to the United States.

But he quoted Kido as saying just that: Japanese-Americans "have been proclaiming their loyalty - the time to prove their true feelings has arrived." Eight paragraphs into the story, Silverman underscored the distinction made by the photo of Fujii; Kido, he said, "speaks for most of the 150,000 Japanese in this country.

Most of them - 70 per cent of them - are American, born in this country." As if reassuring his readers that their Japanese-American neighbours were not a threat, Silverman made clear that "most of them have never seen Japan, can't read or speak Japanese".

Older Japanese, including Toyoji Abe, publisher of the New World-Daily Sun, a Japanese-language newspaper, know "that their children owe no loyalty to Japan: They are Americans." Silverman quoted Abe as saying that he hoped "to remain in this country as a law-abiding resident, co-operating wherever possible with the American authorities," an attitude he claimed was shared by other Japanese-Americans.

Upon hearing of Pearl Harbor, Silverman wrote, "these men swallowed the most bitter pill they could imagine. They discovered their new country was attacked by their old country, and they made their decisions. They went American". Patriotism and loyalty were also the themes of a four-column San Francisco Chronicle photo of a group of Japanese-American soldiers huddled around a car, listening to war reports on the radio.

The banner above the photo read "Japanese Would Fight Japan," even though the soldiers were correctly identified in the caption as Japanese-Americans. "In a few months," the caption read, "they may be fighting on, and against, the soil their parents left." But like Kido and Abe, quoted in Silverman's story, "there was no hesitancy in this group," the caption read. "The attack was treacherous. The counter-attack should be relentless."

For the moment, Japanese-Americans were still a significant part of the news frame constructed by journalists covering the impact of Pearl Harbor. They had been given the chance to show their patriotism, even if journalists had in effect deployed their loyalty in order to help officials maintain order and cohesion. In addition, these early stories served a more destructive purpose: they marginalized - or, as Gitlin might argue, "domesticated"- Japanese-

Americans, even though they posed no threat, and were, for the most part, loyal citizens.

In their coverage, journalists created two groups of Japanese-Americans: the officials and the masses; only official, high-ranking Japanese-American officials were quoted, a finding consonant with Donohue, Tichenor, and Olien's claim that conflict is reported only when it involves "dominant powers or power blocs".

If there was any anti-American sentiment on the part of Japanese-Americans, it was not covered. Moreover, the average Japanese-American citizen appeared in stories as a cartoon-like, flag waving caricature. With this part of the story established, journalists were now primed to "sound the alarm" about the threat allegedly posed by Japanese nationals.

They soon moved beyond Japanese-American patriotism, beyond what Barthes (1973) calls "inoculation." Reporters allowed Japanese-Americans - for Barthes, "radical voices" - "a controlled moment of speech," one which ensured that "the social body [was] strengthened and not threatened by the contrast between it and the radical".

The guard dog function also offers a possible explanation for journalists' willingness to cover this angle: reporters often act as "fair weather friends for those with marginal positions of power". Journalists shed light on Japanese-American patriotism only until the government developed a policy for dealing with them.

Further, even in stories with a patriotic themes, reporters cited "official" Japanese-American sources in order to better manage the story, a practice that would continue, even when Japanese-Americans were nearly absent from the pages of these newspapers.

Eventually, the lives of Japanese-Americans would be "exnominated," to use Barthes' term. Homages to Japanese-American loyalty would end abruptly as coverage focused on the government's effort to win the war. Journalists continued their extensive coverage of roundup efforts. A page one headline in the December 8 Chronicle announced "Japanese in the U.S.: S.R Joins the Nation in Rounding Up Suspicious Characters and Some Business Men".

The reporter gave the local roundup a sense of national context, leading with "federal agents and troops moved into Japanese communities from San Francisco to Norfolk, Virginia, [and] Alaska to the Panama Canal shortly after noon yesterday and took into custody an undisclosed number of Japanese nationals."

The Chronicle story touched on incarceration efforts in San Diego, Sacramento, and New York. Police blocked off little Tokyo in Los Angeles, referred to in the story as "headquarters for 60,000 Japanese in Southern California. The Times reporter noted that "traffic was halted on First Street" in Little Tokyo in order to "prevent incidents". The Chronicle reported that "a number of people were picked up" by law enforcement officials, a fact missed or not included in the Little Tokyo story by the Times reporter.

The focus here is still on individual law enforcement officials exerting power, as Donohue, Tichenor, and Olien would argue. Nowhere is the structure from which their power emanates examined or challenged. Moreover, reporters were writing less about Japanese-Americans as individuals; Japanese-Americans were reduced to the number of people rounded up during a raid.

This suggests a corollary to the "guard dog" function: while conflict is reported to the extent that it affects individuals, those creating the conflict - even if that conflict is imagined or unrealized - are represented by journalists as a group of faceless, nameless individuals.

As law enforcement officials rounded up Japanese nationals, journalists began to engage in what Fiske calls "claw back"; they attempted to mediate this turn of events "into the dominant value system without losing [its] authenticity". The language used by the Chronicle reporter in the story cited earlier, for example, reinforces a positive image of law enforcement officials. The reporter wrote that a Japanese man "was hustled" into the local immigration station; FBI agents "swooped down" on a predominantly Japanese part of San Francisco.

Agents also arrested a man who was the "head man" of the local Japanese "colony" and who was also the editor of a Japanese newspaper. The article also gives a glowing description of how law enforcement officials "threw a blockade around the big Japanese fishing villages" on Terminal Island in Los Angeles Harbor.

Japanese fishermen coming home from the day's work "were herded into wire enclosures" by soldiers. To be sure, government officials were acting outside their traditional roles by rounding up Japanese-Americans, which in part explains the extensive coverage by journalists, the guard dog theory argues. Reporting would become even more intense when the federal government moved into the uncharted territory of internment.

STEPPING OUTSIDE TRADITIONAL ROLES

For the moment, the loyalty theme had simply outlived its usefulness. Officials now prepared to step outside of their traditional roles - a key condition for the emergence of "guard dog" reporting. In addition, government officials now supplied journalists with a steady stream of information about the arrests, which enabled journalists to more effectively manage the story.

In the Los Angeles Times, there was an unmistakable end to its recognition of Japanese-American patriotism. On December 9, it ran a lengthy page-nine article on the State Council of Defense's rejection of Governor Culbert Olson's plan to stave off potential riots by restricting Japanese nationals and Japanese-Americans to their homes.

The council was motivated more by pragmatism than by tolerance. Olson's restriction, the story noted, "might endanger the supply of vegetables and fruits to the public". Olson was quoted as saying that citizens "can expect anything since the occurrences of yesterday." It was the council's duty, he said, "to watch that no part of the civilian population be caught unaware or unprotected from any possible attack from the air or invasion."

Olson also outlined "action that should be taken to alleviate any tension in the situation crated by the 10,000 Japanese living in this area". Here, Olson sounds almost rancorous, perhaps because taken as a whole, the Times article is balanced. For example, the reporter emphasized the economic ramifications of detaining Japanese nationals and Japanese-Americans.

A December 13 Times photo showed JACL Anti-Axis Committee headquarters with a sign in its window reading "America - We Are Ready."

The photo's caption told readers that the organization would "turn over to authorities all `consorts of enemy.'" But after publication of the photo, which appeared under the heading "Japanese-Americans Ready to Fight Enemies," the Times fell silent on the loyalty issue.

Its readers began seeing stories about Japan and its people with charged headlines like "Japan Fanaticism Began in 559 B.C." and "Japan Pictured as Nation of Spies". In that first wave of photos, reporters allowed Japanese-Americans to reach out to the reader and show their loyalty; in the last Times photo, Japanese-American loyalty was reduced to a sign on a storefront.

It is worth noting that only one person appeared in the photo - a sudden change from the groups of Japanese-Americans professing loyalty in earlier photos. An accompanying article told readers that 500 Japanese and Japanese-Americans attended a meeting in which a state official told the farmers in the crowd to keep "tilling their fields and bringing their produce to market".

The New York Times' December 9 story on Japanese-American loyalty ran under a two-deck, one-column headline in the back of the issue's first section - a much less prominent position than those occupied by the Chronicle and Los Angeles Times stories. The chair of the American Committee for Protection of the Foreign Born said that "the foreign-born people of the United States will rally to the national cause with full loyalty in the present crisis" .

The story talked about guarantees of loyalty from German, Italian, and Japanese-Americans in the form of telegrams to FDR. The Times' pedestrian approach to the story is attributable to a comparatively small Japanese-American population in the eastern United States and in New York City. A day earlier, the Times ran a photo essay titled "The New War in the Pacific: Japanese and Chinese Reactions."

Reactions captured in the photos came from a group of Chinese diplomats giving the thumbs up sign in front of the Japanese Consulate, from a Japanese official burning boxes of papers outside the Japanese embassy in Washington,

D.C. (with the caption "Japanese waste no time in burning State papers on the grounds of their embassy"), and in two photos of Japanese officials representatives of the "dominant power" allegedly threatening our safety - leaving the Japanese consulate in New York, one with a police escort.

Japanese Americans still appeared in news stories and photos, but their marginalization by journalists continued. Reporters failed to explore why Japanese-Americans were in a position to have to profess their loyalty. Loyalty was embodied by patriotic Japanese-Americans gathered around a radio, and, later, by Japanese officials being escorted from the consulate.

In a subsequent story, Los Angeles Times writer Thomas Hamilton quoted First Lady Eleanor Roosevelt as saying she saw no reason "why Japanese with `good' records meaning `no criminal or anti-American record' - had anything to fear, whether they were long-time residents or had only just arrived." In the same article, Hamilton detailed Nicholas Biddle's order to the FBI to arrest "a selected group of Japanese aliens", but also quoted him as saying that mass arrests would be "unwise".

Hamilton does frame the issue as a discussion of the system-the structure -in place to deal with questions of loyalty, but builds the story on quotes from powerful individuals. Hamilton's story, along with a shorter December 10 Times story about the number of Japanese-American arrests in the United States to that point, details the "organized challenge," albeit an imaginary one, that Donohue, Tichenor, and Olien discuss as being at the heart of the guard dog function.

In fact, the government made extensive and successful use of the manufactured challenge; journalists responded to the uncertainty with more intense coverage of the "alien" issue. When government officials stepped even further outside their "traditional roles" and began to discuss internment, the guard dog barked even louder. We see this in a Times story in the December 10 issue. An adjoining two-column photo shows a group of Japanese Americans being taken into custody by sailors in Norfolk, Virginia.

In the story, the Times reported that an order from FDR that German and ItalianAmericans be caught in "the FBI dragnet" along with Japanese-Americans since "an invasion or predatory incursion is threatened upon the territory of the United States" by the other two Axis powers. FDR had to make this proclamation in order to invoke a federal law that allowed him to order the arrest of enemy aliens on sight.

Officials were now threatening the rights of innocent people - clear movement, Donohue, Tichenor, and Olien would argue, outside "the traditional roles of political conflict." The New York Times joined the Chronicle and Los Angeles Times in intensifying coverage of the issue.

On December 9, a New York Mmes story described the government's first sweep, telling readers that the arrests "of disloyal Nipponese still are being made as part of protective moves against any possible fifth column action". The December 10 New York Times story talked of "roundups" and the FBI's "sudden swoops" and resulting arrests.

A second December 9 story in the New York Times told of civilian officials "striking swiftly throughout Los Angeles and Southern California" to take 500 "alien Japanese" into custody. True to the guard dog function, the story told of individuals in power roles struggling to deal with the problem: "Deputy sheriffs, led by Undersheriff Jack Ross, and California highway patrolmen, combed the farm houses and Japanese vegetable growers dormitories through the Santa Maria, Guadalupe, and Lompoc valleys".

On December 13, a two-deck headline in the New York Times announced: "2,541 Axis Aliens Now in Custody." The first eight paragraphs of the accompanying story focused on Biddle, the official source, including his reminder to citizens that aliens were "dangerous to the peace and safety of the nation".

Thus, in less than a week, print reporters had raised the issue of Japanese-American patriotism, removed it from the news frame, and diminished Japanese-Americans by quoting only official sources, and by focusing on efforts of law enforcement officials and the federal government to control a problem that didn't exist.

By reporting on what Donohue, Tichenor, and Olien might call an "externally based conflict," journalists cleared the way for the government to take its nascent Japanese-American policy to the next level. As discussed in the next section, journalists would continue to encourage the "reinforcement of local cohesion" discussed by Donohue, Tichenor, and Olien.

Readers of these newspapers soon began seeing inaccurate and inflammatory reports of fifth column activity along with the arrest summaries. Having to deal with this threat was portrayed by reporters as beyond the government's traditional role - beyond its control, as Donohue, Tichenor, and Olien discuss. It was as if these "guard dog" reporters were offering a bit of breathing room to a government struggling to get its act together.

Coverage of the threat soon intensified, and was clearly biased in favour of government officials. The Los Angeles Times reported that Charles Ishii, president of the Regional American Japanese Public Service Association, had been arrested despite his earlier statement that Japanese-Americans were loyal. The story's subhead diminished Ishii: "Asiatic, who had pledged loyalty, found with guns".

In the same issue, the Times had laid the groundwork for reports of fifth column activity in the United States by running a story on Japanese troops landing in the Philippines "with the probable help of `fishermen' fifth columnists" near the entrance to Manila Bay.

The level of sourcing deemed acceptable by journalists working at the time is seen in the story's third paragraph: "the report of the landing on Lubang, some sixty miles southwest of the big American naval base of Cavite, was not confirmed officially, but enough credence was placed in it that defence officers were trying urgently to contact the provincial Governor."

The reporter here fails to define "credence," and does not inform readers who supported the account. For the Chronicle, the ensuing days were marked by the continuing count of detained aliens. On December 9, a page eight headline read: "The Alien Roundup: 200 S.F. Policemen Begin Looking for Germans and Italians". Subheads inserted in the story included "The Big Take" and "Fresno Arrests."

The reporter imbued the story with a decidedly misanthropic flavour: The arrests netted Japanese nationals, as well as some Japanese citizens of the United States, in Los Angeles, Seattle, San Diego, Sacramento, Fresno, Stockton, various other Pacific Coast and inland points, and on the Eastern Seaboard. Hawaii jailed 391 Japanese.

The word "netted" gives the impression that Japanese-Americans were little more than animals. The reporter also wrote that "guards were stationed in front of 100 Japanese business houses, throttling their operations." An agent from the Department of the Treasury was quoted by the reporter as saying he and his colleagues had thwarted numerous attempts to remove financial documents from Japanese-owned businesses.

It should be noted, however, that the call for tolerance and recognition of loyalty did not completely disappear; it moved for a time to the Chronicle's editorial pages. A December 9 Chronicle editorial acknowledged that "some Japanese-born, legally barred from naturalization, are at heart strong for American ideals.

However, in the same editorial, the paper argued that "some American-born Japanese, hence citizens (written as if this was a sudden development), are reasonably suspect for alien sympathy." The paper warned its readers that "there is no excuse to wound the sensibilities of any persons in America by showing suspicion or prejudice" ("This is a Tough Time," 1941).

Doing so, the editorial continued, "is a help to the fifth column spirit." Moving the loyalty argument to a different section of the paper allowed reporters and editors to manage and at the same time marginalize it. The issue was no longer important enough to be covered regularly, or to occupy space on the news pages.

Reporters were now occupied with fifth column activity, and with the government's movement outside of its traditional role to deal with it, as Donohue, Tichenor and Olien would argue. In his seminal work on news media portrayal of the left, Gitlin argues that the news media often "limit the terms of effective opposition".

Here, reporters were, to apply Gitlin's term, slowly "defining away" Japanese-Americans, and were doing so based on a false characterization the threat to national security - that they had a role in creating. Reporters had first placed Japanese-Americans in the position of having to defend themselves, and were now marginalizing their attempts to do so.

In the same issue, a letter to the editor detailed its writer's relationship with a fiercely loyal Japanese-American family. The writer urged tolerance: We Americans of European descent, we so-called whites, must choose. We can give the lead to the ill-willed, the stupid and the prejudiced intelligent among us, and so hurt and bewilder 100,000 fellow citizens. Or, repudiating our ugly intolerances, we can by mere quiet decency towards superficially "different" Americans, strengthen both army and navy with the equivalent of $100,000,000 worth of equipment.

Two days later, the Chronicle published a letter from Nori Ikeda of San Francisco. Ikeda pledged his support to Roosevelt's war policy and condemned the attack on Pearl Harbor. He said he spoke for all Japanese Americans "in saying that we are ready to do our share in the defence of the United States. We ask you to have faith in our loyalty to America, our country, and to believe in our desire to do what we can to promote unity of will and action in this national emergency".

Some readers were moved by these expressions of devotion. In a letter to the Chronicle, San Francisco resident Sylvia Brown asked: "Isn't there something that can be done about those feeble-minded `patriots' who go about venting their childish emotions upon our good and loyal Japanese citizens?"

But by the time these letters were published, journalists had successfully minimized reaction to the official stance on Japanese-Americans. Soon, even fewer voices rose to defend Japanese-Americans.

FUNCTION OF JOURNALISM IN COVERAGE

Print journalists at first halfheartedly played the celebrated role of "watchdog," in some cases urging readers to be tolerant of Japanese-Americans. But their tolerance, and their time in the "watchdog" role, lasted only until the government put the finishing touches on its policy to deal with alleged fifth column activity, a policy which culminated in the internment. From that point on, print journalists assumed the role of "guard dog," acting as the government's sentry, patrolling for threats to the official version of events that unfolded after Pearl Harbor.

Donohue, Tichenor, and Olien outlined the "guard dog" function as it relates to political reporting, but I argue that it is of particular relevance here. "Guard dog" journalists act as "sentries" for groups who hold power and who have the ability to create their own security systems - in this instance, the federal government, local and state officials, and the military.

Guard dog reporting takes place "when external forces present a threat to local leadership". In writing favorably about dominant groups, journalists tend to "concentrate on individuals while accepting the structure," a tendency seen clearly (and discussed in more detail later) in reporting on the alleged Japanese-American threat to national security. Through their interaction with and dependence on local leaders for information, journalists are trained to suspect potential intruders, and sometimes, as is the case here, "sound the alarm" for reasons that the dominant group may initially be unable to understand.

This inability arises when the authority within the power structure is divided or when part of the power structure is made uncertain by an organized challenge. Along the way, groups who lack power and influence receive little attention from "guard dog" journalists. How a journalist gathers information and writes stories is shaped by the nature of the structure being served and by whom the dominant groups label a threat.

When there is consensus in a community, the guard dog "sleeps," stirring only when an external threat to local leadership materializes. Conflict is reported "in a constrained way and only on certain issues and under certain structural conditions" - in short, when there is conflict between "dominant powers or power blocs". Further, "where different local groups have conflicting interests," Donohue, Tichenor, and Olien argue, "the media are more likely to reflect the views of the more powerful groups".

Such protection highlights "the functions of externally based conflict for reinforcement of local cohesion". Coverage emphasizes the role of dominant groups in addressing issues and correcting problems faced by the community. The guard dog function rejects as "unrealistic" the "watchdog" role of the press taught in so many university journalism classes as a guiding principle for journalistic practice.

The media are not autonomous; they operate as part of the power structure; as such, they "have neither the inclination nor the power to challenge those dominant groups, unless they are already under challenge by other forces". Unable to develop social policy or motivate political action, the media are left to report on actions taken by dominant groups.

If, as in the case of alleged "fifth column" activity explored in this monograph, "these groups and agencies are concerned primarily with an external threat, that will be the agenda of the media.". Questions from reporters that seem to challenge the official view of an event or issue amount to "role playing" driven more by attacks from "contending powers" than by a journalist's desire to expose corruption or challenge action taken by a corporation or agency.

The "guard dog" theory of reporting also runs counter to the view that reporters are little more than "lapdogs," - submissive, dependent, and oblivious to all interests except those of powerful groups. While a "guard dog" journalist does defer to authority, he or she is not completely subservient to dominant interests. In times of conflict, the work of a "lapdog" journalist would amount to little more than a "defence of the powerful against outside intruders," while the "guard dog" reporter would look for opportunities to report conflict between dominant groups. How deferent a journalist is "depends upon the nature of the community structure as well as on the concentration of power in the larger society".

Finally, the guard dog theory rejects the notion that the media are "equal co-actors" in society's power structure, able to motivate support for policies created by the government, their influence so palpable "that only unusually strong institutions and leaders can counter it". In actuality, reporters are "dependent on the dominant powers" and act to protect "the local power establishment".

Reporters pay a great deal of attention to "nation and society - their persistence, cohesion, and the conflicts and divisions threatening their cohesion". The "tug of war" between the media and dominant powers seen by some is in reality "a result of reporting and reflecting the conflicting views among divided political or economic bodies".

A secondary theoretical strand for this chapter comes from Fiske's work on news as text. Fiske argues for the study of news as a form of discourse - "a set of conventions that strive to control and limit the meanings of the events it conveys". A string of events like those that unfolded after Pearl Harbor are, to use Fiske's term, "unruly." Journalists struggled to make sense of events and to gather information on which to build coverage.

This analysis also explores how journalists applied some of the "strategies of containment" discussed by Fiske to try and routinize coverage of the issues. It is argued, for example, that the government's take on the Japanese American threat became the dominant narrative strand in news coverage of this period; that is, it was "nominated," to use Barthes' term.

Coverage that promoted fairness and tolerance in dealing with Japanese-Americans was "exnominated" once the government took steps to implement its policy for dealing with the Japanese-American issue. For an event to be newsworthy, Fiske argues, it must pertain to "elite" people; it must also be "negative" and "surprising". Of the Japanese-Americans quoted in early coverage, many were prominent business owners and organization officials-the "elite," it could be argued, of the Japanese-American community.

Not only did this reliance on elite sources make it easier for journalists to manage early coverage of the crisis, it also gave them the means to begin marginalizing Japanese-Americans. When journalists began paying more attention to the government's version of events, they all but stopped using Japanese-Americans as sources. Instead, they looked only to prominent government and military officials for the lion's share of their information.

As Fiske notes, "the socially powerful tend to be familiar to us as individuals, the powerless or the voices of opposition are familiar mainly as social roles, which are filled by a variety of forgettable individuals". Donohue,

Tichenor, and Olien conclude their discussion of the "guard dog" function with a series of hypotheses formulated to guide further exploration of journalistic practice:

In any structure, the intensity of press reporting and editorializing about a public issue is directly proportional to the degree to which top power positions are uncertain as a result of organized challenge.

Media are more likely to report attacks on individuals in power roles than attacks on power structures. Guard dog media reporting is less intense when the strategies of powerful actors are confined to the traditional roles of political conflict. Media coverage tends to be evaluated as more favorable among groups and occupations occupying more established and dominant power positions, compared with groups and organizations having less established power.

Questioning of the guard dog role is more likely in a highly pluralistic structure than a less pluralistic one. The balance of the monograph will be a test of these hypotheses built on coverage by journalists at three of the nation's most important newspapers of alleged "fifth column" activity by Japanese-Americans.

This case study of the "guard dog" function of the press is built on a textual analysis of the New York Times, San Francisco Chronicle, and Los Angeles Times from December 8, 1941-the day after the attack on Pearl Harbor - to February 19, 1942, the day FDR issued Executive Order 9066.

In all, the main news sections of seventy-two issues of each newspaper were reviewed. The New York Times was selected because of its reputation as the nation's "newspaper of record." The Los Angeles Times and Chronicle were included because they were, and continue to be, two of the most widely read newspapers on the West Coast.

Articles, columns, and letters to the editor that discussed Japanese-Americans, alleged fifth column activity, or calls for or against evacuation of Japanese-Americans were analysed for recurring thematic elements and thematic changes. The goal of the analysis was to chart the emergence of the "guard dog" function, and to show how journalists framed coverage of the alleged Japanese-American threat to national security.

President Franklin D. Roosevelt's decision in 1942 to intern more than 140,000 Japanese-American citizens is one of the darkest chapters in the nation's history. Constitutional rights were trampled; possessions were seized, lives destroyed - all in the name of eliminating a nonexistent threat to national security. Justification for Roosevelt's action came from fabricated reports of potential "fifth column" activity by Japanese-Americans from military officials bent on marshaling support for the United States' entry into World War II.

Issued by Roosevelt on February 19, 1942, Executive Order 9066 empowered the Secretary of War to "exclude any and all persons, citizens, and aliens, from designated areas in order to provide security against sabotage, espionage, and fifth column activity". Immigrants born in Japan (Issei) and second generation Japanese-Americans (Nisei) were not allowed to work or travel anywhere on the West Coast.

They were rounded up and sent first to "assembly centres," and then to one of ten relocation centres run by the civilian-staffed War Relocation Authority. On December 7, Roosevelt empowered Attorney General Francis Biddle to have the FBI arrest a set number of enemy aliens. On December 8, the Department of justice closed the borders of the United States both to enemy aliens and to "all persons of Japanese ancestry, whether citizen or alien".

By December 11, nearly 1,400 Japanese-Americans, by then classified as "dangerous enemy aliens," had been taken into custody. The Aliens Division of the Department of Justice, created by Congress in 1940, maintained lists of aliens who would be interned once war began. The Aliens Division was run by John Franklin Carter, a former journalist.

It was Carter who sent FDR a report from West Coast businessman Curtis Munson in which Munson claimed that while most Issei and Nisei were loyal to the United States, "there are still Japanese.who will tie dynamite around their waist and make a human bomb out of themselves".

Despite Munson's report, military officials at first concluded that "widespread sabotage by Japanese is not expected" and that "identification of dangerous Japanese in the west coast is reasonably complete". Nevertheless, 3,000 enemy aliens-half of them Japanese -were interned during the week following Pearl Harbor; the Treasury Department soon froze their bank accounts.

On December 19, 1941, General John DeWitt made the first military proposal for internment. The strongest advocates for internment would include then California Attorney General Earl Warren, later a revered champion of civil rights during his time on the Supreme Court, and DeWitt, who, along with Secretary of War Henry Stimson, encouraged Roosevelt to pursue evacuation as a viable means of ending the Japanese-American "threat" to national security.

Warren told a Congressional committee in February 1942 that Japanese-American sabotage and treachery would inevitably surface: "I believe that we are being lulled into a false sense of security.our day of reckoning is bound to come". In fact, DeWitt lied in his report to Roosevelt about the existence of the threat, a lie left unchallenged for more than four decades, until a federal appeals court ruled that the statute of limitations did not cancel the claims of Japanese-American evacuees whose property was seized before they were interned.

The Supreme Court relied on incomplete evidence when it held that possible subversive activities justified the evacuation of Japanese-Americans, the appeals court ruled. A key purveyor of this "incomplete evidence," according to a number of historians and institutions acting on behalf of Japanese-

Americans, was the print media. Acting far more pliant than the "guard dog" described by Donohue, Tichenor, and Olien, journalists were willing pawns in the government's attempts to paint Japanese-Americans as a threat to national security. Anecdotal evidence cited in accounts written by these historians offers some support for this claim. The Los Angeles Times, for example, announced on December 8 that California was "a zone of danger".

"We have thousands of Japanese here," a Times reporter wrote, "some, perhaps many are good Americans. What the rest may be we do not know, nor can we take a chance in the light of yesterday's demonstration that treachery and double-dealing are major Japanese weapons". After Pearl Harbor, Daniels contends, the Los Angeles Times called on "alert keen-eyed citizens" to finger what were surely "spies, saboteurs, and fifth columnists in their midsts". And it was not the first time that newspapers on the West Coast had attacked Asian-Americans.

In 1905, the San Francisco Chronicle lashed out at Asian immigrants in a series of articles supporting attempts by California's political parties and the American Federation of Labour to end immigration from China and Japan. Stories from the Chronicle carried headlines like "Crime and Poverty Go Hand in Hand with Asiatic Labour" and "Japanese a Menace to American Women".

Four decades later, an immediate call came from a number of journalists to deal decisively with the potential Japanese-American threat; according to Hosokawa, "other voices took up the cry as the days passed, until newspaper and radio commentators were baying like a pack of wolves on a hot trail."

West Coast newspapers "abandoned [their] tradition of supporting the underdog, seeking the truth, unmasking the demagogues, and demanding fair play". Syndicated columnist Henry McLemore brashly called for internment: "herd `em up, pack `em off, and give `em the inside room in the badlands". No journalist was more ardent about evacuation than Scripps-Howard columnist Westbrook Pegler, who advocated putting all Japanese-Americans under surveillance and suspending their habeas corpus rights.

For every hostage killed by the Axis powers, Pegler argued, the United States should kill "100 victims out of [American] concentration camps". At the time, however, the federal government was not actively considering evacuation. In a memo to Roosevelt, Attorney General Nicholas Biddle said that an attack on the West Coast by the Japanese was not imminent.

Hysteria, "and, in some instances, the comments of the press and radio announcers have resulted in a tremendous amount of pressure being brought to bear" on Warren and California Governor Culbert Olson, Hoover said in a memo to Biddle.

But joining Pegler in warning readers about the potential for a Japanese attack on the West Coast was revered columnist Walter Lippmann. At DeWitt's request, Lippmann, in his February 20, 1942 column, told his readers that he agreed with Warren, who argued that because the Japanese and Japanese-Americans were all the more dangerous since they had not yet engaged in any surreptitious activity. Inactivity, Lippmann wrote, was "a sign that the blow is well-organized and that it is held back until it can be struck with maximum effect".

More than twenty years later, Lippmann stood by his work: "There is no doubt that the rights of the [Japanese-American] citizens were abridged by the measure, but I felt then, and still do, that the temper of the times made the measure justified". Lippmann's quick assent to DeWitt's wishes contradicts his standing in the eyes of many scholars as "the most wise and forceful spokesman for objectivity" in journalism.

Indeed it was Lippmann who wrote that "men who have lost their grip upon the relevant facts of their environment are the inevitable victims of agitation and propaganda. The quack, the charlatan, the jingo, and the terrorist can flourish only where the audience is deprived of independent access to information".

The government and the military capably filled the role of charlatan as the period between Pearl Harbor and Executive Order 9066 unfolded, encouraging stories of decisiveness even as they wavered about the correct course of action. But for their part, reporters did not, to use Hosokawa's words, begin "baying like a pack of wolves on a hot trail."

They gradually fell into the role of "guard dog" discussed by Donohue, Tichenor, and Olien, focusing for at least a short time on the patriotism shown by Japanese-Americans. Only as the crisis unfolded - and the government deployed a policy to deal with it - did print reporters shift coverage to the fifth column threat fabricated by officials. We turn now to a detailed textual analysis of how this coverage unfolded.

DOMINANT POWER POSITIONS

The federal government soon accelerated dissemination of fifth column reports. A page one story in the December 11 Chronicle said that the Army "had ringed the Nation with men and steel sufficient to `meet any threat' of invasion." As before, reporters told readers that the threat was directed at law enforcement officials, not the power structure, as Donohue, Tichenor, and Olien would argue.

It was reported that a group of unknown individuals had set a series of brush fires that resembled arrows, one pointing to the Bremerton Navy Yard in Washington, the other to Seattle. As a result, the story said, "the Fifth columnist search was on in the region of Post Angeles, Washington". The New York Times on December 11 ran a six-paragraph story on the alleged incident on page 25. Two days earlier, the Los Angeles Times ran a page one story reporting the Army's announcement that two groups of enemy aircraft had been spotted near San Francisco Bay. An army general told the Chronicle that the planes "were turned back at the Golden Gate". DeWitt was quoted in the New York Times story on alleged incident as saying that those who believed there was no danger were "inane, idiotic, and foolish".

"Remember that San Francisco is so full of military objectives that the whole city is a military objective," DeWitt said, suggesting later that "it might have been `a good thing' if the visitors dropped some bombs". Such an event, DeWitt said, attacking opposition to the American war effort, "might have awakened some of the fools in this community who refuse to realise this is a war".

On December 13, the New York Times discussed reports of "unidentified planes" near San Diego and speculated about a possible air base "in sparsely settled Lower California, where border rumors have placed large concentrations of large Japanese". Nowhere in these articles do reporters describe their attempts to confirm the military's reports; they rely solely on military and government sources, or, in the case of the New York Times, or what were referred to by the reporter as "local Mexican sources."

In Chronicle stories published on December 11, reporters, having established a dominant narrative about Japanese-Americans for their readers, now took a more misanthropic tone; it is at this point that references to "Japs" and "Nips" begin appearing in their stories.

A turning point in the coverage was a press conference held by Secretary of the Navy Frank Knox on December 15, 1941 upon his return from examining the carnage at Pearl Harbor. Referring to Japanese-Americans living in Hawaii, he told reporters that "the most effective fifth column work of the war was done there". Some have argued that Knox lied to reporters about fifth column activity in order to convince Americans that getting involved in the war was the wisest course of action.

But as 1941 ended, journalists continued to intensify their reporting of alleged fifth column activity. There were even fewer signs of even-handedness; gone were accounts of Japanese-American loyalty; the use of Japanese-Americans as sources for stories waned.

The Chronicle on December 22 published an editorial in which it recognized a "proof of loyalty" offered by a group of Japanese-Americans in San Francisco who had organized a special chapter auxiliary to the Red Cross. Nisei, the editorial said, "are not to blame for defects of any persons in their groups."

According to the editorial, "it is actions, not antecedents that count." Hypocrisy teems from this statement. Acting in their guard dog role, these newspapers had been propagating false and exaggerated reports from the government of the kind of "actions" alluded to in the Chronicle editorial. Japanese-Americans should not have felt the need to create their own Red Cross chapter, the editorial's writer claimed.

"If it seems to distinguish them by their own action as a unit apart, it is a distinction already forced upon them by the hysterical judgement of many Americans." Such a sentiment must have been little comfort to Japanese-Americans in the Bay Area, especially since the effort by reporters to frame the crisis in a way that supported the government was probably at the root of much of the "hysterical judgement" referred to by the author.

The next day, Chronicle columnist Dorothy Thompson repeated the warning uttered by Knox at his December 15 press conference: "There is a monstrous fifth column in the United States - just as there was a fifth column in Hawaii, which contributed to the disaster at Pearl Harbor.". Thompson asked: "Have those people been found, and are they still not operating?"

Thompson later gave vivid evidence of the news media's guard dog role when she wrote, "one of the greatest weapons that can be used against them is the press publicity, clarification of their methods, so that the people themselves can see what's going on". Thompson laid bare the news media's work as sentry - saying, in effect, that reporters were now part of the war effort, and that the government could count on their unstinting support.

As Donohue, Tichenor, and Olien note, "media coverage tends to be evaluated as favorable among groups.occupying more established and dominant power positions". Officials would have no cause to evaluate press coverage of their efforts as anything other than favorable. The successful marginalization of Japanese-Americans by the press, done to galvanize support for the war, had left no room for "questioning the guard dog role" played by reporters.

In an article published the same day, the New York Times offered apparent confirmation of Thompson's claims, reporting on page four the arrest of 273 alleged fifth columnists in Hawaii. As had become common practice, the Times article cited only government officials. The reporter referenced the Knox press conference, but reassured readers that "there were no Fifth Columnists among the members of the armed services in Hawaii".

Our institutions, thanks to the presence of "great persons" like DeWitt and Knox were safe. But the threat still loomed; while most of the Japanese-Americans in Hawaii were loyal, the article reported, some had "provided the enemy with valuable military information".

As the year ended, the Chronicle continued to publish stories about successful containment of the threat. On December 27, Biddle ordered all aliens to turn over all cameras and radios or face internment in what the Chronicle referred to as "concentration camps."

A short page one article on December 28 was headlined "Aliens Must Surrender Their Radios"; the next day, the newspaper ran a detailed article about the nearly 5,000 radios turned over by "axis aliens" to San Francisco police. In the middle of the article, the reporter cited a government report that "enemy fifth columnists" had contacted enemy forces from Washington -

"presumably Pacific raiders and undersea boats which have been attacking West Coast ships".

The New York Times on December 29 ran a two-column photo showing two elderly Japanese-American residents turning over a radio to a San Francisco police officer under the heading "Japanese Aliens Comply with U.S. Order." The rest of the Chronicle article read like a how-to guide for marginalized Japanese-Americans: "if an alien is in doubt about what he should do to comply with the order, he should turn in his camera or radio at once.

Resolve all doubts in favour of the Government." Reporters had allowed the government to organize and give life to the challenge, and were now content to report the success the government enjoyed in managing the challenge. The sentry was still at its post. In a year-end article appearing in the New York Times, United Press reporter Wallace Carroll provided vivid evidence that journalists continued to act as "sentries" for the government even after Japanese-Americans had been completely marginalized. In a story headlined "Japanese Spies Showed the Way for Raid on Vital Areas in Hawaii," Carroll gave the most detailed account of the alleged fifth column activity.

Recall again that there was absolutely no evidence of such activity. Carroll's main contentions, based on a visit to Honolulu, were (1) that large arrows were cut in sugar cane fields to pinpoint military objectives; (2) that a Japanese man arrested for operating a short-wave radio during the attack on Pearl Harbor was a frequent visitor to a U.S. Army post; (3) that Japanese vegetable sellers were aware of movements in and out of port by the U.S. Navy; and (4) that ads, "innocent looking and accepted by newspapers in good faith, may have contained code messages to the fifth columnists".

Carroll's reports were never corroborated. Carroll did tell his readers that the article "was not intended as an indictment of all Japanese in Honolulu." For the most part, he wrote, "they were industrious and well-behaved. But enough of them were fifth columnists to make the attack successful."

Carroll showed the lack of any boundary between reporter and sentry when he wrote: "The facts, if presented to the American people now, may help put them on alert in other potential areas of danger". Carroll's article is noteworthy in at least one other respect: it was written in the first person. Journalists tend not to write stories using this voice because it damages their credibility by creating the appearance of bias.

Carroll carried the approach through to the end of the piece, when he warned readers that there was still work to be done: "When I left Honolulu ten days ago, I was informed that Japanese members of the Territorial Guard still were stationed at reservoirs, power plants and other public utilities. Japanese-Americans still held positions in the post office and telephone service."

Coverage of fifth column activity by all three papers in January and February 1942 became even more inflammatory as calls began to come for internment -

a larger step clearly outside the "traditional roles of political conflict" discussed by Donohue, Tichenor, and Olien. Stories continued to dehumanize Japanese-Americans. The Los Angeles Times reported on January 14 that a Japanese-American gardener was denied his chance to sue his landlord because he was unable to prove his citizenship.

The next day, a California Superior Court judged ruled that "foreignborn Japanese" lacked legal standing. The January 18 Times reported that Koshiro Endo, a teacher, had been arrested by the FBI. The three-paragraph story ran under the headline, "Jap Educator Seized by the FBL" The FBI refused comment on the reason for the arrest, a point apparently not challenged by the reporter who wrote the story.

On January 22, the Times ran an Associated Press story in which California Congressman Leland Ford called for immediate internment of all Japanese-Americans. Ford acknowledged that the issue was "rather touchy in some quarters due to the fact many Japanese are native-born,"-which, of course, would make them American citizens, a distinction lost on Ford and omitted by the AP reporter, who was content to run portions of Ford's statement verbatim.

The reporter made little or no effort to contextualize Ford's statement, listing Ford's opinions without challenge: "He feels that these native-born Japanese may not be any more loyal than are the foreign born," the story says. "He develops the fact that other loyal Americans are enlisting in the Army and Navy and Air Force."

The writer continued. Since so many other Americans are making sacrifices, "he believes is it not asking too much of the Japanese to make theirs in the form of permitting themselves to be placed in concentration camps, although they may be loyal." Once again acting as "guard dog," the reporter is framing the purported threat as it affects a single "great person" - in this case, Ford.

As support grew for our involvement in the war, reporters continued to intensify the language they used in their stories to refer to the efforts underway to detain Japanese-Americans. On January 30, the Chronicle began what became an almost daily page one report under some variation of the heading "Alien Restrictions."

The newspaper reported that Biddle had ordered that San Francisco's "strategic waterfront districts" be "swept clean" of enemy aliens. Japanese-Americans would be banned from twenty-nine "forbidden zones" along the West Coast. Biddle warned local officials to let the federal government handle the removal of aliens, since it was "in possession of all the facts" regarding their threat to national security.

A follow-up story the next day on demands by members of Congress to give the War Department authority to clear "strategic areas" carried the massive headline "Rigid Rules Hit S.F. Aliens". A three-deck subhead told readers that

"Subversive Elements Will Be Crushed." The Chronicle reporter proudly wrote that "America's long— ridiculed attitude of sweetness and light to enemy aliens has been forever blasted out of existence". For the first time, enemy aliens saw: the grim spectre of concentration camps, mass evacuation of families, revocation of business licenses, doctors and dentists thrown out of work, a savage hunt to crush secret organizations.

Government measures were grouped together by the Chronicle reporter and referred to for the first time as an "anti-alien programme." A page one story from the Los Angeles Times on January 28 shows a more reserved tone, despite its inflammatory headline - "Eviction of Jap Aliens Sought":

Southland authorities yesterday urged upon President Roosevelt and governmental agencies that all Japanese aliens be evicted immediately from Los Angeles Harbor and from the vicinity of defence plants and aircraft factories,

Much later in the article, the reporter, discussing the forced removal of Japanese-Americans from city jobs, makes a significant change in the news frame. To this point, reporters had at least sporadically acknowledged the possibility that some Japanese-Americans were loyal to the United States.

Quoting Los Angeles County Manager Wayne Allen, the reporter eliminates any vestiges of tolerance: "It is difficult if not impossible to distinguish loyal from disloyal Japanese." Citing this response is the work of a guard dog now in complete support of the official version of the Japanese-American issue.

Remaining signs of the balance seen in earlier stories were now gone. Under a two-deck headline that read "Speedy Moving of Japs Urged," Times reporter Kyle Palmer on December 31 described a call by local members of Congress on the Justice Department to take a stronger stance on evacuation.

In the lead, Palmer told readers that local members of Congress had taken "sharp issue with the leisurely programme" set up by Justice "for evacuating enemy aliens and possible sympathizers".

Waiting until the middle of February to evacuate Japanese-Americans, Palmer wrote, "might precipitate rather than prevent serious acts of sabotage". Local members of Congress urged Roosevelt to turn over control of all enemy aliens to the War Department.

At first glance, the guard dog seems to be wandering from its post. In actuality, however, only the master has changed. Here, the reporter focuses on the concern of local officials that the federal government was not acting quickly enough to deal with the problem.

The reporter frames the story as a disagreement among "power blocs" - a tendency of guard dog reporting posited by Donohue, Tichenor, and Olien. Nowhere do reporters cite reaction from the JACL or from Japanese-Americans in the area.

Thus, as officials accelerated their efforts to create a plan of evacuation, the people directly affected by that plan - Japanese-Americans - had been all but eliminated from the news frame, their presence lost to extensive coverage of squabbling among dominant institutions still at odds over the correct course of action.

Rather than explore the competing versions of the plan, or probe their potential impact, journalists in effect looked on while the conflict among power blocs simmered.

THE "CONTENDING POWERS" GIVE IN

When federal officials completed their plans for dealing with JapaneseAmericans, journalists, who had long since abandoned objective portrayals of Japanese-Americans, embraced the return to stability. Criticisms of the plan from local and state officials - "contending powers," as Donohue, Tichenor and Olien call them - would continue, but federal officials soon moved decisively towards internment.

One of the first newspapers to fully endorse evacuation was the San Diego Union. On January 20, 1942, the paper started a series of editorials attacking the Japanese for Pearl Harbor. Later, Union editorial writers concluded that there was no way to determine the loyalty of Japanese-Americans. A Sacramento Bee reader argued that the Japanese "were forcing other races off the land, including whites from pioneer families".

In the Santa Rosa Press Democrat, a reader asked "Biologically and economically, is the Jap fitted (sic) to mingle in American life?" Los Angeles newspaper columnist Lee Shippey, prophetically advocated creating "a number of big, closely watched truck farms on which Japanese-Americans could earn a living and assure us a steady supply of vegetables".

In a February 1 front-page editorial (like the article written in the first person, a rarity for most newspapers), the Chronicle provided clear evidence that its reporters were ready to endorse whatever measures the government would implement: "In time of war, the way to escape politics and hysteria is to leave it to the constituted authorities. And that means, in this case, the Federal authorities".

Now that the threat had been identified, it was up to the government, buttressed by nearly two months of staunch support from print journalists, to deal with the problem. Journalists had seen the government through its indecision, as Donohue, Tichenor, and Olien argue, and now believed it was ready to act. Ironically, however, the Chronicle stopped far short of endorsing internment.

While it supported removal of Japanese-Americans from "designated strategic areas," the newspaper stressed that "it was not necessary to imitate Hitler by herding whole populations, the guilty and the innocent together, into even humane concentration camps" State and local officials should not adopt such a policy, nor should citizens "take `the law' -or, rather the absence of it-into their own hands." Instead, the editorial concluded, everyone should "leave it to the Government".

The Chronicle's zealotry continued to show in its headlines; the newspaper began almost every story on evacuation with a headline that included the words "aliens," "enemy aliens," or "alien roundup." The Los Angeles Times mixed reports of successful evacuation with stories of fifth column activity. On February 3, the Times ran two photos of Japanese-Americans on page six.

The first, under the banner, "Nipponese Get Free Trip to Immigration Stations" pictured a group of Japanese-Americans being transported to a detention station on Los Angeles' Terminal Island "on one of Uncle Sam's free bus rides." Gone were the happy pictures of loyal Japanese-Americans listening to the radio for war news.

Instead, readers of the Times saw an FBI agent questioning a Japanese-American man (in the other February 3 Times photo). The agent, the caption read, "instructed the man to go to his home." In an adjoining Associated Press story, Earl Warren was quoted as saying that the West Coast was "wide open to any kind of sabotage or fifth column activity".

Warren told a meeting of California law enforcement officials that there had already been "numerous violations" of California's Alien Land Act. Ventura County officials were soon joining in the call for evacuation, the Times reported the next day. "Our gravest danger," according to a county official quoted in the story, "is from native-born Japs who still worship the Emperor".

According to county officials, "it is impossible to know those Japanese who are loyal to the United States." On February 6, the Times reported that H.A. Van Norman, the chief engineer of Los Angeles' Bureau of Water Works and Supply in 1934 had received a request from the Japanese consulate for information on the city's water supply. This was convincing evidence, the Times reporter wrote, of a plot to do damage to the water system. The letter, reproduced across three columns, would be part of the evidence gathered by Martin Dies, a member of Congress, of fifth column activity dating back before Pearl Harbor. The story reported "growing dissatisfaction" with the federal government for failing to: take more drastic action in connection with not only the Japanese espionage activities in prewar times but in the seeming lack of speed and effectiveness with regard to the current handling of the alien problem on the Coast. Dies, who chaired the House Un-American Activities Committee, would release a report on "the extent of Nipponese espionage in this country," the Times reported on page six of the same issue.

The report, which included information gathered before Pearl Harbor, supported charges "that Federal authorities failed to take necessary precautions and prevented his group from disclosing the extent of the Japanese spy ring". Quoting only Dies, the story reported that Japanese citizens allowed to enter this country for business reasons - so-called "treaty traders" - had "energetically collected information which would have been of tremendous value to an enemy nation," the Times reported. Further, the Dies report revealed that Nisei were allegedly forced to belong to organizations called "Kens" which demanded that they send money to Japan. Another Times evacuation story reported Mayor Bowron's concern that "if there is intrigue going on, and it is reasonably certain that there is, right here is the hotbed, the nerve centre, of the spy system, of planning for sabotage".

Local officials had no idea what the federal government was going to do to address the problem, Bowron said. City officials wanted to cooperate with their federal counterparts, "but it appears to us that no one in authority in the federal government knows what to do."

Here, at least part of the "organized challenge" to dominant institutions was coming from local officials. Coverage of the challenge intensified because these individuals clearly were acting outside their traditional roles. Later, the Times reporter underscored the changing definition of loyalty; under the subheading "Country First," the reporter asked "How to tell them apart?"

According to Bowron, "the answer is locked in the hearts of the Japanese-Americans in our midst." The Times would later quote Bowron as saying that he believed Abraham Lincoln would have ordered internment of Japanese-Americans. As journalists continued to report the conflict between these "power blocs,", their treatment of JapaneseAmericans worsened. On February 6, the New York Times described a meeting between Olson and Japanese-American officials. The story also highlighted the claim by petroleum industry officials that a "sabotage plot" was in place, one that "awaits only the `zero hour' before being put into effect".

Times reporter Davies quoted Bowron as saying that "they should be put to work." Olson said that while he didn't endorse Bowron's plan, he thought there was "no middle ground for Japanese citizens."

If they weren't prepared to show complete loyalty, he said, they "ought to be concentrated." Later in the Times story, Olson is quoted as saying that he would appoint a committee of Japanese-Americans "to cooperate in drafting plans for an evacuation programme of lesser proportions."

JACL President Saburo Kido said his organization was willing to help, but "appealed against any denial of constitutional rights" to Nisei.

The use of Kido as a source and the inclusion of the JACL were rare in coverage of the evacuation issue. During the period leading up to Executive Order 9066, journalists for all three newspapers typically used only JACL officials to represent the Japanese-American side of the story. In its story detailing reaction to the order, the New York Times used only a prepared statement from JACL officials Kido and Mike Masoaka which pledged cooperation with the government and which urged calm among its members. Japanese-American citizens were not asked for their reaction. By February 7, both the Los Angeles Times (page six) and the Chronicle (page four) ran an AP story in which Olson told a conference of Japanese-American leaders that the only way they could help themselves was by working to help the United States to defeat Japan.

"The government of Japan will be made to surrender and disarm and will be wiped out," Olson said. "There isn't any middle ground for Japanese citizens". While Chronicle reporters moved through February 1942 writing glowing reports about successful "alien roundups," its editorial writers mixed a bit of tolerance with caution, and even a bit of self-examination. In a February 6 editorial, the Chronicle said that there was little hysteria over alleged fifth column activity.

"Perhaps there is even too little of it," the editorial noted. It was government officials and journalists who were "seeking to capitalize on the supposed excitement of others, which is mostly a figment of their own imaginations." Donohue, Tichenor, and Olien note that placing blame on the media often occurs as a controversy develops.

But these expressions are "simply instrumental for keeping the media under control, to prevent damage". Chronicle columnist Chester Rowell said evacuation was necessary, but added that state and local officials may have been acting too zealously. "In war, the presumption of innocence shifts, and it is for the non-citizen resident to establish his loyalty, rather than for the authorities to prove his lack of it," he wrote. State and local officials must cooperate with the federal government, he said, with federal officials deciding on the appropriate course of action. As before, coverage focused on the competing "power blocs" discussed by Donohue, Tichenor and Olien. "When it gets into local hands, pressure group politics and personal headline seeking also get in," Rowell said. Rowell's comment echoes the sentiment felt by local officials who had tired of waiting for the federal government to act.

As Donohue, Tichenor, and Olien contend, groups with less power tend to look less favorably at media coverage of their efforts. But despite these warnings, Rowell reminded his readers that "the danger, of course, is real. If German and Japanese consulates in California were not engaged in fifth column activities, they were the only exceptions in the world."

With a sound structure for addressing the threat issue finally in place, journalists soon began preparing readers for internment. On February 12, the Chronicle reported that imposition of martial law was imminent. As law enforcement officials continued their successful "raids on enemy aliens," legislators in Washington, D.C., were drafting legislation for a compulsory licensing system, to be administered by the U.S. Army.

The Times ran a page-one story on a renewed call by legislators from the west for immediate evacuation of "all persons of Japanese lineage". The licensing system had been scrapped in favour of an exercise of Presidential authority that would "dispose of the problem with less cumbersome machinery". A February 13 story in the Chronicle revealed that nearly 35,000 enemy aliens had not registered with the federal government. True to its guard dog function, the Chronicle reporter placed the onus on the backs of the unregistered aliens. No mention was made of inefficiencies in the registration process. The Chronicle reporter wrote that citizens groups in southern California were not taking the news of the discrepancy well: they were "planning reprisals against all enemy aliens and against many citizens of Japanese parentage". Less than a week later, Roosevelt issued Executive Order 9066. More than 120,000 Japanese-Americans were rounded up and sent to 10 internment camps.

Print journalists from the New York Times, the Los Angeles Times, and the San Francisco Chronicle had in effect helped the government work through its period of indecision by marginalizing Japanese-Americans, by focusing on the acts of officials as individuals rather than as part of a larger structure, by accepting without question the government's manufactured challenge, by focusing on disagreement among "power blocs," and, finally, by offering their endorsement of the policy that, once finalized, would eventually lead to the internment. The guard dog function of the press developed by Donohue, Tichenor, and Olien provides a strong theoretical foundation for understanding the work of journalists in the period between Pearl Harbor and the internment of Japanese-Americans and offers support for the hypotheses posed by the authors at the end of their article.

Reporters at the newspapers studied here did not, as Daniels and others have argued, fall in line behind government officials and leap to the conclusion that Japanese-Americans on the West Coast represented a threat to national security. A more complex picture emerges: newspaper reporters initially gave Japanese-American citizens the chance to show their loyalty to the United States. Soon, however, the government began disseminating unsubstantiated reports of fifth column activity. Print reporters then assumed the role of "sentry" discussed by Donohue, Tichenor, and Olien and began changing the news frame to support the actions and policies of officials who had fabricated the Japanese-American threat in order to mobilize support for our involvement in the war.

After showing some tolerance for Japanese-Americans, print reporters began "working not for the entire community, but for "those particular groups who have the power and influence to create and control their own security systems". Reporters were soon conditioned by officials to suspect "all potential intruders" and "sound the alarm for reasons that individuals in the master household.can neither understand nor prevent".

The "master household" (government officials) clearly understood the "reasons" for the alarm; it had in fact created them. Reporters at these newspapers soon encouraged suspicion of JapaneseAmericans. Some, like the columnist Westbrook Pegler, brashly took up the fifth-column cause; most journalists simply acted as sentries. As the federal government moved closer to enacting an internment plan, journalists began framing Japanese-Americans as a threat to national security. It is this threat. purely manufactured, that became the "organized challenge" to which officials soon responded.

Attacks by local and state lawmakers on the federal government's plans for dealing with JapaneseAmericans were framed as dominant groups, or "power blocs," as Donohue, Tichenor and Olien call them, looking for a way to show that their plans to control the situation would be the most effective. Reporters helped manufacture the uncertainty that leads to intensified coverage in support of dominant institutions, as Donohue, Tichenor and Olien argue.

Reporters also framed stories about the fifth column threat as an attack on individuals - citizens, law enforcement officials, and government officials. Figures like FDR, Eleanor Roosevelt, Biddle, Bowron, Dies, DeWitt, and Olson - "great persons," as Donohue, Tichenor and Olien call them dominated the coverage.

Rarely did reporters give readers a context against which to judge the actions and motives of officials. These individuals embodied a structure that was never called into question. The real victims Japanese-American citizens on the West Coast - were marginalized by reporters; they Lost their voice as stories of loyalty gave way to hysteria, calls for evacuation, and reports of the "running tab" of alien arrests.

Their opposition to internment was imbued with a distinct "sideshow" flavour so that the distinction between supporters and opponents of evacuation was made to seem "natural" - a matter of "common sense," as Gitlin would argue. Reporters used few Japanese-American citizens as sources. The JACL became their official voice - often the only entity cited by reporters in stories published in the days leading up to the internment.

On those rare occasions when reporters cited Japanese-Americans, they were diminished and marginalized; pejorative terms were often used to describe their physical characteristics. Intensity of reporting increased as the government contemplated moving outside what Donohue, Tichenor and Olien would call "the traditional roles of political conflict." Thankfully, attempting to strip citizens of their Constitutional rights is not an everyday occurrence.

Thus, as local, state, and federal officials crafted, discarded and revised evacuation plans, reporting, at least on the West Coast, picked up in intensity. The Chronicle, for example, offered readers its almost daily digest of "alien" arrests. The guard dog's strongest presence is in the inequity of coverage reviewed here. Japanese-Americans, reporters told their readers, represented a threat to our dominant institutions. In fact, the threat - the "organized challenge" discussed by Donohue, Tichenor, and Olien-was a complete fabrication. Reporting clearly framed the crisis (and defined the enemy) in a way that supported the official version of events. Sadly, such conduct by journalists in times of crisis seems to be the rule, not the exception, even as reporters bask in the glow of their work during the Watergate crisis and the Vietnam War. Journalists routinely endorse official versions of events - they seem to play the role of "guard dog" once a story is under control, when it is no longer "unruly," even if that unruliness is manufactured by official sources. The glow of Watergate obscures the fact that most news - including news produced through investigative reporting - is the product of routines built on a few key elements: journalists have values, but conceal them by adhering to the ideal of objectivity; journalists favour "statements of fact which are observable and unambiguous"; and they construct a view of reality "which reinforces official viewpoints", Thus, print reporters covering the aftermath of Pearl Harbor may simply have been waiting for the government to come up with an "observable" and "unambiguous" version of the Japanese-American threat.

Further, Protess, Cook, Doppelt, Ettema, Gordon, Leff, and Miller note that FDR had an amicable relationship with the press - much like Ronald Reagan's - and that this might have caused journalists to look the other way when the call first came for internment.

Thus, there is little evidence print journalists acted as "watchdogs" until the government came up with that policy-there were no investigations of how Japanese-Americans were treated by government officials, for example. Instead, the period between Pearl Harbor and Executive Order 9066 was a journalistic holding pattern. Journalists waited until they could resume dependence on official sources of information. Herman and Chomsky explain that journalists "are drawn into a symbiotic relationship with powerful sources of information by economic necessity and reciprocity of interest". Here, the story was still forming; the Japanese-American issue arose while journalists were still trying to make sense of the attack on Pearl Harbor, and of the American response to it.

If we accept the "guard dog" theory of reporting, it made sense for them to seek out official sources of information - journalists knew these sources, and believed them to be credible. As Fishman notes, "[r]eporters operate with the attitude that officials ought to know it is their job to know.a newsworker will recognize an official's claim to knowledge not merely as a claim, but as a credible, competent piece of knowledge".

But Herman and Chomsky see this as something journalists do as a matter of routine; it does not happen only as a reaction to crisis. "The media need a steady, reliable flow of the raw material of news," they argue. Any tolerance shown for Japanese-Americans was more a product of the absence of an "official line" and the need to meet deadlines than a desire to portray events in an unbiased fashion. As Donohue, Tichenor, and Olien explain, the "[m]edia do not have the capacity to innovate in devising social policy or political action, but must necessarily deal with ideas and actions generated among the powerful groups." If, as here, the dominant groups "are concerned with an external threat, that will be the agenda of the media.".

The guard dog theory leaves little, if any, room for the investigative reporting "binges" Schudson describes. Nevertheless, journalists point to their work in the Vietnam War as an example of strong investigative reporting, claiming that it triggered an adversarial relationship between journalists and the government.

But reports from Vietnam served only to galvanize burgeoning opposition to the war, opposition that was beginning to attract a great deal of coverage. Hallin argues, for example, that "political divisions at home," not the horrific images of the war reported by the news media, caused "the collapse of America's will" to continue fighting in Vietnam. Applying the guard dog theory, it could be argued that the military simply did a poor job of conveying its assumptions about Vietnam - its version of the war - to the public through the news media.

The military failed to contain reporters, as it would less then a decade later in Grenada and then in the Persian Gulf. But even if writers like Schudson, Bagdikian, and Chomsky are correct, and the news media are "primarily an establishment institution with few ambitions to rock establishment boats,", the Watergate myth of the zealous investigative reporter empowered by the "watchdog" role still carries a great deal of power in the field and with news consumers. The news media have come under fire for their willingness to accept the restrictions on coverage imposed by the military in the various stages of conflict in the Persian Gulf. Such restrictions by the military would have been wasted on reporters covering the Japanese-American issue; they intensified their "guard dog" coverage once the government had crafted its policy.

Journalists responded to the Persian Gulf restrictions with perfunctory attacks, acting almost as if they did not want to anger military officials. By addressing the problem in this fashion, reporters underscored the military's success in moving the debate away from questions about the government's Persian Gulf policy. This is not to say that today's journalists invoke Watergate with any consistency. As Rosenstiel explains, journalists "trot out" the myth of investigative reporting "on occasions when it's triggered, when it's appropriate, when we think it's safe, when we're not leading public opinion too much, when all the conditions and all the stars line up".

Even the term "muckraker" came from an official source. Most of the time, journalists are quite willing to rely on established sources of information - especially today, when so many news organizations are part of conglomerates. Journalists did not simply decide en masse to endorse the government's policy towards Japanese-Americans; this analysis reveals that reporters initially gave Japanese-Americans the opportunity to profess loyalty to the United States.

But these stories amounted to little more than a "holding pattern;" journalists abandoned stories of loyalty and patriotism once officials made more sense of the tragedy and put into place a strategy- one built on bigotry and rumor - to deal with the issue. Once a coherent strategy emerged, journalists settled into the role of sentry.

As Donohue, Tichenor, and Olien note, the "occasional tendency to turn on one of the masters in a pluralistic power structure and yet protect their house is fundamental to the guard dog conception of media".

Bibliography

A. Kumar: *Social Change : Through NGOs*, Anmol Publication, Delhi, 2003.

A.S. Shukla: *Journalism Today : Concepts and Practices*, Rajat Publications, Delhi, 2010.

Ajay Das: *Journalism : Editing and Reporting*, Omega Publication, Delhi, 2010.

Ajay Das: *Mass Media And Journalism*, Omega Publications, Delhi, 2010.

B. Manna: *Mass Media and Laws in India*, Naya Prokash Publication, Delhi, 1998.

C.S. Shrivastava and R.K. Parekh: *Media Journalism*, Crescent Publishing Corporation, Delhi, 2012.

Deepak Kumar: *Journalism and Information Technology*, Surendra Publications, Delhi, 2010.

Diwakar Sharma: *Public Relations : An Emerging Specialised Profession: Text and Case Studies*, Deep and Deep Publication, Delhi, 2004.

Gurdarshan Singh: *Major Trends In Commercial Journalism In The World*, Arise Publication, Delhi, 2006.

Hari Mohan Agarwal: *Journalism in Practice*, Reference Press, Delhi, 2005.

Iqbal S. Sachdeva: *Public Relations : Principles and Practices*, Oxford University Press, Delhi, 2009.

Jaya Chakravarty: *Journalism : Concept, Approaches and Global Impact*, Sarup & Sons., Delhi, 2007.

Jitendra Kumar Singh: *Modern Journalism : Issues and Trends*, APH Publication, Delhi, 2009.

K C Sharma: *Journalism in India : History, Growth, Development*, Regal Publication, Delhi, 2007.

K Chandrakandan; J Venkata Pirabu; C Karthikeyan & N Anandaraja: *Mass Media and Interpersonal Communication for Social Awakening*, Authors Press, Delhi, 2001.

Kapil Desai: *Media Ethics And Social Change*, Swastik Publications, Delhi, 2010.

Karun Shetty: *Journalism in Transition*, Pacific Publication, Delhi, 2011.

Krishna Menon: *Media Communication and Photo Journalism*, Manglam Publication, Delhi, 2008.

M H Syed: *Journalism : News and News Coverage*, Anmol Publication, Delhi, 2006.

M. Kumar: *Social Change : Theory and Practice*, Mohit Publications, Delhi, 2010.

M.S. Bisht: *Journalism, Advertisement and Public Relations*, Cyber Tech Publications, Delhi, 2011.

Manoj Suresh Goel: *Mass Media And Social Change*, M.D. Publications, Delhi, 2009.

N.C. Pant: *Modern Journalism : Principles and Practice*, Kanishka Publication, Delhi, 2002.

Namita Agrawal: *Mass Media and Communication : Career Opportunities*, Book Enclave, Delhi, 2012.

Narendra Arya: *Media and Journalism Laws*, Anmol Publcation, Delhi, 2011.

Narendra Ojha: *Mass Media and Communication*, ABD Publication, Delhi, 2006.

Naval Prabhakar and Narednra Basu: *Mass Media : Origin and Development*, Commonwealth Publication, Delhi, 2007.

Naval Prabhakar and Narendra Basu: *Journalism : Editing, Reporting and Feature Writing*, Commonwealth Publication, Delhi, 2007.

Naval Prabhakar and Narendra Basu: *Journalism and Mass Communication*, Commonwealth Publication, Delhi, 2007.

Naval Prabhakar and Narendra Basu: *Mass Media and Contemporary Social Issues*, Commonwealth Publication, Delhi, 2007.

Naval Prabhakar and Narendra Basu: *Public Relations : Principles and Functions*, Commonwealth Publication, Delhi, 2007.

Nayyar Shamsi: *Mass Media and Democracy*, Anmol Publication, Delhi, 2006.

R. Choudhary: *Journalism Ethics*, Centrum Press, Delhi, 2010.

Rahul Mudgal: *Journalism and Law*, Sarup & Sons, Delhi, 2009.

S N Das Gupta: *Journalism : A Digital Literacy Guide*, ALP Books, Delhi, 2009.

S.C. Sharma and Sweta Bakshi: *Modern Journalism and Mass Communication*, A.K. Publication, Delhi, 2009.

Stuart Allan: *Journalism : Critical Issues*, Rawat Publication, Delhi, 2008.

Suraj Singh: *Liberalization and Journalism*, Centrum Press, Delhi, 2010.

T. Rajsekhar: *Journalism Administration*, Sonali Publication, Delhi, 2008.

T.J.S. George: *Lessons in Journalism: The Story of Pothan Joseph*, Viva Books, Delhi, 2007.

Tony Harcup: *Journalism : Principles and Practice*, Sage Publication, Delhi, 2009.

Veena Sharma: *Journalism with New Challenge*, ALP Books, Delhi, 2012.

Index